The Legal and Policy Challenges of Student Dress and Grooming Codes

The Legal and Policy Challenges of Student Dress and Grooming Codes

Balancing Rights and Responsibilities

Todd A. DeMitchell

ROWMAN & LITTLEFIELD
Lanham • Boulder • New York • London

Published by Rowman & Littlefield
An imprint of The Rowman & Littlefield Publishing Group, Inc.
4501 Forbes Boulevard, Suite 200, Lanham, Maryland 20706
www.rowman.com

86-90 Paul Street, London EC2A 4NE

British Library Cataloguing in Publication Information Available

Library of Congress Cataloging-in-Publication Data

Names: DeMitchell, Todd A., author.
Title: The legal and policy challenges of student dress and grooming codes : balancing rights and responsibilities / Todd A. DeMitchell.
Description: Lanham, Maryland : Rowman & Littlefield Publishers, [2024] | Includes bibliographical references and index. | Summary: "DeMitchell explores the case law and policies of this persistent and ever-evolving problem in their latest volume on legal issues in public schools"—Provided by publisher.
Identifiers: LCCN 2024000101 (print) | LCCN 2024000102 (ebook) | ISBN 9781475874419 (cloth) | ISBN 9781475874426 (paperback) | ISBN 9781475874433 (ebook)
Subjects: LCSH: Dress codes—Law and legislation—United States. | Freedom of expression—United States. | Students—United States—Uniforms. | Students—Civil rights—United States.
Classification: LCC KF4770 .D46 2024 (print) | LCC KF4770 (ebook) | DDC 344.73/0793—dc23/eng/20240117
LC record available at https://lccn.loc.gov/2024000101
LC ebook record available at https://lccn.loc.gov/2024000102

Also by Todd A. DeMitchell

Todd A. DeMitchell

- *Teachers and Their Unions: Labor Relations in Uncertain Times*
- *Educators at the Bargaining Table: Successfully Negotiating a Contract That Works for All*
- *Labor Relations in Education: Policies, Politics, and Practices*
- *Negligence: What Principals Need to Know about Avoiding Liability*

Todd A. DeMitchell and Richard Fossey

- *The Challenges of Mandating School Uniforms in the Public Schools: Free Speech, Research, and Policy*
- *Student Dress Codes and the First Amendment: Legal Challenges and Policy Issues*
- *The Limits of Law-Based School Reform: Vain Hopes and False Promises*

Todd A, DeMitchell, Richard Fossey, and Terri A. DeMitchell

- *Raising a Cautionary Flag: Educational Malpractice and the Professional Teacher*

Todd A. DeMitchell and Mark A. Page

- *Threading the Evaluation Needle: The Documentation of Teacher Unprofessional Conduct*

Contents

Preface

An Update on Student Rights and School Responsibilities

> "From the earliest days of organized society . . . matters of appearance and dress have always been subjected to control and regulation, sometimes by custom and social pressures, sometimes by legal rules. A variety of reasons justify limitation on this interest. . . . [J]ust as the individual has an interest in a choice among different styles of appearance . . . so also does a society have a legitimate interest in placing limits on the exercise of that choice."[1]

Stanford law professor Richard Thompson Ford provocatively wrote in his 2021 book *Dress Codes: How the Laws of Fashion Made History* that "[w]e are free to wear anything we choose, but slaves to the judgment of others."[2] He captures the balancing act of the liberty to select what to wear with the reality of judgment through laws, regulations, social pressure, and shaming.

For example, airlines have been enforcing regulations about what the flying public may or may not wear on their planes.[3] While many of the restrictions target women (short skirts, low-cut blouses, sheer skirts, leggings, bikini bottoms, and crop tops), some target baggy pants/sagging pants and Speedos.[4]

Even the "most magical place on earth" enforces a dress code for its visitors. Several patrons have reported being dress-coded at Disney theme parks.[5] One incident uploaded to TikTok showed a twenty-three-year-old woman being escorted by park staff to receive a yellow Walt Disney World T-shirt to replace her lace-up crop top.[6]

And staid, conservative places have also enforced dress regulations. In 1938, Helen Hulick, a twenty-eight-year-old kindergarten teacher refused to wear a dress to court, where she was appearing as witness in a burglary case in Los Angeles. Hulick appeared in court wearing slacks. She was ordered by Judge Arthur S. Guerin postponed the trial and order Hulick to go home and return properly attired in a more "acceptable outfit." She stated that she had been wearing slacks since she was fifteen and was comfortable in them, and besides, she only owned one formal dress. Furthermore, she said, "I will come back in slacks, and if he puts me in jail, I hope it will help to free women forever of anti-slackism."[7]

When Hulick appeared in slacks for the third time, Guerin jailed her for five days for contempt of court and required her to appear in court wearing a denim dress. A protest resulted in the appellate court overturning the judge's rule against wearing slacks. Several months later, Hulick appeared in front of Guerin wearing a formal evening gown.

Some municipal dress code regulations carry penalties. Ford offers several examples of such clothing bans. He writes, "The bikini was an instant sensation but also an instant cause of moral panic."[8] Cities in Europe, Australia, and the United States banned bikinis as "a hazard to public morality and decency" in the 1950s. Recently the bikini restriction has resurfaced. In 2022, Sorrento, Italy, a picturesque coastal town near Pompeii and Naples, banned walking around shirtless and in swimwear. The mayor stated that the ban was necessary to restore "decorum" and "decency" and the reputation and quality of life of the town. The fine for a dress code violation was set at £425.[9]

Some sixty-odd years after the appearance of the bikini, cities and towns in Germany, France, Italy, and Morocco banned the burkini as indecent. The burkini first appeared in 2004 and is worn by some Muslim women. It is essentially a full-body one-piece bathing suit designed so that women can go in the water.[10] This is an odd policy in that it requires women to wear less, when many policies and social mores expect women to wear more.

Another clothing choice targeted by ordinances is sagging pants. In Flint, Michigan, sagging pants violated the city's disorderly conduct and indecent exposure ordinances, which carry up to a year in jail and fines of $500. Albany, Georgia, reported in 2010 that it had issued 187 citations and collected $3,916 in fines from individuals wearing pants or skirts more than three inches below the top of the hips.[11]

Even fitness clubs and gyms, where relaxed dress is expected, dress codes have not disappeared. In Ontario, a woman and her husband were working out at their gym when a supervisor informed the woman that her appearance was making other patrons uncomfortable. The employee explained that "her chest was too big for her tank top, and members complained."[12] She felt humiliated, and she and her husband left the gym.

In 2023, the Missouri House of Representatives joined the list of places that are attempting to push back against the trend away from casualness and informality to a more "traditional" time. The House debated the proper attire that women legislators should wear on the floor of the state capitol.[13] The debate did not include the attire of the male legislators, centering instead on what types of layers of clothing must cover female legislators' arms. Female legislators now can wear cardigans as their second layer of clothing to cover their arms.

Dress codes are found in various places in society (businesses, restaurants, and private clubs, for example), and public decency laws generally refer to nudity and sexual activity in view of the public.[14] The US Supreme Court in *Barnes v. Glen Theatre, Inc.*, a case involving nude dancing, held that public nudity is not an expression protected by the First Amendment, thus affirming state decency laws outlawing public nudity.[15]

Our society has become more casual in many aspects. Relaxed dress standards are a visible marker of this trend away from formalism. While the expected dress for flying has changed from men in suits and women in dresses to a more relaxed look, so have other public venues experienced the loosening of dress expectations. At the extreme, or as a glimpse of the future, is the "new naked dressing" of the high fashion runway and Hollywood red carpet.[16] However, as seen by the observations from airlines, gyms, and theme parks, the shift to a more casual look does not mean that anything can be worn, especially at school.

In an interesting twist, strictly scripted dress codes have occasionally been used to push for more casualness. The International Handball Federation dress code states that women in the beach game "must wear a bikini bottom with a tight-fitting top." In the 2021 European Beach Handball Championship held in Varna, Bulgaria, on the Black Sea, the Norwegian national women's handball team refused to wear bikini bottoms, instead opting for shorts that resembled thigh-length biker shorts.

The team stated that the bikini bottoms made them feel "unnecessarily sexualized and uncomfortable." (The code stated that clothing could not cover more than 10cm of their butts.)[17] The team was chastised and fined for covering up. However, starting in January 2022, the code was changed to require women athletes to wear "short tight pants with a close fit" and a body-fitting tank top.[18]

The place most likely to come to mind in any discussion of dress codes code is the public school. The tension between what students want to wear to school and what school administrators will allow is part of the daily routine for many, if not most, schools across the nation.[19] According to one report, "Dress codes have always been a point of contention in public schools. Teachers, students, parents, and administrators struggle, often against each other, to determine what is appropriate for school and who should get to decide."[20]

And the controversy surrounding student attire is not just limited to the schoolyard. Brecklynn Willis, a member of her high school swim team in Anchorage, Alaska, had competed in four events in a competition. After winning a heat, a race official disqualified her, deeming that her swimsuit had shifted position and exposed "too much of her backside."[21] The official said that the girl's school-issued swimsuit didn't fit her properly, violating a modesty rule. The Anchorage School District lobbied to have the disqualification thrown out as "heavy-handed and unnecessary." The Alaska School Activities Association reversed the disqualification.

DRESS CODES IN THE PUBLIC SCHOOLS: ADMINISTRATORS ON THE HIGHWIRE

K–12 EDUCATION: DEPARTMENT OF EDUCATION SHOULD PROVIDE INFORMATION ON EQUITY AND SAFETY IN SCHOOL DRESS CODES

October 25, 2022
Congressional Addressees
Nearly every public school district in the nation requires students to adhere to a dress code. School dress codes provide overall guidelines for how students are expected to dress for school; establish rules about clothes, hair, and accessories; and lay out disciplinary consequences for violating the dress code. For example, students who violate a school's dress code may be asked to change clothes, be sent home, or be suspended from school.

Jacqueline M. Nowicki, Director
Education, Workforce, and Income Security Issues
United States Government Accountability Office
GAO-23-105348 K–12 Education, (October 2022), 1,
https://www.gao.gov/assets/gao-23-105348.pdf.

Scholars and the courts have long recognized public schools as essential. Noted educational researchers David Tyack and Larry Cuban wrote that dialogue and debate about the goals of education are a "potent means of defining the present and shaping the future"; they are "one way that Americans make sense of their lives."[22] Similarly, the US Supreme Court has regarded education as a matter of extreme importance. In *Plyler v. Doe*, the court wrote, "We have recognized the public schools as a most vital civic institution for the preservation of a democratic system of government and as the primary vehicle for transmitting the values on which our society rests."[23]

Control of this vital institution rests with elected local school boards. School boards have broad discretion in the management of their schools. The authority to prescribe and control conduct in the schools is comprehensive.[24] However, that authority is not without limits. Actions taken in the public schools "must be exercised in a manner that comports with the transcendent imperatives of the First Amendment."[25] Thus, decisions made by school boards and carried out by educators must not conflict with the constitutional rights of students who attend the school. Policies that control student attire are often subject to this imperative.

"The very nature of public education requires limitations on one's personal liberty in order for the learning process to proceed."—*Richards v. Thurston*, 424 F.2d 1281, 1285 (1st Cir. 1970)

The Rise of Dress Codes and Resulting Litigation

Tensions around changes in student attire and school officials hewing to community standards of appropriate dress arose in the 1960s and during a period of expanding personal freedom. Former expectations for behavior were being challenged and loosened. In response, school authorities as "representatives of those generations and norms pushed back, adopting increasingly formal and specific guidelines for student dress, hair length, and facial hair."[26] The stage was set for litigation as school boards sought to maintain traditional standards for school dress and students sought to gain more personal freedom regarding what they wore to school.

Student challenges to school dress codes are now almost a staple in public schools, sometimes moving from the principal's office to the courts and social media platforms. Most often, the plaintiff student argues that the messages proclaimed on their clothing or the clothing itself are constitutionally protected under the First Amendment. Indeed, in *Tinker v. Des Moines Independent Community School District*, the Supreme Court ruled more than fifty years ago that public school students do not "shed their constitutional rights to freedom of speech or expression at the schoolhouse gate."[27] Numerous lower court decisions have ruled that students' constitutional right of expression may include the messages they proclaim on their clothing.

Nevertheless, in the years since the *Tinker* case was decided, the Supreme Court has made clear that students' right to free expression is not unlimited when they are at school. As Chief Justice Warren Burger stated in *Bethel School District No. 403 v. Fraser*, "The undoubted freedom to advocate unpopular and controversial views in schools and classrooms must be balanced against the society's countervailing interest in teaching students the boundaries of socially appropriate behavior."[28] Further, as one federal district court asserted, public school students' right to free speech must be "balanced against the need to foster an educational atmosphere free from undue disruptions to appropriate discipline."[29]

Over the years, the Supreme Court has sketched out some of the limits on students' constitutional right to freedom of expression while they are in the public school environment. In the *Bethel* case, the court held that schools have the authority to censor student speech that is vulgar, lewd, or profane.[30] In *Hazelwood School District v. Kuhlmeier*, the court stated that schools can regulate student speech that is school sponsored.[31] And in *Morse v. Frederick*, the Supreme Court upheld the right of school authorities to ban student expression that promotes or celebrates the use of illegal drugs.[32] Most recently, the court held that while schools may regulate some off-campus speech, their authority is more limited than it is with on-campus speech.[33]

These Supreme Court decisions have helped school administrators understand the limits of their constitutional authority when they seek to regulate student speech, including speech on students' clothing. Nevertheless, disputes continue to arise between students and school officials regarding what students wear to school. Again and again, the federal courts have been called on to determine whether a student has a First Amendment right to wear a particular item of clothing that school officials seek to ban as being in violation of their school's student dress code.

Thus, educators are required to balance two sometimes conflicting responsibilities: On the one hand they are charged with providing high-quality education in a safe, orderly, and nonabusive environment. On the other hand, they are required to respect their students' constitutional right to freedom of expression, which they sometimes exercise through messages on their clothing as well as their choice of clothing.

School districts win some of these court cases and they lose others. Examples of cases they have won include *Gano v. School District No. 411*, in which a federal district judge upheld the suspension of a student who wore a T-shirt showing three school administrators inebriated,[34] and *Baxter v. Vigo County School Corporation*, in which the suspension of a Lost Creek Elementary School student for wearing T-shirts that read "Unfair Grades," "Racism," and "I Hate Lost Creek" was upheld.[35]

Examples of student victories include a federal court of appeals decision in Pennsylvania ruling that students have the constitutional right to wear bracelets that proclaim, "I ♥ Boobies" to show their support for breast cancer awareness[36] and a federal district court decision in Wisconsin that awarded a preliminary injunction against a school principal who disciplined a student for wearing clothing that was not banned by the school's dress code. In the latter case, a freshman received an in-school suspension for wearing T-shirts depicting weapons, even though the school's dress code did not specifically prohibit wearing clothing depicting images of weapons. Using the *Tinker* standard, Judge Lynn Adelman found that the school district failed to meet its burden of showing a reasonable belief of substantial disruption resulting from wearing the T-shirts.[37]

Dress codes sit at that intersection of students' constitutional right to free speech and the compelling need for public schools to establish and maintain a suitable learning environment for their students.[38] Schools, like the wider society, reflect transitions of expectations. A 2019 *Wall Street Journal* noted that "[c]lothing once considered taboo is now permitted as more districts across the U.S. relax student dress code policies."[39] This trend of relaxed standards runs alongside the push to restrict student attire choices through mandated school uniforms. We will explore these tensions between rights and responsibilities and between casualness and formality in student appearance.

OVERVIEW OF THE BOOK: A CONTINUING TENSION OVER RIGHTS AND RESPONSIBILITIES

Student Dress Codes and the First Amendment: Legal Challenges and Policy Issues was published in 2014.[40] This 2024 volume builds on the prior work and expands it. This book, *The Legal and Policy Challenges of Student Dress and Grooming Codes: Balancing Rights and Responsibilities*, updates case law and legal challenges from the last decade. As stated above, the tension between the trend toward more casualness in personal attire is clashing with the institutional need for conformity of standards and support of community mores.[41] This tension is most visible in the schools, where students' desire to express their identities clashes most visibly with the schools' responsibility to maintain order, decorum, and standards of decency in the learning environment.

Specifically, issues of gender and race that have gained attention in the interval between 2014 to the present, such as the gendering of dress codes, with the weight of regulations falling most heavily on the exposed shoulders of female students, are addressed. The rise of dress code violations associated with hairstyles—most notably, the issue of braids and locs—is also explored. This book also includes a chapter on school uniforms. These additions round out the exploration of restrictions on student appearance, which focuses on the legal and policy issues pertaining to student dress codes and grooming.

The book is organized into ten chapters. The first two chapters set the stage for the rest of the book. Chapter 1, discusses the controversy about student expression through clothing choices and the challenges that confront public school educators who seek to respect the constitutional rights of their students while enforcing policies designed to ensure the efficient delivery of educational services and the protection of a proper learning environment for students. Chapter 2 examines the five US Supreme Court decisions on the constitutional rights of students to engage in free speech while at school, and more recently, away from school, as well as other free speech cases that impact symbolic expression at school.

The next four chapters review case law on the types of messages that have resulted in court cases. For example, in chapter 3, types of banned clothing—including pants, hats, and gang-associated clothing as well as depictions of sex and drugs—are discussed. The chapter explores some of the broad issues of controversial in-school communications via student appearance and dress codes.

Chapter 4 focuses on a persistent and emotional issue, Confederate iconography.[42] The public display of the Confederate battle flag and other Southern Civil War symbols has often led to violence, discord, and disruption. It is important for educators to know the impact of these symbols while seeking the balance between rights and responsibilities "as they strive to provide a safe and welcoming environment for all of their students."[43]This chapter discusses the controversy and case law of dress code regulations and Confederate symbols.

Chapter 5 focuses on controversial issues such as banned products, images of weapons, and political messages. The last chapter in this exploration of messages, chapter 6, examines targeted messages and analyzes messages about sex, including abortion and sexual orientation.

The next two chapters explore gender and hair regulations. Chapter 7 discusses the rising concern about dress codes that target female students by sexualizing female attire and placing the responsibility on female students for the actions of male students. Chapter 8 explores the reaction to hair styles of racial and ethnic groups.

Chapter 9 shifts from dress codes that prohibit specific aspects of student appearance to mandatory school uniforms that require students to wear specific attire. This chapter provides an overview of the rationale for school uniforms and the litigation on school uniforms. The following question is posed: "Are school uniforms a real remedy for the thorny problems that beset our public schools or are they just a placebo that masks the heavy lifting that real achievement and school cultural change require?"[44]

In the final chapter, recommendations are offered to school authorities regarding how to draft student dress codes that will pass constitutional muster and balance the rights and responsibilities of both students and educators.

In addition, the book attempts to bring the policy implications of dress code regulations into focus.

In this concluding chapter, I argue for a balance between the rights of students to express themselves at school and the responsibilities of educators to maintain a safe, orderly, and respectful school environment, arguing for an even-handed, nondiscriminatory application of reasonable rules across gender, racial, ethnic, and religious lines.

The public school is a special place with a unique and critical mandate. Students enter the schoolhouse gate with constitutional rights, but those rights are neither as fulsome as they are outside of the gate nor coextensive with those of adults. Their attenuated rights are not just a function of age, they are also a function of the obligation of the state to protect the civil rights and civil liberties of its citizens. The state, through its public schools, acts as both educator and sovereign, requiring the yielding of some rights that students may exercise outside the schoolhouse gate.

For example, an individual's right to the freedom of expression has the greatest latitude when government acts as the sovereign. When the state acts as the employer, the employee's rights are not as robust. Similarly, when the state acts as an educator to its students, the students' rights are circumscribed in the unique setting of the school. A public school is a special place, reserved for learning, and rules regulating speech in the public square may not be appropriate for regulating speech in the classrooms of public schools.

The US Supreme Court has recognized the legitimate limitations on student constitutional rights within the schoolhouse gate, writing that the rights of students must be "applied in light of the special characteristics of the school environment"[45] and "the constitutional rights of students in public school are not automatically coextensive with the rights of adults in other settings."[46] Students' right to wear what they want to wear and the responsibility of school officials to create a proper educational environment are both exercised within the unique environment of the public school.

Students have venues for expressing their views while at school in student clubs, school newspapers, and appropriate forums for student discussions and debates. Unfettered choice of clothing choices is not and should not be one of those expressive venues. It is not so outside the schoolhouse gate and cannot be so within the schoolhouse gate. It is a special place of work and study. It has a special societal purpose serving as a public good for society, an educated populace, and a private benefit for the individual. In order to achieve the former, reasonable restrictions must be placed on the latter.

The challenge is to thread the needle of defining and maintaining a culture that recognizes the rights of students while providing an environment that is supportive as well as conducive to teaching and learning within a safe environment, both physically and emotionally. Although, dress codes are "based on social norms and expectations which exist to perpetuate the status quo,"[47] many educators believe that these norms and expectations are necessary to maintain a school environment that is conducive to learning.

However, there is a dynamic tension between the aims of education—the enculturation of the individual into the existing society and the important role of accelerating and stimulating social change: "Education is a struggle between tradition and aspiration."[48] The challenge of threading the needle for developing and enforcing dress code expectations is to recognize the legitimacy of stitching together both rights and responsibilities.

> "Nobility is defined by the demands it makes on us—by obligations, not by rights."—Jose Ortega y Gassett, *Revolt of the Masses* (1929), Chapter 7 Noble Life and Common Life, Or Effort and Inertia, https://dn790005.ca.archive.org/0/items/TheRevoltOfTheMasses/The%20Revolt%20of%20the%20Masses.pdf.

NOTES

1. *Miller v. School District No. 167, Cook County, Illinois,* 495 F.2d 658, 664 (7th Cir. 1974).

2. Richard Thompson Ford, *Dress Codes: How the Laws of Fashion Made History* (New York: Simon and Shuster, 2021), 364.

3. Hannah Frisberg, "The Airline Dress Codes Oliva Culpo and Others Don't Know About," *New York Post* (January 22, 2022), https://nypost.com/2022/01/14/the-airline-dress-codes-olivia-culpo-and-others-dont-know-about/. (Note: Oliva Culpo is former Miss Universe.)

4. Hannah Sampson, "Recent Incident over Attire Highlights Ambiguity in Airline Dress Codes," *Washington Post* (July 11, 2019), https://www.washingtonpost.com/travel/2019/07/11/recent-incident-over-attire-highlights-ambiguity-airline-dress-codes/.

5. See Disneyland, "Theme Parks—Frequently Asked Questions: Q. What is the best way to dress for a day at the parks?" (n.d.), https://disneyland.disney.go.com/faq/parks/dress/.

6. Julia Ranney, "Woman Sparks Tiktok Debate over 'Inappropriate' Disney Dress Code Violation," Yahoo! Life (March 24, 2022), https://www.yahoo.com/lifestyle/disney-world-park-dress-code-tiktok-153938819. html.

7. Katharina Buczek, "In 1938, This Los Angeles Teacher Made History after Refusing to Wear a Dress in Court—And Was Even Jailed for Wearing Slacks," *CHIPCHICK* (August 26, 2022), https://www.chipchick.com/2022/08/in-1938-this-los-angeles-teacher-made-history-after-refusing-to-wear-a-dress-in-court-and-was-even-jailed-for-wearing-slacks.html.

8. Ford, *supra* note 2, 281.

9. Jack Newman, "Italy's Sorrento Resort Bans BIKINIS: Wearing Swimwear Could land You a £425 Fine for 'Indecency,'" *Daily Mail* (July 7, 2022), https://www.dailymail.co.uk/news/article-10991927/Italys-Sorento-resort-bans-BIKINIS-Wearing-swimwear-land-425-fine-indecency.html; emphasis in original.

10. Ford, *supra* note 2, 280–81.

11. Ibid., 197–98. The Fort Worth public transportation authority announced their new policy prohibiting from wearing sagging pants that exposed their underwear or buttocks by posting the following: "Pull-Em Up or Find Another Ride." Ibid., 198.

12. Arianna Jeret, "Why a Gym Employee Told a Woman That Her Tank Top Made People Uncomfortable," *Your Tango* (May 19, 2022), https://www.yourtango.com/self/why-woman-gym-said-tank-top-made-people-uncomfortable.

13. Jack Suntrup, "Dress Code for Women Legislators Debated in Missouri House," *St. Louis Post-Dispatch* (January 12, 2023), https://www.stltoday.com/news/local/govt-and-politics/dress-code-for-women-legislators-debated-in-missouri-house/article_a1dcfd3e-abf5–5722-acd1–11275dae9ede.html.

14. See *Justia*, "Public Indecency" (October 2021), https://www.justia.com/criminal/offenses/sex-crimes/public-indecency/. However, restrictions on dress have focused on more than just public decency seeking to reinforce the mores of the society. In the lamentable history of America's institution of slavery, Ford writes, "the laws of American slave states prohibited Black people from dressing 'above their condition." Ford, *supra* note 2, 14.

15. *Barnes v. Glen Theatre, Inc.*, 501 U.S. 560, 568 (1991). Chief Justice William Rehnquist, citing *Bowers v. Hardwick*, 478 U.S. 186, 196 (1986), said, "The law, however, is constantly based on notions of morality, and if all laws representing essentially moral choices are to be invalidated under the Due Process Clause, the courts will be very busy indeed." "Thus," the chief justice continued, "the public indecency statute furthers a substantial government interest in protecting order and morality." *Barnes v. Glen Theatre, Inc.*, 501 U.S. at 570.

16. Vanessa Friedman, "Naked Dressing Has You Covered," *New York Times* (October 20, 2022), https://www.nytimes.com/2022/10/20/style/naked-dressing.html. The reporter writes,

> Nor, said Ms. Rabinovitch-Fox, is it "about the feminine body necessarily. It's just about the body. It's about, I have the right to expose myself the way I want to."
>
> Indeed, the idea of bodily "rights" comes up again and again when designers talk about the new naked.

Ibid.

17. Scott McDonald, "Norway Women's Beach Handball Team Says Mandatory Bikini Rule Is Too Cheeky," *Newsweek* (July 19, 2021), https://www.newsweek.com/norway-womens-beach-handball-team-says-bikini-rule-too-cheeky-them-1611278.

18. Caroline Radnofsky, "Norway's Beach Handball Team Wins Fight over Sexist Uniform Rules," NBC News (November 1, 2021), https://www.nbcnews.com/news/

world/norways-beach-handball-team-win-fight-sexist-uniform-rules-rcna4218: "Norwegian Handball Federation President Kåre Geir Lio called the change 'both a real and symbolic step' toward combating gender inequality in the sport." Ibid.

19. The United States is not the only nation which has dress code controversies. For example, Japan's strict school uniform regulations has faced some recent pushback. The Japanese government has had restrictive regulations, known as *buraku kōsoku* or "black rules," dating back to the 1870s when they established a regulated system of education. In 2017 a high school student sued the Osaka Prefecture Government for causing mental distress when the school repeatedly demanded that she dye her hair black from its natural brown to black. A group was searching for "solutions to draconian rules to reduce stress for both students and teachers." Takagi Kyōko, "New Organization Takes on Unreasonable Rules in Japan's Schools," Nippon.com (June 28, 2018), https://www.nippon.com/en/currents/d00414/.These regulations have also included the color of the student's underwear (white, so that it does not show through) and ponytails. The ponytail restriction was designed so that the nape of female students' necks do not "sexually excite male students," similar to the underwear restriction. Brooke Kato, "Japanese Schools Ban Ponytails Fearing They Might "Sexually Excite" Men," *New York Post* (March 10, 2022), https://nypost.com/2022/03/10/japanese-schools-ban-ponytails-fearing-they-sexually-excite-men/. See chapter 7 for a discussion about restrictions on female attire based on forecasted sexual responses by male students.

20. Alyssa Pavlakis and Rachel Roegman, "How Dress Codes Criminalize Males and Sexualize Females of Color," *Kappan* 100, no. 2 (2018), https://kappanonline.org/pavlakis-roegman-dress-codes-gender-race-discrimination/.

21. Ryan Prior and Doug Criss, "A Young Swimmer Was Disqualified after a Race for How Her Swimsuit Fit Her Body. The Outcry Led to a Reversal," CNN (September 12, 2019), https://www.cnn.com/2019/09/11/us/high-school-swimsuit-disqualified-alaska-trnd/index.html. The association had sent put a previous memo that there was a trend of male and female high school athletes intentionally rolling up their swimsuits "in such a way as to expose the athlete's buttocks." Ibid.

22. David Tyack and Larry Cuban, *Tinkering Toward Utopia: A Century of Public School Reform* (Cambridge, MA: Harvard University Press 1997), 42.

23. *Plyler v. Doe*, 457 U.S. 202, 221 (1982).

24. *Board of Education, Island Trees Union Free School District No. 26 v. Pico*, 457 U.S. 853, 863–64 (1982).

25. Ibid., 864.

26. Deborah M. Ahrens and Andrew M. Siegel, "Of Dress and Redress: Student Dress Restrictions in Constitutional Law and Culture," *Harvard Civil Rights-Civil Liberties Law Review* 54 (2019): 56. The authors write,

> When educators issued edicts telling male students how long their hair could be or forbidding women to wear pants to school, they were mobilizing one of their weapons (authority over formal school discipline) in the service of a larger cultural conflict that was playing out in many venues and contexts across the nation.

Ibid.

27. *Tinker v. Des Moines Independent Community School District*, 393 U.S. 503, 506 (1969).

28. *Bethel School District No. 403 v. Fraser*, 478 U.S. 675, 681 (1986).

29. *Bivens v. Albuquerque Public Schools*, 889 F. Supp. 556, 559 (D. N. M. 1995).

30. *Bethel School District v. Fraser*, 478 U.S. 675 (1986).

31. *Hazelwood School District. v. Kuhlmeier*, 484 U.S. 260 (1989).

32. *Morse v. Frederick*, 551 U.S. 393 (2007).

33. *Mahanoy Area School District v. B.L.*, 141 S. Ct. 2038 (2021). Justice Stephen Breyer, speaking for the majority, identified the school's standing of in loco parentis as one of those special characteristics. Ibid., 2044–45.

34. *Gano v. School District No. 411*, 674 F. Supp. 796 (D. Idaho 1987).

35. *Baxter v. Vigo County School Corporation*, 26 F.3d 728 (7th Cir. 1994).

36. *B. H. v. Easton Area School District*, 725 F.3d 293 (3d Cir. 2013).

37. *Schoenecker v. Koppman*, 349 F. Supp.3d 745 (E. D. Wis. 2018). However, in another federal Eastern District Wisconsin case, Judge William Griesbach found *Schoenecker* "unpersuasive." *N.J. by Next Friend Jacob v. Sonnabend*, 536 F.Supp.3d 392, 403 (E. D. Wis. 2021). The issue *Jacob*, like *Schoenecker*, was the display of images of weapons. Griesbach held that the dress code ban on images of weapons was reasonable and furthered important pedagogical goals, such as reducing student aggression. Ibid, 408. See chapter 5 for a discussion of these cases.

38. The Supreme Court has recognized that schools have a "compelling interest in having an undisputed school session conducive to the students' learning" (*Grayned v. City of Rockford*, 408 U.S. 104, 119 (1972).

39. Tawnell D. Hobbs, "Schools Relax Dress Codes in Bid to End Body Shaming," *Wall Street Journal* (July 13, 2019), https://www.wsj.com/articles/schools-relax-dress-codes-in-bid-to-end-body-shaming-11563010202.

40. Richard Fossey and Todd A. DeMitchell, *Student Dress Codes and the First Amendment: Legal Challenges and Policy Issues*, (Lanham, MD: Rowman and Littlefield, 2014).

41. Ford, *supra* note 2, 371, writing, "Fashion may not help us fight the enemies of humanity. But it gives us a glimpse of what we are fighting for."

42. For example, in March 2023, a Republican Florida state senator filed an amendment to SB 668 that provides a list of flags that would be permitted to be displayed by Florida's governmental entities, including public schools. While the amendment did not specifically mention the rainbow pride flag or other LGBTQ symbols, it was viewed by many as excluding those flags, similar to Florida HB 1011, which does exclude LGBTQ flags from the list of approved flags. However, the amendment did include the Confederate flag in the list of approved flags that can flown over public schools. The author, a retired Green Beret veteran, withdrew the amendment, stating that he does not have Confederate sympathies and that the amendment was filed in an error. However, the immediate uproar and response to remove the amendment underscores the sensitivity to Confederate iconography. Darragh Roche, "Republican Lawmaker Says He Filed Confederate Flag Legislation 'in Error,'" *Newsweek* (March 16, 2023), https://www.newsweek.com/republican-lawmaker-says-he-filed-confederate-flag-legislation-error-1788136.

43. Todd A. DeMitchell and Richard Fossey, "The Battle over the Confederate Flag in Our Schools: Heritage or Oppression?" *Education Law Reporter* 352 (2018): 937.

44. Todd A. DeMitchell, Commentary, "School Uniforms: There Is No Free Lunch," *Teachers College Record* (December 14, 2006), ID Number 12891.

45. *Tinker v. Des Moines Independent Community School District*, 393 U.S., 506.

46. *Bethel School District No. 403 v. Fraser*, 478 U.S., 682.

47. Deanna J. Glickman, "Fashioning Children: Gender Restrictive Dress Codes as an Entry Point for the Trans* School to Prison Pipeline," *Journal of Gender, Social Policy & the Law* 24, no. 2 (2016): 284. Glickman argues that dress codes come at the cost of the gender identity of trans* students, with long-term negative consequences.

48. Todd A. DeMitchell, "Tinkering Toward Utopia, or Dystopia? A Philosophical/Policy Perspective on Educational Reform," *International Journal of Educational Reform* 5, no. 3 (1996): 357.

Acknowledgement

I acknowledge and with great gratitude thank my friend and colleague Richard Fossey, JD, EdD, Paul Burdin Professor Emeritus, University of Louisiana, Lafayette for his encouragement and assistance with the development of this book. Together we wrote *Student Dress Codes and the First Amendment: Legal Challenges and Policy Issues* (2014) and *The Challenges of Mandating School Uniforms in the Public Schools* (2015), plus a number of law reviews and legal commentaries. When I approached Richard about revisiting our earlier work, Richard encouraged me to undertake the revisions and additions to update the current state of public school student dress and grooming codes. He generously offered to edit and critically review the book but declined the larger role given the demands on his time and competing responsibilities.

While I take sole responsibility for the content of the book, I acknowledge that without the decades of working with Richard on student dress and grooming codes as well as related legal topics, this book would not have been written. While I reluctantly accepted his decision to take a different role, I recognize and value our career-long collaboration and continuing friendship. This book is a continuation of our collaboration on the important legal topics in education.

1

What to Wear to School?

Student Choice and School Restrictions: The Controversy

> "Dress codes have always been a point of contention in public schools. Teachers, students, parents, and administrators struggle, often against each other, to determine what is appropriate for school and who should get to decide."[1]

> "No absolute right to an unfettered choice of appearance has ever been recognized."[2]

The morning ritual begins for students when they are confronted with their daily morning challenge: first, what is clean enough to wear to school, and second, is it something I must wear (a school uniform) or is it something that must I not wear (a dress code)? The morning ritual also begins for school administrators, who must sort out potential violations of the dress code, which students colloquially call being "coded" (when an educator at school asks a student "to either remove or cover a clothing item").[3]

Since the 1960s, the seemingly innocuous morning question of what to wear to school today has been anything but simple. As students push for greater freedom of choice for their clothing choices and appearance, school administrators must find the educational and legal balance between what clothing and appearance is acceptable and what is not. The morning question of what to wear to school has often moved from merely vexing and benign to being draped in constitutional considerations as students assert their free speech and other rights.

Attending to issues of short skirts, baggy pants, exposed underwear, and controversial T-shirts all too often have been a staple in the morning ritual of many school administrators. Students' answers to the perennial question of what to wear to school have often moved from their clothes closet to the principal's office and sometimes to the courtroom. Noted school law scholars Martha M. McCarthy, Nelda H. Cambron-McCabe, and Suzanne Eckes assert that "fads and fashions in hairstyles and clothing have regularly evoked litigation as educators have attempted to exert some control over pupil appearance."[4]

The controversy over what can be worn at school persists. Because this controversy most often involves assertions of a violation of student free speech rights as well as growing number of challenges regarding enforcement and discriminatory practices,[5] there is a pathway to the courts to review the school's dress decisions and policies.[6]

"Unlike the United Kingdom, the United States has a largely unwritten history of public school dress norms and restrictions. As best as scholars have been able to determine, dress norms and expectations were ubiquitous in American education up until the late 1960s, but formal dress codes were surprisingly rare and public school uniforms were almost—perhaps entirely—unheard of. . . . Anecdotal evidence suggests that school officials resorted to disciplinary action to rein in a recalcitrant or non-conforming student, but tended to do so in a limited and ad hoc way, very rarely establishing a formal dress code."—Deborah M. Ahrens and Andrew M. Siegel, "Of Dress and Redress: Student Dress Restrictions in Constitutional Law and Culture," *Harvard Civil Rights-Civil Liberties Law Review* 54 (2019): 55

Law professor Stephen R. Goldstein wrote in 1969, "In light of the number of recent cases on the subject of school control of hair and dress and the general ferment concerning the issue, it is startling to note that there are only a handful of hair and dress cases predating the 1960s."[7] One of the earliest examples of the controversy of student appearance that ended up in the courts occurred one hundred years ago. The Mississippi Supreme Court in 1921 held a school regulation reasonable which required pupils in an agricultural high school to wear khaki uniforms while attending school and when visiting public places within five miles of the school.[8] It was deemed a reasonable regulation within the scope of the school board to adopt. This occurred in a time of wide discretion recognized by the courts.[9]

Hewing to the reasonableness standard, the Iowa Supreme Court in the same year found a school regulation requiring students to wear a cap and gown at graduation. However, the court held that it was unreasonable to deny the student a diploma for not wearing a cap and gown. The court ordered the school district to grant the student her diploma and a certificate of her grades but left the cap and gown requirement in place.[10]

Two years later, *Pugsley v. Sellmeyer* was decided in a split decision (2–1). The case was a dispute between a school and a student about student dress. In that case, Pearl Pugsley was suspended for wearing face powder. The Arkansas Supreme Court refused to overturn the school's decision, stating, "Courts have other more important functions to perform than that of hearing complaints of dissatisfied pupils of the public schools against rules and regulations promulgated by the school boards for the government of the schools."[11]

The majority held that the dress code did not involve "oppression" or "humiliation."[12] As suggested by this and subsequent decisions, these early courts were reluctant to substitute their judgment for that of school boards, even if the court believed that the regulation was "unwise" or "inexpedient."[13] However, the dissent asserted that Pearl was eighteen years old and school rule forbidding a student of her age from wearing talcum powder as a cosmetic was unreasonable and an abuse of authority. "Useless laws diminish the authority of the necessary one," the dissent concluded.[14]

Until the late 1960s, most courts adopted the Arkansas Supreme Court's stance on student attire and maintained a basic hands-off approach to the regulation of student appearance as long as the regulation was reasonable. Times have changed, although, as seen in *Pugsley*, school officials and students do not always share the same opinion of what is appropriate to wear to school.

A DRESS CODE OR A SCHOOL UNIFORM: THE SCHOOL'S RESPONSE TO STUDENT APPEARANCE

> "Trying to regulate teen wardrobes is a fool's errand. Most everyone agrees that students should be clothed; beyond that, it gets tricky."—Starshine Roshell, "The Ugly Sexism of School Dress Codes," *The Week* (July 2, 2016), http://theweek.com/articles/633222/ugly-sexism-school-dress-codes

When the US Supreme Court decided the *Tinker v. Des Moines Independent Community School District* case in 1969,[15] it may not have realized that it had reopened the courts to lawsuits brought by students that were essentially closed by *Pugsley* in 1923. In the years following the *Tinker* decision, students and their parents have filed numerous lawsuits challenging the authority of school authorities to ban messages on students' clothing as well contesting prohibitions on student appearance.

The Tinker children's expression had consisted of a political statement—opposition to the war in Vietnam—which they communicated by wearing black arm bands. But in the years following the Supreme Court's *Tinker* decision, the federal courts have reviewed disputes between students and school administrators involving clothing-based student speech on a wide range of issues—politics, drugs, sexuality, and even the Confederate battle flag—within the special environment of the public school. The courts also reviewed issues over restrictions over hair length and wearing hair in braids and locs.

As it happened, the *Tinker* case was decided about the time the T-shirt was evolving from a utilitarian men's undergarment to a fashionable item of clothing for both men and women. Moreover, beginning in the 1960s, people increasingly began wearing T-shirts with messages, and these messages ranged from profound political and social statements to humorous gag lines and bawdy expressions of sexual humor.[16] Indeed, when one reviews a half century of First Amendment lawsuits brought by students against school districts, a great many of them revolve around controversial messages on students' T-shirts worn in public schools.

The public school is special place for students, and it is a workplace for educators, administrators, and other employees. Students have a place where they work, study, play, and interact with peers as part of the state's commitment to them. Teachers instruct, supervise, and maintain an environment that is conducive to student safety and an environment conducive to their students' work.

Most of the work performed by professionals often involves one-on-one interactions of short duration but occasionally of more protracted duration in highly focused situations such as surgery or a trial. However, teacher interactions with their students have prolonged, focused contact: "Probably no other professional group has such extended times with their client/patient."[17] These actions have a range of formal and informal interactions.

While students congregate informally in many places, such as a mall, park, playgrounds, beaches, and so on, the school, whether public or private is not an informal gathering place with relaxed expectations and rules for appearance.

Educators have a professional and a legal obligation to secure the legal and constitutional rights of their charges. The school is a truly unique environment, and that uniqueness brings challenges such as what dress and appearance is appropriate and conducive to meeting the purposes for compulsory education.

As noted above, within this unique environment a dynamic tension exists between students push for their rights and the educators' responsibilities to those students. For example, students have a constitutional right to free speech under the First Amendment, a right they do not relinquish when they walk through the schoolhouse gate. However, as the Supreme Court observed in *Cornelius v. NAACP Legal Defense and Educational Fund*,

> Even protected speech is not equally permissible in all places and at all times. Nothing in the Constitution requires the government freely to grant access to all who wish to exercise their right to free speech on every type of Government property without regard to the nature of the property or to the disruption that might be caused by the speaker's activities.[18]

Although students are considered "persons" and are therefore entitled to constitutional protections, their protected rights of speech and expression are limited. Chief Justice Burger asserted "that the constitutional rights of students in public school are not automatically coextensive with the rights of adults in other settings."[19] Forms of expression allowed by adults may be prohibited to children in a public school.

The push by students to express themselves at school through their choice of clothing challenges two kinds of school regulations. First, students' demands to choose their attire often conflict with school dress codes, which define the clothes that cannot be worn. Clothes that do not adequately cover the buttocks, breasts, and bellies and clothes that are revealing, advertise alcohol or drugs, or create or are likely to disrupt the school are often targets of dress codes.[20] Sometimes the controversy is over the content the clothing communicates. For example, in 2022, a father, on behalf of his daughter, sued a Michigan school district when it prevented her from wearing a hat with an image of an AR-15 and the slogan "Come and Take It."[21]

Dress codes have seldom been associated with school reform. They are more of a response to behavior or messages that can be distracting or disruptive. For example, a federal district court in Massachusetts noted that dress codes can protect students from "an environment of unrelenting winks, snickering, and sexual proddings."[22]

Second, student clothing choices may also challenge school policies that mandate what students must wear to school. In other words, a school district with a school uniform policy may see its policy challenged on First Amendment grounds by students who insist they have a constitutional right not to wear a uniform while they are in school.

Requiring students to wear uniforms to school, student plaintiffs assert, restricts their right to expressive conduct through their choice of clothing. While school uniforms often conjure visions of private,[23] often Catholic[24] schools where girls wear plaid skirts and boys wear ties and jackets, most public school uniforms require that specific colors such as khaki and blue be worn.

When defending their student dress codes in court, most school districts do not attempt to justify their dress codes based on research or policy arguments that such policies improve student achievement. Rather, school districts generally justify their dress codes on the grounds that such codes prevent

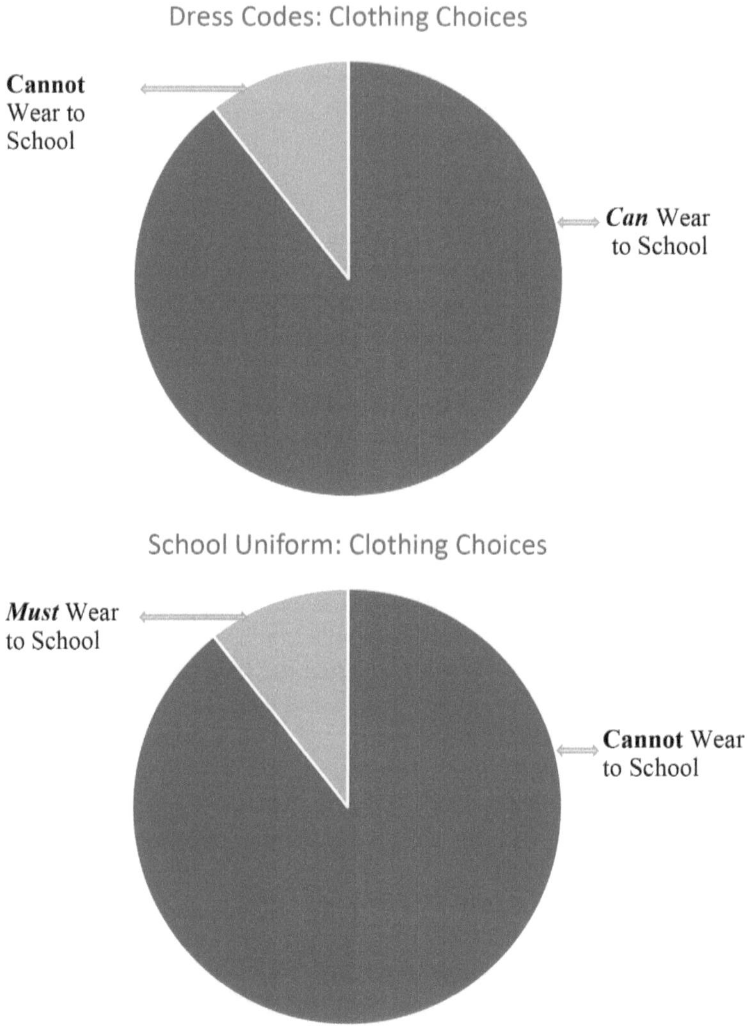

Figure 1.1 Dress Codes Versus School Uniform Clothing Choices

disruptions caused by certain types of clothing and support the learning environment. They argue that dress codes help students focus on learning by banning provocative clothing and advertisements for illegal behavior such a drug use or alcohol consumption.

The arguments for not allowing students to wear certain advertisements or banning clothing that is too revealing are not aimed at improving attendance, achieving better results on standardized tests, or developing community spirit. Rather, school authorities adopt dress codes with the simple goal of creating a purposeful learning environment that reflects community values.

Dress code advocates do not assert that banning sagging pants (precariously worn to reveal colorful boxers), crop-top T-shirts, or torn jeans will result in anything more than a more businesslike environment for students and adults.

The US Government Accountability Office (GAO) in October 2022 found that the top two frequently stated reasons for adopting a dress code are eliminating distractions (73 percent) and student safety (72.8 percent). The least frequent reason was preventing gang violence (5.3 percent). The following example of dress code rationales was provided: "*Suburban School District*: the student dress code is intended to create and preserve a positive climate for teaching and learning . . . and preserve school order and safety."[25]

The policy objectives of a student dress code and the rationale for adopting a school uniform code are similar, but with differences. Schools generally adopt dress codes to maintain a disciplined learning environment and to protect the school environment from inappropriate influences, whereas schools that introduce student uniform codes often do so with the specific goal of enhancing student achievement. Chapter 9 will continue the discussion on school uniforms.

THE BALANCING ACT

> "How do we balance school interests in educational mission and student interest in identity formation and self-determination? How do community norms and expectations influence school decisionmaking?"—Meredith Johnson Harbach, "Sexualization, Sex Discrimination, and Public School Dress Codes," *University of Richmond Law Review* 50 (2016): 1040

For many students, what to wear to school is an innocuous question that is often answered by locating something in the closet that is clean (or reasonably clean). For other students, the decision about what to wear to school involves the student's personal beliefs and values and is linked to the student's nascent development of self and personal values. For example, Aloysius Dreaming Bear brought a lawsuit against his school district hoping to win the right to wear his traditional Lakota clothing to his high school graduation instead of the required cap and gown.[26]

School officials and students do not always share the same opinion of what is appropriate to wear to school. But if a school chooses to adopt a specific policy that restricts what students may wear to school, that policy must comport with established and guaranteed constitutional freedoms.

There are legitimate reasons for schools to adopt student dress codes. Some of these reasons involve safety (no chains, spiked collars, and flip-flops).

Schools have a legitimate concern, for example, about students wearing loose clothing around machinery commonly found in industrial arts classes.

Other concerns involve the impressionable age of the students and the inappropriateness of certain types of dress (revealing clothes, clothes that advertise drugs and alcohol). One high school in New England expressed its desire for modesty by developing a student dress code around what school officials and students called the "4 Bs"—bellies, butts, breasts, and boxers.[27] You can have them; you just can't show them.

And some school officials adopt dress codes to prohibit clothes that can cause disruptions, interfere with the school mission, or glorify gangs. Many schools have policies that prohibit students from wearing clothing that celebrates the illegal use of drugs or alcohol, and some have codes that prohibit students from wearing clothing associated with gang activity. One high school principal in a small New England town describes his school's dress code in the following way:

> We have a very vague dress code. We really only try to deal with imagery and/or slogans that are for illegal activities (alcohol, drugs, violence, hate language, etc.). We do not dress code students (male or female) in regards to clothing length, skin exposure, etc. We receive pushback administratively for our perceived lax enforcement of dress code but we feel it helps to create a more positive and inclusive culture in our school.[28]

Community standards have influenced several dress code cases. In 1987, students sued an Ohio school district for refusing to allow them to attend a prom dressed as a person of the opposite sex.[29] A federal court found no First Amendment violation, however. In the court's view, schools have the authority to enforce dress regulations that teach community values and promote school discipline.

The same year, an Illinois student challenged a school rule, invoked to curtail gang activity, against males wearing earrings.[30] Like the Ohio students, the plaintiff lost this case. However, community standards change. In 2010, a female student brought suit when she was denied the opportunity to attend her prom with her girlfriend wearing a tuxedo. The federal district court found that the student's free speech rights were abridged, asserting that the "expression and communication of her viewpoint is the type of speech that falls squarely within the purview of the First Amendment."[31]

One legal commentator has asserted that the "'[t]he Achilles' Heel' of dress codes is the difficulty in defining what is proper attire in the classroom without violating the basic constitutional rights of students."[32] While public school students enjoy some degree of freedom of speech within the schoolhouse gates, the courts have recognized that this freedom must be balanced against the need to foster an educational atmosphere free from undue disruptions.

Moreover, although some student clothing clearly conveys a particular message—T-shirts proclaiming political messages, for example—not all clothing choices have enough expressive content to be protected by the Free Speech Clause of the First Amendment.

For example, in a New Mexico case involving a student's asserted constitutional right to wear "sagging pants," a federal judge concluded that most people would not interpret the wearing of droopy pants as conveying a message. Moreover, the judge noted, the "communication of ideas must be measured against substantial and compelling societal goals such as safety, decency, individual rights of other citizens, and the smooth functioning of government."[33]

However, in Utah, Emalyce Kee, who is Navajo and Rosebud Sioux, was told in 2021 that she could not wear a beaded graduation cap with an eagle plume: "She wondered what the difference was between her cultural regalia and other students wearing candy necklaces or gold jewelry, or even Hawaiian leis."[34] She hid her custom cap under her cap and donned it when her name was called and walked in it.

About a year later, on April 14, 2022, Utah governor Spencer Cox signed into law HB 30 Student Tribal Regalia Use Amendments, making it illegal to deny Native American students the opportunity to wear their cultural regalia to their graduation. The law pertains to students enrolled or eligible to be enrolled as a member of a tribe. Tribal regalia means a tribe's traditional dress and includes recognized objects of cultural significance such as tribal symbols, beads, and feathers.[35]

CONCLUDING THOUGHTS

While students possess free speech rights, those rights can sometimes be constitutionally abridged within the special environment of the public school, and those rights must be balanced against the legitimate interests of school authorities. This book explores the contours of that legal balance as articulated by the courts.

Without a doubt, considerable litigation starting in the 1960s has established that the once benign and mundane issue of what students choose to wear to school is now draped with constitutional considerations. The constitutionality of student dress codes has been litigated in federal courts all over the United States. In just over a half century of litigation, students have expanded their school wardrobe and grooming rights. However, not all dress decisions of students are cut from constitutional cloth.

Judges are often sympathetic to the special nature of the schoolyard and are unwilling to adopt the dress mores of the shopping mall, seeking to keep from trivializing the Constitution. However, they also often reflect a respect for student constitutional rights inside the schoolhouse gate. We will next lay the Supreme Court foundation for student free speech rights, the core issue asserted in cases of restrictive dress codes from LGBTQ+ positions, to images of weapons, sagging pants, the Confederate flag, sexualization of female students, natural hair, and school uniforms explored in following chapters.

"It is worth remembering that, whether this decision is correct or not, no other court system in the world today, and none that has existed in the history of the world, would take so much time to address the concerns of two high school students sent home over their T-shirts. Whatever the outcome, claims of violation of free expression are given the greatest attention, even when they arise in miniature, by this country, this judicial system and this court."—*Pyle v. South Hadley School Committee,* 824 F. Supp. 7,11 (D. Mass.1993)

NOTES

1. Alyssa Pavlakis and Rachel Roegman, "How Dress Codes Criminalize Males and Sexualize Females of Color," *Phi Delta Kappan* 100, no. 2 (September 24, 2018): 54–58, https://kappanonline.org/pavlakis-roegman-dress-codes-gender-race-discrimination/. The authors continue,

> Recent headlines in the popular press highlight stories of girls and young women who were forced to wear a sweatshirt over a tank top during a heat wave, put tape over their nipples if they were not wearing a bra, or remove hair extensions. In the era of Black Lives Matter and #MeToo, these news stories highlight ways that seemingly neutral school policies may inequitably impact students based on their gender and race.

Ibid.

2. *Miller v. School District*, 495 F.2d 658, 664 (7th Cir. 1974).

3. Pavlakis and Roegman, *supra* note 1, ibid.

4. Martha M. McCarthy, Nelda H. Cambron-McCabe, and Suzanne Eckes, *Public School Law: Teachers' and Students Rights*, 7th ed. (Boston: Pearson, 2014), 113.

5. For a discussion and analysis of dress codes using an intersectional feminist critical race lens, see Jennifer L. Martin and Jennifer N. Brooks, "Loc'd and Faded, Yoga Pants, and Spaghetti Straps: Discrimination in Dress codes and School Push-out," *International Journal of Education Policy & Leadership* 16, no. 19 (2020): 1–19, http://journals.sfu.ca/ijepl/index.php/ijepl/article/view/1047.

6. These controversies are costly to school districts and taxpayers. For example, in a 2008 case, a student sued her school district on First Amendment grounds after school authorities banned her from wearing or displaying slogans advocating the fair treatment of gay and lesbian students. The student won her suit, which resulted in a judgment of $1 against the school district, obviously a trivial amount. Attorneys' fees and other litigation expenses, however, cost the school district $325,000. (*Gilman v. School Board. for Holmes County*, 567 F. Supp. 2d 1359, 1365 [N. D. Fla. 2008]) These are not inconsequential costs to an educator's disciplinary decision.

7. Stephen R. Goldstein, "The Scope and Sources of School Board Authority to Regulate Student Conduct and Status: A Nonconstitutional Analysis," *University of Pennsylvania Law Review* 117, no. 3 (1969): 399 (n. 88).

8. *Jones v. Day*, 127 Miss. 136, 89 So. 906 (1921).

9. Describing the history of board discretion, the Note author wrote, "First, school boards have been endowed with statutory authority to operate and manage learning institutions in any manner they deem necessary for the educational instruction of the students; the courts have recognized that the management of schools is not a judicial function." Notes, "High School Hair Regulations," *Valparaiso University Law Review* 4, no. 2 (1970): 402. Similarly, I. N. Edwards wrote, "It should be said, however, that the courts are very reluctant to declare a board regulation unreasonable, and in no case will they pass on its wisdom or expediency." I. N. Edwards, "Recent Judicial Decisions Relating to the Powers of Boards of Education," *School Review* (June 1924): 447, https://www.journals.uchicago.edu/doi/pdf/10.1086/437998.

10. *Valentine Independent School District*, 191 Ia. 1100 (1921).

11. *Pugsley v. Sellmeyer*, 250 S. W. 538, 539 (Ark. 1923). The school regulation banned students from wearing transparent hosiery, face paint, or immodest dress. Ibid., 539–40.

12. Ibid.

13. Newton Edwards, "Legal Authority of Boards of Education to Enforce Rules and Regulations," *Elementary School Journal* 31, no. 6 (1931): 446.

14. *Pugsley v. Sellmeyer*, 250 S.W., 540.

15. 393 U.S. 503, 514 (1969).

16. Charlotte Brunel, *The T-Shirt Book* (New York: Assouline, 2002), 112; Alice Harris, *The White T* (New York: Harper Style, 1996), 44.

17. Todd A. DeMitchell, Richard Fossey, and Terri A. DeMitchell, *Raising a Cautionary Flag: Educational Malpractice and the Professional Teacher* (Lanham, MD: Rowman and Littlefield, 2022), 39. See chapter 2 for a discussion of the context of education and educators as members of a learned society, 19–52.

18. 473 U.S. 788, 799–800 (1985).

19. *Bethel School District No. 403 v. Fraser*, 478 U.S. 675, 682 (1986).

20. However, *Tinker v. Des Moines Independent Community School District*, 393 U.S. 503, 514 (1969), essentially found that student, passive, nondisruptive political speech (wearing a black armband in protest of the war in Vietnam) during school hours is protected speech.

21. Jennifer Chambers, "Durand Third-Grader's Father Sues School over Right to Wear Hat Depicting AR-15 Rifle," *Detroit News* (May 13, 2022), https://

www.detroitnews.com/story/news/education/2022/05/13/durand-third-grader-father-sues-school-over-right-wear-hat-ar-15-rifle-image/9767159002/. The father, Adam Stroub, is seeking a preliminary and permanent injunction prohibiting the elementary school from restricting her speech by preventing her from wearing her hat, and nominal damages.

22. *Pyle v. South Hadley School Committee*, 861 F. Supp 157, 170 (D. Mass. 1994).

23. Michael Firmin, Suzanne Smith, and Lynsey Perry, "School Uniforms: A Qualitative Analysis of Aims and Accomplishments at Two Christian Schools," *Journal of Research on Christian Education* 15 (2006): 143–68, https://www.tandfonline.com/doi/abs/10.1080/10656210609485000.

24. See Susan McBrayer, "The School Uniform Movement and What It Tells Us about American Education: A Symbolic Crusade, by David L. Brunsma," *Catholic Education* (September 2007), https://digitalcommons.lmu.edu/ce/vol11/iss1/12/: "The plaid uniform has been culturally synonymous with Catholic schools. Today, however, uniforms have become less formal, replacing dress shirts for polo shirts emblazoned with the school name or mascot. Sweaters and blazers have given way to sweatshirts in many Catholic schools. Administrators and teachers may have initiated this change in keeping with the more secular phenomenon of 'business casual.' Furthermore, rising tuition, declining enrollment, and a change in demographics may have also contributed to new trends in the Catholic school uniform."

25. Jacqueline M. Nowacki, *K–12 Education: Department of Education Should provide Information on Equity and Safety in School Dress Codes* (Washington, DC: US Government Accountability Office GAO-23–105348 K–12 Education, October 2022), 16, https://www.gao.gov/assets/gao-23-105348.pdf.

26. *Dreaming Bear v. Fleming*, 714 F. Supp. 2d 972, 975 (D. S. D. 2010).

27. Email communication discussing the "4 Bs" dress code in the possession of the author from Ashley Mancusi (January 16, 2013).

28. This communication (October 17, 2022) is in the possession of the author.

29. *Harper v. Edgewood Board of Education*, 655 F. Supp. 1353 (S. D. Ohio 1987).

30. *Olesen v. Board of Education of School District No. 228*, 676 F. Supp. 820 (N. D. Ill. 1987). In *Hines v. Caston School Corporation*, 651 N.E.2d (Ind. Ct. App. 1995), suit was brought by a male elementary school student challenging a school policy banning the wearing of earrings by boys. The suit was brought under due process and equal protection grounds, not free speech. The court held that the law was reasonably related to the desire of the community's schools to reflect its values and instill discipline. Wearing earrings by males was considered inconsistent with community standards.

31. *McMillen v. Itawamba County School District*, 702 F. Supp. 2d 699, 705 (N. D. Miss. 2010). For a discussion of proms and LGBT students, see Suzanne Eckes, Todd DeMitchell, and Richard Fossey, "Commentary: A White Sports Coat and A Pink Carnation: Protecting the Legal Rights of LGBT Students to attend the Prom,"

Teachers College Record (March 29, 2013), ID Number 17072. Also see *Doe ex rel. Doe v. Yunits*, No. 001060A, 2000 WL 33162199 (Mass. Super. Oct. 11, 2000), in which a Massachusetts public school district was enjoined from prohibiting a male student from attending school wearing female clothes and accessories.

32. Rob Killen, "The Achilles' Heel of Dress Codes: The Definition of Proper Attire in Public Schools," *Tulsa Law Journal* 36 (2000): 459–86. Killen concludes, "If school districts must restrict students' appearance to maintain discipline in the learning environment, instead of relying on inherently weak dress codes, school boards should consider enacting uniform policies, which have a proven record of success." Ibid., 486.

33. *Bivens v. Albuquerque Public Schools*, 899 F. Supp. 556, 559 (D. N. M. 1995).

34. Alastair Lee Bitsoi, "She Was Told She Couldn't Wear Her Tribal Regalia at Graduation. She Wore It Anyway," *Salt Lake Tribune* (April 20, 2022), https://www.sltrib.com/news/2022/04/20/native-student-denied/. A similar event in Saskatchewan, Canada, also resulted in legislation to protect indigenous culture. Isabella Kulak, an eleven-year-old member of the Cote First Nation wore a handmade ribbon skirt, an important part of the identity and history of many indigenous women. Isabella was told that her skirt was inappropriate to wear for her school's "formal day." In response to Isabella's activism, a bill was presented to the Senate titled National Ribbon Skirt Day in honor of indigenous women and girls. The Senate bill describes the ribbon skirt as a "centuries-old spiritual symbol of womanhood, identity, adaption and survival and . . . a way for women to honour themselves and their culture. Tom Yun, "Indigenous Girl Shamed for What She Wore to School Pushes for National Ribbon Skirt Day," CTV News (January 9, 2022), https://www.ctvnews.ca/lifestyle/indigenous-girl-shamed-for-what-she-wore-to-school-pushes-for-national-ribbon-skirt-day-1.5733286.

35. HB 30, Utah Code Section 1. Section 53G-4–412 (2022), https://le.utah.gov/~2022/bills/static/HB0030.html.

2

The First Amendment

Student Appearance and Expressive Conduct

> It is perhaps, the most basic of questions in First Amendment jurisprudence: what constitutes speech?[1]

From the early days of the common school movement which evolved into our current system of public education, students were not afforded the constitutional protections that were possessed by adults. Reasonableness was the near universal standard for the regulation of student conduct. The courts were "very reluctant to declare a board action unreasonable": even when the court believed that the rule was "unwise" or "inexpedient."[2] The Fifth Circuit of Appeals opined, "It is not the job of federal courts to determine the most effective way to educate our nation's youth."[3]

For example, in a 1908 case, the Supreme Court of Wisconsin upheld the suspension of a student who ridiculed his teachers in a poem published in the local newspaper. The court stated that school authorities must be invested with a broad authority to discipline students "unless it has been illegally or unreasonably exercised."[4]

Students did not always possess the right to free speech. In fact, "the United States Supreme Court did not even apply the Bill of Rights to public school students until the 1940s."[5] The courts imposed little or no obligation on the public schools to respect the constitutional rights of their students, essentially adopting the position that they had none.

However, in 1943, the US Supreme Court recognized the liberty interests of students in the important flag salute case during World War II, holding that "educating the young for citizenship is reason for scrupulous protection of Constitutional freedoms of the individual, if we are not to strangle the free mind at its source and teach youth to discount important principles of our government as mere platitudes."[6] Next, the 1967 Supreme Court decision in

Shelton v. Tucker made clear that students enjoyed constitutional rights in the school environment, writing, "The vigilant protection of constitutional freedoms is nowhere more vital than in the community of American schools."[7]

Furthermore, continuing the development of constitutional rights for students, the US Supreme Court found in 1975 that students have a constitutional right to due process before being suspended or expelled from school.[8] However, students have not been successful in asserting that paddling (corporal punishment) rises to the level of a constitutional violation under the Eighth Amendment's prohibition against cruel and unusual punishment.[9] And in 1985 the court asserted that students have a constitutional right to privacy under the Fourth Amendment, which they do not give up when they come on school grounds, and school officials cannot disregard that right simply because they desire to search a student's person or possessions.[10]

Students gained recognition for constitutional rights, but do students possess a constitutional right of freedom of expression to wear clothes of their choice to school? A corollary question is, what constitutes expression in the choice of attire? The issue of student speech is important because, as Nelda Cambron-McCabe stated, "[s]chool officials confront students' speech rights on a daily basis in public schools."[11]

Gaining an understanding of the role that the First Amendment rights of public school students is imperative to a fulsome discussion of the legal controversy of dress codes. The legal controversy rests on a foundation of a student's assertion that "dress can qualify as conduct that meets the standard of symbolic speech, which is entitled to First Amendment protection."[12] It is noteworthy that no student dress code case has been argued before the US Supreme Court. However, the high court has provided some guidance with respect to the parameters of student freedom of expression at school.

The controversy over what students wear to school and their appearance at school, as previously noted, most often involves whether and to what extent students' sartorial choices are protected by their First Amendment rights. An understanding of students' First Amendment right to free speech in the school environment is a necessary predicate for a discussion about the constitutionality of school regulations of student attire and appearance.

THE SPECIAL CHARACTERISTICS OF THE PUBLIC SCHOOL

"The Supreme Court has repeatedly emphasized that public education is paramount in preparing children for civic engagement in a democratic system and has deemed education an essential component in the maintenance of 'the fabric of society.' Because education is viewed as necessary for the preservation of our democracy, the provision and administration of public schools is at the zenith of the State's functions."—Amanda Harmon Cooley, "Inculcating Suppression," *Georgetown Law Journal* 107 (2019): 372

Various courts have carved out a special niche in our society for the public schools based "on the so-called 'special characteristics' of the elementary and secondary environment."[13] Actions that a student may take outside the schoolhouse gate often may not be taken inside that gate. The Supreme Court, in the seminal student free speech case *Tinker v. Des Moines Independent School District*, held students do not "shed their constitutional rights to freedom of speech or expression at the schoolhouse gate."[14]

While acknowledging that public school students have the First Amendment right of free speech, that right is exercised within the special characteristics of the school environment. A balance is sought between students' rights and the preservation of the educational process.[15] "Free expression rights may be limited by policies that are reasonably designed to take into account the special circumstances of the educational environment."[16] The courts have cabined students' First Amendment rights by giving deference to school administrators' judgment as to what speech is appropriate in the context of the public school.[17]

COURTS SEEK THE PROPER BALANCE

Historically, the courts have been loath to intervene in the decisions of school boards unless it can be shown that the board acted in an arbitrary, capricious, discriminatory, or unreasonable manner. Courts have heeded the admonition of the Supreme Court, writing, "We previously have cautioned that courts lack the 'specialized knowledge and experience' necessary to resolve 'persistent and difficult questions of educational policy.'"[18] School boards have a substantial interest in creating and maintaining a safe and effective learning environment; the courts seem to leave them to difficult tasks.

An example of this balance of public school student rights and the responsibilities of the school is found in the Fourth Amendment search-and-seizure cases in schools. The constitutional right to be free from unreasonable seizures is different inside the schoolhouse gate than it is outside the gate. The Supreme Court, in the seminal 1985 student search-and-seizure case *New Jersey v. T.L.O.*, held that students' have a constitutional right to be free from unreasonable search and seizure but that given the special nature of the public school, that right was less than that for a citizen who was not a student.[19]

Thus, while student expectations of privacy are legitimate,[20] equally legitimate is the school's "need to maintain an environment in which learning can take place."[21] This balance between the privacy interests of students and the "substantial" need of educators to maintain order in the school, the Supreme Court wrote, is found in the standard of reasonable suspicion for a legal search as opposed to the stricter standard for the police of probable cause.

Although students are considered "persons" and are therefore entitled to constitutional protections, these protected rights of speech and expression are limited. Chief Justice Burger asserted "that the constitutional rights of students in public school are not automatically coextensive with the rights of adults in other settings."[22] Forms of expression allowed by adults may be prohibited to children in a public school. Public school children enjoy some measure of freedom of speech within the schoolhouse gates, but that freedom "is balanced against the need to foster an educational atmosphere free from undue disruptions to appropriate discipline."[23]

Students' constitutional right to free speech is not unfettered. The right must be balanced against the need of the state to provide an efficient system of public education. Public schools inculcate fundamental values necessary to the maintenance of a democratic society. Schools have broad discretion in inculcating fundamental values into their programs and have wide discretion in choosing the curriculum to reflect those values.[24]

Students have the right to free speech in public schools. That right is balanced against the legitimate demands that the schools provide an environment conducive to learning and protecting the rights of all students. Restrictions are placed on minors that are greater than those placed on adults.[25] But what is the student's right to free speech?

THE FIRST AMENDMENT RIGHT TO FREE SPEECH

The First Amendment to the United States Constitution states, in pertinent part, that "Congress shall make no law . . . abridging the freedom of speech or of the press."[26] The importance of free speech to the concept of what it means to be an American cannot be overstated. The right to free speech builds a foundation for the relationship between citizens and their government. It is a right that neither the Magna Carta of 1215 nor the English Bill of Rights of 1689 protected for citizens. (However, the English Bill of Rights protected free speech for members of Parliament.)

The right to free speech is characterized as the touchstone, the wellspring of individual liberty. Free speech is a hearty, robust right, not a mere shadow of a right that hues to bland, uneventful speech.[27]

For example, Justice Benjamin N. Cardozo described the freedom of speech as "the matrix, the indispensable condition of nearly every other form of freedom."[28] More than eight decades ago, the Supreme Court wrote, "Freedom of speech and freedom of press, which are protected by the First Amendment from infringement by Congress, are among the fundamental personal rights and liberties which are protected by the Fourteenth Amendment from invasion by state action."[29] In 1995 the Supreme Court opined that the purpose of the Bill of Rights generally and the First Amendment particularly "is to protect unpopular individuals from retaliation and their ideas from suppression at the hand of an intolerant society."[30]

Professor Alexander Meiklejohn echoes these sentiments from the Supreme Court about the importance of free speech to the individual but adds the dimension he deems necessary for self-government. He writes, "The unabridged freedom of public discussion is the rock on which our government stands."[31] Similarly, the court wrote that free speech serves society by allowing the "uninhibited, robust, and wide-open debates about matters of public importance that secures an informed citizenry."[32]

Consequently, the right to free speech in our society is extensive and robust.[33] Supporting this view, Justice Oliver Wendell Holmes observed, "[I]f there is any principle of the Constitution that more imperatively calls for attachment than any other it is the principle of free thought—not free thought for those who agree with us but freedom for the thought we hate."[34]

Another example of the breadth and depth of the First Amendment right to free speech is found in a Supreme Court case involving race-baiting speech. The high court wrote "[a] function of free speech under our system of government is to invite dispute. It may indeed best serve its high purpose when it induces a condition of unrest, creates dissatisfaction with conditions as they are, or even stirs people to anger. Speech is often provocative and challenging."[35]

Law professor Cass Sunstein offers an interesting view of the limitations of government to regulate speech, especially political speech. He wrote that "government cannot insult the moral autonomy of its citizens by stopping them from hearing what other people say—especially if the reason that government acts is its fear that citizens will be influenced or persuaded by what is said."[36]

Speech is a major vehicle for citizens to participate in democratic self-governance: "[T]here is practically universal agreement that a major purpose of [the First] Amendment was to protect the free discussion of governmental affairs."[37] Consequently, "debate on public issues should be uninhibited, robust, and wide-open."[38]

Nevertheless, freedom of speech is not an absolute constitutional right in every situation.[39] As the Supreme Court observed in *Cornelius v. NAACP*,

> Even protected speech is not equally permissible in all places and at all times. Nothing in the Constitution requires the government freely to grant access to all who wish to exercise their right to free speech on every type of Government property without regard to the nature of the property or to the disruption that might be caused by the speaker's activities.[40]

THE LIMITS OF FREE SPEECH

However, as robust as the right of free speech is under our Constitution, it is not without limits. Indeed, the Supreme Court, writing more than one hundred years ago, asserted that the right of free speech, while "sacred and vital," "is not absolute, it is subject to restriction and limitation."[41]

Content of the Speech

"If there is a bedrock principle underlying the First Amendment, it is that the government may not prohibit the expression of an idea simply because society finds the idea itself offensive or disagreeable."[42] Thus, government restrictions on speech that are based on the content of the speech face a presumption of invalidity when reviewed by the courts. An assessment of whether a regulation is content related or content neutral depends on "whether the government has adopted a regulation of speech because of disagreement with the message it conveys."[43]

Professor Erwin Chermerinsky writes, "All speech, regardless of its content, must be treated the same by government. To allow the government to target particular views or subjects permits the government to greatly distort the marketplace of ideas."[44] Essentially, given the power of government over individuals, it cannot overpower the message that it disagrees with and trumpet the message that it prefers; otherwise, "government may effectively drive out certain ideas or viewpoints from the marketplace."[45] Government regulations must be neutral regarding the content of the message or they must meet the highest burden of strict scrutiny analysis in order for the regulation to pass constitutional muster.

An example of government suppressing speech through a content-related regulation is found in *R. A. V. v. St. Paul*, in which the St. Paul Bias-Motivated Crime Ordinance was struck down.[46] The Supreme Court held that a bias-motivated crime ordinance violated the First Amendment because it punished fighting words motivated by race, color, creed, religion or gender hostility but not those motivated by other reasons. The ordinance punished certain viewpoints but not others, and the government may not regulate speech "based on hostility—or favoritism—towards the underlying message expressed."[47]

The ordinance was used to prosecute someone for burning a cross on the lawn of an African American family. While the Supreme Court, in a somewhat fractured opinion, found the act to be reprehensible, it also found that that the ordinance suppressed speech.

Governmental agencies that promulgate content-related regulations that suppress speech on a disfavored topic come to the courts with a heavy burden of proving constitutionality, while content-neutral regulations may shoulder a lighter load. If a dress code is considered content neutral—in other words, it is not aimed at suppressing the content of specific speech—it has a greater chance of success. An example of a content-neutral regulation is the dress code passed by the Waxahachie Independent School District, which prohibited shirts displaying any printed message other than messages pertaining to school spirit that were approved by the school principal.

In essence, virtually all shirt-based speech was prohibited; thus, the regulation did not single out a particular message to suppress. The policy was neutral regarding all content of the speech as well as the viewpoint of the speech.[48] The Fifth Circuit Court of Appeals, in a lawsuit challenging the constitutionality of the dress code, asserted that "[t]he District was in no way attempting to suppress any student's expression through its dress code—a critical fact based on earlier student speech cases—so the dress code is content-neutral."[49]

In *Linmark Associates, Inc. v. Town of Willingboro*, the Supreme Court noted that laws regulating the time, place and manner of speech are different than those regulations that prohibit speech.[50] Time, place, and manner restrictions that do not treat speech differently based on the content of the speech and leave open ample alternative means of expression typically do not violate free speech rights. For example, school regulations that designate the places and times in which students can distribute literature need to be reasonable and nondiscriminatory. The regulations must apply uniformly to all speech (content neutral), and for a school, the regulations must be related to the function of the school.[51]

Unprotected Speech

Free speech is indeed a critical right that is vigorously protected in our society. It is a right that is often used as the example of what it means to be an American and to be free. However, the right to free speech is not absolute. The courts, when reviewing free speech challenges, must parse the difference between the regulation of speech and the suppression of speech. They "are not the same, either in purpose or result."[52] Regulation is permissible when government is not trying to suppress the content of ideas, except in very specific circumstances such as fighting words,[53] incitement to riot producing imminent lawless action,[54] defamation,[55] child pornography,[56] obscenity,[57] and true threats.[58]

Moreover, the Supreme Court has made clear that the free speech rights of students while at school are not as full-bodied as the free speech rights of adults. Even though students do not shed their constitutional right to free speech at the schoolhouse gate,[59] school officials have the authority to put some restrictions on student speech, as outlined in five Supreme Court decisions, which will be discussed in the next section.

THE SUPREME COURT AND STUDENT FREE SPEECH CASES

As discussed above, public schools have a long history of not recognizing that minors possess constitutional rights. Until the middle of the twentieth century, the courts imposed little or no obligation on the public schools to respect the constitutional rights of their students.

An early example of the move to recognize the constitutional rights of minors took place in a non-school setting. The Supreme Court held that a fifteen-year-old facing delinquency prosecution must be afforded due process rights.[60] "The case [, *In re Gault*,] is viewed as a turning point in the constitutional rights of juveniles."[61] It can be viewed as part of the general trend of the Warren Court's concern starting with the desegregation cases of the 1950s and spreading to the unequal treatment of minority populations.[62]

The free speech rights of public school students developed and are still developing since the move to increase the rights and protections of individuals. The chronology of the five major Supreme Court decisions starting in 1969 is explored below.

> "School boards, not federal courts have the authority to decide what constitutes appropriate behavior and dress in public schools."—*Canady v. Bossier Parish School District*, 240 F.3d 437, 441 (5th Cir. 2001)

The Black Armband as Symbolic Protest: *Tinker v. Des Moines Independent Community School District*

It has been more than fifty years since the Supreme Court historically extended the protection of the First Amendment to students inside the schoolhouse gate.[63] In 1965, John and Mary Beth Tinker and Chris Eckhart were suspended by Des Moines school officials for wearing black armbands to school in protest of the Vietnam War. The school administration had learned about the Tinker children's planned protest in advance and hastily developed and implemented a policy targeting the protest. They were suspended when they refused to take off the armbands.

The three students sued in federal court, arguing that the First Amendment gave them the right to express themselves in a quiet and dignified way, but a federal district court dismissed their complaint. On appeal, the Eighth Circuit Court of Appeals heard the case *en banc* (a hearing before all the circuit judges), but the court was equally divided and thus affirmed the trial court's dismissal of the students' constitutional claims. The two students then proceeded to the US Supreme Court to press their case that they had a constitutional right to quietly and passively wear a two-inch-wide black armband in protest of the war in Vietnam.

Martha McCarthy, noted school law professor, described *Tinker* as the Magna Carta for student free speech rights.[64] Furthermore, as the Supreme Court observed in *Grayned v. Rockford*, *Tinker* is the "touchstone" case when the courts "consider[] the question of how to accommodate First Amendment rights within the special characteristics of the school environment."[65]

In *Tinker v. Des Moines Independent Community School District*, the Supreme Court reversed the lower courts' decisions and recognized the Tinker children's right to wear black armbands to school in protest of the Vietnam War. The Supreme Court wrote, "Our problem lies in the area where students in the exercise of their First Amendment rights collide with the rules of the school."[66]

The Supreme Court declared that "[s]tudents in school as well as out of school are 'persons' under the Constitution. They are possessed of fundamental rights that the state must respect, just as they themselves must respect their obligations to the state,"[67] although school officials possess "the comprehensive authority . . . to prescribe and control conduct in the schools."[68]

However, the court found limits to the control that can be exerted over public school students, asserting,

> In our system, state-operated schools may not be enclaves of totalitarianism. School officials do not possess absolute authority over their students. . . . In our system, students may not be regarded as closed-circuit recipients of only that which the State chooses to communicate. They may not be confined to the expression of those sentiments that are officially approved.[69]

The Supreme Court found that school authorities could not justify the prohibition of student expression at school unless the conduct would "materially and substantially interfere with the requirements of appropriate discipline in the operation of the school" or "collid[es] with the rights of others."[70] The court asserted that "undifferentiated fear or apprehension of disturbance" cannot trump this "hazardous freedom" and replace it with rigid regimentation.[71]

Using this line of reasoning, a restriction on student clothing that arguably has some symbolic or explicit expression must be supported by a finding that the clothing would "materially disrupts classwork or involves substantial disorder."[72] Second, student speech may be prohibited when it involves a "collision with the rights of other students to be secure and to be let alone."[73] This standard raised the question of whether all clothing choices are protected as long as they do not create a material and substantial disruption.

However, the court in *Tinker* may reveal less support for an expansive view of students' rights to wear any clothing of their choice. First, the Supreme Court acknowledged the requirements of appropriate discipline in the operation of schools. Furthermore, and more importantly, the high court wrote,

> The problem posed in the present case does not relate to regulation of the length of skirts or the type of clothing to hairstyle or department. It does not concern aggressive, disruptive, action or disruptive action or even group demonstrations. Our problem involves direct, primary First Amendment rights akin to "pure speech."[74]

Courts have cited *Tinker* many times over the years in cases involving the free expression rights of public school students in their choice of clothing and appearance and whether that choice disrupts the school's activities, including instruction.[75] Unfortunately, not all of these cases involved issues as noble as the one the Tinkers brought forward. For example, a federal district court judge in Massachusetts noted that dress codes can protect students from an "environment of unrelenting winks, snickering, and sexual proddings."[76] The expert witness for the student plaintiffs in that case agreed that sexual innuendos in an educational environment can make students uncomfortable and can interfere with their ability to study.

Nevertheless, although the Supreme Court differentiated between pure speech and clothing issues, courts have cited *Tinker* for the proposition that a student's choice of style of clothing may carry the protection of the United States Constitution. For example, the Fourth Circuit of Appeals, applying *Tinker*, supported a student wearing a T-shirt with the three black silhouettes holding rifles, with "NRA" stamped over the silhouettes. The court found that the T-shirts were not disruptive.[77] Similarly, cases involving wearing the Confederate flag often use the *Tinker* test to resolve the issue.[78]

Lewd, Vulgar, and Offensive Student Speech: *Bethel School District v. Fraser*

Since the *Tinker* decision first acknowledged the free speech rights of students in the school environment, three more Supreme Court decisions "[have] expanded the kinds of speech schools can regulate."[79] Some consider *Tinker* as the "high water mark" for student free expression and the subsequent Supreme Court decisions as a retrenchment.[80]

Seventeen years after *Tinker*, the Supreme Court decided a case that would dramatically impact students' rights of expression at school. In *Bethel School District No. 403 v. Fraser*[81] the Supreme Court ruled that school officials could sanction a high school student for using lewd, vulgar, or offensive sexual metaphors during a political speech at a school assembly. Matthew Fraser gave a nomination speech filled with graphic, explicit sexual language but no profanities. Some students in the school assembly "hooted and yelled" and made sexual gestures in response to his speech, while other students sat bewildered and embarrassed.

After a due process hearing with the assistant principal, Fraser received a three-day suspension for using obscene language in violation of the school's discipline code, and he had his name removed from the candidate graduation speaker list.[82] Fraser contested the discipline in federal district court, alleging a violation of First Amendment right to free speech.

The district court held for Fraser, asserting that the school's disruptive conduct rule was vague and overbroad. It awarded Fraser $278 in damages and $12,750 in litigation costs and attorneys' fees. The school district appealed but lost before the Ninth Circuit Court of Appeals. The circuit court found that Fraser's speech was "indistinguishable" from Tinker's armband.[83]

In declaring that the school district had the authority to sanction Fraser for his vulgar speech, the Supreme Court chose not to apply the *Tinker* standard of material and substantial disruption, and instead fashioned a new analysis and test. The Supreme Court stated emphatically that the public schools have the duty to "inculcate[s] the habits and manners of civility."[84] This fundamental value of civility, the court pointed out, must take into account the "sensibilities of others."[85]

As one commentator opined, "This statement, coupled with *Tinker's* collision with the rights of others, tends to support dress codes aimed at supporting a civil school environment."[86] As the Supreme Court pointed out in *Fraser*, our nation's leaders have rules against offensive expression in our legislative halls, where vigorous political debate often occurs. Could the Supreme Court expect no less degree of civility in our schools? Or, as the Supreme Court put it, "Can it be that what is proscribed in the halls of Congress is beyond the reach of school officials to regulate?"[87]

The Supreme Court in *Fraser* held that "[t]he determination of what manner of speech in the classroom or in a school assembly is inappropriate properly rests with the school board."[88] Thus, the court upheld a school district's right to prohibit speech that is lewd, vulgar, or, laced with sexual innuendo.

"Surely it is a highly appropriate function of public education to prohibit vulgar and offensive terms in public discourse."[89]

Furthermore, the court affirmed that the constitutional rights of students in public schools are not automatically coextensive with the rights of adults in other settings. While adults have wide freedom in matters of public discourse, it does not follow that the same latitude must be permitted to children in P–12 public school. As cogently expressed by Judge Jon O. Newman and quoted by the Supreme Court, "the First Amendment gives a high school student the classroom right to wear Tinker's armband, but not Cohen's jacket."[90]

The Supreme Court's rationale in the *Fraser* decision was applied by the Sixth Circuit Court of Appeals, which held that a Marilyn Manson T-shirt of a three-headed Jesus with the wording "See No Truth, Hear No Truth, Speak No Truth" was vulgar, offensive, and contrary to the mission of the school.[91] Because the T-shirt was vulgar, the Sixth Circuit reasoned, it was not necessary to determine whether wearing the T-shirt to school might disrupt the school environment.

The federal district court in Massachusetts, responding to a dress code dispute involving Coed Naked T-shirts, wrote, "[U]nless federal courts are to take on the task of assessing, each morning of the school year, the latest creations of the adolescent imagination . . . [,] the limits on vulgarity in secondary schools, assuming a general standard of reasonableness, are to be defined by school administrators, answerable to school boards and ultimately to the voters of a community."[92] This places the authority for defining what expressive conduct is acceptable in a school environment squarely on the shoulders of those who bear the daily responsibility for that school environment.

The Supreme Court acknowledged in both *Tinker* and *Fraser* that students possess the constitutional right to free speech. However, that right is neither as robust as that which they have outside the schoolhouse gate nor as robust as that of adults. The court "affirmed that the constitutional rights of students in public schools are not automatically coextensive with the rights of adults in other settings."[93] Thus, the court views the school as a special place.

The Imprimatur of the School: *Hazelwood School District v. Kuhlmeier*

Fraser reduced some of the reach of *Tinker* by adding speech that is lewd, vulgar, and offensive to the types of speech that school authorities can ban without violating the First Amendment. Thus, in addition to student speech that school authorities reasonably believe is disruptive, school officials can ban speech that is patently offensive. A third important Supreme Court case, *Hazelwood School District v. Kuhlmeier*,[94] followed *Fraser* by adding further restrictions on student speech.

Hazelwood involved the free speech rights of students. This was the first time that the Supreme Court heard a case about student expression and the school's curriculum.[95] In this case, student contributors to a school newspaper published as part of a journalism class contested the principal's deletion of material from the newspaper prior to its publication. The Supreme Court started with a free speech forum analysis. Free speech has the greatest latitude in traditional public forums such as streets and parks, which have been used for purposes of assembly and communication.[96] Public schools do not possess these attributes, the majority asserted. If the school is not a public forum, then "school officials may impose reasonable restrictions on the speech of students, teachers, and other members of the school community."[97]

Since the school was not an open forum for indiscriminate student speech, the school newspaper, as part of its curriculum (the speech of the school), was not a forum for indiscriminate student speech. The school, as a forum for speech, is "reserved for its intended purpose of creating supervised learning experiences."[98] The *Hazelwood* court found that the school had authority over such school-sponsored publications as theatrical productions and "other expressive activities that students, parents, and other members of the public might reasonably perceive to bear the imprimatur of the school."[99] The Supreme Court held that educators do not offend the Constitution by exercising editorial control over school-sponsored expression "so long as their actions are reasonably related to legitimate pedagogical concerns."[100]

Deference to school authorities was given full weight when the court reasoned, "We thus recognized that the determination of what manner of speech in the classroom or in school assembly is appropriate properly rests with the school board rather than the federal courts."[101] Consequently, "[a] school need not tolerate student speech that is inconsistent with its 'basic educational mission. . . . '"[102] Nevertheless, the court has not retreated from the core principle that public school students enjoy some measure of free speech rights inside the schoolhouse gate. In some ways, the *Fraser* Court has returned to a reasonableness standard, at least for this free speech test, that we saw in *Pugsley* but appeared to have vanished with *Tinker*.

Students have the right to freedom of speech in school, but that right must be balanced and is neither absolute nor expansive. The fourth public school student free speech case moves the fulcrum further from *Tinker* and toward administrative prerogative.

Bong Hits 4 Jesus: *Morse v. Frederick*

The fourth Supreme Court student speech case is *Morse v. Frederick*.[103] It is probably best known by "BONG HITS 4 JESUS" the inscription of a fourteen-foot banner unfurled at a school activity. On January 24, 2002, the

Olympic Torch Relay passed through Juneau, Alaska, on the way to the Salt Lake City Winter Olympics. The route went past the Juneau-Douglas High School. The principal allowed the students and staff to view the event outdoors as part of a school-sponsored event. School supervision was provided.

Joseph Frederick, a student at the school, was late for class and joined some of his classmates across the street from the school. When the torchbearers and camera crew came by, Frederick and several of his friends unfurled the "BONG HITS 4 JESUS" banner so they could be filmed by the television crew. Frederick wanted to get attention. He did. He got the attention of the press, the principal, a federal district court,[104] the Ninth Circuit Court of Appeals,[105] and the United States Supreme Court.[106]

The banner could be easily seen across the street at the school. Upon seeing the banner, Principal Deborah Morse immediately crossed the street and demanded that the students take down the banner. All of the students, with the exception of Frederick, complied. Frederick was ordered to the principal's office and was subsequently suspended. The principal asserted that the banner advocated the use of illegal drugs, which was in violation of the school's policy. Frederick sued in federal court.

The federal district court granted summary judgment for the defendant.[107] The Ninth Circuit Court of Appeals reversed,[108] and the Supreme Court reversed the Court of Appeals.[109] The high court discussed the standards of *Tinker*, *Fraser*, and *Hazelwood* but found them inadequate to the issue at hand. The court instead turned to another line of Supreme Court cases to anchor its decision. The message of Frederick's banner could reasonably be construed as condoning or advocating drug use, even though Frederick contended that the words were "nonsense meant to attract the television cameras."[110]

Consequently, cases involving drug use at school were used as a foundation for the analysis. Specifically, two prior Fourth Amendment student drug testing cases, *Vernonia School District 47J v. Acton*[111] and the *Board of Education v. Earls*,[112] were cited as authority. These cases held that the drug testing policies of students who participate in extracurricular activities were constitutional.

Noting that the problem of drugs remained a serious one, the Supreme Court held that because the public school was a special place and because of the governmental interest in stopping student drug use, schools were allowed to "restrict student expression that they reasonably regard as promoting illegal drug use."[113] In fact, the court asserted, "failing to act would send a powerful message to the students in [the principal's] charge . . . about how serious the school was about the dangers of illegal drug use."[114]

Chief Justice John Roberts, who wrote the majority opinion in the case, emphasized that drug use among the nation's youth was a serious problem and that school districts had an important interest in deterring drug use among school children. "Congress has declared that part of a school's job is educating students about the dangers of illegal drug use," Roberts wrote. He continued,

> It has provided billions of dollars to support state and local drug-prevention programs . . . and required that schools receiving federal funds under the Safe and Drug-Free Schools and Communities Act of 1995 certify that their drug prevention programs 'convey a clear and consistent message . . . that illegal use of drugs is wrong and harmful.'"[115]

Moreover, Roberts pointed out, the Juneau school board and thousands of school boards all over the United States had adopted policies to deter the illegal use of drugs among students. Thus, in the Supreme Court's majority view as expressed by Roberts, the special characteristics of the school environment and the strong governmental interest in stopping student drug use allow schools to "restrict student expression that they reasonably regard as promoting illegal drug use."[116]

Roberts acknowledged the challenges that school administrators face. "School principals have a difficult job, and a vitally important one," he wrote.

> When Frederick suddenly and unexpectedly unfurled his banner, Morse had to decide to act—or not act—on the spot. It was reasonable for her to conclude that the banner promoted illegal drug use—in violation of established school policy—and that failing to act would send a powerful message to the students in her charges, including Frederick, about how serious the school was about the dangers of illegal drug use. The First Amendment does not require schools to tolerate at school events student expression that contributes to those dangers.[117]

In short, the Supreme Court's majority opinion in *Morse v. Frederick* strongly affirms the authority of school officials to ban student expression in the school environment or at school-sponsored activities that officials reasonably interpret as promoting illegal drug use. Although the *Morse* case dealt with a banner, not a T-shirt, this authority clearly includes the right to prohibit students from displaying drug promoting messages on their clothing. Moreover, although the Supreme Court's opinion did not mention the illegal use of alcohol, the opinion's reasoning at least implies that school authorities can prohibit student expression that celebrates or promotes the underage use of alcohol as well as expressions that promote illegal drugs.

Thus, school administrators should make sure their school policies explicitly state that student expression that promotes or celebrates the use of illegal drugs or alcohol is prohibited in the school environment and all school-sponsored functions. Then, if "BONG HITS 4 JESUS" or a similar drug-celebrating phrase appears on a banner or a student's T-shirt, school officials can constitutionally rely on that policy to take appropriate action to remove the offending message from the school environment without offending the First Amendment.

The impact of *Morse* on student free speech is a subject of discussion among scholars and will likely take a number of years of lower decisions to flesh out its place among the three previous major cases.[118] However, one commentator opined that *Morse* does not mark a major shift in student free speech and instead "exemplifies continued conflicting ideologies among jurists."[119] And, as two school law commentators conclude, "this decision does not expand students' expression rights."[120]

The Supreme Court has fashioned four tests that are used in student free speech cases. Typically, courts review speech that is lewd, vulgar, or offensive using *Bethel.* School-sponsored speech is analyzed under *Hazelwood*, and all other speech is reviewed under the *Tinker* standard. Under *Morse*, student speech that promotes unlawful activity such as drug use is not protected in a public school. It can be asserted that the *Tinker* disruption prong is a results-based standard while *Morse* is a content-based standard.

Student free speech is not absolute, nor is it expansive or coextensive with the speech of adults. Students have the right to freedom of speech in school, but that right must be balanced with the interests of the school to efficiently and effectively provide instruction to their students.

The Student Off-Campus Snapchat and the Missed Opportunity: *Mahanoy Area School District v. B. L.*[121]

Social media is ubiquitous, and nowhere is this is more recognizable than with the nation's youth. While principals try to limit its intrusion into their schools, potentially the largest challenge is off-campus use finding its way past the schoolhouse gate. This is true for students[122] as well as faculty.[123] A common lament from school administrators, school board members, and school law scholars is the lack of guidance from the Supreme Court in defining the limits of responsibility that can be exercised in response to student off-campus speech. The Supreme Court in 2021 finally took a student off-campus speech case, but did it provide the needed guidance?

B. L., at the end of her freshman year, tried out for her public school's varsity cheerleading squad as well a position as a right fielder on a private softball team. She was not selected for either. However, she was offered a spot on the junior varsity cheerleading squad. She did not accept the decision "with good grace," especially when she found out that an entering freshman was placed on the varsity cheerleading squad.

That weekend, while at a local convenience store, she posted on her smartphone two images on her Snapchat story. The feature allows any person in the user's "friend" group (about 250 friends) to view the images for twenty-four hours. The first image showed B. L. and a friend with their middle fingers raised with the caption: "Fuck school fuck softball fuck cheer fuck everything." The second image contained an upside-down smiley face and a caption that read: "Love how me and [another student] get told we need a year of jv before we make varsity but tha[t] doesn't matter to anyone else."[124]

At least one of the members of her group took pictures of the posts and shared them members of the cheerleading squad. One of those students shared the photos with her mother, who was a cheerleading squad coach. Several members of the cheerleading team were upset about the posts, and questions about the posts surfaced in an algebra class. The cheerleading coaches decided that the posts contained profanity in connection with the extracurricular activity, in violation of team and school rules, and suspended B. L. from the cheerleading squad for the upcoming year. Her apologies did not move the coaches, athletic director, principal, superintendent, and school board to remove the suspension. B. L. and her parents filed a lawsuit in federal district court.

The district court granted a temporary restraining order compelling the school to reinstate B. L. to the cheerleading team. The court, in granting the subsequent motion for summary judgement, found that B. L.'s Snapchat "had not caused a material and substantial disruption."[125] The court ordered her disciplinary record to be expunged and awarded nominal damages and attorneys' fees.

The Third Circuit Court of Appeals affirmed the lower court's conclusion but broke with the rationale for the decision—the application of the *Tinker* test. The panel majority held that the freedom to discipline students for on-campus speech that may be protected elsewhere does "not apply to off-campus speech" which is "outside school-owned, operated, or supervised channels and that is not reasonably interpreted as bearing the school's imprimatur."[126] The appellate court found that the *Tinker* standard did not apply and that off-campus student speech was essentially beyond the reach of the school. The school district filed a petition for certiorari. The Supreme Court granted the petition.

After reviewing the four Supreme Court decisions on student speech, the court reiterated the *Tinker* holding that the special characteristics of the public school call for "special leeway" in regulating student speech that occurs under its supervision. Breaking with the holding of the Third Circuit's analysis of the limit of *Tinker*, Justice Breyer for the majority wrote that "the special characteristics that give schools additional license to regulate student speech always disappear when a school regulates speech that takes place off campus. The school's regulatory interests remain significant in some off-campus circumstances."[127] Thus, under some circumstances, schools can regulate student speech.

The majority listed several of the circumstances that may give "additional license" to the school to regulate student off campus speech. Below are several of the circumstances that the court cited from briefs and amici:

- "[s]erious or severe bullying or harassment targeting particular individuals;
- threats aimed at teachers or other students;
- the failure to follow rules concerning lessons, the writing of papers, the use of computers or participation in other online school activities;
- and breaches of school security devices, including material maintained within school computers."[128]

In addition, the court cited from B. L. and her supporting amici briefs for several distinctions that would allow for school intervention. They include, treating as on campus speech which can be subject to regulation based on the previous four Supreme Court decisions, the following:

- "the school's immediate surroundings;
- travel en route to and from school;
- all speech taking place over school laptops or on a school's website;
- speech taking place during remote learning;
- activities taken for school credit;
- and, communications to school e-mail accounts or phones.'[129]

The majority, using several different sources, cited conditions under which schools could exercise discretion over certain student off campus speech actions. However, the Supreme Court does not beyond just cataloging what others offer. The majority wrote, following the lists of speech circumstances that would allow for school regulation: "We are uncertain as to the length or content of any such list of appropriate exceptions or carveouts to the Third Circuit majority's rule."[130] However, the majority found that the leeway regarding the special characteristics of the public school concerning student off-campus speech "is diminished."[131]

The Supreme Court failed to give a clear definition of what circumstances may aid school administrators who are the first responders ascertaining whether student speech that occurs off campus meets the requirements of those special circumstances and is unprotected. The omission is clear to school administrators who seek guidance for the legal issues they regularly confront.

It was also clear to Justice Clarence Thomas. In his dissenting opinion, Thomas spoke to the conundrum that the majority found a rationale for extending school discipline beyond the schoolhouse gate to regulate student speech but did not offer a path to defining it with reasonable guardrails protecting against unconstitutional application. He wrote, "But the Court's foundation is untethered from anything stable, and courts (and schools) will almost certainly be at a loss as to what exactly the Court's opinion today means."[132]

The majority, while holding that in this case the school administrators violated B. L.'s constitutional protections, stated, "We leave for future cases to decide where, when, and how these features mean off-campus location will make the critical difference. This case can, however, provide one example."[133] The court concluded its analysis affirming the judgment of the Third Circuit that B. L.'s free speech rights were abridged by the school; it did not agree with the reasoning of the appellate court, but neither did it fashion a test to replace it.

"Thus, we do not now set forth a broad highly general First Amendment rule stating just what counts as "off campus" speech and whether or how ordinary First Amendment standards must give way off campus to a school's special need to prevent, *e.g.*, substantial disruption of learning-related activities or the protection of those who make up a school community."—*Mahanoy Area School District v. B. L.*, 141 S.Ct. 2038, 2045 (2021)[a]

[a] These two *Mahanoy* carveouts of student free speech reflect the *Tinker* test of material and substantial disruption or collision with the rights of others.

NON-EDUCATION FREE SPEECH CASES

The five student free speech tests fashioned by the Supreme Court reflect the finding that the public school is a special place. Consequently, because it is special, the constitutional tests must address that context. While the first big four cases dominate student free speech analysis, there is an emerging use of non-education jurisprudence to work through the balancing act of student free speech with school efficiency and effectiveness. Non-education cases, which have primarily been used in school uniform cases but have also surfaced in dress code cases, will be discussed next.

These cases are important in school uniform and dress code cases because they focus on what constitutes speech. If some activity is not considered speech, the protection of the First Amendment Free Speech Clause cannot be asserted. The centrality of this initial analysis is found in *Tinker*. In *Tinker*, the Supreme Court first had to find that students have a constitutional right to free speech and then decide whether the black armband was symbolic speech. The court decided in the affirmative in both situations. Wearing the black armband in protest of the war in Vietnam is a symbolic act "akin to pure speech."[134] The most pertinent non-education cases are next.

"Ideas spread by symbols as well by words."—Louis Fisher and Katy J. Harriger, *American Constitutional Law*, vol. 2: *Constitutional Rights: Civil Rights and Civil Liberties*, 10th ed. (Durham, NC: Carolina Academic Press, 2013), 484

Burning a Draft Card: *United States v. O'Brien*[135]

In 1966, David Paul O'Brien and three companions burned their draft cards on the steps of the South Boston courthouse in a symbolic gesture against the draft. O'Brien was attacked by members of the crowd. Several agents of the Federal Bureau of Investigation who were part of the crowd ushered O'Brien and his companions into the safety of the courthouse, where O'Brien was arrested. He was later indicted, tried, convicted, and sentenced in federal court. His act violated the 1948 (amended in 1965) Universal Military Training and Service Act, which made it an offense to alter, destroy, or mutilate a draft card. He sued, alleging his free speech rights were suppressed by the statute.

The Supreme Court faced the issue of whether O'Brien's conduct was speech. Chief Justice Warren, writing for the court, stated, "We cannot accept the view that an apparently limitless variety of conduct can be labeled 'speech' whenever the person engaging in the conduct intends thereby to express an idea."[136] The intent to communicate through conduct does not automatically transform that conduct into free speech protected by the First Amendment.

Even arguing that burning the draft card was speech, O'Brien had to prevail on the postulation that the statute's purpose was to suppress speech.[137] The Supreme Court asked whether the statute furthered an important or substantial governmental interest that is unrelated to the suppression of free expression and that any "incidental" restriction is no greater than is necessary to meet the governmental interest.[138] The court found that the statute met a substantial governmental interest that was not related to the suppression of speech. Therefore, when O'Brien burned his draft card he frustrated the governmental interest of the selective service.

The *O'Brien* test, considered an intermediate test, asks whether the disputed governmental regulation is justified by ascertaining if the (1) regulation furthers a governmental interest, which is (2) unrelated to the suppression of free speech and (3) if the government's interest is greater than any incidental suppression of speech. The use of *O'Brien* to ascertain whether the dress code or school uniform policy furthers a governmental regulation (maintaining a proper educational environment, improving test scores, reducing violence, or improving attendance, for example) asks whether the regulation is intended to suppress student speech, and if there is any suppression of student speech, whether it is necessary to achieve the school's objectives for the code or uniform.[139] A number of circuits have used *O'Brien* in their analysis.[140] Whereas *Tinker* reviews the conduct and effect of the conduct, *O'Brien* reviews the regulation.

An example of the application of the *O'Brien* test is found in a Kentucky high school. Atherton High School's School Based Decision Making Council set school policy to support an environment that maximized student achievement. The council addressed a rising concern of student dress including gang identification attire as well as violence. As a result, a dress code was enacted which limited clothing choices and prohibited clothing logos except the school's logo. Medallions and necklaces were also banned. Students who alleged the dress code prevented expressive conduct by limiting clothing choices brought a free speech lawsuit.

The federal district court applied the *O'Brien* test to the content-neutral dress code policy.[141] The court first concluded that school officials have an "important and substantial interest in creating an appropriate learning environment by preventing gang presence and limiting fights in school."[142] Second, there was no intent to suppress student speech. Third, any suppression of student speech was incidental and was outweighed by the goal to create a safe and peaceful learning environment. The court took note in this part of the analysis that the dress code policy "does not prohibit alternative and more specific student expression through badges, buttons and other means."[143] In other words, student speech was not totally stifled by the policy; there were alternative means for student expression. The court concluded that the dress code was reasonably related to a legitimate objective.

The Peace Symbol and the American Flag: *Spence v. Washington*[144]

On appeal from the Supreme Court of Washington, the Supreme Court heard the case of a college student who responded to the recent invasion of Cambodia and student killings at Kent State University by affixing, through removable tape, a large peace symbol to the American flag. He hung the flag upside down outside his apartment window. His purpose was to associate the flag with peace instead of war and violence. His action violated a Washington statute forbidding the exhibition of the American flag with attached or superimposed figures or symbols. He was convicted of violating the statute.[145]

The court, citing *Tinker*, noted that the symbol of the flag and peace sign were symbols of expression: "[I]t was a pointed expression of anguish by appellant about the then-current domestic and foreign affairs of his government. An intent to convey a particularized message was present, and in the surrounding circumstances the likelihood was great that the message would be understood by those who viewed it."[146] Consequently, the court cast the case as one of prosecution of an idea through an activity. It is interesting to note that the court found *O'Brien* to be "inapplicable" because no other governmental interest unrelated to expression was advanced or supported by the Washington statute.[147]

Spence meant to communicate his ideas using the American flag. Thus, he sought to communicate using the symbolism of the flag his protest. His act "was not an act of mindless nihilism."[148] It was the sort of communication through symbols that was "short-cut from mind to mind."[149]

The *Spence* test states that for forms of expression to qualify as expression, and thus protection under the First Amendment, there must be "imbued with elements of communication" having a "particularized message" that would most likely be understood. Essentially, *Spence* established a test for the constitutional protection of the use of symbols as speech. It is important to note that in *Spence*, the court found a lowered governmental interest in controlling expression because the speech took place on private property rather than on property over which the government exercised supervisory control.[150] This may have implications for schools, where school authorities do exercise control over student expression inside the schoolhouse gate that it could not exercise outside the gate.

However, *Spence* has been used in school settings. An example is *Isaacs v. Board of Education*, in which a student asserted that her headwrap celebrated her African American and Jamaican heritage and thus should be exempt from the school's no hats/headgear policy.[151] The plaintiff student failed *Spence*. While the student intended it as a particularized message about her culture, her headwrap was not likely perceived by others as containing that message. It is worth noting that the *O'Brien* test was also was applied, which found that the policy passed constitutional muster and that the interest of securing an appropriate learning environment in which the restriction on student speech was not greater than necessary to achieve its goal.[152] This case will be discussed further in chapter 3.

Burning the American Flag: *Texas v. Johnson*[153]

In 1984, Gregory Lee Johnson unfurled the American flag in front of the Dallas city hall during the time that the Republican National Convention was taking place in the city. He doused the flag with kerosene and set it on fire.[154] He was part of a group of around one hundred demonstrators who were protesting policies of the Reagan administration. There was no disruption or breach of the peace following the flag burning. Johnson was arrested, charged, and convicted of violating the Texas penal code, which made it a crime to desecrate a venerated object. The Court of Appeals of Texas affirmed the conviction, but the Texas Court of Criminal Appeals reversed, recognizing Johnson's speech as symbolic given the circumstances.

The US Supreme Court granted certiorari and heard the case. The court began by asking the question of *Spence*, whether Johnson's expressive conduct was speech. Next the court followed *O'Brien* and asked whether the state's regulation was related to the suppression of free expression. Symbolic expression of *Tinker*, joined with the communicative conduct related to the American flag, bracketed the analysis of *Texas v. Johnson*.

First, Johnson's burning of the American flag was related to a political demonstration that coincided with the Republican Party's renomination of Ronald Reagan and was not a random act: "The expressive, overtly political nature of [Johnson's] conduct was both intentional and overwhelmingly apparent."[155] Second, the court held that government "has a freer hand in restricting expressive conduct than it does in restricting the written or spoken word."[156]

However, in the instant case, the court asserted that government cannot appropriate specific symbols to only be used only for the purposes designated by government "to communicate a limited set of messages would be to enter territory having no discernible or defensible boundaries."[157] It was not the state's end to preserve the flag as the symbol of our country with which the justices took issue; it was their means of criminalizing the behavior of a citizen using the symbol for a message different than the state preferred. The court did not believe that the special role that the American flag plays was endangered by the act of a solitary person.

The flag is a symbol with great meaning: meaning that transcends and is resilient to most Americans. The Supreme Court called for more speech not less speech when it wrote, "The way to preserve the flag's special role is not to punish those who feel differently about these matters. It is to persuade them that they are wrong."[158] The individual's right to free speech encompasses the communication of "offensive and disagreeable" ideas.[159]

The court's analysis took it through *O'Brien* and *Spence*. Basically, applying *Spence*, the court in *Texas v. Johnson* asked two questions: First, is there an intent to convey a particularized message? If this question is answered affirmatively, the court next asks whether there is a likelihood that the message will be understood by the people who view the message.[160]

An example of the use of *Texas v. Johnson* is found in the New Hampshire case *Governor Wentworth Regional School District v. Hendrickson*.[161] This case, discussed in greater detail in chapter 4, revolved around an ongoing dispute between two groups of students in a New Hampshire high school—the "gay students" and the "rednecks." Tensions escalated between the groups and took a turn when the rednecks would occasionally give the Nazi salute and a "Seig Heil" response upon encountering members of the gay students. The group retaliated by wearing patches to school depicting a circle with the swastika in the middle with a diagonal line through it.

The principal was concerned about a further escalation of tension, which could lead to a disruption and banned the wearing of the patches according to the school's dress code. A lawsuit was filed. At trial the court used *Johnson* to ascertain that the patches were symbolic speech and *Tinker* to establish a reasonable forecast of a material and substantial disruption. The patch was lawfully banned.

Cases involving student dress and free speech use *Spence* and *Johnson*. Both cases involve an analysis of symbolic expression to ascertain if it contains constitutional dimensions of speech. The tests ask the same essential two questions. There is no discernible pattern for the choice of one of these tests over the other. Both are acceptable analytical tools in student free speech cases that involve symbolic speech. Both also occurred after *Tinker* and both arose out of non-school criminal cases.

THE SUPREME COURT AND WHAT STUDENTS WEAR TO SCHOOL

There are six U.S. Supreme Court cases that are used for free speech issues associated with public school dress and grooming codes. Three of the cases arose within the public schools (*Tinker, Fraser*, & *Hazelwood*) and three arose in non-public school settings (*O'Brien, Spence*, & *Johnson*). Another Supreme Court case, *Mahanoy*, is applicable to student speech which occurs off campus and thus likely will have little effect on dress and grooming code litigation. Taken together, the Supreme Court has fashioned, albeit in an ad hoc fashion, a discernible pathway for dress code and school uniforms. However, this is a poor substitute for a fully articulated standard issued by the Supreme Court. The following are some constitutional considerations.

- Symbolic expression is protected as pure free speech if it is intended to convey a particularized message and there is a high likelihood that those who view the message will understand the message. (*Tinker*, *Spence*, and *Johnson*)
- School regulations that pertain to student choice of attire must support an important or substantial governmental interest that is unrelated to the suppression of free expression and that any "incidental" restriction is no greater than is necessary to meet the governmental interest. (*O'Brien*)

- Student expression that carries the imprimatur of the school shall be considered under the legitimate pedagogical concern. (*Hazelwood*)
- Student dress that is lewd and vulgar is prohibited. (*Fraser*)
- Student speech or attire that promotes drug use is not protected speech. (*Morse*)
- Student speech that creates a material and substantial disruption, whether or not it meets the other standards, will not be found to be protected speech. (*Tinker*)
- The ability of school authorities to discipline students for their off-campus speech is diminished. (*Mahanoy*)

The exploration of these Supreme Court student free speech standards will assist in reading the following chapters.

NOTES

1. Clay Calvert, "Fringes of Free Expression: Testing the Meaning of 'Speech' amid Shifting Cultural Mores & Changing Technologies," *Southern California Interdisciplinary Law Journal* 22 (2013): 547.
2. Newton Edwards, "Legal Authority of Boards of Education to Enforce Rules and Regulations," *Elementary School Journal* 31 (1931): 466.
3. *Canady v. Bossier Parish School Board*, 240 F.3d 437 444 (5th Cir. 2001).
4. *State ex rel. Dresser v. District Board of School District No. 1* (St. Croix Falls), 135 Wis. 619, 628 (1908).
5. David L. Hudson Jr., *The Silencing of Student Voices: Preserving Free Speech in America's Schools* (Nashville, TN: First Amendment Center, 2003), 6.
6. *West Virginia State Board of Education. v. Barnette*, 319 U.S. 624, 637 (1943).
7. *Shelton v. Tucker*, 364 U.S. 479, 487 (1967).
8. *Goss v. Lopez*, 419 U.S. 565 (1975).
9. *Ingraham v. Wright*, 430 U.S. 651 (1977).
10. *New Jersey v. T.L.O.*, 469 U.S. 525 (1985).
11. Nelda Cambron-McCabe, "Students' Speech Rights in an Electronic Age," *Education Law Reporter* 242 (2009): 493.
12. Katherine Say, "Differing Viewpoints under the First Amendment: Students versus School Authorities," *Oklahoma City University Law Review* 28 (2003): 905, 906.
13. Mary-Rose Papandrea, "Student Speech Rights in the Digital Age," *Florida Law Review* 60 (2008): 1086. The author wrote, "[T]he Court has relaxed the applicable standard of review in four specific settings: the military, prisons, public employment, and schools. In each context, the Court has stated that the special circumstances of these institutions warrant broad deference to the decision to restrict speech." Ibid., 1086–87.
14. *Tinker v. Des Moines Independent School District*, 393 U.S. 503, 505 (1969).
15. *LaVine v. Blaine School District*, 257 F.3d 981, 988 (9th Cir. 2001).

16. Martha M. McCarthy, Nelda H. Cambron-McCabe, and Stephen B. Thomas. *Public School Law: Teachers' and Students' Rights*, (Boston: Allyn and Bacon, 1998):114–15.

17. *Denno v. School Board of Volusia County*, 959 F. Supp. 1481 (M. D. Fla. 1997).

18. *Board of Education v. Rowley*, 458 U.S. 176, 208 (1982), citing San Antonio Independent School District v. Rodriguez, 411 U.S. 1, 42 (1973).

19. 469 U.S. 325 (1985).

20. Ibid., 338.

21. Ibid., 340.

22. *Bethel School District No. 403 v. Fraser*, 478 U.S. 675, 682 (1986).

23. *Bivens v. Albuquerque Public Schools*, 889 F. Supp. 556, 559 (D. N. M. 1995).

24. *Board of Education v. Pico*, 457 U.S. 853, 869 (1982).

25. *See Ginsberg v. New York*, 390 U.S. 629 (1968).

26. US Constitutional Amendment I. James Madison in his speech before the House of Representatives on June 8, 1789, supporting amendments to the Constitution, proposed, "The people shall not be deprived or abridged of their right to speak, to speak, to write, or to publish their sentiments: and the freedom of the press, as one of the great bulwarks of liberty, shall be inviolable." Barry, W. T, and James Madison. *James Madison to W. T. Barry, August 4*. August 4, 1822. Manuscript/Mixed Material. https://www.loc.gov/item/mjm018999/.

27. See *Snyder v. Phelps* 131 S. Ct. 1207 (2011) (protecting hateful speech at military funerals).

28. *Palko v. Connecticut*, 302 U.S. 319, 327 (1937).

29. *Lovell v. City of Griffin*, 304 U.S. 444, 450 (1938).

30. *McIntyre v. Ohio Elections Commission*, 514 U.S. 334, 357 (1995).

31. Alexander Meiklejohn. *Free Speech and Its Relationship to Self-Government* (New York: Harper, 1948), 91.

32. *New York Times Company v. Sullivan*, 376 U.S. 254, 270 (1964).

33. See *Texas v. Johnson*, 491 U.S. 397 (1989) (burning the American flag as a protected form of speech).

34. *United States v. Schwimmer*, 279 U.S. 644, 654–55 (1929) (Holmes, J.. dissenting).

35. *Terminello v. Chicago*, 337 U.S. 1, 4 (1940).

36. Cass R. Sunstein, "Academic Freedom and Law: Liberalism, Speech Codes, and Relevant Problems," in *The Future of Academic Freedom*, ed. Louis Menard (Chicago: University of Chicago Press 1996), 96.

37. *Mills v. Alabama,* 384 U.S. 214, 218 (1966).

38. *New York Times v. Sullivan*, 376 U.S. 214, 218 (1964).

39. *Whitney v. California*, 274 U.S. 357, 373 (1927) ("although the rights of free speech and assembly are fundamental, they are not in their nature absolute.").

40. 473 U.S. 788, 799–800 (1985).

41. *Gilbert v. State of Minnesota*, 245 U.S. 325, 332 (1920).

42. *Texas v. Johnson*, 491 U.S. 397, 414 (1989).

43. *Ward v. Rock Against Racism*, 491 U.S. 781, 791 (1989).

44. Erwin Chermerinsky, "Content Neutrality as a Central Problem of Freedom of Speech: Problems in the Supreme Court's Application," *Southern California Law Review* 70 (2000): 55–56.

45. *Simon & Shuster, Inc. v. Members of the New York State Crime Victims Board*, 502 U.S. 105, 116 (1991).

46. *R. A. V. v. St. Paul*, 505 U.S. 377 (1992).

47. Caroline Mala Corbin, "The First Amendment Right against Compelled Listening," *Boston University Law Review* 89 (2009): 958–59.

48. "A viewpoint-neutral restriction on content is one that is evenhandedly applied without regard to the specific message being advocated." *Moms for Liberty v. Brevard Public Schools*, 582 F. Supp. 3d 1214, 1219 (M. D. Fla. 2022).

49. *Palmer v. Waxahachie Independent School District*, 579 F.3d 502, 510 (5th Cir. 2009).

50. *Linmark Associates, Inc. v. Township of Willingboro*, 431 U.S. 85 (1977).

51. See *Perry Education Association v. Perry Local Educators' Association*, 460 U.S. 37 (1983) for a discussion of an open forum, a limited forum, and closed forum.

52. *Poulos v. New Hampshire*, 345 U.S. 395, 408 (1953).

53. *Chaplinsky v. New Hampshire*, 315 U.S. 568 (1942).

54. *Brandenburg v. Ohio*, 395 U.S. 444 (1969).

55. *Beauharnais v. Illinois*, 343 U.S. 250 (1952).

56. *New York v. Ferber*, 458 U.S. 747 (1982).

57. *Miller v. California*, 413 U.S. 15 (1973).

58. *Virginia v. Black*, 538 U.S. 343 (2003).

59. *Tinker v. Des Moines Independent Community School District*, 393 U.S. 503 (1969).

60. *In re Gault*, 387 U.S. 1 (1967).

61. "*In re Gault* Establishes Due Process Rights for Juveniles," *Constitutional Law Reporter* (October 13, 2017), https: //constitutionallawreporter.com/2017/10/13/In-re-gault-due-process/.

62. Donna M. Bishop and Hillary B. Farber, "Joining the Legal Significance of Adolescent Developmental Capacities with the Legal Rights Provided by *In re Gault*," *Rutgers Law Review* 60 (2007): 132–33.

63. *Tinker v. Des Moines Independent Community School District*, 393 U.S. 503 (1969).

64. Martha McCarthy, "Student Expression Rights: Is a New Standard on the Horizon?" *Education Law Reporter* 216 (2007): 15–34.

65. 408 U.S. 104, 117 (1972).

66. Ibid., 507.

67. *Tinker v. Des Moines Independent Community School District*, 393 U.S., 511.

68. Ibid., 507.

69. Ibid.

70. Ibid., 513. Justice Hugo Black's dissent lamented that the case was "wholly without constitutional reasons" and "subjects all the public schools in the country to the whims and caprices of their loudest-mouthed, but maybe not their brightest, students." Ibid., 525 (Black, J., dissenting).

71. Ibid., 508.

72. Ibid., 513.

73. Ibid., 508. The use of the second prong has been spotty. The Third Circuit Court of Appeals wrote, "The precise scope of *Tinker*'s 'interference with the rights of others' language is unclear." *Saxe v. State College Area School District*, 240 F.3d 200, 217 (3d Cir. 2001). However, see Richard Fossey, Todd A. DeMitchell, and Robert LeBlanc, "*Harper v. Poway Unified School District*: Schools Can Ban Demeaning Speech Toward Vulnerable Students Without Offending the First Amendment," *Education Law Reporter* 211 (2006):559–72, for an analysis of a Ninth Circuit Court of Appeals decision on demeaning speech by wearing a T-shirt to school directed towards LGBTQ students. The T-shirt read on the front, "BE ASHAMED" and "OUR SCHOOL EMBRACED WHAT GOD HAS CONDEMNED," and on the back it read, "HOMOSEXUALITY IS SHAMEFUL Romans 1:27." The appellate court used the second prong of *Tinker* to uphold the school ban students from wearing T-shirts "that flaunt demeaning slogans, phrases or aphorisms relating to core characteristics of particularly vulnerable students and that may cause them significant injury." Ibid., 560, citing *Harper v. Poway Unified School District*, 445 F.3d 1166, 1171 (9th Cir. 2006).

74. Ibid., 507–8 (internal citations omitted).

75. See for example, *Sypniewski v. Warren Hills Reg. Bd. of Educ.*, 307 F.3d 243, 257 (writing, "Where a school seeks to suppress a term merely related to an expression that has been proven disruptive, it must do more than simply point to a general association."); *Guiles v. Marineau*, 461 F.3d 320 (2d Cir. 2006) (overturning the suspension of a student for wearing a T-shirt depicting President George W. Bush negatively, finding no disruption of the learning process); *Chambers v. Babbitt*, 145 F. Supp. 2d 1068, 1072 (D. Minn. 2001) (holding that the school district was unable to establish a connection between fights and car vandalism were in response to a student wearing a T-shirt that said "Straight Pride.").

76. *Pyle v. South Hadley School Committee*, 861 F. Supp. 157, 170 (D. Mass. 1994). The controversial T-shirts read: "See Dick Drink. See Dick Drive. See Dick Die. Don't' be a Dick" and "Coed Naked Band: Do It to the Rhythm." The dress code, among other restrictions, prohibited clothing that "[h]as comments, pictures, slogans, or designs that are obscene, profane, lewd, or vulgar." At 163.

77. *Newsome v. Albemarle County School Board*, 354 F.3d 249 (4th Cir. 2003).

78. For a discussion of Confederate flags, free speech, and *Tinker*, see chapter 4.

79. *Palmer ex rel. Palmer v. Waxachie Independent School District*, 579 F.3d 502, 507 (5th Cir. 2009).

80. *Morgan v. Swanson*, 659 F.3d 359, 374 (5th Cir. 2011).

81. 478 U.S. 675 (1986).

82. Ibid., 678.

83. Ibid., 679.

84. Ibid., 682.

85. Ibid.

86. Todd A. DeMitchell, "School Uniforms and the Constitution: Common Dress in an Uncommon Time," *Education Law Reporter* 157 (2001): 7.

87. *Bethel School District No. 403 v. Fraser*, 478 U.S., 682.

88. Ibid., 683.

89. Ibid., 682. See, also, *New Jersey v. T.L.O.*, 105 S.Ct. 733, 742 (1985) asserting, while adults have wide freedom in matters of public discourse, it does not follow that "the same latitude must be permitted to children in public school."

90. *Bethel School District No. 403 v. Fraser*, 478 U.S., 683. In *Thomas v. Board of Education, Granville Central School District*, 607 F.2d 1043, 1057 (2nd Cir. 1979), Judge Newman referred to Cohen's jacket, which had "Fuck the Draft" lettered on the back, citing *Cohen v. California*, 403 U.S. 15, 21 (1971).

91. *Boroff v. Van Wert City Board of Education*, 220 F.3d 465, 471 (6th Cir. 2000), *cert. denied* 532 U.S. 920 (2001).

92. *Pyle By & Through Pyle v. South Hadley School Committee*, 861 F. Supp. 157, 170 (D. Mass. 1994).

93. *Bethel School District No. 403 v. Fraser*, 478 U.S., 682.

94. 484 U.S. 260 (1988).

95. Lucinda Housley Luetkemeyer, "Silencing the Rebel Yell: The Eighth Circuit Upholds a School's Ban on Confederate Flags," *Missouri Law Review* 75 (2010): 996.

96. *Hazelwood School District v. Kuhlmeier*, 484 U.S., 267.

97. Ibid.

98. Ibid., 270.

99. Ibid., 271.

100. Ibid., 273.

101. Ibid., 267.

102. Ibid., 266 (quoting *Fraser*, 478 U.S. at 685).

103. 551 U.S. 393 (2007).

104. *Frederick v. Morse*, 2003 U.S. Dist. LEXIS 27270 (D. Alaska, May 27, 2003).

105. *Frederick v. Morse*, 439 F.3d 1114 (9th Cir. 2006).

106. *Morse v. Frederick*, 551 U.S. 393 (2007).

107. *Frederick v. Morse*, 2003 WL 25274689 (D. Alaska May 27, 2003).

108. *Frederick v. Morse*, 439 F.3d 1114 (9th Cir. 2006).

109. *Morse v. Frederick*, 551 U.S. 393 (2007).

110. If Frederick's words were meaningless, could they constitute speech? If they were not speech could his right to free speech be abridged when there was no speech? Does a string of words without communicative intent constitute speech?

111. 515 U.S. 646, 661 (1995) ("Deterring drug use by schoolchildren is an 'important-indeed, perhaps compelling interest.'").

112. 536 U.S. 822, 834 (2002) ("The drug abuse problem among our Nation's youth has hardly abated since *Vernonia* was decided in 1995. In fact, evidence suggests that it has only grown worse.").

113. *Morse v. Frederick*, 551 U.S., 408.

114. Ibid., 410. See Justice Samuel Alito's concurrence, "The special characteristic that is relevant in this case is the threat to the physical safety of students. . . . Students may be compelled on a daily basis to spend time at close quarters with other

students who may do them harm. Experience shows that schools can be places of special danger." Ibid., 424 (Alito, J., concurring).

115. Ibid., 408.

116. Ibid.

117. Ibid., 409–10.

118. For example, see, David Schimmel, "*Morse v. Frederick*: Did the Supreme Court Weaken or Strengthen Student Freedom of Expression?" *Education Law Reporter* 226 (2008): 557; Kathleen Conn, "The Long and the Short of the Public School's Disciplinary Arm: Will *Morse v. Frederick* Make a Difference?" *Education Law Reporter* 227 (2008): 1.

119. JoAnna S. Thomas, "The Emerging Dichotomy of the Educational Institution: Expression and Authority in Public Schools under Morse v. Frederick, 127 S. Ct. 2618 (2007)," *Nebraska Law Review* 88(1) (2009): 180–203, 198.

120. Justin M. Bathon and Martha M. McCarthy, "Student Expression: The Uncertain Future," *Educational Horizons* (Winter 2008): 82, https://files.eric.ed.gov/fulltext/EJ781667. pdf.

121. 141 S.Ct. 2038 (2021).

122. See, e.g., Mollie McQuillan and Suzanne Eckes, "A Legal Update: When Social Media Posts Cause Students Emotional Harm," *Education Law Reporter* 399 (2022): 14–21.

123. See Suzanne E. Eckes, Todd A. DeMitchell, and Richard Fossey, "Legal Matters for Educators: A Lesson on Social Media," *Principal Leadership* 22, no. 7 (March 2022): 54–55; Mark Paige and Todd A. DeMitchell, "Arbitration Litigation Concerning Teacher Discipline for Misuse of Technology: A Preliminary Assessment," *Education Law Reporter* 296 (2013): 22–41.

124. *Mahony Area School District v. B.L.*, 141 S.Ct. 2038, 2043 (2021).

125. Ibid., 2044.

126. Ibid., citing the Court of Appeals decision; see 964 F.3d 170, 189 (2020).

127. Ibid., 2045.

128. Ibid.

129. Ibid.

130. Ibid.

131. Ibid., 2046.

132. Ibid., 2063 (Thomas, J., dissenting).

133. Ibid., 2046.

134. *Tinker v. Des Moines School District*, 393 U.S., 505.

135. 391 U.S. 367 (1968).

136. Ibid., 376.

137. Ibid.

138. Ibid., 377.

139. Geoffrey A. Starks makes a case for the use of *O'Brien* in place of *Tinker* when the school policy is content neutral, which is how a mandatory school uniform is often characterized. He argues that *O'Brien* is the better analytical tool because it applies the appropriate level of scrutiny and "it is better calibrated to confer the proper level of deference upon school officials." "*Tinker's* Tenure in the School Setting:

The Case for Applying *O'Brien* to Content-Neutral Regulations," *Yale Law Journal Online* (August 30, 2010), http://yalelawjournal.org/the-yale-law-journal-pocket-part/constitutional-law/tinker's-tenure-in-the-school-setting: -the-case-for-applying-o'brien-to-content% 11neutral-regulations/.

140. See, e.g., *Palmer v. Waxahachie Independent School District*, 579 F.3d 502 (5th Cir. 2009); *Jacobs v. Clark County School District*, 526 F.3d 419 (9th Cir. 2008); *Blau v. Fort Thomas Public School District,* 401 F.3d 381 (6th Cir. 2005).

141. *Long v. Board of Education of Jefferson County*, 121 F. Supp. 2d 621 (W. D. Ky. (2000); affrm'd 2001 U.S. App. Lexis 18103 (6th Cir. 2001).

142. Ibid., 626.

143. Ibid.

144. 418 U.S. 405 (1974).

145. Three Seattle police officers observed the flag from the street. The officers arrested the owner with no disruption or altercation. There was no evidence that the flag attracted any attention on the street nor did Spence do anything to draw attention to the flag. Ibid., 406 409.

146. Ibid., 410–11.

147. Ibid., 415 n. 8.

148. Ibid., 410.

149. Ibid., citing *West Virginia State Board of Education*, 319 U.S. at 632.

150. Ibid., 411.

151. 40 F. Supp. 2d 335 (D. Md. 1997).

152. *Isaacs*, 40 Supp. 2d at 338.

153. 491 U.S. 397 (1989).

154. Ibid., 399. The protestors chanted, while the flag burned, "America, the red, white, and blue, we spit on you." Ibid.

155. Ibid., 406.

156. Ibid., 407.

157. Ibid., 417.

158. Ibid., 419. The court concluded, "We do not consecrate the flag by punishing its desecration, for in doing so we dilute the freedom that this cherished symbol represents." Ibid., 420.

159. Ibid., 414.

160. Ibid., 404.

161. 421 F. Supp. 2d 410 (D. N. H. 2006).

3

The Clothes Are the Message

Headlines often capture the emergence of an issue as well as the breadth of an issue.

Below are a few recent headlines on student appearance.

- "Hays school board asked to remove satanism reference in dress code."[1]
- "Prom dress policing is tough on kids."[2]
- "The pandemic put school dress codes into perspective: 'We want to control our lives.'"[3]
- "Black student can't attend Texas graduation over his long locs, lawsuit says."[4]
- "She was told she couldn't wear her tribal regalia at graduation. She wore it anyway."[5]
- "Police detain, release four Grossmont High School students after dress code protest 'escalated.'"[6]

While many school dress codes have been the target of student protests at school and the subject of litigation in courts, at least one school district is swimming against the tide. In 2022, the Forney Independent School District in the Dallas–Fort Worth metroplex in Texas passed what some would describe as a restrictive dress code: that clothing with a hood—whether it be a sweatshirt, jacket, or coat—will not be allowed inside school buildings. In addition, pre-K through fourth grade students can wear dresses, skirts, and skorts but then age out of that "privilege." The school district asserts that it will "bring a more professional atmosphere to the classroom and set children up to be good professionals as they mature."[7]

However, a number of school districts are moving in the opposite direction toward loosening strict dress codes. Some school districts responded to complaints and actions by students and parents lobbying to reduce what they consider unreasonable and discriminatory dress code regulations. The *Wall Street Journal* has reported that "[c]lothing once considered taboo is now permitted as more districts across the U.S. relax student dress code policies, deemed disproportionately targeted at female students, and move to gender-neutral equitable dress codes."[8]

K–12 EDUCATION: DEPARTMENT OF EDUCATION SHOULD PROVIDE INFORMATION ON EQUITYAND SAFETY IN SCHOOL DRESS CODES

Recent reports and research studies have garnered national attention and have shed light on concerns with certain elements of dress codes, including those that are unclear or overly strict, require expensive purchases, or prohibit items associated with cultural or racial identity, such as banning head coverings or traditionally Black hairstyles. In addition, some of these studies have noted that having different dress codes for girls and boys can present obstacles for transgender and nonbinary students. Some school districts have responded to dress code controversies by revising their dress codes—sometimes citing a commitment to equity and inclusion when doing so—or by switching to uniforms.

Jacqueline M. Nowicki, Director
Education, Workforce, and Income Security Issues
United States Government Accountability Office
GAO-23-105348 K–12 Education, (October 2022), 1,
https://www.gao.gov/assets/gao-23-105348.pdf.

The move to critically assess the fairness and utility of dress codes is probably the result of an accumulation of stories of female students disproportionately being singled out for discipline over male students that started to appear in the popular press, adding to the pressure for policy action. It's not one single event; rather we see the news reporting a number of shaming incidents based on student attire.

For example, Chicago's Evanston Township High School administration, in response to student protest over a dress code that discriminated along gender and racial lines, listened to their students' concerns. The principal, Marcus Campbell, stated, "We needed to look at getting a new dress code, and we wanted to make sure it was body-positive and didn't marginalize students."[9]

One high school principal in a New England small town describes his school's dress code, which responded to concerns about the impact of dress codes, in the following way:

> We have a very vague dress code. We really only try to deal with imagery and/or slogans that are for illegal activities (alcohol, drugs, violence, hate language, etc.). We do not dress code students (male or female) in regards to clothing length, skin exposure, etc. We received pushback administratively for our perceived lax enforcement of dress code but we feel it helps to create a more positive and inclusive culture in our school.[10]

The administration took the tack of addressing the issue through enforcement with a concern for how the message transmitted by a dress code impacts the culture of the school.

In a New Jersey middle school, female students were tired of "being shamed" for wearing comfortable clothes during warm weather. They launched a campaign with the Twitter hashtag "#IAmMoreThanADistraction," challenging schools to focus their attention on reducing the objectification of the female body.[11]

In another example, eighth grader Sophia Trevino started wearing a protest T-shirt to school after she and fifteen other girls were dress-coded on the first day of school. Sophia was dress coded because when she put her hands down by her thighs, her fingertips were lower than the rip in her distressed jeans. She started wearing a yellow T-shirt to school on Fridays that stated,

DRESS CODES ARE
SEXIST
RACIST
CLASSIST[12]

Sophia's protest focused on the dress code for singling out girls making them responsible for boys' actions. She said, "In schools, they think that the boys are just drooling over our shoulders and our thighs. They aren't. They don't care. And even if they do, that's their fault. That's theirs."[13] This theme will be explore further in chapter 7.

The Friday protest, which included between fifty and sixty students, plus their petition to change the dress code to something more inclusive and gender-neutral led to extensive media coverage. A month later, the school district appeared to have deleted the fingertip language (although the school district denied that there was any change).[14] Protests in some cases have led to a relaxation of some of the rules, especially those that appear to target females and students of color.[15]

In Clovis, California, a handful of male students at Buchanan High School wore dresses to protest the school's dress code. A high senior said, "Our district's dress code should not favor or discriminate any gender [*sic*]. We believe everyone should be able to express themselves equally. A boy with long hair is no less of a hard worker than a girl with long hair."[16] However, soon afterward, the school went against recommendations that would have allowed boys to wear earrings and have long hair and would have removed language that stated that dresses and skirts are to only be worn by girls. It is interesting that no boys were disciplined for wearing dresses during the day of protest.[17]

What is appropriate student clothing and appearance is contested, and it is an enduring contest. Old complaints remain and new concerns arise. The epigraph at the beginning of the chapter gives an indication of some emerging complaints. What is consistent is the role of politics in debating and determining the public policies for public schools and the yardstick wielded by the courts to determine rights and responsibilities.

A RECENTLY UPDATED MIDDLE SCHOOL DRESS CODE IN A SMALL NEW ENGLAND TOWN: COMMUNICATION WITH THE PRINCIPAL

"We changed our procedures this year to omit any gender discrimination. I've also told staff we either all police it or no one does. Thus far, we've had less than 5 issues and it was only to buttocks being exposed. We also dealt with a few weapon imagery issues."

The following is the updated middle school dress code.

APPEARANCE & DRESS

As part of the general culture of respect for the two fundamental rights that govern all school conduct, we expect our community members to maintain an appearance that is suitable for the teaching and learning environment. We do not maintain or enforce a specific "dress code" beyond the protection of these rights, which includes the following requirements:

1. All clothing must comply with the health code of the State of New Hampshire and must not create a safety issue.
2. Any clothing with images of or references to alcohol, tobacco, illegal drugs, obscenities, violence, sex, gang identification, or which

advocate prejudice or harassment of any race, religion, national/ethnic group, age, sex, sexual orientation, or disability are prohibited.

3. Items of dress that in the judgment of the school staff pose a potential danger or may cause a substantial disruption to the learning environment are prohibited.Students who do not meet expected standards may be asked to change their clothing and their legal guardian will be notified.[a]

[a] This communication from the principal was received by the author on October 20, 2022, A copy of the communication is in his files.

For example, Illinois passed Public Act 102-0360 (2022), commonly known as the Jett Hawkins Law. The law was passed in response to a story about four-year-old Jett's braids and later his ponytail as violating his school's dress code. Awareness was raised, prompted by his mother, about the stigmatizing of children's hair, when for many it is an extension of who individuals are and is deeply connected to racial and cultural identity. The law bans dress code requirements from "discriminating against hairstyles historically associated with race, ethnicity, or hair texture."[18] We will return to this topic in chapter 8.

In the last chapter, we reviewed the US Supreme Court's decisions about the free speech rights of students. As discussed, the court has placed constitutional limitations on the authority of school officials to censor students' speech while they are at school—although they can certainly ban disruptive speech, lewd speech, and speech that celebrates or promotes illegal drug use or other illegal behavior. School authorities can also stop student speech that carries the imprimatur of the school. This set of education cases focuses on the student (disruption or the classification or content of the communication).

We reviewed the leading non-education cases that provide an emerging standard for judging the constitutionality of the school rule (*O'Brien*) and whether the communication reaches constitutional standing (*Spence* and *Johnson*). These non-education free speech standards will be applied to dress codes as applicable.

In spite of the articulation of these various free speech tests, it is noteworthy that the US Supreme Court has not decided any cases involving student attire, refusing to review lower court decisions on the subject. Therefore, guidance for navigating the path between protecting constitutional rights and providing an environment conducive to student learning and student safety is left to the lower courts. Frequently, the lack of guidance from the Supreme Court has led to conflicting decisions, with constitutional rights being defined differently from one federal circuit to the next.

NONSPECIFIC STUDENT MESSAGES

Over the years, students have filed numerous lawsuits challenging school bans on specific messages conveyed on student clothing. As we will see in the next two chapters, students have claimed a right to proclaim messages on their clothing that state their opposition to abortion, their loyalty to the antebellum South, their attitudes about drugs, their positions on homosexuality, and a variety of other social and political issues.

In a time of concern for civility in society, respect for legitimate authority, and security for schoolchildren, the debate about dress codes and uniforms has often been sharp. Do we as a society value the rights of students to wear clothes of their choice to school even if they are considered vulgar and offensive by others and are filled with sexual innuendo, or are issues of clothing and appearance at school too trivial to lay claim to the limited resources of the courts and overstretched educators? In other words, do students possess a constitutional right of freedom of expression to wear clothes of their choice to school?

A corollary question is what constitutes constitutionally protected expression. "Clearly, under most circumstances, one's choice of clothing is no more or less than expression of individuality and general sense of self."[19] The complaining student bears the burden of demonstrating that the conduct is "sufficiently imbued with elements of communication"[20] to receive First Amendment protection. In other words, is the choice of wearing an "Aloha" shirt sufficiently expressive that the reasonable person would know what communication is being made by wearing the "Aloha" shirt?

Students have also filed lawsuits in which they have claimed a First Amendment right to wear clothing that conveys no textual or graphic message; it is the clothing itself that is the message of their identity. In the *New York Times*, journalist Jan Hoffman writes, "Dress is always code, particularly for teenagers eager to telegraph evolving identities."[21]

> "All this is too much for some educators, who say high school should not be a public stage to work out private identity issues. School, they say, is a rigorous academic and social training ground for the world of adults and employment."—Jan Hoffman, "Can a Boy Wear a Skirt to School?" *New York Times* (November 6, 2009), https://www.nytimes.com/2009/11/08/fashion/08cross.html

In essence, students in these cases argue that their clothing choices are expressions of their individuality, their personal tastes, their personalities, or their affiliation with a particular ethnic group, and that these expressions are protected under the Free Speech Clause of the First Amendment.

Reviewed below is a case in which a female student claimed a First Amendment right to wear a red, white, and blue necklace to school to show her support for the war in Iraq. In another, a student argued that she had a First Amendment right to wear a headwrap to school as an affirmation of her African American heritage, even though school authorities claimed that the headwrap violated the school's "no hats" rule. And in another case, a male student claimed a constitutional right to wear sagging pants to show his affiliation with hip-hop culture.

In deciding these cases, the courts often looked to Supreme Court decisions that spelled out when an individual's conduct had some expressive element that entitled it to First Amendment protection. The Supreme Court has made clear that not all conduct is protected by the First Amendment. To bring a free speech claim based on conduct and not words, claimants must pass a two-part test discussed in the previous chapter: First, they must show that their conduct "conveys a particularized message," and second, they must show that there is a great likelihood that the message will be understood by those who view it.[22]

In *United States v. O'Brien*, the Supreme Court also made clear that governmental agencies may enforce a regulation that infringes on speech so long as the regulation enforces a substantial government interest unrelated to the suppression of free expression and is narrowly drafted so as to achieve that interest without infringing on First Amendment rights more than necessary.[23]

Therefore, students who claim a broad First Amendment right to wear the clothing of their choice must first show that their clothing conveys some "particularized message" that others who view the message will understand. They then must show that the dress code that infringes on their clothing choice furthers no substantial governmental interest or that it is drafted in such a way that it infringes on the student's freedom of expression more than is necessary.

These are high hurdles for students to overcome in challenging student dress and grooming codes on constitutional grounds. As will be seen from a review of the cases in this chapter, students seldom succeed when they challenge a school district's dress code on constitutional grounds.

CLOTHING AS A SYMBOL

In chapter 2, the Supreme Court cases on symbolic speech were discussed, starting with the seminal case *Tinker v. Des Moines Independent School District*,[24] finding that a black armband worn in protest of the war in Vietnam was "akin to pure speech." Furthermore, non-education American flag Supreme

Court cases (*Texas v. Johnson*[25] and *Spence v. Washington*[26]) are also defining the free speech contours for dress codes and school uniforms. A finding of symbolic speech is the beginning of the inquiry and not the end.

The context of the speech is important, and where the student speech takes place is a critical factor because of the special nature of the school: "In the public school arena, the free expression rights of students are balanced by the corresponding interest of furthering the educational mission of schools."[27] The plaintiff student bears the burden of proving that his or her expression warrants First Amendment protection using Supreme Court standards. Bald assertions of a speech right are insufficient.

The Case of the Sagging Pants: *Bivens v. Albuquerque Public Schools* (1995)

In *Bivens v. Albuquerque Public Schools*, Richard Bivens, a ninth grader at Albuquerque's Del Norte High School, received a long-term suspension after he repeatedly refused to comply with his school's dress code, which prohibited students from wearing sagging pants.[28] The school district maintained that its prohibition against sagging pants was justified since the wearing of sagging pants was associated with gang activity.

Bivens sued the Albuquerque school system, arguing that he was not associated with a gang and that the pants reflected his identification and link with his Black identity, Black culture, and the styles of Black urban youth. More specifically, Bivens maintained that wearing sagging pants "is part of a style known as 'hip hop,' whose roots are African American, and it represents a fashion statement for blacks and Hispanics extensively."[29]

A federal trial court acknowledged that some types of expressive conduct enjoy constitutional protection, such as the Tinker children's black armbands. Nevertheless, the court asserted, "[n]ot every defiant act by a high school student is constitutionally protected speech."[30] While public school students enjoy some degree of freedom of speech within the schoolhouse gates, it is balanced against the need to foster an educational atmosphere free from undue disruptions. In order to be entitled to constitutional protection, expressive conduct must pass the two-part test devised by *Texas v. Johnson*, discussed in chapter 2: "First, the actor must intend to convey a particularized message, and second, there must be some likelihood that the message would be understood by those who observe the conduct."[31]

Granting that Bivens met the first prong of intentionality, the court was unpersuaded that he could prevail on the record before the court on the second prong, understanding the message of the expressive conduct. In the court's opinion, Bivens's sagging pants failed the second part of the two-part test. Whatever message Bivens intended to convey by wearing sagging pants was not readily apparent to those who saw his pants sag, exposing his underwear, the court concluded. If sagging is just a fashion trend of adolescents, then it would be devoid of a particularized message that would have a likelihood to be understood by others seeing the sagging pants. Therefore, his First Amendment claim failed.

Bivens also raised a second constitutional argument—that the school district's dress code was unconstitutionally vague and did not give him fair notice of the type of clothing that was prohibited. The court wrote: "I reject the notion that a school dress code prohibiting sagging must be expressed in inches or millimeters, any more than other styles prohibited by the dress code must be quantified exactly." The court noted that the dress code also prohibited "short shirts," "half-shirts," and "inappropriate tank tops" without stating precisely what those terms meant. The court saw no constitutional infirmity on a vagueness ground, concluding that "[t]he need to maintain appropriate discipline in schools must favor more administrative discretion than might be permitted in other parts of society."[32]

Headwraps: *Isaacs v. Board of Education of Howard County* (1999)

Other students have claimed a broad constitutional right to choose their school clothing like the right to wear sagging pants that Bivens unsuccessfully asserted. One contested area of student dress is hair coverings. (Hair and hairstyles will be discussed in chapter 8.) The US Government Accounting Office's October 2022 report on dress codes estimated that over 80 percent of the dress codes prohibited head coverings such as "hats, hoodies, bandanas, and scarves" and 44 percent of dress codes ban hair wraps.[33]

An example is found in *Isaacs v. Board of Education of Howard County*. Shermia Isaacs, a ninth grader in a Maryland high school, sued her school district after the assistant principal prohibited her from wearing a multicolored headwrap to school on the grounds that the headwrap violated the school's "no hats" policy.[34]

In considering Shermia's claims, a federal trial court first applied the same two-part test that another federal court had utilized in the *Bivens* case. Did Shermia intend to convey a particularized message when she wore her headwrap to school? And if so, would that message be generally understood by those who viewed it? Thes are essentially the Supreme Court tests from *Spence* and *Johnson*.

Shermia admitted that she occasionally wore the headwrap to school for the purpose of covering her hair when she was not satisfied with its appearance. Nevertheless, she and her mother consistently maintained that Shermia's primary motivation for wearing the headwrap "was to say symbolically 'I celebrate my African-American and Jamaican heritage.'"[35]

The court was not entirely satisfied that Shermia's headwrap met either part of the two-part test, but the court concluded that the headwrap did constitute symbolic speech. Even so, the court noted, the school district's prohibition against Shermia's headwrap would be upheld if the school's "no hats" policy furthered an important governmental interest.

In the court's view, the school district had articulated an important governmental interest in enforcing its policy, which was to provide "a safe, respectful school environment that is conducive to education and learning."[36]

The court articulated the ways in which the school district's governmental interests were furthered by the "no hats" rule:

> [H]ats can (i) cause increased horseplay and conflict in the hallways, (ii) obscure the teacher's view of the student wearing the hat or view of the students sitting behind that student (and as a result can cause the teacher to miss signs of substance abuse or other health problems), (iii) obscure students' view of the blackboard, (iv) allow students to hide contraband, and (v) foster a less respectful and focused climate of learning."[37]

The court found the school district's justifications to be valid and not irrational or arbitrary, as Shermia contended. Furthermore, the court said it was abundantly clear that the school district enforced its "no hats" rule for reasons unrelated to the suppression of free expression. In the court's view, the rule's restriction on expression was no greater than necessary to further the school's interest. Finally, the court pointed out that Shermia had alternate means of expressing her message within the school's dress code, including the wearing of traditional African dress or jewelry to class.

Shermia further argued that the school's refusal to allow her to wear a headwrap to school violated her constitutional right to be secure in her person. In support of that argument, she cited a decision by the Fourth Circuit Court of Appeals that had found "that a person's right to wear his hair as he wishes is 'an aspect of the right to be secure in one's person guaranteed by the due process clause."[38]

Responding to this creative argument, the court pointed out that there was an evident distinction between hairstyle and clothing:

> Clearly . . . , a public school's restrictions on headgear are far less intrusive on this personal freedom than similar restrictions on hairstyle. Headgear, like other clothing and unlike hair, is easily removed and replaced. Shermia is free to wear her headwrap outside of school and, apparently, is even free to wear the headwrap to and from school. The rule simply requires that she leaves the headwrap in her locker during the school day.[39]

In any event, the court went on, a determination that Shermia's desire to wear a particular headgear is entitled to some constitutional protection would not end the constitutional inquiry: "Personal freedoms are not absolute; they must yield when they intrude upon the freedom of others."[40] In the court's opinion, "[t]he reasons advanced by the school system for its 'no hat' restriction sufficiently and reasonably establish the need for the restriction's relatively minor infringement on personal freedom."[41]

Finally, the court paid careful attention to Shermia's argument that her headwrap lacked the characteristics that made other hats disruptive. It was true, the court admitted, that her headwrap "is less likely to block her face than other hats, and it would be harder to remove and throw around the hallway or classroom."[42] It was also true, the court acknowledged, that Shermia's headwrap had not caused a disruption during the few hours she wore it while at school. Indeed, the court conceded, "[n]o one contends that a hat or headwrap would be constantly disruptive in class."[43]

Furthermore, her argument that allowing religious headgear undermined the content-neutral regulation also did not prevail. The court asserted that as a threshold matter, religious headgear is not symbolic speech; instead "it is worn not to express a message to others but because of a mandate derived from a doctrine of reverence for a deity."[44] Even assuming that religious headgear is symbolic speech, it would receive increased constitutional protection because it implicated more than one constitutional right and would thus be considered as deserving hybrid constitutional protection for free speech and free expression.

Nevertheless, the court said, the fact that no problems arose during the brief time Shermia wore her headwrap in school did not determine the outcome of the case. The relative likelihood of disruption was great enough in the court's mind to justify the school system's "no hat" rule. "Furthermore," the court concluded, "it would be entirely unrealistic to ask school administrators . . . to decide on a hat-by-hat basis whether a particular hat poses sufficient danger of disruption."[45] Indeed, in the court's opinion, Shermia's argument that the school should be required to make administrative decisions about individual hats was unreasonable.

A Red, White, and Blue Necklace: *Grzywna v. Schenectady Central School District* (2006)

In *Grzywna v. Schenectady Central School District*, a mother sued the school district where her twelve-year old daughter (known only as Jane Doe) attended school, claiming the district had violated her daughter's First Amendment rights by prohibiting her from wearing a homemade red, white, and blue beaded necklace.[46] According to the mother, her daughter wore the necklace "to show her support for the soldiers serving in Iraq (including certain members of her family) and to demonstrate her love of country."[47] School officials justified the ban on the grounds that the necklace was considered gang-related and that school policy prohibited the wearing of gang-related items at school.

The school district responded to the suit by filing a motion to dismiss. School authorities argued that wearing the necklace to school was not constitutionally protected since wearing the necklace conveyed no particularized message and it was unlikely that anyone seeing Jane Doe wearing the necklace would understand that she was communicating a message. The school district also rejected the mother's argument that its dress code was unconstitutionally vague.

A federal trial court denied the school district's dismissal motion without giving much of an indication about how it might ultimately rule in the case. The court concluded that it could not be said with certainty in the early phase of the lawsuit whether Jane Doe had a constitutional right to wear the necklace. Jane herself maintained that wearing the necklace conveyed a particularized expressive message, and the court determined that it could not be said for certain that viewers would fail to understand that:

> [I]t cannot be questioned that Plaintiff's wearing of the red, white and blue necklace coincided with the ongoing war in Iraq and that there is public debate about that war. While plaintiff claims that she was showing support for her country, for her family members who served in Iraq, and for her support of members of the military in general, people do not automatically associate the colors red, white and blue (or a red, white, and blue beaded necklace) as necessarily demonstrating support for the troops.[48]

Thus, the court concluded, using *Texas v. Johnson*, that it was simply unclear at the early stage of the litigation "whether anything about the necklace itself or the context in which Plaintiff wore the necklace gave any particular meaning to it."[49] Merely intending to express an idea is not sufficient for the conduct to be considered speech. The court also declined to rule definitively on Jane Doe's claim that the school district's student dress policy was unconstitutionally vague.

WEARING WHAT I LIKE TO SCHOOL

A Constitutional Right to Wear Blue Jeans to School? *Bannister v. Paradis*

In *Bannister v. Paradis*, an old federal court case out of New Hampshire, a federal court was asked to decide on the constitutionality of a school board policy that prohibited students from wearing "dungarees" to school.[50] Kevin Bannister, a sixth grader, wore blue jeans to school in violation of the "no dungarees" rule and was sent home.

Antonio Paradis, the school principal, defended the school district's dress code in court. As summarized by the court:

> [Paridis] testified that discipline in school is essential to the educational process, and that proper dress is a part of a good educational climate. It was his opinion that if students wear working or play clothes to school, it leads to a relaxed attitude and such an attitude detracts from discipline and a proper educational climate. Mr. Paradis stated further that students with patches on their clothes and students with dirty clothes, regardless of the type of clothing, should be sent home.[51]

Principal Paradis's testimony was supplemented by the school board chairman, an airline pilot. The chairman asserted that "California students had poor academic records and that this was due to the sloppy and casual attire worn by them to school."[52] As the trial court pointed out, the chairman did not provide any basis for claiming that California students had poor academic records.

In a 1970 decision that perhaps reflected the expansive spirit of the 1970s regarding individual rights, a federal trial judge expressed no patience with the school board's dress code. "There is no evidence that the wearing of dungarees of any color had every caused any disturbance at the school or given rise to any disciplinary problems," the court observed. "Kevin's wearing of blue jeans did not cause any disturbance and there was no disciplinary problem involved except the one involving Kevin himself." Therefore, the court stated, "It can be fairly concluded that wearing clean blue jeans does not constitute a danger to the health or safety of other pupils and that wearing them does not disrupt the other pupils."[53]

The judge in the case was bound by a First Circuit decision that had recognized a constitutional right of a student to choose the length of his hair. Based on the language of that opinion, the court concluded that "a person's right to wear clothes of his own choosing provided that, in the case of a schoolboy, they are neat and clean, is a constitutional right protected and guaranteed by the Fourteenth Amendment."[54]

The court acknowledged that the right to wear blue jeans to school did not rank very high on "the scale of values of constitutional liberties."[55] Nevertheless, in the court's view, the school had not been able to show that the wearing of blue jeans "inhibited or tended to inhibit the educational process."[56] Thus, the court ruled in Kevin's favor, finding "that the defendants have not justified the intrusion on the personal liberty of Kevin Bannister, small as that intrusion may be, and that the prohibition against wearing dungarees is unconstitutional and invalid."[57] The court concluded by enjoining the school district from enforcing its rule against students wearing dungarees to school.

Although the court struck down the school district's ban on blue jeans, it did not prohibit all school restrictions on student clothing. Specifically, the court said this:

> We realize that a school can, and must, for its own preservation exclude persons who are unsanitary, obscenely or scantily clad. Good hygiene and the health of the other pupils require that dirty clothes of any nature, whether they be dress clothes or dungarees, should be prohibited. Nor does the Court see anything unconstitutional in a school board prohibiting scantily clad students because it is obvious that the lack of proper covering, particularly with female students, might tend to distract other pupils and be disruptive of the educational process and school discipline.[58]

It should be remembered that the *Bannister* case was decided before the Supreme Court decisions discussed earlier in this chapter that laid out a two-part test for determining when an individual's conduct has an expressive element that entitles it to constitutional protection. Specifically, the *Bannister* court did not ask whether Kevin Bannister was conveying a "particularized message" by wearing blue jeans or whether people seeing him wear the jeans would understand that he was engaged in expression simply because he was wearing jeans.

Do Parents Have the Right to Decide What Their Children Wear to School? *Blau v. Fort Thomas Public School District*[59]

Robert Blau, a lawyer and parent of Amanda Blau, sued Fort Thomas Public School District, claiming the dress code at his daughter's middle school violated Amanda's constitutional rights and his constitutional rights as Amanda's father. Blau raised three constitutional challenges: (1) the dress code violated Amanda's First Amendment right to free expression; (2) the code violated Amanda's substantive due process right to wear the clothes of her own choosing; and (3) the code violated Blau's substantive due process right to direct the upbringing of his child, including the control his child's dress.

The dress code been developed by the middle school's Site Based Decision Making Council, which consisted of two parents, three teachers, and the principal. Although the code was not as restrictive as a school uniform code, it contained a number of detailed restrictions on student dress, which were summarized by the court:

- clothing that is too tight, revealing, or baggy, as well as tops and bottoms that do not "overlap";
- "hats, caps, scarves, or sweatbands" except on "special event days" such as "spirit" or "reward" days;
- non-jewelry chains and chain wallets;
- clothing that is "distressed" or has "holes in it";
- "visible body piercing (other than ears)";
- "unnaturally colored hair that is distracting to the educational process," including "blue, green, red, purple [or] orange" hair;
- "clothing that is too long, flip-flop sandals, or high platform shoes";
- pants, shorts or skirts that are not of "a solid color of navy blue, black, any shade of khaki, or white";
- "shorts, skirts, or skorts" that do not "reach mid-thigh or longer";
- "bottoms made with stretch knits, flannel, or fleece such as sweatpants, jogging pants, or any type of athletic clothing" as well as "baggy, sagging, or form-fitting pants";
- tops that are not "a solid color" and are not "crew neck [style], polo style with buttons, oxford style, or turtleneck";
- tops with writing on them and "logos larger than the size of a 'quarter.' . . except 'Highlands' logos or other "Highlands Spirit Wear'";
- tops that are not "of an appropriate size and fit"; and
- "form-fitting or baggy shirts" or "any material that is sheer or lightweight enough to be seen through."[60]

After Blau filed the lawsuit, the council modified the dress code, making it less restrictive in some ways but more restrictive in others. The modified code prohibited blue jeans as well as tops with plunging or revealing necklines, and it added a provision prohibiting any clothing that promoted drugs, alcohol, tobacco, or sex or that displays offensive or degrading images. The modified code liberalized the restrictions on pants, skirts, and shorts, permitting any color, and permitted striped or patterned tops.

In bringing the lawsuit, Amanda did not claim a desire to communicate a particular message through her clothing. Rather, she said, "she want[ed] to be able to wear clothes that 'look[] nice on [her],' that she 'feels good in' and that express her individuality."[61] Nor had she sued on religious grounds. Neither Amanda nor her father claimed the code was incompatible with their religious beliefs. The father's chief complaint was that the dress code inhibited his daughter's "ability to wear clothing that she likes."[62]

A trial court dismissed the lawsuit on the school district's motion for summary judgment, finding no constitutional violations in the school district's dress code. The Blaus appealed to the Sixth Circuit Court of Appeals, which affirmed the trial court's dismissal.

The Sixth Circuit began its legal analysis by stating flatly that the school district had the authority to enforce its dress code under Sixth Circuit's own precedent. In a 2000 decision, the court had said that a school district could enforce a dress code that banned "offensive illustrations" by banning a student from wearing a nihilistic Marilyn Manson T-shirt.[63] Thus, "it surely follows that a school district may enforce a dress code that regulates the types of pants and tops students may wear and may do so with respect to a student who does not wish to convey 'any particular message' through her clothing but simply wants to wear clothes that 'look nice' on her."[64]

The Sixth Circuit then went on to ask a more basic question: Does the First Amendment cover a claim such as Amanda's at all? "The protections of the First Amendment do not generally apply to conduct in and of itself," the court pointed out.[65] "To bring a free-speech claim regarding actions rather than word, claimants must show that their conduct 'conveys a particularized message' and 'the likelihood [is] great that the message [will] be understood by those who view[] it."[66]

In the court of appeals' view, the complaints against the dress code at Amanda's school did not give rise to a constitutional claim because they had not met the burden of showing that the First Amendment protected Amanda's conduct, "which in this instance amounts to nothing more than a generalized and vague desire to express her middle-school individuality." As the Sixth Circuit explained, the First Amendment simply does not protect Amanda's "vague and attenuated notions of expression—namely, self-expression through any and all clothing that a 12-year-old may wish to wear on a given day."[67]

The Blaus also argued that the school dress code was constitutionally overbroad because it suppressed a substantial amount of protected conduct that other students might engage in. But the Sixth Circuit rejected this claim as well. Courts will sustain a governmental regulation that restricts expressive conduct, the Sixth Circuit pointed out, using *Spence* and *Johnson*, if (1) the regulation was adopted for reasons not related to the suppression of expression, (2) the regulation furthers an important or substantial governmental interest, and (3) the regulation does not burden expression more than necessary to further the governmental interest.

In the Sixth Circuit's view, the dress code at Amanda's school passed constitutional muster. Contrary to the Blaus' assertions, the court concluded that the code had not been adopted for the purpose of suppressing speech. Rather, the school's Site Based Decision Making Council had adopted the code to enhance school safety, improve the learning environment, promote good behavior, enhance students' self-esteem, bridge socioeconomic differences between families, and reduce clothing costs for families. In the court's view, these were important governmental interests.

Furthermore, the Sixth Circuit was convinced that the school's dress code did not suppress more expressive conduct than was necessary to further its interests. The code restricted students' dress only during school hours, so students were free to wear what they wished in the evenings and on weekends. In addition, the school offered adequate alternative outlets for expression. For example, the court noted, students could write for the school newspaper, participate in extracurricular activities, and wear buttons expressing their viewpoints.

Having disposed of the First Amendment claims, the court next turned to Amanda's claim that the dress code violated her substantive due process rights under the Fourteenth Amendment. The court quickly dismissed this claim, pointing out that the dress code clearly had a rational basis and Amanda's asserted right to wear what she wanted to school was not a fundamental constitutional right that would require stricter judicial scrutiny.

Finally, the court considered Robert Blau's interesting argument that the dress code violated his substantive due process right to control the upbringing of Amanda, which included a constitutional right to choose her clothing. Blau based this argument on two Supreme Court cases, both decided in the 1920s, which had recognized the constitutional right of parents to direct the education of their children.[68]

The Sixth Circuit rejected this argument, emphatically ruling that the holdings in these old cases could not be stretched to include the constitutional right of parents to exempt their children from school dress codes. "While parents may have a fundamental right to decide *whether* to send their child to a public school," the court emphasized, "they do not have a fundamental right generally to direct *how* a public school instructs their child."[69] On the contrary, the court wrote,

> [w]hether it is the school curriculum, the hours of the school day, school discipline, the timing and content of examinations, the individuals hired to teach at the school, the extracurricular activities offered at the school, or, as here, a dress code, these issues of public education are generally committed to the control of state and local authorities.[70]

The Supreme Court in the touchstone case cited for the parental right to direct the upbringing of their child provides the foundation for Sixth Circuit's statement above. In 1925 the court wrote, "No question is raised concerning the power of the state reasonably to regulate all schools, to inspect, supervise and examine them, their teachers and pupils."[71] The First Circuit Court of Appeals affirmed this position seventy years later, stating,

> If all parents had a fundamental constitutional right to dictate individually what the schools teach their children, the schools would be forced to cater a

> curriculum for each student whose parents had genuine moral disagreements with the school's choice of subject matter. We cannot see that the Constitution imposes such a burden on state educational systems, and accordingly find that the rights of parents as described in *Meyer* and *Pierce* do not encompass a broad-based right to restrict the flow of information in the public schools.[72]

Blau v. Fort Thomas Public School District is a particularly important case for two reasons. First, contrary to most of the cases reviewed in this chapter, *Blau* is a federal court case decided at the appellate level. Although the Sixth Circuit Court's opinion is binding precedent only within the boundaries of the Sixth Circuit (the states of Kentucky, Ohio, and Tennessee), it may be persuasive in other federal circuits when they consider student free speech issues.

In addition, the *Blau* decision is important because the court considered a broad range of constitutional challenges against a school dress code, including the argument that parents have a substantive due process right to control the dress of their children while at school. Indeed, it is hard to imagine any new constitutional theory that could be presented to defeat a school's dress code other than the ones raised by Robert Blau and his daughter. Thus, from the perspective of school districts and school leaders, the *Blau* decision is a particularly good decision.

An Objection to Bland Clothing: *Bell v. Anderson Community Schools*

In *Bell v. Anderson Community Schools*, an unpublished case decided in 2007, a federal trial court in Indiana relied heavily on the Sixth Circuit's *Blau* opinion to reject a constitutional attack on a school district's dress code.[73] The Anderson Community Schools adopted a dress code containing detailed restrictions on student dress, somewhat similar to those that were approved in *Blau*, including a requirement that students wear "pants, trousers, capris, skirts, skorts, or jumpers that are black, navy, or khaki colored."[74] The dress code did not require students to buy specific brands or styles of clothing or dictate the exact articles that students were required to buy.

Scott and Laura Bell, parents of five children who were enrolled in the school system, filed a lawsuit objecting to the code on constitutional grounds. They claimed they lacked the clothing the new code required and would have to buy a completely new wardrobe for each child. In addition, they complained "that being able to wear the clothes they want is fundamental to their children's 'freedom of speech, expression, and freedom of happiness.'"[75] Specifically, the Bells claimed that wearing the "bland colors" that the dress code proscribed would "promote and or increase their emotional orders as well as depression." They also argued that their children should be free to choose clothing that was "best suited to their personality."[76]

The Bells filed their suit without an attorney, and the federal trial judge admitted having difficulty determining the legal theories under which they were proceeding. Nevertheless, the court denied their claims, relying heavily on the Sixth Circuit's *Blau* decision.

In *Blau*, the Indiana court noted, the Sixth Circuit had ruled that the First Amendment did not protect a student's right "to wear whatever she desired" and upheld a school district's dress code against constitutional challenge.

The Indiana court found the *Blau* decision persuasive. "The Bells have not shown that their children wish to convey any particularized message at all," the court wrote. "They have only hinted that this Dress Code will affect their children's 'freedom of expression' and that wearing 'such bland colors will promote or increase their emotional disorders as well as depression.'"[77] Such vague and attenuated notions of expression are not protected by the First Amendment, the court ruled.

Another case that also found the *Blau* position persuasive regarding "vague and attenuated notions of self-expression through clothing" is *Bar-Navon v. Brevard County School Board*.[78] In an unpublished opinion, the Eleventh Circuit Court of Appeals upheld a dress code that set out this standard:

> Pierced jewelry shall be limited to the ear. Dog collars, tongue rings, wallet chains, large hair picks, chains that connect one part of the body to another, or jewelry/accessories that pose a safety concern for the student or others shall be prohibited.[79]

Danielle Bar-Navon, then a sixteen-year-old tenth grade student at Viera High School, had piercings located on her tongue, nasal septum, lip, navel, and chest. She brought suit when she was suspended and prohibited from wearing the pierced jewelry. She did not intend to make a political or religious statement with her piercings. However, she asserted that her piercings were an expression of her "individuality," "non conformity and wild side," her "openness" to new ideas, and her "readiness to take on challenges in life."[80]

While noting that students enjoy some measure of the constitutional right to free speech within the special characteristics of the public school environment, the plaintiff student carried the burden of showing that she had a protected expressive right to wear jewelry that communicated her individuality. Citing *Spence* and *Johnson*, the court of appeals questioned whether the piercings implicated free speech protection of the First Amendment. However, setting aside their skepticism, they assumed some measure of communication in the piercings and used an intermediate scrutiny analysis.

The dress code, the appellate court asserted, furthered legitimate educational objectives: "The School Board sought to avoid extreme dress or appearance which might create a school disturbance or which could be hazardous to the students or others."[81] The court concluded that the jewelry limitation was narrowly tailored and there was ample alternatives for student speech.

It is interesting to note this analysis posits an *O'Brien*-type analysis but does not reference it. Accepting that the dress code, as applied to Bar-Navon's piercings, would create a disturbance (*Tinker*), there was no discussion of a disruption or of a reasonable forecast of disruption. Similarly, there was no discussion of the health hazard posed by the piercings. In fact, the only health issue that arose was when Bar-Navon replaced her piercings with plastic studs colored to match her skin tone. She developed an infection in her lip.

The court found a modicum of speech in the plaintiff's piercings but sidestepped a *Tinker* analysis and cited *Hazelwood*'s admonition that the determination of what speech is appropriate inside the schoolhouse gate "properly rests with the school board rather than the federal courts."[82] Whether the student's message merited protection as speech or whether it was speech was not addressed. The analysis focused on whether the dress code pursued a legitimate governmental interest in a narrow manner allowing for alternative student Danielle's free speech rights. The court answered in the affirmative. Consequently, the student's free speech rights were not abridged.

GANGS AND GANG ATTIRE

Dress codes have often targeted gangs in the schools, while school uniform policies focus on improving discipline, which sweeps curbing violence into its goals. Dress codes have explicit policies that address gangs, while school uniforms implicitly but not necessarily explicitly address gangs. School uniforms are considered a positive response to gangs because all gang members must wear the same clothing in the same colors, thus reducing their color identification with a specific gang.

Restricting Gang Attire

Gang activity at school negatively impacts the safety of all students.[83] According to the National Gang Center, "Gang members do not leave their conflicts, attitudes, and behaviors outside the school doors. Some of the most dangerous gang activities in any community may take place in and around local schools."[84] Gangs have identifiers that distinguish them from non–gang members and other gang members. These identifiers include gang attire, hand signs, colors,[85] and tattoos.[86] Several states have passed legislation aimed at curbing gang activity at school by imposing dress code restrictions on wearing gang-related apparel.

The organization National School Safety and Security Services identified aspects of gangs that implicate potential antigang dress codes, colors, and tattoos.[87] For example, Iowa passed the following school dress code statute:

> The general assembly finds and declares that the students and the administrative and instructional staffs of Iowa public schools have the right to be safe and secure at school. Gang-related apparel worn at school draws attention away from the school's learning environment and directs it toward thoughts and expressions of violence, bigotry, hate, and abuse. (Iowa § 279.58)[88]

Schools must take reasonable steps to safeguard their students from foreseeable harm. Those steps must comport with the constitutional freedoms that students bring with them when they enter the schoolhouse gate while recognizing that the rights of students are not coextensive with those of adults. In an effort to combat violence, many states allow school districts to enact regulations targeting gang-related apparel. The idea is to restrict the symbols associated with gang membership so that a gang member cannot outwardly identify him- or herself as a part of a gang, thus reducing the likelihood of violence. These regulations also protect non-gang students from being mistakenly targeted by gang members as a rival.

The following is an example of a gang-related dress code for elementary school students from the Parma City School District in Ohio:

> The presence of any apparel, jewelry, accessory, notebook, or manner of grooming, which by virtue of its color, arrangement, trademark, or any other attribute, denotes membership in a group or gang is prohibited. (Board of Education Policy 5511A)

It is interesting to note that the gang-related section for secondary school students is slightly different. It reads, "Inappropriate insignias, emblems, and/or gang-related colors shall not be worn during the school day or at school functions." It is unknown why the difference in policy. The elementary school student policy is more explicit in defining the restrictions.

The questions raised by gang-related dress code restrictions are twofold: First, are they effective or do they just target gang wannabes with real gang members finding subtle new ways of identification of membership? Second, do they violate the constitutional rights of students? Whether gang-related dress codes are effective in curbing violence at school is beyond the scope of this discussion. The second issue of constitutional violations will be discussed because if the policy violates students' constitutional rights, the effectiveness of the policy does not matter; it is unconstitutional and, therefore void.

A major legal concern, in addition to free speech, regarding gang-related dress codes is whether they violate the substantive due process rights of students. Under the Fourteenth Amendment, public schools may not adopt rules or regulations which violate the substantive due process rights of their students. An important aspect of substantive due process is vagueness. The void for vagueness doctrine of the Fourteenth Amendment prevents arbitrary and discriminatory enforcement.[89] A regulation is void on its face when it is so vague that persons of common intelligence must necessarily guess at its meaning and its application.[90]

In other words, a regulation/policy violates due process guarantees if a reasonable person would not know what to refrain from doing or what must be done to comport with the law, rule, or regulation. If it does not meet this standard, it is vague. If the rule is vague, it does not provide fair notice or warning. A second substantive due process consideration is whether the regulation or policy is overbroad sweeping in protected activity, thus rendering the protected activity unprotected.[91] Comporting with the requirements of substantive due process is a challenge for gang-related dress codes.

The Rosary and Gang Identification

An example of a gang-related dress code policy that ran afoul of substantive due process is found in New Caney High School in Montgomery County, Texas. The policy prohibited gang-related attire in school or at school-related events. Under the enforcement of the policy, the wearing of rosaries outside of the shirt was considered gang-related apparel. Rosaries were not specifically listed as gang apparel in the policy.[92] However, a police officer, the gang liaison officer, identified gang members of the United Homies as wearing rosaries within the area of the school district.

Even though school authorities stated that two students who wore rosaries to school for several months were not members of a gang, nor were they ever misidentified as gang members,[93] they were told that for their safety, they could not wear their rosaries outside of their shirts while at school. The students brought suit in federal district court.

The court in *Chalifoux v. New Caney Independent School District*, specific to the void for vagueness doctrine, found the policy violated substantive due process. The policy lacked a specific definition for gang apparel and thus did not provide adequate notice of what is prohibited, and it "provided excessive discretion to law enforcement officials in defining the parameters of its ban on gang-related apparel."[94] This definition, the court asserted, revealed little about what conduct is prohibited. Without a definition, students did not receive notice of prohibited conduct such as wearing a rosary on the outside of the shirt. In addition, the gang-related dress code placed too much discretion to define violations of the ban on gang-related apparel in the hands of officials.

In addition, the court found that the policy infringed on First Amendment rights of speech and a sincere expression of religious beliefs because not all gang members wore rosaries, and not all individuals who wore rosaries were gang members.

The Cross Tattoo

Brianna Stephenson, as an eighth grader, tattooed a small cross between her thumb and index finger. The cross was not intended as a religious symbol. It was also not intended as gang identification. Brianna did not have a record of disciplinary problems; in fact, she was considered by her teachers to be conscientious and diligent. Despite having a learning disability, she preserved and made the honor roll. She wore the cross tattoo without incident for thirty months. That changed when her high school, West High School, experienced an increase in gang activity with violence and intimidation.

The school district, in response to the problem of gangs, developed the "Proactive Disciplinary Position K–12." The policy stated, in pertinent part, that "[g]ang related activities such as display of 'colors,' symbols, signals, signs, etc., will not be tolerated on school grounds."[95] Soon after the policy was implemented, a school counselor with whom Brianna was meeting saw the tattoo and informed the associate principal.

It was determined that the tattoo of the cross was a gang symbol even though there was no evidence that Brianna was involved in gang activity and no other student filed a complaint about her tattoo being a gang symbol. Brianna was suspended for one day. In the subsequent meeting with Brianna and her parents, the associate principal informed them that Brianna had to either remove or alter the tattoo or face a ten-day suspension.

Brianna, concerned that altering the tattoo would make it bigger and the school authorities and others could consider the alteration to be a gang symbol, decided to undergo laser treatment to remove the tattoo, leaving a scar in place of the tattoo. Brianna sued following the removal of the tattoo, arguing in part that the gang-related policy violated her due process because the policy was void for vagueness.

The case found its way to the Eighth Circuit Court of Appeals.[96] The appellate court held that the policy was void for vagueness. The fact that the term "gang" was not defined rendered the policy defective. The court asserted that without a definition of "gang" and the prohibited "colors," "symbols," "signals," and "signs," the policy does not have its central definition to which colors, symbols, signals, and signs can be applied. "Accordingly, the District must 'define with some care' the 'gang related activities' it wishes students to avoid."[97]

In the court's view, the regulation failed to define the term at all and consequently failed to provide meaningful guidance for those who enforce it.[98] Applying this standard, the court found that the policy failed to provide adequate notice of what conduct is prohibited. The court stated that "the District regulation violates the central purposes of the vagueness doctrine because it fails to provide adequate notice regarding unacceptable conduct and fails to offer clear guidance for those who apply it. A person of common intelligence must necessarily guess at the undefined meaning of 'gang related activities.'"[99]

In addition, as in *Chalifoux*, discussed above, the policy provided virtually unfettered discretion for school authorities and police officers to define gang-related activity/symbols in any way they chose.[100] Because the term lacked a working definition, it failed to provide meaningful guidance for educators who enforce the policy.

Gangs and Sports Teams

Jeglin v. San Jacinto Unified School District considered whether a California school district could pass a rule prohibiting students from wearing clothing that bore "writing, pictures, or any other insignia which identifies any professional sports team or college on school district campuses or at school district functions."[101] The school district adopted the policy to curtail gang activity and applied it to all school campuses, including the high school, the middle school, and the district's four elementary schools.

Several students challenged the policy. For example, Marvin Jeglin wore a Chicago Bears jacket to the middle school, Ariel Jeglin wore a blue sweatshirt identifying the University of California, Los Angeles to her elementary school, and Darcee Le Borgne wore a University of San Diego sweatshirt to the high school. All were told their clothing violated the school district's dress code and that they would be disciplined if they disregarded the school district's policy against wearing clothing that displayed an affiliation with a college, a university, or a professional sports team.

The students sued, claiming a violation of their First Amendment rights, and a federal trial court applied the *Tinker* standard to the undisputed facts of the case. Under *Tinker* and binding precedent in the Ninth Circuit Court of Appeals, the court said, it was clear that public school students have a right to freedom of speech which is not shed at the schoolhouse gates. However, "[t]he interest of the state in the maintenance of its education system is a compelling one and provokes a balancing of First Amendment rights with the state's efforts to preserve and protect its educational process."[102] The court tipped the balance toward the preservation and protection of the school. In the court's view, this right "encompasses the wearing of clothing that displays a student's support of a college or university or professional sports team."[103]

Nevertheless, the court continued, schools can censor student speech if they reasonably forecast the speech will trigger a substantial disruption in the school environment. In the case before it, San Jacinto school officials argued its rule was justified because the wearing of clothing affiliated with a college or a sports team was linked to gang activity. The court considered the evidence of gang activity at all three school levels. Regarding the elementary schools, the court ruled that the school district had offered no evidence of gang presence in any of the district's four elementary schools. In the court's view, there was no justification for applying the school district's restrictive dress code to the elementary school population.

At the middle school level, the court found only negligible evidence of gang activity. Therefore, the court ruled that the school district's rule against clothing affiliated with athletic teams and colleges was an unwarranted infringement on the First Amendment rights of middle school students.

The court heard conflicting evidence regarding gang activity at San Jacinto High School. Several students testified that gang members did not wear clothing affiliated with sports teams or colleges to display their gang affiliations, but school authorities presented evidence to the contrary. In the end, the court concluded that the school district had carried its burden of showing a gang presence, "albeit of undefined size and composition,"[104] at the high school and a need to enforce its restrictive dress code at the high school level as a means of preventing possible disruption. Therefore, the court permitted the school district to enforce its dress policy at the high school level.

Jeglin v. San Jacinto Unified School District is a somewhat difficult to categorize. It could be argued that the case is about targeted student speech, since each of the students who sued had worn clothing to school that identified their affiliation with a particular sports team or college. On the other hand, it appears the students were motivated more by a desire to establish a broad constitutional right to right choose their clothing rather than a drive to proclaim their allegiance to specific sports organizations.

Discussion: Dress Code Response to Gangs

School administrators have a legal and a professional duty to take reasonable steps to respond to the violence associated with gang activity at school. The question is whether a dress code aimed at gang-related apparel is reasonable and workable. Given the susceptibility of such dress codes to fail the test of vagueness, is it a workable approach? Does a gang-related dress code provide sufficient notice and definition of what is prohibited?

Once a restriction is in place, many gangs morph their identifying symbols and signs for the specific purpose of keeping them secret from authorities raising the question of effectiveness. The court in *Stephenson*, the cross tattoo case above, captured this conundrum, writing, "Sadly, gang activity is not relegated to signs and symbols otherwise indecipherable to the uninitiated. In fact, gang symbols include common, seemingly benign jewelry, words and clothing."[105] Red and blue are colors of the Blood and Crips but they also the colors of the American flag.

A better approach is to focus energy and resources for immediate responses to any acts that endanger or tend to endanger students or staff. It is a response to a violent or intimidating act that is most important, not the response to the color of the clothes of the individual.

Dress codes, as discussed above, can implicitly target violence by focusing on gang identifiers, albeit with checkered success. School uniforms do not target violence at school but tacitly encompass school violence associated with student attire; instead, many ban gang identification by requiring a sameness in clothing that does not allow for identification as an individual or a member of a group or a gang. Mandatory school uniforms do not distinguish between gang members, members of a band, or members of the Girl Scouts or Boy Scouts, nor do they distinguish between speech that glorifies war or celebrates peace.

CONCLUSION

In this chapter, we looked at cases in which students challenged school dress codes on First Amendment grounds. In contrast to the cases discussed in the next two chapters, students in these cases did not claim a right to proclaim a specific textual or graphic message. Rather, they claimed a right to wear clothing that expressed their personality or affiliation with an ethnic or minority culture, reflected their personality, or, in one case, simply made the student feel good.

None of these cases ruled that school districts are prohibited by the First Amendment from imposing a dress code. Even the case of *Bannister v. Paradis*, in which the court struck down a school code's ban on blue jeans, affirmed a school district's right to impose a dress code to enforce standards of modesty and cleanliness. Cases in which students assert a right to wear clothes that they want to school try to don a cloak of constitutional free speech with little success.

If there is no message that can be understood, the statement cannot rise to the level of protected speech. In fact, the court in *Blau v. Fort Thomas Public*

School District raised the concern that elevating clothing as a notion of protected self-expression "would risk deprecating the First Amendment in cases in which a 'particularized message' does exist."[106] As seen in our discussion of relevant cases above, the threshold of what constitutes speech is important. In instances involving student symbolic speech or general expressive rights communicated through clothing choices, such as sagging pants, headwraps, jeans, colorful clothes, and piercings, what constitutes speech is critical. *Tinker*, *Spence*, and *Johnson* provides a framework for analysis.

Thus far, the Supreme Court has not decided the constitutionality of a student dress code as a general matter. In *Tinker*, the court only considered the constitutionality of a school rule that prohibited students from wearing black armbands, which the court recognized as symbolic speech.

Nevertheless, the Supreme Court's *Tinker* decision indicated that it recognized a constitutional distinction between a school's prohibition against a student's clearly expressive message, such as the Tinker children's black armbands, and a dress code intended to promote modesty or deportment. The court pointed out that the *Tinker* case did "not relate to regulation of the length of skirts or the type of clothing, to hair style, or deportment," suggesting that general dress code regulations are constitutionally permissible.[107]

In the next three chapters, we will look at lawsuits brought by students who were barred from communicating targeted messages about a particular topic. These topics include Confederate iconography, drugs, firearms, and politics, followed by sex, abortion, and sexual orientation.

NOTES

1. KNSS 98.7/1330, Wichita, Kansas (July 25, 2022), https://www.audacy.com/knss/news/local/hays-school-board-asked-to-remove-satanism-in-dress-code. A parent asked that references to Satanism be removed as a dress code prohibition based on the school district's nondiscrimination policy regarding religion. The family had belonged to the Satanic Temple for a number of years.

2. Kelly Wallace, CNN Health (April 21, 2017), https://www.cnn.com/2017/04/21/health/prom-dress-shopping-too-sexy-skimpy-parents/index.html.

3. Alia Wong, *USA Today* (December 22,2021), https://www.usatoday.com/story/news/education/2021/12/22/school-dress-code-protests-covid-pandemic/8942425002/?gnt-cfr=1.

4. Kaitlyn Alanis, *Fort Worth Star-Telegram* (April 29, 2022), https://www.star-telegram.com/news/nation-world/national/article260892187.html.

5. Alastair Lee Bitsoi, *Salt Lake Tribune* (April 20, 2022), https://www.sltrib.com/news/2022/04/20/native-student-denied/. Emalyce Kee, who is Dine (Navajo) and Rosebud Sioux, brought a beaded graduation cap with an eagle plume and was denied permission to wear it even though other students were allowed to wear candy

necklaces, gold jewelry, and Hawaiian leis. Soon afterward Utah governor Spencer Cox signed HB 30 into law, making it illegal to deny Native American students the opportunity to wear cultural regalia during "academic milestones." Ibid.

6. Karen Kucher, Karen Pearlman, and Alex Riggins, *San Diego Union Tribune* (September 13, 2021), https://www.sandiegouniontribune.com/news/public-safety/story/2021-09-13/police-respond-to-grossmont-high-after-student-protest-escalates. The protest appears to have been a response to a "change.org petition created Sunday, which appeared to be written by a senior at the high school, indicated students were upset by portions of the dress code viewed as misogynistic and sexist." Ibid. See also Brooke leigh Howard, "Hoodie Ban Fuels Wild Brawls and 10 Arrests on High School Campus," Yahoo! Life (November 4, 2022), https://www.yahoo.com/lifestyle/hoodie-ban-fuels-wild-brawls-201545986.html. After the protests, the school board amended the rule:

> Starting Friday November 4th, students will be permitted to wear hooded sweatshirts during the school day," a statement announcing the decision read. "However, the original rule that hoods may not be worn on heads while in district schools still stands. Failure to adhere to this rule will result in disciplinary action for each infraction.

Ibid.

7. Matt Delaney, "School District in Texas Orders Kids to Wear Professional Attire: No Hoodies, Skirts or Dresses," *Washington Times* (June 24, 2022), https://www.washingtontimes.com/news/2022/jun/24/school-district-texas-orders-kids-wear-professiona.

8. Tawnell D. Hobbs, "Schools Relax Dress Codes in Bid to End Body Shaming," *Wall Street Journal* (July 13, 2019), https://www.wsj.com/articles/schools-relax-dress-codes-in-bid-to-end-body-shaming-11563010202.

9. Nadra Nittle, "Students Are Waging War on Sexist and Racist School Dress Codes—And They're Winning," *Vox* (September 13, 2018), https://www.vox.com/the-goods/2018/9/13/17847542/students-waging-war-sexist-racist-school-dress-codes.

10. The communication (October 17, 2022) with the high school principal is in the possession of the author.

11. "Girls Fight Back against Gender Bias in School Dress Codes," *NEA Today* (January 6, 2016), http://neatoday.org/2016/01/school-dress-codes-gender-bias/.

12. Isabella Grullon Paz, "'Sexist,' 'Racist,' 'Classist': Georgia 8th Grader Challenges School Dress Code,'" *New York Times* ((September 6, 2021), https://www.nytimes.com/2021/09/04/us/politics/mask-dress-code-protest.html. The Cobb County School District in a statement said "that the district's rules for student dress 'encourage a focus on learning for all 110,000 students in Cobb, not on what students prefer to wear.'" Ibid.

13. Ibid.

14. Ibid. The fingertip language stated that "'all shorts, skirts and dresses must be fingertip length'—meaning when students hold their arms at their sides, their longest finger must still touch fabric. The code also specifies that 'no skin may be exposed above the fingertip.'"

15. For an interview with a fourteen-year-old who describes the successful process ("Learning to ask for help and thinking of wider impact") that she used to change her middle school dress code and the dress codes of sixteen other schools, see "How I Changed My School District's Sexist Dress Code When I Was 14," *Fast Company* (February 17, 2022), https://www.fastcompany.com/90721072/how-i-changed-my-school-districts-sexist-dress-code-when-i-was-14.

16. Mackenzie Mays, "Teen Boys Don Dresses to Protest School Dress Code," *Miami Herald* (February 3, 2016), https://www.miamiherald.com/news/nation-world/national/article57871978.html.

17. Ibid. However, a female sophomore wore a shirt within the bounds of the dress code but wrote in rainbow colors across the back "dress codes suck." She was coded.

18. "Student Care: Jett Hawkins Law," *Illinois State Board of Education* (n.d.), https://www.isbe.net/Pages/Jett-Hawkins-Law.aspx. The law identifies braids, locs, and twists.

19. *Bear v. Fleming*, 714 F. Supp. 2d 972, 983 (D. S. D. 2010).

20. *Spence v. Washington*, 418 U.S. 405, 409 (1974).

21. Jan Hoffman, "Can a Boy Wear a Skirt to School?" *New York Times* (November 6, 2009), https://www.nytimes.com/2009/11/08/fashion/08cross.html.

22. *Spence v. Washington*, 418 U.S. 405, 411 (1974); *Texas v. Johnson*, 491 U.S. 397, 404 (1989).

23. 391 U.S. 367 (1968)

24. 393 U.S. 503 (1969).

25. 491 U.S. 397 (1989).

26. 418 U.S. 405 (1974).

27. *Littlefield v. Forney Independent School District*, 268 F.3d 275, 283 (5th Cir. 2001).

28. 899 F. Supp. 556 (D. N. M. 1995).

29. Ibid., 561. For a discussion of sagging pants as "a message of fashionable disobedience," see Onika K. Williams, "The Suppression of a Saggin' Expression: Exploring the 'Saggy Pants' Style within a First Amendment Context," *Indiana Law Journal* 85 (2010): 1173 "Wearing saggy pants should be viewed as an unconventional, expressive form of conduct that deserves First Amendment protection." Ibid., 1172.

30. 899 F. Supp. 560 (D. N.M. 1995).

31. Ibid., citing *Texas v. Johnson*, 491 U.S. 397, 404 (1989).

32. Ibid., 563.

33. Jacqueline M. Nowacki, *K–12 Education: Department of Education Should provide Information on Equity and Safety in School Dress Codes* (Washington, DC: US General Accounting Office GAO-23–105348 K-12 Education, October 2022), 14, https://www.gao.gov/assets/gao-23-105348.pdf.

34. 40 F. Supp. 2d 335 (D. Md. 1999).

35. Ibid., 336.

36. Ibid., 338.

37. Ibid.

38. Ibid., 339, quoting *Massie v. Henry*, 455 F.2d 779, 783 (4th Cir. 1972).
39. Ibid.
40. Ibid. (internal citation and quotation marks omitted).
41. Ibid.
42. Ibid.
43. Ibid., 340.
44. Ibid., 338.
45. Ibid.
46. 489 F. Supp. 2d 139 (N.D. N.Y. 2006).
47. Ibid., 142.
48. Ibid., 145.
49. Ibid., 146.
50. 316 F. Supp. 185 (D. N.H. 1970).
51. Ibid., 186.
52. Ibid., 187.
53. Ibid., 186.
54. Ibid., 188.
55. Ibid.
56. Ibid.
57. Ibid., 189.
58. Ibid., 188–89.
59. 401 F.3d 381 (6th Cir. 2005).
60. Ibid., 385–86.
61. Ibid., 386.
62. Ibid.
63. *Boroff v. Van Wert City Board of Education*, 220 F.3d 465 (6th Cir. 2000).
64. *Blau v. Fort Thomas School District*, 401 F.3d at 388.
65. Ibid.
66. Ibid., citing *Spence v. Washington*, 418 U.S. 405, 411 (1974) and *Texas v. Johnson*, 491 U.S. 397, 404 (1989).
67. Ibid., 390.
68. See *Meyer v. Nebraska*, 262 U.S. 390 (1923) (statute prohibiting the teaching of school subjects in any language other than English was an arbitrary interference with parents' right t control the education of their children); *Pierce v. Society of Sisters*, 268 U.S. 510 (1925) (statute requiring all children between the ages of 8 and 16 to attend a public school unreasonably interfered with parents' right to direct the upbringing of the children. For a discussion of the parental right to direct and the responsibility of the state to educate its citizens, see Todd A. DeMitchell and Joseph J. Onosko, "A Parent's Child and the State's Future Citizen: Judicial and Legislative Responses to the Tension over the Right to Direct an Education," *Southern California Interdisciplinary Law Journal* 22 (2013): 591–635. The authors conclude, "A school district's democratically elected representatives and hired professional educators must be allowed to fashion a curriculum that comports with the community's political and educational decisions about what knowledge is of the greatest worth for its citizens." Ibid., 635.

69. *Blau v. Fort Thomas Public School District*, 401 F.3d at 395 (emphasis by the court).

70. Ibid., 395–96.

71. *Pierce v. Society of Sisters*, 268 U.S. 510, 534 (1925).

72. *Brown v. Hot, Sexy and Safer Productions, Inc.*, 68 F.3d 525, 534 (1st Cir. 1995).

73. No. 1:07-cv-00936-JDT-WTL, 2007 U.S. Dist. LEXIS 57428 (S.D. Ind. Aug. 6, 2007).

74. Ibid., 4 (LexisNexis pagination).

75. Ibid., 5.

76. Ibid.

77. Ibid., 22.

78. 290 Fed. Appx. 273, 276 (11th Cir. 2008).

79. Ibid., 274.

80. Ibid., 275.

81. Ibid., 277.

82. Ibid.

83. For a listing of state statutes and gangs, see http://www.streetgangs.com/laws/statesdefined.html.

84. Michelle Arciaga, Wayne Sakamoto, and Errika Fearby Jones, "Responding to Gangs in the School Setting, *National Gang Center Bulletin* 1 (November 2010), http://www.nationalgangcenter.gov/Content/Documents/Bulletin-5.pdf.

85. Ibid., 11–12.

86. National School Safety and Security Services, *Gangs and School Safety*, http://www.schoolsecurity.org/trends/gangs.html.

87. Ibid.

88. For a listing of other state statutes and school gang-related apparel, see http://https://nationalgangcenter.ojp.gov/legislation/apparel.

89. *Smith v. Goguen*, 415 U.S. 566, 573 (1974).

90. *Connally v. General Construction Company*, 269 U.S. 385, 391 (1926).

91. *Broaderick v. Oklahoma*, 413 U.S. 601, 615 (1973).

92. *Chalifoux v. New Caney Independent School District*, 976 F. Supp. 659, 664 (S.D. Tex. 1997). The policy stated:

1. Oversized apparel, including baggy pants which are worn low on the waist; overalls with one strap unfastened; pants that are cut off below the knees and worn with knee socks. (Pants should fit at the waist and have properly sewn hems).
2. Any attire which identifies students as a group (gang-related) may not be worn to school or school-related activities.
3. Baseball caps, hair nets, bandanas, sweatbands.

93. Ibid., 667.

94. Ibid., 669.

95. Ibid., 1308.

96. *Stephenson v. Davenport Community School District*, 110 F.3d 1303 (8th Cir. 1997).

97. Ibid., 1310.
98. Ibid., 1310.
99. Ibid., 1311.
100. The court wrote, "Thus, the essentially unfettered discretion of these individuals placed a high school student in the unenviable position of removing her tattoo by scarring her body or suffering suspension from her educational pursuits for ten days and face possible expulsion. The District regulation, therefore, violates a central purpose of the vagueness doctrine that if arbitrary and discriminatory enforcement is to be prevented, laws must provide explicit standards for those who apply them. Ibid.
101. 827 F. Supp. 1459, 1460 (C.D. Calif. 1993).
102. Ibid., 1461.
103. Ibid.
104. Ibid., 1462.
105. *Stephenson v. Davenport Community School District*, 110 F.3d at 1311.
106. *Blau v. Fort Thomas Public School District*, 401 F.3d at 390.
107. *Tinker v. Des Moines Independent Community School District*, 393 U.S. 503, 507–08 (1969).

4

Symbols

The Confederate Battle Flag in the Public Schools

> A person gets from a symbol the meaning he puts into it, and what is one man's inspiration is another's jest and scorn.[1]

On Thursday morning, February 23, 2023, at Porter Ridge High School in North Carolina, a student snapped a picture of a student's truck flying the Confederate battle flag. The picture was uploaded on social media and created an instant angry reaction from several parents. One parent commented that "the flag itself isn't necessarily the issue, but rather the symbolism behind it and the fear it can create."[2] After administrators talked with the students involved, they voluntarily removed the flag.

Symbols matter: "Public symbolism has profound implications for the citizens of the public body represented by the symbol."[3] They convey messages that often trigger strong emotional responses—both negative and positive. The Statute of Liberty, for example, is a powerful symbol conveying deeply held beliefs that America welcomes people from all over the world—those "huddled masses yearning to breathe free."[4]

On the other hand, a noose is a powerful symbol linking America's violent past with current injustices. The Anti-Defamation League considers it a general hate symbol, writing, "The hangman's noose has become to be one of the most powerful visual symbols directed against African Americans, comparable in the emotions that it evokes to that of the swastika for Jews."[5]

"Ideas spread by symbols as well by words."[6] The message associated with a symbol, however, may be contested by groups of people who have different interpretations of the symbol. The Confederate flag is a symbol, often a powerful one. But a symbol of what? The Confederate battle flag, for example, incites strong tensions between students who see the flag as a symbol of Southern heritage and others who see the flag as a symbol of oppression.

A federal district judge, writing in 1997, acknowledged the conflicting interpretations of the Confederate when he wrote,

> Undoubtedly, the Confederate battle flag does not represent the same thing to everyone. . . . There are citizens of all races who view the flag as a symbolic acknowledgment of pride in Southern heritage and the ideals of independence. Likewise, there are citizens of all races who perceive the flag as embodying principles of discrimination, segregation, white supremacy and rebellion.[7]

Monuments and other iconography of the Confederacy and slavery are facing increased scrutiny for their place in the public square. On June 9, 2020, Margaret Huang, president and chief executive officer of the Southern Poverty Law Center, sent a letter to all armed forces requesting that they follow the example of the Marine Corps, which banned all Confederate iconography from all of its bases and installations. She wrote,

> Our public entities should no longer play a role in distorting history by honoring a secessionist government that waged war against the United States to preserve white supremacy and the enslavement of millions of people. We must act now to bury the myth of the Lost Cause once and for all.[8]

In 2020, Richard Fossey and I wrote, "The arc of history is bending towards the elimination of public praise and acknowledgement of the Confederate states' actions and actors."[9] The "Lost Cause" may be finally and truly be lost.

THE CONFEDERATE BATTLE FLAG: A SYMBOL OF PRIDE OR OPPRESSION?

"To many who are aware of the immeasurable suffering that resulted from slavery and the civil War, displaying this [Confederate] flag today represents an expression of continuing contempt for the rights of African-Americans to participate fully and equally in American Society."—*West v. Derby Unified School District #260* 23 F. Supp. 2d 1220, 1233 (D. Kan. 1998)

In this chapter we will explore student clothing that displays a Confederate flag—usually the iconic Confederate battle flag. Without question, Confederate flags are controversial. Again and again, the federal courts have been called on to determine whether students have a First Amendment right to display a Confederate flag on their clothing while at school. A surprisingly large number of these cases have reached the federal appellate court level, which is an indication of how strongly some students and parents feel about the right to display a Confederate flag.

Confederate flag litigation in the federal courts dates back to the early 1970s, and it is not necessary to examine all of these cases in detail to understand the present state of the law on the constitutionality of school prohibitions against students wearing Confederate flags on their clothing while at school.[10] For example, the federal Eastern District Court in 1970 wrote, "The Confederate battle flag, since the decision by the U.S. Supreme Court on May 17, 1954 in *Brown v. Board of Education* (Brown I) has become a symbol of resistance to school integration and, to some, a symbol of white racism in general."[11] In this section, we will examine some of the recent federal appellate court decisions on symbolic speech associated with the Confederal battle flag.

As will be seen, schools win most of these cases. In general, the courts have applied *Tinker*'s substantial disruption test to the facts of these cases and have supported school authorities' decision to ban the Confederate flag if they have evidence that displaying the flag will likely trigger a substantial disruption in the school environment, such as racial turmoil.

Before starting our discussion of the appellate court cases, it is important to note that in summer of 2020, the Oregon Department of Education issued a ban on "hate symbols" such as the noose, Confederate flag, and swastika. An Oregon Department of Education official stated that these symbols "are being used to bully and harm students and staff, and this is particularly true for students of color."[12]

West v. Derby Unified School District (2000)[13]

A student known as T.W. was suspended from school after he drew a Confederate battle flag during his math class; he did not display the flag on his clothing. Previously T.W. had received a three-day suspension for calling another student "blackie," in addition to other disciplinary infractions.

The school district had previously adopted a rule against displaying the Confederate flag and other racially offensive symbols, an action it took in response to significant racial tensions at the high school. Racist graffiti had appeared on the high school campus, with some using the N-word, and one fight had erupted over a student wearing a Confederate flag headband while some Black students wore shirts with an "X," denoting support of Malcom X's teachings. Moreover, racial tensions had been exacerbated by the off-campus activities of the Ku Klux Klan and Aryan Nation.[14]

T.W.'s parent sued, alleging several constitutional violations characterizing the drawing as "peaceful and nonthreatening" without intent to harass or intimidate. However, the trial court found that T.W. "knowingly and intentionally violated the policy against possession of [Confederate] symbols."[15]

The Tenth Circuit Court of Appeals first dismissed as meritless T.W.'s argument that his intent was not established. The court asserted that school officials, with the countless disciplinary issues they regularly face, are not compelled under due process to prove that students possess *mens rea* akin to criminal intent. T.W. had received all of the process that he was due.[16]

Turning to T.W.'s free speech claim, the appellate court held that school officials had not violated T.W.'s First Amendment rights, since they "had reasonably concluded that possession or display of the Confederate flag images . . . would likely lead to a material and substantial disruption of school discipline."[17] School officials, after establishing a reasonable forecast of disruption, need not wait to take action until a disruption occurs; they need not wait until a "full-fledged brawl" has broken out before acting.[18]

The school district had passed a ban on displays of the Confederate flag, the court ruled, not merely to avoid discomfort and unpleasantness, but to avoid the possibility of serious racial conflict in the schools. Indeed, the lower court had specifically found that the school district had a reasonable basis for concluding that the Confederate flag is a symbol that "is racially divisive or creates ill will or hatred."[19] Thus, in the court's opinion that was affirmed by the court of appeals, school officials had not violated T.W.'s free speech rights when it sanctioned him for knowingly drawing a Confederate flag while at school, in violation of school policy.

Scott v. School Board of Alachua County (2003)[20]

Two high school students defied their school principal's unwritten ban on the display of Confederate flags and were suspended. They sued, but a Florida federal court upheld the suspension. The students then appealed, raising several legal arguments, including the argument that there was insufficient evidence of substantial disruption to justify their suspension.

The Eleventh Circuit of Appeals affirmed the trial court's decision, adopting part of it verbatim. In essence, the Eleventh Circuit affirmed the principal's Confederate flag ban under two principles. First, school officials had produced enough evidence of racial tensions to justify the ban under the *Tinker* standard on the grounds that they feared a substantial disruption if the flag was displayed.

Second, relying on *Bethel School District v. Fraser*,[21] the court noted that a school's essential mission includes the responsibility "to teach students of differing races, creeds and colors to engage each other in civil terms rather than in terms of debate highly offensive or highly threatening to others."[22] In the court's opinion, there was "no evidence that the school district [had] attempted to suppress civil debate on racial matters." Rather, "the district had concluded that the display of certain symbols that have become associated with racial prejudice are so likely to provoke feelings of hatred and ill will in others that they are inappropriate in the school context."[23]

Essentially, the *Scott* appellate court concluded that the Confederate flag, when displayed in the school environment, could be viewed as offensive and uncivil speech and could be banned under *Fraser*'s offensive speech standard without regard to whether the speech might cause a substantial disruption. The court focused on the content of the message (*Fraser*) and not the response to the message (*Tinker*).

Barr v. Lafon (2008)[24]

Students challenged a school district's rule prohibiting students from displaying the Confederate flag on their clothing while at school and took their lawsuit to the Sixth Circuit Court of Appeals. As explained by the high school principal at a school assembly, he would not allow students "to have Rebel flags or symbols of [the] Rebel flag on their clothing, or anything else that was a disruption to the school."[25] Students sued, arguing they had a First Amendment right to express their Southern heritage by displaying the Confederate flag on their clothing, but a federal trial court was unsympathetic and dismissed their case.

On appeal, the students argued that the school district had engaged in viewpoint discrimination, prohibiting some racially divisive symbols but not others and banning racially divisive speech but not racially inclusive speech. In particular, the students charged the school with prohibiting students from displaying the Confederate flag on their clothing but allowing African American students to wear clothes that displayed an image of Malcolm X.

The Sixth Circuit agreed with the students that if there were evidence that the school district had selectively enforced its dress code against the Confederate flag but not against other racially divisive symbols, it would be compelled to reverse the trial court's decision in the school district's favor.[26] But in fact, the court concluded, the students had produced no more than "a scintilla of evidence" that this was the case. In the court's view, there simply was no genuine issue of material fact that the school district enforced a prohibition against displaying the Confederate flag while allowing students to wear clothing with Malcolm X iconography.[27]

Moreover, in the Sixth Circuit's opinion, there was ample evidence that school officials reasonably foresaw substantial disruption if students came to school wearing clothing that depicted the Confederate flag. "This is not a case in which the school acted upon undifferentiated fear or apprehension of disturbance," the court emphasized.[28] Rather, "in a context of high racial tensions, race-related altercations, and threats of violence," school authorities reasonably feared the flag would disrupt the school's educational process.[29]

B.W.A. v. Farmington R-7 School District (2009)[30]

In a decision out of Missouri, the Eighth Circuit Court of Appeals upheld a school district's ban on student clothing depicting the Confederate flag. Three students, identified only by initials, sued the Farmington School District after they were sent home for wearing various items of clothing that displayed the Confederate flag, including a belt buckle that contained an image of the flag and the words "Dixie Classic."

As explained by the court, Farmington's school superintendent had banned students from displaying the Confederate flag on their clothing prior to the suspensions. He took this action due to several racially charged incidents that had taken place during the previous school year. "In the first incident, a white student urinated on a fourth grade black student while allegedly saying 'that is what black people deserve.'"[31] In the second incident, white students showed up at a black student's residence and made racial comments. A fight ensued, and later people drove around the black student's home "screaming racial epithets and threatening to burn down the home."[32] In a third incident, Farmington varsity basketball players allegedly made racial slurs toward two black players on an opposing team during a basketball tournament, which led to an investigation by the US Justice Department's Office of Civil Rights.

The students sued the school district, alleging a violation of their constitutional rights, but a federal district court granted the school district's motion to dismiss the suit. On appeal, the Eighth Circuit affirmed. Based on the prior incidents of racial conflict, the court concluded that Farmington school officials reasonably forecast that there would be substantial disruption if the Confederate flag is displayed at the high school.

A.M. v. Board of Trustees of Burleson Independent School District (2009)[33]

Similarly, the Fifth Circuit Court of Appeals backed a Texas school district that prohibited two high school students from carrying purses on campus that displayed the Confederate flag. The students sued and sought an injunction against the school ban. A Texas federal court denied their motion for an injunction and dismissed their suit, finding sufficient evidence that school officials reasonably anticipated a disruption if the Confederate flag was displayed on campus.

On appeal, the Fifth Circuit summarized the school district's considerable evidence supporting their claim that the Confederate flag would likely provoke a substantial disruption if displayed on campus:

> There is ample, uncontroverted evidence that elements of the BHS student body have continually manifested racial hostility and tension. This tension has become evident in the various events described above, including racially hostile graffiti and vandalism, multiple disciplinary referrals involving racial epithets, and a physical confrontation between white BHS students and the African-American students of another high school. Some of these elements included the use of the Confederate flag, including the incidents in which a white HS student waved the flag in the direction of an opposing school's predominantly African-American volleyball team. As recently as spring 2006, Confederate flags were flown over the flagpole on Martin Luther King Jr. Day and a white student simulated the lynching of an Africa-American student.[34]

Even if those incidents "[did] not rise to the level of 'substantial disruption' under *Tinker* (thus justifying the ban based on past actual disruption)," the court observed, "they serve as a factual basis for administrators' forecast that disruptions might occur if students were allowed to display racially charged symbols such as the Confederate flag."[35]

In sum, the court concluded that school officials reasonably anticipated that displays of the Confederate flag would create a substantial disruption at Burleson High School. Moreover, contrary to the students' contention, it was not necessary for school officials to show that display of the flag had caused a disruption in the past before imposing a ban on its display.

Defoe Ex Rel. Defoe v. Spiva (2010)[36]

The Anderson County School District in Tennessee, like many school districts throughout the nation, adopted a student code of conduct that included regulations on student dress. The dress code stated that student attire "or appearance, which tends to draw attention to an individual rather than to a learning situation, must be avoided."[37] The code banned clothing and accessories that displayed racial or ethnic slurs, gang affiliations, vulgar or suggestive language or images, and promotions of products that students are not legally entitled to purchase or possess, such as alcohol, illegal drugs, and tobacco.[38]

School authorities claimed that racial tension had existed at the district's Clinton High School dating back to 1956, when the school was first integrated. For that reason, the school banned the Confederate flag, which school officials said "would be a distraction to any student offended by it and could result in some sort of dangerous disagreement resulting from conflict or violence."[39]

On October 30, 2006, Tom Defoe, a student, wore a T-shirt that depicted the image of the Confederate flag. When school officials asked him to remove the T-shirt or to turn it inside out, he refused. He was sent home. Six days later, he wore a belt buckle to school with a Confederate flag displayed on it. He was subsequently suspended from school.[40]

On November 20, 2006, Tom, with his parents, sued the school district for a violation of his free speech rights. A weeklong jury trial was conducted during the summer of 2008. The jury was unable to reach a unanimous verdict. The federal district court judge granted summary judgment for the defendant school district.[41] The plaintiff student and his parents appealed to the Sixth Circuit Court of Appeals.

On appeal, a three-judge panel affirmed the trial court's decision in favor of the school district. In a concurring opinion, one judge acknowledged that the Confederate flag is subject to various interpretations. On one hand, the battle flag is seen by some as conveying "a noble message," signifying "honor for one's ancestors who fought bravely . . . for independence from the industrialized North."[42] But on the other hand, the Confederate flag "is doubtless *perceived* by many, if not most, student viewers in today's high schools in the United States as a statement of racial hostility—comparable to a slogan that says 'Blacks should be slaves' or 'Blacks are inferior.'"[43]

Certainly, in the concurring judge's opinion, "[a] plainly reasonable interpretation of a Confederate flag T-shirt or jacket is one of racial hostility or contempt, regardless of the subjective intent of the wearer."[44]And even if a student displayed a Confederate flag without intending to communicate racial hostility, "a school administrator cannot practically administer a rule that permits such clothing sometimes and prohibits it other times, depending on the intent of each individual wearer."[45]

The *Defoe* case illustrates the challenges that educators face as they attempt to honor the free speech rights of students while maintaining a safe and orderly educational atmosphere. Unfortunately, in recent years, public school districts are increasingly being sued by students and their parents based on claims that school authorities violated a student's free speech rights under the First Amendment by enforcing a student dress code that restricted a student's choice of clothing.

Hardwick v. Heyward (2013)[46]

Finally, we have the Fourth Circuit's 2013 opinion in *Hardwick v. Heyward*, the latest federal appellate court decision to consider whether high school students have a First Amendment right to display a Confederate flag on their clothing while at school. In that case, the Fourth Circuit concluded that a South Carolina school district did not violate the free speech rights of

Candice Hardwick when it prohibited her from wearing a number of shirts that depicted the Confederate flag over a period of three school years.

In 2003, Candice was a middle school student in the Latta School District (LSD), a small school system in South Carolina. The town of Latta had a heritage of slavery and segregation, and its schools were not desegregated until the 1970–1971 school year[47]. At the time of the litigation, LSD's student enrollment was approximately sixteen hundred, about equally divided between white and African American students.

Latta Middle School and Latta High School both had student dress codes. The middle school dress code stated that student dress would generally be considered appropriate so long as it did not "distract others, interfere with the instructional program, or otherwise cause disruption."[48] The policy then went on to describe clothing that would be deemed inappropriate: "clothing that displays profane language, drugs, tobacco, or alcohol advertisements, sexually innuendoes or anything else deemed to be offensive."[49]

LSD's high school dress code was similar to the middle school policy. The high school code provided that

> students are to come to school in a neat and clean manner each day. Dress is casual, but some styles, which may be appropriate outside of school, are clearly inappropriate for schools. Students may not wear the following: . . . . Shirts with obscene/derogatory sayings.[50]

During the 2002–2003 school year, Candice had the first of a series of confrontations with school officials over her clothing. In early 2003, the middle school principal directed Candice to remove her "Southern Chick" shirt, which displayed a Confederate flag.

During the following school year (2003–2004), school officials told Candice to remove a "Dixie Angels" shirt, a "Southern Girls" shirt, and a shirt honoring African American Confederate soldiers. All these shirts depicted a Confederate flag. Candice also wore a shirt displaying the American flag with the words "Old Glory" and "Flew over legalized slavery for 90 years!"

In late February 2004, Candice came to school wearing a shirt that depicted Robert E. Lee and the Confederate flag. She was given an in-school suspension after she refused to change shirts. The following month, Candice came to school wearing a "Girls Rule" shirt that displayed a Confederate flag. She changed shirts on this occasion after school authorities directed her to do so.

At some point in this ongoing confrontation, Candice's parents wrote a letter to John Kirby, the LSD superintendent, informing him that they approved of Candice's clothing choices, which reflected Candice's heritage and religious beliefs. LSD's school board chairman, Harold Kornblut, responded to the letter, telling the parents that LSD was justified in banning Candice's

Confederate flag clothing based on a long history of racial tensions in the school district and the likelihood that other students might interpret the flag's meaning differently from the way Candice interpreted it.

In 2004, Candice began attending Latta High School, where the Confederate flag controversy continued. In May 2005, the high school principal removed Candice from class for wearing a shirt that proclaimed "Daddy's Little Redneck" and—like several of Candice's previous shirts—displayed a Confederate flag.

Candice then produced four more "protest" shirts. The principal prohibited these shirts as well, although not all the protest shirts contained pictures of the Confederate flag. For example, one protest shirt stated: "Honorary Member of the FBI: Federal Bigot Institutions."[51]

Unable to get LSD to change its position on her choice of Confederate flag–themed clothing, Candice sued her middle school principal, her high school principal, and the school district's board of trustees, claiming a violation of her constitutional rights under the First and Fourteenth Amendments. A federal trial court dismissed most of Candice's claims on the defendants' motion for summary judgment, and Candice filed her first appeal.

In its initial ruling, the Fourth Circuit ruled that it did not have jurisdiction over Candice's case since the trial court had not ruled on all of Candice's claims. Specifically, the trial court had not ruled on the so-called protest shirts that Candice wore—some of which did not contain images of the Confederate flag. The trial court then ruled on the protest shirt issues, dismissing Candice's suit in its entirety, and Candice filed her second appeal.

In its second decision on Hardwick's case, the Fourth Circuit Court of Appeals affirmed the trial court's dismissal. In the Fourth Circuit's opinion, the record contained "ample evidence from which the school officials could reasonably forecast that all of these Confederate flag shirts would materially and substantially disrupt the work and discipline of the school."[52] The court rejected Candice's argument that the Confederate flag shirts had in fact created no disruptions at LSD. "That the shirts never caused a disruption is not the issue," the court explained. "[R]ather the issue is whether school officials could reasonably forecast a disruption because of her shirts."[53]

Similarly, the appellate court rejected Candice's argument that the shirts merely symbolized her heritage and religious faith. "Again," the court reiterated, "the proper focus is whether school officials could predict that the Confederate flag shirts would cause a disruption."[54]

Finally, the court wrapped up its First Amendment analysis by ruling that school authorities reasonably predicted that one of her protest shirts—a shirt depicting the American flag along with the words "Old Glory" and "Flew over legalized slavery for 90 years!"—was likely to cause a substantial disruption even though the shirt did not display the Confederate flag.[55] The court also ruled that the school district's speech codes were not unconstitutionally vague or overbroad.

The *Hardwick* decision is notable because the Fourth Circuit ruled that the Latta School District reasonably anticipated that Candice's Confederate flag depictions could cause a substantial disruption at school even though her controversial shirts, worn over a period of three school years, apparently caused no disruptions. In addition, the court found that one of Candice's T-shirt carried the potential for disruption even though it did not display a Confederate flag.

SUMMARY COMMENTS

One interesting aspect of the Confederate flag cases is the odd alliances that the Confederate flag controversies have formed. The American Civil Liberties Union and the Sons of Confederate Veterans as well as Southern Legal Resource Center have joined in opposing the school bans on Confederate symbols. "Though such groups fall on squarely opposite sides of the political spectrum," one commentator observed, "they are unified by their concern that student free speech is eroding, and *Tinker*'s original principles are slowly unraveling with each decision upholding such bans."[56]

However, a strong trend has emerged toward banning the Confederate flag from school campuses. In the legal debate about whether Confederate images are symbols of heritage or symbols of oppression, the courts have generally concluded that the Confederate flag symbolizes racial oppression, which can lead to disruption.[57] Several appellate decisions from about a decade ago were explored. However, it is important to not leave the chapter with the impression that Confederate flags are no longer an issue in schools. In January 2021, a student faced disciplinary action for displaying a Confederate flag on his truck while it was on campus.[58]

"The school administrators released the following statement on the incident:

We respect the rights of individuals to express their views, however, those views and expressions may directly conflict with our legal obligation to ensure a non-discriminatory and non-harassing environment for our students and staff."—Van Tieu, "Rocklin Student Disciplined for Displaying Confederate Flag at School Sparks Debate," ABC10 (January 21, 2021), https://www.abc10.com/article/news/local/rocklin/rocklin-student-disciplined-displaying-confederate-flag/103-54049eaa-629e-4033-84ca-6b5b065beb0d

Moreover, despite the fact that many students may wish to display a Confederate flag as a symbol of Southern heritage and not to communicate racial animus, most courts have concluded that schools still have the authority to ban their presence on school grounds. As a Sixth Circuit judge observed in one of these cases, "even if [an] individual student meant no hostility or contempt, a school administrator cannot practically administer a rule that permits such clothing sometimes and prohibits it other times depending on the intent of each individual wearer."[59] The Confederate flag communicates a message of divisiveness and racism and is in conflict with public school values of nondiscrimination and inclusion of all students.

NOTES

1. *West Virginia State Board of Education v. Barnette*, 319 U.S. 624, 632–33 (1943).

2. "Parents Angry after Confederate Flag Flown at Union County High School," 3 WBTV (February 23, 2023), https: //www.wbtv.com/2023/02/24/parents-angry-over-confederate-flag-flown-union-county-high-school/. The students were not disciplined, the school did not have a policy prohibiting Confederate flags.

3. Robert J. Bein, "Stained Flag: Public Symbols and Equal Protection," *Seton Hall Law Review* 27 (1998): 913.

4. Emma Lazarus, "The New Colossus" (1883), https: //poets.org/poem/new-colossus.

5. "Noose," Anti-Defamation League (n.d.), https://www.adl.org/education/references/hate-symbols/noose.

6. Louis Fisher and Katy J. Harriger, *American Constitutional Law*, vol. 2: *Constitutional Rights: Civil Rights and Civil Liberties*, 10th ed. (Durham, NC: Carolina Academic Press, 2013), 484.

7. *Sons of Confederate Veterans, Inc. v. Glendening*, 954 F. Supp. 1099, 1103 (D. Md. 1997) (internal quotation marks and internal citation omitted).

8. Editor, "A Legacy of Lies: 'Lost Cause' Myth Distorted Civil War History to Infect America's Soul with White Supremacy," *Milwaukee Independent* (June 12, 2020), http://www.milwaukeeindependent.com/articles/a-legacy-of-lies-lost-cause-myth-distorted-civil-war-history-to-infect-americas-soul-with-white-supremacy/.

9. Todd A. DeMitchell and Richard Fossey, "Scrubbing the Confederacy from the Public Schools: Now Is the Time," *Education Law Reporter* 378 (2020): 15. For an additional discussion of confederate flags in the public schools, see Todd A. DeMitchell and Richard Fossey, "The Battle over the Confederate Flag in Our Schools: Heritage or Oppression?" *Education Law Reporter* 352 (2018): 937–60. See this article for a discussion of the elimination of public school use of confederate symbols such as school names (Johnny Reb), the singing of "Dixie" at school functions, and the use of the Confederate battle flag as a school symbol.

See also for a discussion of Confederate iconography, Todd A. DeMitchell and Richard Fossey, "Confederate Monuments Do Not Constitute Speech by the Sons of Confederate Veterans: *McMahon v. Fenves*," *Education Law Reporter* 389 (2021): 683–89:

> Our nation's history of slavery is not erased by removing the symbols of the Confederacy and its record of enslaving forcibly removed Africans; they will forever be a part of who we are as a people and a nation. Removing Confederate iconography from the public square is not aimed at erasing our history. Rather, it is aimed at no longer honoring those who fought against the United States in an insurrection to sustain a system of human slavery.

Ibid., 688–89.

10. For an early case involving wearing clothing depicting the Confederate flag to school, see *Melton v. Young*, 465 F.2d 1332 (6th Cir. 1972), in which an appellate court held that a school could reasonably forecast that wearing a jacket to school with the emblem of the Confederate flag would cause a material disruption. However, see *Banks v. Muncie Community Schools*, 433 F.2d 292 (7th Cir. 1970), in which the Seventh Circuit Court of Appeals upheld the school district policy, which allowed students of a new school in Muncie, Indiana, to vote on their symbols and mascot. The students voted for the Rebels and selected a symbol that resembled the Confederate flag. Suit was brought alleging that the symbols were inflammatory and discouraged African American students from participating in extracurricular activities. The federal district court found no racial discrimination but characterized the matter as "tyranny by the majority." The plaintiff also lost on appeal. The court of appeals found the symbols "offensive and that good policy would dictate their removal." Ibid., 299. However, the court did not find a constitutional violation and opined that the board policy of allowing students to make choices allowed that they would make good choices as well bad choices.

11. *Smith v. St. Tammany Parish School Board*, 316 F. Supp. 1174, 1176 (E.D. La. 1970) (internal citations omitted). The court concluded:

> The retention of Confederate flags in a unitary school system is no way to eliminate racial discrimination "root and branch" from the system. The Confederate battle flags *must* be removed from all schools in the St. Tammany Parish school system. Accordingly.

Ibid., 1176–77; emphasis in original.

12. Rob Manning, "Oregon Bans Confederate Flag, Other Hate Symbols from Public Schools," OPB (September 16, 2020), https: //www.opb.org/article/2020/09/19/confederate-flag-ban-schools-oregon/. Cheri Helt, a Republican representative, said, "The Confederate flag is a symbol of treason, racism, and white supremacy. It has no place in Oregon." Ibid.

13. 206 F.3d 1358 (10th Cir. 2000).

14. Ibid., 1362.

15. Ibid., 1363 (quoting the federal district court).

16. Ibid., 1365.
17. Ibid., 1366 (quoting the federal district court).
18. Ibid., 1367.
19. *West v. Derby Unified School District #260*, 23 F. Supp. 2d 1223, 1233 (D. Kan. 1998).
20. 324 F.3d 1246 (11th Cir. 2003).
21. 478 U.S. 675 (1986).
22. *Scott*, 324 F.3rd at 1249 (internal citations and quotation marks omitted).
23. Ibid.
24. 538 F.3d 554, 557 (6th Cir. 2008).
25. Ibid., 557.
26. Ibid., 574.
27. Ibid., 575.
28. Ibid., 567 (internal quotation marks omitted).
29. Ibid.
30. 554 F.3d 734 (8th Cir. 2009). Farmington High School had a predominantly white student population of approximately eleven hundred, with only fifteen to twenty of those students African American.
31. *B.W.A.*, 554 F.3d at 736. The Black student withdrew and attended another school.
32. Ibid.
33. 585 F.2d 214 (5th Cir. 2009).
34. Ibid., 222.
35. Ibid.
36. 625 F.3d 324 (6th Cir. 2010).
37. Ibid., 326.
38. Ibid.
39. Ibid., 327.
40. Ibid., 329 (Rogers, J., concurring).
41. Ibid., 330 (Rogers, J., concurring).
42. Ibid., 339 (Rogers, J., concurring).
43. Ibid. (Rogers, J., concurring) (emphasis in original).
44. Ibid. (Rogers, J., concurring).
45. Ibid. (Rogers, J., concurring).
46. 711 F.3d 426 (4th Cir. 2013).
47. Ibid., 438.
48. Ibid., 430.
49. Ibid.
50. Ibid.
51. Ibid., 432.
52. Ibid., 438 (internal citations and internal quotation marks omitted).
53. Ibid., 439.
54. Ibid.
55. Ibid., 440.

56. Lucinda Housley Luetkemeyer, "Silencing the Rebel Yell: The Eighth Circuit Upholds a Public School's Ban on the Confederate Flags," *Missouri Law Review* 75, no. 3 (2010): 1007. The author concluded,

> The court in *B.W.A.* was faced with the unenviable task of determining the appropriateness of the actions taken by Farmington, Missouri school officials who were placed between the proverbial "rock and a hard place" by having to choose between the possibility of quashing legal student speech or allowing a potentially dangerous disruption to occur. The case established that when school officials reasonably suspect material and substantial disruption to the learning environment, they may constitutionally restrict the free speech rights of students, including prohibiting the display of the Confederate flag, even if the flag has not yet been the cause of any actual disruption.

Ibid., 1013.

57. Dress codes targeting the Confederate battle flag are not the only retrenchment in the symbol of the "Old South." There is a decided movement towards removing Confederate mascots from public schools. For example, after a principal in Fairfax, Virginia, decided to ban the school's Confederate flag logo, the caricature "Johnny Reb," and the team name the Rebels, suit was brought by students. The principal banned the symbols even though there was no history of disruption associated with the symbols. The Fourth Circuit in a second appellate hearing upheld the decision to eliminate the Confederate symbols. The court concluded that school officials "have the authority to disassociate the school from controversial speech even if it may limit student expression" (*Crosby v. Holsinger*, 852 F.2d 801, 802 [4th Cir.1988]). A school, over the objection of its students, may choose the symbols that it wants associated with its name.

58. Van Tieu, "Rocklin Student Disciplined for Displaying Confederate Flag at School Sparks Debate," ABC10 (January 21, 2021), https://www.abc10. com/article/news/local/rocklin/rocklin-student-disciplined-displaying-confederate-flag/103–5404 9eaa-629e-4033–84ca-6b5b065beb0d.

Similarly, in May 2022, around the time of the school massacre in Uvalde, Texas, although not planned as a statement about the Uvalde shooting, two University High School students in Normal, Illinois, displayed a large Confederate flag on their parked truck in the school parking lot. On the flag were images of assault rifles with the words "Come and Take It." The display was not well received, with one student cutting down the flag and throwing it in a dumpster. Charlie Schlenker, "Confederate Flag and Gun Rights Taunt Caused Furor at University High School," WGLT (May 26, 2022), https://www.wglt.org/local-news/2022–05–26/confederate-flag-and-gun-rights-taunt-causes-furor-at-university-high-school.

59. *Defoe ex rel. Defoe v. Spiva*, 625 F.3d 324, 339 (6th Cir. 2010) (Rogers, J., concurring). The appeals panel used *Tinker* to forecast disruption as a basis for enforcing a ban on the display of the Confederate flag on clothing, backpacks, or notebooks. For example, students hung a Confederate flag in the hallway of the school when two African American students enrolled. At a basketball game with another school, the students threw Oreo cookies at a biracial player form the other team.

However, the concurring opinion, which the majority accepts as governing if there are any differences between the two opinions, used Morse as the guide. Ibid., 326. Judge Rogers asserted in his concurrence,

> A public high school that can put reasonable limits on drug-related speech by students can put reasonable and even-handed limits on racially hostile or contemptuous speech, without having to show that such speech will result in disturbances.

Ibid., 338.

5

Targeted Messages on Students' Clothing

Drugs, Firearms, and Politics

> Public symbolism has profound implications for the citizens of the public body represented by the symbol.[1]

> In a case involving images of firearms worn to school, the federal district court in Wisconsin wrote: "The 'can of worms' out of which these [dress code] cases arise was opened by the Supreme Court in *Tinker v. Des Moines Independent Community School District*, 393 U. S. 503 (1969)."[2]

When the US Supreme Court decided the *Tinker* case in 1969, it may not have realized that it had opened the floodgates to a new type of lawsuit against school districts—what we might call "T-shirt litigation." In the years following the *Tinker* decision, students and their parents have filed numerous lawsuits challenging the authority of school authorities to ban messages on students' clothing. The Tinker children's expression consisted of a political statement—opposition to the war in Vietnam—which they communicated by wearing black arm bands. These legal disputes over student attire involve unique facts and unique student messages. In this chapter, we will explore political and social topics such as images of firearms as well as banned substances for students, such as drugs and alcohol. These categories of student clothing disputes will be separately discussed in this chapter.

POLITICAL MESSAGES AND MESSAGES ON SOCIAL ISSUES

The Supreme Court's *Tinker* decision involved pure political speech: opposition to the Vietnam War, which students expressed symbolically by wearing black armbands at school. When the Supreme Court issued its opinion in the case, it seems likely the justices anticipated that future conflicts between students and schools over students' free speech rights would involve serious political and social issues.

Thus, when reviewing student speech expressed on their clothing, it is appropriate to begin with clothing messages on social and political topics. As we will see, when federal courts have evaluated these cases, they have usually looked to *Tinker* for guidance and asked whether the students' speech created a substantial disruption in the school environment.

"At least in high school, a political message does not justify a vulgar medium."—*Pyle v. South Hadley School Committee*, 861 F. Supp. 157 (D. Mass. 1994).

For example, in *Barber v. Dearborn Public Schools*, Breton Barber, a student at Dearborn High School in Dearborn, Michigan, wore a T-shirt to school that displayed a photograph of President George W. Bush along with the phrase "International Terrorist."[4] Barber said, "I wore the shirt to spark discussion among the students in an issue I cared deeply about."[5]

Breton's school had a sizeable Arab population, and the school principal, Judith Coebly, feared Barber's message would offend these students, who by and large supported Bush's policies in the Middle East. These events took place as the United States prepared to invade Iraq in 2001, and Coebly also feared Breton's shirt would exacerbate tensions at the school, where some students had ties to military families. Thus, she prohibited Breton from wearing the T-shirt to school.

Breton, with the American Civil Liberties Union of Michigan, sued the Dearborn school district and asked the court for an injunction requiring school authorities to allow him to wear his "International Terrorist" T-shirt at school. In response, Dearborn school authorities argued that they reasonably believed Breton's T-shirt would create a substantial disruption at his high school when they banned the shirt, and thus it could be constitutionally banned under the *Tinker* standard.

A federal court was not persuaded, however, and granted Breton his injunction. The court pointed out that there was no evidence of any disturbance or disruption at the high school on the day Breton wore his controversial T-shirt. The school defendants maintained that the T-shirt controversy had created a "media frenzy," which provided an additional justification for banning the shirt, but an assistant principal admitted that "there [had] not been any kind of demonstration, disruption, or commotion as a result of the media's presence."[6]

Finally, the court rejected Coebly's argument that the imminent prospect of war between the United States and Iraq had created tensions that justified the ban. "Clearly the tension between students who support and those who oppose President Bush's decision to invade Iraq is no greater than the tension that existed during the United States' involvement in Vietnam between supporters of the war and war protesters," the court observed.[7]

Similarly, a T-shirt depicting Bush with the description "Chicken Hawk in Chief" and linking him to alcohol and drugs, while in poor taste, was constitutionally protected.[8] Zachary Guiles was a seventh-grade student when he first wore the T-shirt with the picture of Bush wearing a helmet with his face superimposed on the body of a chicken. Surrounding the president were pictures of oil wells and dollar signs. Off to the side of the president, the T-shirt depicted three lines of cocaine with a razor blade, and one of his wings was attached to a martini glass. The back of the T-shirt had the same picture as the front but also included smaller print accusing the President of being a crook, a cocaine addict, a draft dodger, and a drunk driver.[9] At least one student complained about the T-shirt. When Zachary was asked to tape over the offending images, turn the shirt inside, out or change it, he refused and was suspended.

Zachary brought suit, seeking to enjoin the school from enforcing the dress code with regard to his T-shirt.[10] The federal district court found the images offensive or inappropriate under *Bethel* and declined to issue an injunction (the political nature of the T-shirt was not contested by the school administrators). However, the court also held that the school violated Zachary's free speech when it censored the word cocaine. The dress code survived, but the suspension did not and was ordered expunged. Both parties appealed.

The Second Circuit Court of Appeals first reviewed the applicability of *Tinker*, *Fraser*, and *Hazelwood* to the case. *Hazelwood* was rejected because the student's T-shirt was not school sponsored. The court broke with the district court over the use of *Fraser*. The appellate court argued that the district court overreached when it applied *Fraser*'s standards. The T-shirt did not contain vulgar, obscene, or profane language. It did not rise to the level of being offensive under *Fraser* because it did not contain any sexual innuendo or profanity. The court asserted that the plainly offensive standard must be part and parcel of the speech that is lewd, vulgar, and indecent.[11] The court concluded that the alcohol and cocaine pictures may cause displeasure and may be insulting and in poor taste, but they are not plainly offensive, "especially when considering that they are part of an anti-drug political message."[12]

Having dismissed *Hazelwood* and *Fraser*, only one Supreme Court test was left standing. The court found that the T-shirt was not disruptive under *Tinker*. There was no disruption and there was no reasonable forecast of disruption. The Second Circuit Court of Appeals granted the injunction permitting Zachary to wear his T-shirt and his record was expunged. It is important to note that the dress code was not found unconstitutional; only its application to Zachary's T-shirt was affected.

Speech through student attire has also been litigated in cases involving politics writ small at the school level. In 2007 the Seventh Circuit Court of Appeals heard a class action suit on behalf of twenty-four eighth graders (the "gifties") who were disciplined for wearing a T-shirt that lost a contest for the design of the class T-shirt. The T-shirts were worn as a protest against the way the election was held. The plaintiffs found little sympathy for their cause with the court of appeals. The students, a group of gifted students, wore their T-shirts on the day that mandatory tests were being held, figuring that "the school would not take disciplinary action against them on that day, lest that lower the school's average test score (they are gifties after all)."[13] The court asserted that the students had avenues available through which to protest the T-shirt election that were "potentially less disruptive" than wearing the T-shirts in contravention of the principal's orders. In the end, the court held that the students had no protected speech right to wear clothing of their own design: "[C]lothing as such is not—normally at any rate –constitutionally protected."[14]

The Politics of Divisiveness

In *Sypniewski v. Warren Hills Regional Board of Education*, the Tenth Circuit Court of Appeals issued a lengthy and somewhat complicated decision that addressed whether school officials in New Jersey's Warren Hills Regional School District could constitutionally bar Thomas Sypniewski, a high school student, from wearing a T-shirt to school that was emblazoned with Jeff Foxworthy "redneck" jokes.[15] Thomas wore the shirt to school for most of a school day without incident, but he was suspended during the last period after he refused a request by the school's vice principal to turn the shirt inside out.

School authorities claimed that the redneck T-shirt violated the school's dress code, which barred clothing that displayed references to alcohol or sexual innuendo. They also maintained that the "redneck" reference violated the school district's racial harassment policy and might incite racial violence in a school that had had a history of racial tensions.

As the court explained, the school district had adopted its racial harassment policy after experiencing considerable racial tensions involving the display of the Confederate flag on campus and the activities of a student gang known as the "Hicks." School authorities believed the term "redneck" was an identifier for the Hicks and thus "redneck" was a gang identifier.[16]

Thomas and his two brothers (also students in the school district) sued, seeking an injunction against the enforcement of the school's dress code and racial harassment policy. A federal trial judge upheld the constitutionality of the racial harassment policy, and the brothers appealed the ruling to the Tenth Circuit.

On appeal, the Tenth Circuit reversed the trial court, ruling that the Sypniewski brothers were entitled to a preliminary injunction prohibiting the school district from applying its racial harassment policy to prohibit the wearing of the redneck T-shirt. In the appellate court's view, there was "little or no evidence that the word 'redneck' had been used to harass or intimidate, or otherwise to offend."[17] Moreover, the court concluded, the evidence revealed "a history of unproblematic use of the word, and that it was not associated to a significant degree with the Hicks or their behavior."[18]

Although the Tenth Circuit commended the Warren Hills school authorities for making a good-faith effort to deal with racial tensions, they went too far in applying the policy. School officials simply had not established that the shirt might threaten to disrupt the school or that it had violated any particular provision of its racial harassment policy.

A later court opinion involving a gang of rednecks turned out better for the school district. In *Governor Wentworth Regional School District v. Hendrickson*, Paul Hendrickson, a high school student identified as a member of a "gay group," came to school wearing a "No Nazis" patch, which consisted of a swastika over which was superimposed the international "no" symbol—"a red circle with a diagonal line through it."[19] Although the patch was characterized in various ways, Paul himself called it a "'tolerance patch' signifying values of tolerance and acceptance."[20]

As the court explained in detail, Paul's gay group was in an ongoing conflict with a rival group known as the "homophobes" or the "rednecks." School officials had documented several incidents of bullying and threats of violence, and the rednecks sometimes taunted members of the gay group with the Nazi salute, "Seig Heil."[21]

In light of the serious tensions between the gay group and the homophobes, school authorities worried that Paul's "No Nazis" patch might spark a school disruption and even lead to violence. Out of safety concerns, they directed him not to wear his patch to school.

Paul repeatedly refused to comply. At first, he was sent home for the day when he appeared at school wearing the "No Nazis" patch. Eventually he was suspended, with the proviso that he could not return to school wearing the patch. According to the court, Paul was out of school for several days or even weeks.

Eventually, the school district took the extraordinary step of filing a declaratory action in federal court, seeking a judicial ruling that it had the authority to prohibit Paul from wearing the "No Nazis" patch at school. The district then filed for summary judgment, asking the judge to affirm the constitutionality of its conduct.

After an exhaustive analysis, the court sided with the school district, ruling that it had lawfully banned Paul's patch based on reasonable concerns about the patch's potential for a serious disruption at school. As the court put it,

> It was reasonable for school authorities to conclude, under all the circumstances, that if Hendrickson were permitted to wear the patch, it would likely precipitate further discord, tension, harassment, and disruptive, even potentially violent, behavior at school. That in turn would disrupt the educational environment and jeopardize the safety of not only the members of the "gay" and "redneck" groups, but all students, teachers, and staff as well.[22]

Madrid v. Anthony is another federal court decision with themes of tensions between rival groups of students.[23] In that case, students and parents sued the Cypress-Fairbanks Independent School District and David Anthony, the school superintendent, after a high school principal banned students from wearing T-shirts that said, "We Are Not Criminals" and "Border Patrol." The controversy took place in the context of a school walkout at Cypress Ridge High School that was staged by Hispanic students who opposed proposed immigration legislation pending in Congress, which they considered unfair and punitive. Some students, mostly Hispanic, wore "We Are Not Criminals" T-shirts to school on the day of the walkout, which occurred on a Monday.

Claudio Garcia, the high school principal, did not punish the students for the Monday walkout, but he warned them they would be punished if they walked out again. Based on the rumor that white and African American students who opposed the walkout were going to antagonize Hispanic students by wearing T-shirts to school that said, "Border Patrol," Garcia feared a race riot would erupt. Consequently, he banned students from wearing either T-shirt.

Disregarding Garcia's warning, about 130 students walked out of school on Tuesday. These students were suspended, and on Wednesday, school authorities contacted the suspended students' parents and asked them to pick up their children at school.

When the parents arrived at the school, some of them demanded to speak with Garcia. Finding the group too large to meet with in one gathering, Garcia asked parents to make appointments. Some of the parents milled around the school building, and eventually a security officer asked them to leave the premises.

In due course, some parents and students who were involved in these events sued the school district, alleging that the ban on the "We Are Not Criminals" T-shirt violated students' right to free speech and that the request for parents to leave the school building violated their constitutional right to assembly. They also charged school officials with refusing to allow Hispanic students to go to the restroom on the day following the walkout in retaliation for their participation in the immigration protests.

In essence, the Cypress-Fairbanks school authorities admitted that they had prohibited students from wearing T-shirts that expressed their opinions, that they asked parents to leave the school premises, and that they had prohibited students from leaving class on the day after the first walkout, which prevented some of them from using the restroom. Officials argued, however, that they prohibited the T-shirts and barred students from going to the restroom during class on one tense school day to prevent riots. Moreover, they explained, school authorities asked parents to leave the school premises on the day of the student suspensions because they could not meet with so many parents at once and they were statutorily required to protect each student's privacy.

A federal trial judge found the school district's arguments persuasive and granted their motion for summary judgment. Regarding the T-shirt ban, the court ruled that school officials have the authority to prevent problems before they happen; they are not required to wait until a disturbance occurs before acting. In the case before it, the court noted that students had already disrupted the work of the school when they walked out of school on Monday. "The evidence shows school officials held a reasonable belief that wearing the t-shirts at issue would cause further, perhaps even more severe disruption and put student safety at risk," the court wrote.[24]

Thus, in the court's opinion, Garcia's decision to ban the T-shirts was constitutionally permissible under *Tinker*'s substantial disruption standard:

> [F]aced with hundreds of students who were disrupting the educational process and two-thirds of the student body who might have antagonized the Hispanic students by wearing a Border Patrol t-shirt, the Court finds Principal Garcia made the proper decision to ban the t-shirts in order to *protect* the Hispanic students from the animosity of other students, not to harm them by precluding their speech. Based on these facts, the Court reasonably believed it necessary to prohibit students from wearing both t-shirts at issue because the expression on them would exacerbate hostility within the student body and could cause fights that would materially and substantially interfere with the work of the school.[25]

The court also found that school officials acted reasonably when they requested parents to leave the Cypress Ridge High School premises and that their decision to prohibit students from leaving class on the day following the first walkout was also reasonable. Neither action, the court concluded, was motivated by a desire to violate constitutional rights or retaliate against the plaintiffs.

We move now from Texas to California. Live Oak High School is part of the Morgan Hill Unified School District, located south of San Jose. Three of the school's white students sued,[26] alleging a violation of their rights to free expression when they were not allowed to wear American flag shirts on Cinco de Mayo.[27] The assistant principal asked the students to turn their shirts inside out based on his belief that the shirts could reasonably result in disruption.

The federal district court began its analysis by recognizing that courts have struggled to find the right balance for the exercise of student First Amendment rights and the need for the school administration to maintain a safe educational environment. The court applied the *Tinker* two-prong analysis to the facts. Finding no disruption, no classes delayed, no classes interrupted, and no violence reported on the day that Assistant Principal Miguel Rodriquez asked the students to change their shirts, the court used the reasonable forecast section of the disruption prong.

The facts showed that for the previous six years, there had been thirty fights on campus. Some of the fights involved gangs, and other fights were between white and Hispanic students. On the previous Cinco de Mayo, a verbal exchange and altercation between Hispanic and white students erupted over a makeshift American flag placed on one of the trees on campus in response to Mexican students walking around school with the Mexican flag.

On the day the plaintiff students wore the American flag shirts, a female student approached one of the plaintiffs, motioned to the shirt, and said, "[W]hy are you wearing that, do you not like Mexicans?"[28] In addition, several students warned the school administration about potential disruption over the shirts.

Acknowledging that no actual violence or disruption occurred from wearing the American flag shirts, the court noted that the *Tinker* disruption is not an "actual disruption" standard. Rather, the school administrators need only articulate reasonable grounds, more than an inchoate sense of disruption, based on an established fact pattern. The schools need not ignore warnings and wait until violence occurs to act. Principals and assistant principals cannot predict with certainty "which threats are empty and which will lead to true violence."[29]

In this case, the school officials acted reasonably in forecasting that violence could result from students wearing the shirts. The assistant principal asked them to turn their shirts inside out to avoid physical harm and did not abridge the students' free speech rights.

We will conclude this section on divisive student speech, this time focusing on potential religious divisiveness, with a review of *Boroff v. Van Wert City Board of Education*, in which the Sixth Circuit Court of Appeals upheld a school ban on Marilyn Manson T-shirts. The appellate court did not use the *Tinker* standard, which would have permitted the shirts to be banned if they created a substantial disruption in the school environment; instead, it used the *Fraser* standard.[30] The Sixth Circuit said simply that the T-shirts conveyed a message that was contrary to the educational mission of the school and thus, under *Fraser*, they could be banned.

These are the facts of the *Boroff* case. Nicholas Boroff, a senior at Van Wert High School in Ohio, came to school wearing a Marilyn Manson T-shirt, which the Sixth Circuit court described as follows: "The front of the T-shirt depicted a three-faced Jesus, accompanied by the words 'See No Truth. Hear No Truth. Speak No Truth.' On the back of the shirt, the word 'BELIEVE' was spelled out in capital letters, with the letters 'LIE' highlighted. Marilyn Manson's name (although not his picture) was displayed prominently on the front of the shirt."[31]

Marilyn Manson, as the Sixth Circuit opinion explained, was the stage name for "Goth" rock singer Brian Warner and also the name of the band in which he was the lead singer. According to the court, Manson (the individual) was widely regarded as a user of illegal drugs, which he had not denied. Indeed, one of his songs was titled "I Don't Like the Drugs (But the Drugs Like Me)."[32]

At the time of these events, Nicholas's high school had a dress and grooming policy stating that "clothing with offensive illustrations, drug, alcohol, or tobacco slogans . . . are not acceptable."[33] One of the school principal's aides spotted Nicholas wearing the shirt and told him it was offensive. The aide gave Nicholas three choices: He could turn the shirt inside out, he could go home to get a different shirt, or he could leave the school and be considered truant. Nicholas left school.

The following day, Nicholas wore another Marilyn Manson T-shirt to school. That same day, Nicholas and his mother met with the school superintendent, the high school principal, and the principal's aide. The superintendent told mother and son that students would not be permitted to wear Marilyn Manson T-shirts to school.

In defiance of this directive, Nicholas wore different Marilyn Manson T-shirts to school on each of the next three school days. These shirts displayed pictures of Marilyn Manson, whose appearance, the court noted, could "fairly be described as ghoulish and creepy."[34] Each day, school authorities told Nicholas he was not permitted to wear a Marilyn Manson shirt to school.

Less than a month after this dispute erupted, Nicholas's mother filed suit, claiming that school administrators had violated her son's First Amendment right to free expression by refusing to allow him to wear Marilyn Manson T-shirts to school. A federal district court dismissed the suit, and she appealed. At some point in the litigation, Nicholas turned eighteen and his name was substituted for that of his mother in the lawsuit.

On appeal, Nicholas argued that the school's ban on Marilyn Manson T-shirts was unreasonable and pointed out that school officials allowed students to wear T-shirts promoting other bands. He also maintained that there was no evidence that a substantial disruption would arise if he wore a Marilyn Manson T-shirt to school.

The Sixth Circuit rejected these arguments and upheld the trial court's dismissal of his suit. "The standard for reviewing the suppression of vulgar or plainly offensive speech is governed by *Fraser*," the court noted.[35] "The School in this case . . . found the Marilyn Manson T-shirts to be offensive because the band promotes destructive conduct and demoralizing values that are contrary to the educational mission of the school."[36]

Specifically, the court noted that the high school principal "found the 'three-headed Jesus' T-shirt to be offensive because of the 'See No Truth. Hear No Truth. Speak No Truth.' mantra on the front, and because of the obvious implication of the word 'BELIEVE' with 'LIE' highlighted on the back."[37] In the principal's view, which the Sixth Circuit quoted approvingly, "the distorted Jesus figure was offensive, because 'mocking any religious figure is contrary to our educational mission which is to be respectful of others and others' beliefs.'"[38]

One Sixth Circuit judge dissented from the majority's opinion, arguing that the school had engaged in viewpoint discrimination by banning Nicholas's T-shirt because of the viewpoint it expressed on religion. The majority strenuously objected to this interpretation of the evidence. In the majority's opinion, "the record demonstrates that the School prohibited Boroff's Marilyn Manson T-shirts generally because this particular rock group promotes disruptive and demoralizing values which are inconsistent with and counterproductive to education."[39]

FIREARMS: FREE SPEECH AND THE RIGHT TO "DEPICT" ARMS

- There have been 189 school shootings resulting in injury or death since 2018.
- There were 38 school shootings with injury or death in 2023.
- From January 1, 2024, to February 1, 2024, there were seven school shootings in seven states with one sixth grade student and one school employee (principal) killed and 14 people injured. The most deadly shooting (6 injured and two killed) took place at Perry High School, Perry, Iowa on January 4, 2024.

Author, "School Shootings This Year: How Many and Where," *Education. Week* (February 16, 2023), https://www.edweek.org/leadership/school-shootings-this-year-how-many-and-where/2023/01

- The presence of weapons may increase aggression – the "weapons effect."

Brad J. Bushman, "Guns Automatically Prime Aggressive Thoughts, Regardless of Whether a "Good Guy" or "Bad Guy" Holds the Gun, *Social Psychological and Personality Science* 9(6) (2018): 727, https://journals.sagepub.com/doi/abs/10.1177/1948550617722202

Professors and a doctoral student in criminal justice report that incidents since 2010 of guns being brandished or fired at schools have steadily increased, with significant increases in 2018 and 2021, with 2022 being the worst on record, with 318 people shot (fatal or wounded).[40] Responses to these shootings and the compelling need to protect students by securing schools have been the subject of federal, state, and local school district policymaking.[41]

Dress codes are one of the policy mechanisms that local school districts have instituted in response to violence, most likely starting with bans on gang symbols and attire. Dress codes that ban student attire that depicts or is associated with violence have likely been a response to the gun violence that has disrupted our schools. In their efforts to reduce violence in the schools, some school authorities conclude that clothing that depicts weapons or instruments of violence should be banned.

For example, following the April 20, 1999, shooting at Columbine High School that killed twelve students and one teacher,[42] some schools banned trench coats, "Goth"-style clothing, and clothing related to the shock singer Marilyn Manson.[43] Since the Columbine tragedy, student clothing depicting weapons has surfaced as one of the most widespread and divisive dress code controversies in the schools, engendering strong emotions on both sides. Concerns over both the Second Amendment and school shootings often punctuate the dialogue on the dress code bans and surface in the courts.

Dress codes that respond to any depiction of a firearm or weapon have resulted in legal challenges, the diversion of scarce resources, and questionable publicity that may not focus on safety with evidence to support the rationality of these prohibitions. Thus, some opponents of the policies question the wisdom, let alone the common sense, of such policies, raising the argument that the banning of depictions of guns is an emotional response to violence at school rather than a reasonable response.

For example, an Elmhurst High School student came to school wearing a T-shirt that displayed a portion of the Marine Corps Creed ("My Rifle") along with a picture of an M16 rifle between two of the stanzas and the seal of the Marine Corps under the last line of the creed.[44] There were no complaints from students, nor was there any disruption because of the T-shirt. Nevertheless, school authorities told the student that he could not wear the T-shirt to school, citing the dress code that prohibited wearing any clothing that depicted symbols of violence. At the time that the student, David Griggs, wore his T-shirt to school, the community had recently been rocked by the kidnapping, brutal torture, and murder of Cheri Sue Hartman, a student from the same high school.

David brought suit in federal district court for a violation his First Amendment right to free speech. The court held that the prohibition against "symbols of violence" was not overbroad[45] and was reasonably related to a legitimate pedagogical concern of preventing violence at school.[46] However, "a permissible regulation might occasionally be used to censor more speech than the First Amendment allows."[47]

Furthermore, the court asserted that while preventing violence by prohibiting symbols of violence at school is permissible, the application of this dress code section to David's Marine Corps T-shirt is "a bit too far." In the court's view, the T-shirt was not related to the tragic murder of Cherie Sue Hartman or the massacre at Columbine High School (arguments asserted by the school board),[48] and it did not disrupt the school.[49] The policy was constitutional, but its application to David's T-shirt was not, the court held. The judge concluded that there was no rational relationship between stopping violence in the school and the message on David's T-shirt that Marines must fight America's enemies.

Another example of a questionable dress code regarding symbols of violence occurred in Coventry, Rhode Island, in 2010. As part of a school project on a patriotic theme, David Morales, age eight, designed and wore to school a camouflage hat with little plastic army men glued to it to honor the men and women serving in the armed services. David was told to take the cap off because it violated the policy on weapons at school.[50] School authorities acknowledged that David was honoring soldiers, but the toy plastic soldiers on his hat were carrying weapons, in violation of the policy against bringing weapons to school. Several days after the story was reported in the press, the superintendent announced that the policy was being reviewed after Lt. Gen. Reginald Centracchio, among others, chided the school district for its policy.[51]

It is highly doubtful that the students at his school faced a heightened risk of harm because of the five plastic soldiers on David's hat. Real threats should occupy the time, resources, and energy of educators, but little David's hat was not such a threat. As the federal district court in *Griggs* wrote, "A general prohibition on 'apparel depicting . . . symbols of violence' is certainly a reasonable way for the Board to discourage such violence in its schools."[52] However, a rigid, unreasonable response to guns on campus dilutes the power of the message about needed restrictions to maintain a safe school environment.

An Overbroad Weapons Image Policy: Substantive Due Process

Substantive due process is concerned with the substance of the law rule or regulation. The law, rule, or regulation that deprives an individual of life, liberty, or property must be reasonable and consistent with the American sense of fairness. It must be clearly and rationally related to a lawful state function (unless the issue involves a fundamental interest that demands a higher standard of review, and education has not been declared a federal constitutional fundamental interest).[53]

The reasonable person test is used when the issue involves substantive due process. The test asks: "Would a reasonable person understand what to do or not do after reading the law, rule, or regulation?" Substantive due process challenges involve questions of vagueness or overbreadth as well as questions about fundamental fairness (conscious shocking behavior).[54]

We now turn to a couple of substantive due process cases involving students who appeared at school wearing T-shirts depicting firearms. In *Newsome v. Albemarle County School Board*, a 2003 decision, the Fourth Circuit Court of Appeals upheld the right of Alan Newsome, a Virginia sixth grader, to wear a T-shirt to school that depicted figures pointing weapons, finding the school district's policy against student messages related to weapons was unconstitutionally overbroad.[55] As described by the court, the back of Alan's T-shirt, which was purple in color, depicted "three black silhouettes of men holding firearms superimposed on the letters 'NRA' positioned above the phrase 'SHOOTING SPORTS CAMP.'"[56]The front of his shirt "bore a smaller but identical version of the men superimposed on the initials 'NRA,' but no other writing or symbols."[57]

Elizabeth Pitt, assistant principal at Alan's school, saw the T-shirt and had the immediate impression that the silhouette figures were "sharpshooters," which reminded her of the Columbine High School shootings. In her judgment, the images on Alan's T-shirt could "reasonably be interpreted by other middle-school students to promote the use of guns." In addition, she concluded that "the imagery on the t-shirt was at odds with her obligation as a school administrator to discourage and prevent gun-related violence since the images on Newsome's t-shirt conflicted with the message that 'Guns and Schools Don't Mix' and had the potential to create confusion among middle school students over the appropriate boundaries between firearms and schools."[58]

Pitt persuaded Alan to turn the shirt inside out, and later the school district amended its student/parent handbook to prohibit students from wearing "messages on clothing, jewelry, and personal belongings that relate to drugs, alcohol, tobacco, weapons, violence, sex, vulgarity, or that reflect adversely upon persons because of their race or ethnic group."[59]

A few months later, Alan sued the Albemarle County School Board, alleging that his First Amendment rights had been violated when he was directed to turn his shirt inside out and that the school district's dress code was unconstitutionally overbroad and vague. A trial court denied Alan's request for a preliminary injunction, and Alan appealed.

On appeal, the Fourth Circuit reversed the trial court, finding that the school board's dress code, which prohibited all student speech that "related" to weapons, was unconstitutionally overbroad. Instead of *Tinker*'s disruption case, the court of appeals used the substantive due process clause to find for the plaintiff.

The court pointed out that the school district had presented no evidence before the trial court that any student clothing containing a message relating to weapons had ever caused a substantial disruption in the school environment. Moreover, the dress code prohibited the display of "lawful, nonviolent, and nonthreatening symbols of not only popular but important organizations and ideals."[60] By way of example, the court pointed out that the State Seal of the Commonwealth of Virginia depicted a woman "standing with one foot on the chest of a vanquished tyrant, holding a spear."[61] The court also noted the irony of the fact that the school district's own high school mascot was a patriot armed with a musket.

The *Newsome* case certainly highlights the importance of a tightly drafted dress code. Had the policy explicitly prohibited student speech that promotes violence instead of speech that was "related" to weapons, perhaps the school district would have prevailed.

This brings us to *Miller v. Penn Manor School District*, a federal district court opinion with facts somewhat like the *Newsome* case.[62] In this case, Donald Miller, a high school student, wore a T-shirt to school which the court described as follows:

> The T-shirt prominently displays images of an automatic handgun on the front pocket area and back of the T-shirt. The front pocket of the T-shirt is also imprinted with the statement "Volunteer Homeland Security" with the image of an automatic handgun placed between the word "Volunteer" above the handgun and the words "Homeland Security" below the handgun.

> The back of the T-shirt is imprinted with the statement "Special Issue-Resident-Lifetime License, United States Terrorist Hunting Permit, Permit No. 91101, Gun Owner-No Bag Limit" in block letters superimposed over a larger automatic weapon.[63]

Donald obtained the shirt as a gift from his uncle, a member of the US military, who had purchased it from the Fort Benning Post Exchange. At the time of the litigation, Donald's uncle was stationed in Iraq.

Although the case includes a detailed discussion about the Penn Manor School District's dress code and its revisions, the heart of the dispute between Donald and the school district hinged on the fact that school authorities banned Donald's T-shirt because they believed it promoted violence and was unacceptable clothing in the school environment. The district's dress code, as revised, prohibited "messages that advocate violence and mayhem, criminal behavior or the violation of Board policy."[64]

Before the court, Donald argued that his T-shirt's message represented "political and patriotic speech aimed at supporting our troops fighting the war on terror in Afghanistan and Iraq" and was also an expression of support for his uncle, who was fighting in Iraq. The school district countered that it was entitled to ban Donald's T-shirt without a showing of substantial disruption under *Tinker* because it had the constitutional authority "to prohibit student speech that advocates the use of force, violence and violation of law."[65]

The plaintiffs asserted that the dress code and censorship of Donald's T-shirt violated the constitutional rights of every student in the high school as well as the school district. The school district responded by contending that the recent Supreme Court decision in *Morse* granted the right, "without a showing of 'substantial disruption,' to prohibit student speech that advocates the use of force, violence and violation of law."[66] They further argued that the special characteristics of the school environment and the importance of preventing violence in the schools allow "schools to restrict student expression" that can be reasonably interpreted as advocating violence.[67] Furthermore, the defendants asserted that rather than a message of patriotic support for the war on terror,[68] the message on the T-shirt suggested that vigilantism and illegal behavior were promoted.

While finding that elements of the dress code were overbroad or vague, the court concluded that the policy prohibiting the promotion of violence was not overbroad or vague and was thus constitutional. The court wrote, "The impact of violence in schools is so great that it now has equal importance as the issue of illegal drug use in schools."[69]

Judge James Knoll Gardner concluded "that a substantial interest resides in public schools to discourage violence both in the school setting as well as in the community at large as part of the District's overall educational mission."[70] This is the language and underlying foundation of *Morse*: the authority to act before speech leads to violence and harm that runs counter to the mission of the school.

Miller, some fourteen years ago, primarily used *Morse* as the touchstone for analyzing a T-shirt with images of weapons. While the analysis does not focus on images of firearms and instead focus on the message of vigilantism and violence, *Morse* may be an underutilized source for grounding school district arguments for prohibiting messages that encourage or support violence. Dress code policies that specifically identify prohibitions of violence linked to communications associated with weapons as being in opposition to the mission, goals, and curriculum of the school may gain traction in the courts when there is no showing of *Tinker*'s material and substantial disruption standard.

Although the trial court invalidated part of the school district's policies on constitutional grounds, it upheld the district's decision to ban Donald's T-shirt based on the shirt's message, which endorsed the use of violence. "The language of Donald's T-shirt advocates the use of force, violence, and violation of law in the form of illegal vigilante behavior and the hunting and killing of human beings," the court observed. "Accordingly, based on the Supreme Court's post-*Tinker* jurisprudence, I conclude that defendants do not have to demonstrate substantial disruption to restrict Donald from wearing his T-shirt."[71]

Miller v. Penn Manor School District is a significant decision because a federal court upheld a school district's student speech ban without relying on the *Tinker* substantial disruption standard. Although the court did not make clear which judicial precedents it relied upon, it apparently concluded that a school district's interest in preventing violence in schools, like its interest in discouraging student drug use, gave Penn Manor the constitutional authority to ban Donald Miller's T-shirt without the necessity of showing that the shirt was disruptive, or likely to be disruptive, in the school environment.

The *Miller* case, like the *Boroff* case, upheld a school ban on student expression without relying on *Tinker*'s substantial disruption test. Without regard to whether Nicolas Boroff's Marilyn Manson T-shirts disrupted the school environment, the court ruled that the school could prohibit Nicholas from wearing the T-shirts to school on the grounds that they were vulgar, plainly offensive, and contrary to the school's educational mission. Thus, in at least a few instances, *Tinker* was not used and *Fraser* and *Morse* were used, providing additional arrows in the quiver of school districts' response when disruption does not occur in response to the student's attire communication.

Images of Firearms in Wisconsin

The issue of images of firearms surfaced in Wisconsin.[72] The federal Eastern District of Wisconsin heard two cases with similar fact patterns using two different free speech standards with opposite outcomes. The Seventh Circuit Court of Appeals resolved the difference in the district court returning to *Tinker*.

The first case was decided in 2018. Michael Shoenecker, a Wisconsin high school freshman, began wearing two T-shirts to school that prominently featured weapons. He stated that he was a sport-shooting enthusiast and appreciated the Second Amendment's recognition of the right of Americans to possess firearms.[73] One T-shirt had the legend "Celebrate Diversity" with images of a variety of weapons, and the second T-shirt spelled "LOVE" with stylized letters in the form of weapons, including a pistol, a hand grenade, two knives, and a rifle.

The school's principal, John Koopman, told Michael that he could not wear clothing that depicted weapons, even though the dress code did not explicitly ban such clothing. The dress code was later amended to explicitly prohibit clothing that depicts weapons.[74] Suit was brought against Koopman in his individual and official capacity, seeking declaratory and injunctive relief that would allow Michael to wear his T-shirts to school without being disciplined. A short time later, he wore a T-shirt that read, with no images, "IF GUNS KILL PEOPLE, I GUESS PENCILS misspell words CARS drive drunk & SPOONS make people fat."[75]

For a response to this often heard disingenuous assertion, see:

"First, guns are dangerous, despite the National Rifle Association's (NRA) mantra that guns don't kill, people kill. This implies that firearms are benign. This saying is simplistic at the least and disingenuous at the worst. The more accurate statement is that people kill people using guns. Guns in the hands of people kill and maim. . . .

Firearms are designed as weapon and a tool for hunting. If guns are left in their packing boxes and are never handled by people, the NRA would be accurate, guns would not kill. But they are not designed to remain in boxes unpacked and not available for their intended use [, shooting]."—Todd A. DeMitchell and Christine C. Rath, "Another School Massacre, Another Call to Arm Teachers: Raising the Caution Flag Yet Again. A Policy Discussion," *Education Law Reporter* 401 (2022): 709 710.

As a threshold matter, the court found that all three T-shirts constituted speech. Thus, the court selected *Tinker* as the applicable school speech standard. The school district asserted three issues that supported its argument that school officials reasonably concluded that the T-shirts would disrupt the school environment.[76] The court dismissed all three.

First, in the court's view, no connection was established between the T-shirts and a decline in test scores. Similarly, no connection was shown between the T-shirts and an upsurge in truancies. Furthermore, no specific facts were offered that showed that there was a substantial disruption, and no evidence was presented that teachers, who felt uncomfortable about the T-shirts, were negatively affected. Finally, the school district had not been able to show that there was a disruption among students over the T-shirts. In short, the defendant failed to establish that there was a reasonable belief that wearing the T-shirts will "create a threat of substantial disruption."[77]

Three years later the Eastern District heard another firearms image case, *N.J. by Next Friend Jacob v. Sonnabend.*[78] The judge, in this case, reversed course.

In the following case, two separate complaints involving public school students were consolidated.[79] In the first case N.J., a student who attended Shattuck Middle School, on February 12, 2020, wore a shirt that with the inscription "Smith & Wesson Firearms—Made in the USA Since 1852." In addition, the shirt also had a depiction of a revolver. N.J. had been warned previously not to war clothing that depicted firearms and was directed each time to cover the image. It was the image and not the words that violated the dress code.

The dress code stated, in pertinent part, "If a student's attire creates a learning environment that is deemed unsafe for students or staff, the student may be asked to change the clothing that is creating the disruption to the safe learning environment." While the dress code did not specifically identify images or depictions of firearms, the students were told that the "safety concerns related to clothing with weapons images or creating fear and anxiety in students" violated the dress code.[80]

District court judge William Griesbach held that students had reported to teachers and guidance counselors that clothing depicting firearms "made them feel uncomfortable, anxious, and unsafe." He opined that it appeared that students were more sensitive about the depiction of guns in February 2020 after two school shooting incidents had occurred near their school.

The second plaintiff, A.L., a Moraine High School student in a separate school district, wore a T-shirt to school with the words "Wisconsin Carry, Inc." with a handgun tucked behind the inscription, as if the gun was in a holster and the inscription was a belt.[81] The principal and associate principal told A.L. that he must cover the inscription and image of the handgun by zipping up his hoodie.

The school's dress code did not specifically prohibit images of firearms. The principal interpreted the prohibition of images of firearms as inappropriate messages without regard for whether the message was pro-gun or anti-gun. The court noted, as it did in the discussion of N.J., that the students in Kettle Moraine High School reported "being uncomfortable around other students who were wearing clothing that depicted or were associated with firearms."[82] The students' concern about school violence and shootings was heightened by the Waukesha shooting and the posting of a YouTube video that insinuated that an attack on the school was imminent.

The plaintiffs sought an injunction permanently barring the school administration from enforcing a ban on clothing depicting firearms. Both the plaintiffs and the defendants brought motions to the court for summary judgment.

Griesbach, unlike the judge who ruled in *Schoenecker*, eschewed the use of the Supreme Court student speech decisions,[83] including *Tinker*, which the plaintiffs asserted was the appropriate test. The court asserted that the *Tinker* material and substantial disruption test is "not applicable to restrictions on student speech in non-public forums where the restriction is viewpoint neutral"[84]—neither pro-gun nor anti-gun.

The district court framed the issue by asking "whether the restriction on student expression is reasonably related to pedagogical concerns"—the test articulated by the Supreme Court in *Hazelwood*.[85] The Supreme Court held in *Hazelwood*'s legitimate pedagogical test that school officials were entitled to regulate speech that might be reasonably attributable to the school "in any reasonable manner."[86] The court explored two pedagogical concerns to apply to the issue before the court—did the images of the firearms create anxiety and fear, and was the "weapons effect" a further justification of a legitimate pedagogical concern?

First, the court found that while the plaintiff's argument "that mere images of firearms cannot inflict injury on anyone,"[87] they can serve as a reminder of the violence that too often is visited upon schools and students. This reminder of violence "lies at the heart of the school's concerns."[88] While noting that some people enjoy guns and may see them as essential in their lives, many people fear guns, the court asserted. The implementation of the dress code prohibiting wearing images of weapons at school is "not unreasonable," the court concluded regarding the first prong of its analysis.

The second analysis reviewed the weapons effect as a further justification for the challenged dress code restriction. While the weapons effect is not tied to any specific curricular activity that requires the use of pedagogical skill or activities, it was discussed as further evidence of the negative impact of images of firearms engendering fears of violence at school.

The weapons effect posits that guns not only facilitate violence, but they may also stimulate it as well. A 1967 study by Leonard Berkowitz and Anthony Page demonstrated that individuals in the controlled study who saw guns were more aggressive than other participants who did not see firearms and instead saw sports items on the nearby table. They dubbed this phenomenon the "weapons effect."[89] The court held that the school district had a reasonable basis for the "minor" restriction of student viewpoints about firearms in the school, which furthers important pedagogical goals.

Using a two-step process, the court reviewed the evidence on whether the prohibition is justified in addressing the concern about anxiety and fear caused by images of firearms and the effect that images of weapons could have on students and staff. The court found that the prohibition of images of firearms was reasonably related to the concern for the well-being of the school population.

The central question before the Seventh Circuit was whether the district court decision rests on a "doctrinal error."[90] In other words, is the speech forum standard based on the principles of *Hazelwood* the appropriate student speech standard in this case?

For example, *Hazelwood* focused on student speech in a school's journalism class. The Supreme Court noted that a public school is not an open forum for student speech. The school, as a closed forum, is "reserved for its intended purpose of creating supervised learning experiences."[91] The *Hazelwood* court found that school authorities had authority over school-sponsored publications as theatrical productions as well as "other expressive activities that students, parents, and other members of the public might reasonably perceive to bear the imprimatur of the school."[92]

The appellate court reasoned that student T-shirts displaying images of weapons could not be viewed by a reasonable observer as school-sponsored or school-endorsed expression, a requirement of *Hazelwood.* (See chapter 2 for a discussion of *Hazelwood.*) The students' T-shirt endorsements of gun ownership did not convey the imprimatur of the school.

The Seventh Circuit answered its central question with a no, concluding that *Hazelwood* is the wrong standard and that "*Tinker* is the controlling authority."[93] Consequently, the court vacated and remanded the case with instructions to analyze the case under the *Tinker* standard. The decision reinforces the use of *Tinker* in student speech cases, including dress code complaints, thus placing the burden on school administrators to justify speech restriction under *Tinker*'s material and substantial disruption test.

The Application of *Morse v. Fredericks* to the Depiction of Weapons

In *N.J.,* the school's position was that images of weapons negatively impact the school's mission to provide a safe environment for students. As Justice Roberts wrote in *Morse*, "The First Amendment does not require schools to tolerate at school events student expression that contributes to those dangers."[94]

Thus, the question that might have been raised in *N.J.* is whether a student's clothing-that depicts images of weapons is contrary to the mission of the school in the same manner that a student banner celebrating the use of marijuana is contrary to the mission of a school in *Morse*.

Drug use and possession are against the law, although several states have decriminalized the use and possession of small amounts of marijuana. Even in states where marijuana use has been legalized, there are age restrictions on its use, just as there are age restrictions on the use and possession of alcohol and cigarettes. In addition, many high schools and middle schools include instruction that warns students on the health risks of alcohol and tobacco products.

Students who argue that they have the free speech right to promote the use of drugs or alcohol on the clothes they wear to school "have a poor track record in the federal courts. Courts would seem to have no difficulty rejecting these claims under *Morse,* which clearly held that schools need not tolerate student speech that celebrates the illegal use of drugs."[95]

But applying *Morse* to weapons may be a more problematic fit. First, the Second Amendment right to bear arms is often part of a school's curriculum in civics courses that instruct students on the US Constitution and the Bill of Rights. Consequently, a student's written statement in support of or against the Second Amendment or conversely would likely survive constitutional muster absent disruption, and *Morse* most probably could not be applied by school authorities who ban student depictions of firearms or quotations from the Second Amendment or similar language in state constitutions.

For example, A.L.'s T-shirt displayed the text of the Wisconsin Constitution's guarantee of the right to bear arms. Could the shirt have been banned if it only quoted the constitutional right and did not include the image of a weapon?

CLOTHING MESSAGES ABOUT DRUGS AND ALCOHOL

Just as high school students often exhibit a strong interest in sex, many are fascinated with illegal drugs and alcohol. One might think, therefore, that there would be a lot of cases involving students who claim a constitutional right to express their views about drugs and alcohol on T-shirts or other items of clothing.

In fact, there are very few lawsuits in which students have claimed a First Amendment right to proclaim their support of alcohol use or the illegal use of drugs. Perhaps potential plaintiffs realize that such a lawsuit would probably not be favorably received by a federal court.

As the Fourth Circuit noted in a 1980 case involving a school's suppression of an underground student publication that contained an advertisement for drug paraphernalia, an advertisement promoting the use of drugs "encourages action which . . . endanger the health and safety of students."[96] The court ruled that the school principal had the authority to halt distribution of any materials of that nature without regard to whether the publication was likely to create a substantial disruption of school activities.

Relying primarily on *Fraser*, an Idaho federal district court in 1987 decided a motion for a preliminary injunction involving student speech. The issue before the court was whether a student's T-shirt, which contained a caricature of three of his school administrators (the principal, a vice principal, and a dean) drinking alcohol and acting drunk at a homecoming activity, was protected under the First Amendment.[97] The drawing showed each administrator with a different alcoholic beverage and a case of beer sitting nearby. The caption read, "It doesn't get any better than this," referring to a then-current beer commercial.[98]

The caricature was to be transferred to T-shirts that were to be sold during homecoming week. When the plan was discovered, the student was suspended for two days. When the student returned to school, he wore the T-shirt and was sent home and told to change his shirt. Subsequently, the school's decision to take disciplinary action was upheld and not considered a violation of the student's free speech rights.

In an interesting approach that foreshadowed *Morse*, the court focused on student speech that runs counter to the school's educational position on a prohibited substance. The court stated that the schools in Idaho are statutorily directed to teach about the effects of alcohol. The court cited *Fraser* for the proposition that teaching can only occur within a "civilized context" and that teaching occurs when the school, through its educators, "sets the bounds for proper conduct."[99]

The federal district court noted the T-shirt caricature of school administrators consuming alcohol on school grounds. The false depiction of the administrators, graphically accusing them of committing a misdemeanor of drinking alcohol on school grounds, compromised the administrators' status as role models, which caused harm to the administrators.[100] Since the plaintiffs suffered little to no harm, the court ruled that his request for a preliminary injunction was not warranted.

Student advocacy for or advertising for drugs and alcohol through dress code litigation has a poor track record. Students routinely lose, with the courts asserting that the celebration of illegal drugs is contrary to the curricular position of the school (a *Morse* lens) or, as seen in the administrator caricature T-shirt, that the message is offensive (a *Fraser* lens).

CONCLUSION

All the cases discussed in this chapter have one common element. In all cases, federal courts looked to Supreme Court precedent for guidance when determining whether a particular student's clothing-borne expression can be constitutionally censored by school authorities. In most cases, the courts applied the Supreme Court's *Tinker* decision to the facts of their cases, asking whether school authorities reasonably anticipated that a particular student expression might cause a substantial disruption in the school setting.

The Seventh Circuit, in its 2022 decision in *Jacob v. Sonnabend*, clearly identified *Tinker* as the appropriate standard for ruling on students' depictions of firearms that appear on their clothing. Consequently, the court vacated and remanded the district court's ruling, which was based on *Hazelwood.* In rejecting *Hazelwood's* legitimate-pedagogical-concern test for doctrinal error, the appellate court held that, *Kuhlmeier* is plainly limited to "speech that others may reasonably perceive as 'bear[ing] the imprimatur of the school.'"[101] The student T-shirts with images of weapons would not be viewed by a reasonable observer as school-sponsored or school-endorsed expression.

In some cases, courts have looked to *Fraser* and asked whether student expression was vulgar, plainly offensive, or contrary to the educational mission of the school. In one case, a court looked to *Morse v. Frederick* for guidance in a clothing-based student expression case, but the overwhelming majority of student free speech cases involving messages on student clothing are decided under the principles laid down in *Tinker* or *Fraser*. And the concurring opinion in *Defoe ex rel. Defoe v. Spiva* analogized *Morse*'s ban on student drug speech to racial divisiveness in a Confederate flag dress code case. The concurring judge wrote, "If we substitute 'racial conflict' or 'racial hostility' for 'drug abuse,' the analysis in *Morse* is practically on all fours."[102]

Obviously, school districts would do well to have student dress codes that articulate the free speech standards laid out in the Supreme Court's decisions on students' free speech rights. Pursuant to *Tinker*, school policy should include a statement that the school can censor student expression that might reasonably be foreseen to create a substantial disruption in the school environment. Pursuant to *Fraser*, the school should reserve the right to ban student expression that is lewd, profane, indecent, or plainly offensive or that consists of sexual innuendo. Pursuant to *Morse*, policy should prohibit student expression that celebrates or promotes the use of alcohol or the illegal use of drugs or otherwise runs counter to the clearly articulated mission of the school.

NOTES

1. Robert J. Bein, "Stained Flag: Public Symbols and Equal Protection," *Seton Hall Law Review* 28 (1998): 897, 913.

2. On the defendants' motion for judgment on the pleadings, which was denied, Judge Griesbach opined on dress code litigation in general. *N.J. by Next Friend Jacob v. Sonnabend*, Case 1: 20-cv-00227-WCG (E.D. Wisc. 11/6/20) at *5.

4. 286 F. Supp. 2d 847 (E.D. Mich. 2003).

5. "Judge Rules in Favor of Michigan Student's Right to Wear Anti-War T-Shirt to School," ACLU (October 1, 2003), https://www.aclu.org/press-releases/judge-rules-favor-michigan-students-right-wear-anti-war-t-shirt-school#:~:text=In%20granting%20the%20order%2C%20Judge,conveyed%20an%20unpopular%20political%20message.

6. 286 F. Supp. 2d 847, 859.

7. Ibid., 857.

8. *Guiles v. Marineau*, 461 F.3d 320 (2d Cir. 2006).

9. Ibid., 322.

10. The Williamstown Middle High School dress reads, "Any aspect of a person's appearance, which constitutes a real hazard to the health and safety of self and others or is otherwise distracting, is unacceptable as an expression of personal taste. Example [Clothing displaying alcohol, drugs, violence, obscenity, and racism is outside our responsibility and integrity as a school community and is prohibited.]" WMHS Student/Parent Handbook 2003–2004, 13; brackets in original.

11. *Guiles*, 461 F.3d 328.

12. Ibid., 329.

13. *Brandt v. Board of Education of City of Chicago*, 480 F.3d 460, 463 (7th Cir. 2007).

14. Ibid., 465.

15. 307 F.3d 243 (10th Cir. 2002).

16. Ibid., 255.

17. Ibid., 256.

18. Ibid., 257.

19. 421 F. Supp. 3d 410, 411 (D. N.H. 2006).

20. Ibid., 411.

21. Ibid., 414.

22. Ibid., 424.

23. 510 F. Supp. 2d 425 (S.D. Tex. 2007)

24. Ibid., 435.

25. Ibid., 436; italics by the court.

26. *Dariano v. Morgan Hill Unified School District*, 822 F. Supp. 2d 1037 (N.D. Cal. 2011).

27. The fifth of May commemorates the Mexican army's 1862 victory over the France in the Battle of Puebla during the Franco-Mexican War (1861–1867). It is a minor holiday in Mexico but it has evolved into a celebration of Mexican culture and heritage in the United States. Schools, particularly in the Southwest, celebrate Cinco de Mayo with activities. Available at http://www.history.com/topics/cinco-de-mayo.

28. *Dariano v. Morgan Hill Unified School District*, 822 F. Supp. 2d, 1044.

29. Ibid., 1045.

30. 220 F.3d 465 (6th Cir. 2000).

31. Ibid., 467.

32. Ibid., 466.

33. Ibid., 467.

34. Ibid.

35. Ibid., 469.

36. Ibid.

37. Ibid.

38. Ibid.

39. Ibid., 471.

40. James Densley, David Reidman, and Jillian Peterson, "School Shootings Are Already at a Record in 2022—With Months to Go," *Conversation* (October 25, 2022). https://theconversation.com/school-shootings-are-already-at-a-record-in-2022-with-months-still-to-go-192494; "All Shootings at Schools from 1970–Present," K–12 School Shooting Database (accessed November 27, 2022), https://k12ssdb.org/all-shootings.

41. See Todd A. DeMitchell, "Locked Down and Armed: Security Responses to Violence in our Schools," *Connecticut Public Interest Law Journal* 13, no. 2 (2013–2014): 275–99; Todd A. DeMitchell and Casey D. Cobb, "Responses to Violence in Our Schools: An Exploration of Security as a Fundamental of Security as a Fundamental Value," *Brigham Young University Education and Law Journa*l (2003): 459–84.

42. See Todd A. DeMitchell, "School Security: The New Fundamental Value in Educational Policy Making: The Columbine Effect," *ELA Notes* 34, no. 9 (1999): 1, 4–5, 9. "United States Senator Harry Reid (D-Nevada), following the killings in Littleton, Colorado [at Columbine High School,] stated, This is an emergency if anything has ever been an emergency." Ibid., 1.

43. See *Boroff v. Wert City Board of Education*, 220 F.3d 465, 467 (6th Cir. 2000). "One school gave students in-school detention for carrying magazines with gun ads." DeMitchell and Cobb, *supra* n. 41, 469.

44. *Griggs v. Ft. Wayne School Board*, 359 F. Supp. 2d 731, 732–33 (N.D. Ind. 2005).

My Rifle

The Creed of a United States Marine

This is my rifle.
There are many like it, but this one is mine.
My rifle is my best friend.

It is my life.
I must master it as I must master my life.

My rifle, without me, is useless.
Without my rifle, I am useless.
I must fire my rifle true.
I must shoot straighter than
my enemy who is trying to kill me.
I must shoot him before he shoots me.
I will . . . (emphasis in original)

For the complete creed written by Major General W. H. Rupertus following the attack on Pearl Harbor, see http://www.arlingtoncemetery.net/whruper.htm.

45. Ibid., 742. The court acknowledged that the scope of a ban on symbols of violence would be vast. However, even though Griggs put forward many instances in which the policy could be used, the court expressed confidence that administrators would not find every instance objectionable under the policy. For example, the court pointed out that the seal of the court depicted an eagle with arrows (a symbol of violence), but that it was unlikely that administrators would object to its use.

46. Ibid., 743.

47. Ibid.

48. "The Board's principal argument is that, in the wake of tragic school shootings at Columbine High School and elsewhere, it has a 'legitimate pedagogical interest' in discouraging a 'culture of violence.'" Ibid., 744.

49. Ibid., 748.

50. Author, "School Bans Hat Over Toy Soldiers' Guns," CBS News, (June 18, 2010), https://www.cbsnews.com/news/school-bans-hat-over-toy-soldiers-guns/.

51. Associated Press, "Rhode Island School Will Reverse the Ban on Student's Toy Soldier Hat," *Plain Dealer* (June 20, 2010), http://www.cleveland.com/nation/index.ssf/2010/06/rhode_island_school_will_rever.html. The general gave David a medal for recognizing veterans and soldiers. The site contains a picture of David's hat.

52. *Griggs*, 359 F. Supp. 2d 731, 742.

53. See *San Antonio Independent School District, v. Rodriguez*, 411 U.S. 1, 38 (1973) (writing, "We have carefully considered each of the arguments supportive of the District Court's finding that education is a fundamental right or liberty and have found those arguments unpersuasive.").

54. See *Rochin v. California*, 342 U.S. 165, 169 (1972) (holding that substantive due process is violated when government, public school, conduct "offend[s] those canons of decency and fairness." In other words a "sense of justice" (at 173) must not "shock the conscience" (at 172). Similarly, due process is violated when government conduct reaches "a demonstrable level of outrageousness." *Hampton v. United States*, 425 U.S. 484, 495 n.7 (1976).

55. 354 F.3d 249 (4th Cir. 2003).

56. Ibid., 252.

57. Ibid.

58. Ibid.

59. Ibid., 253.
60. Ibid., 259–60.
61. Ibid., 260.
62. 588 F. Supp. 2d 606 (E.D. Penn. 2008).
63. Ibid., 611.
64. Ibid., 615.
65. Ibid., 618.
66. Ibid., 618.
67. Ibid.
68. The court, citing *Morse*, held that Donald's assertion of the patriotic sentiment of the T-shirt "is a description of his motive, not the interpretation of what his T-shirt says." Instead, "[t]he message conveyed is a violent and threatening promotion of vigilante behavior." Ibid., 625.
69. Ibid., 617.
70. Ibid., 627.
71. Ibid., 625.
72. *Jacob v. Sonnabend*, 37 F.4th 412 (7th Cir. 2022).
73. *Schonecker v. Koopman*, 349 F. Supp. 745, 747 (E.D. Wis. 2018). The court heard a motion for a preliminary injunction (plaintiff) and a motion to dismiss (defendant). The plaintiff's motion was granted, while the principal's motion was denied.
74. The amended Markesan High School Handbook 2018–2019 at 24 ECF N0.21-1 reads:

> Clothing or articles displaying obscenities, suggestive slogans and/or images, nudity, gangs, crime, violence, occult worship, slanderous or harassing material, encouragement of disruptive behavior, weapons, beer/alcohol, tobacco, marijuana or other drug designs are prohibited. Ibid., 748.

75. Ibid.
76. Ibid., 752–53.
77. Ibid., 753.
78. *N.J. ex rel. Jacob v. Sonnabend*, 536 F. Supp. 3d 392 (E.D. Wis. 2021), *vacated and remanded*, 37 F.4th 412 (7th Cir. 2022).
79. For a more detailed analysis of the *N.J.* Wisconsin cases, see Todd A. DeMitchell and Richard Fossey, "Images of Firearms and Dress Codes: A Legitimate Pedagogical Concern? No Says the Seventh Circuit Court of Appeals," *Education Law Reporter* 407 (2023): 1–14.
80. *N.J.*, 536 F. Supp. 3d 392, 396. The prohibition of displaying images of firearms applied equally to supportive messages and negative messages. Ibid., 395.
81. Ibid., 397. The back of the shirt, which was covered by A.L.'s hoodie jacket had the following text referring to the Wisconsin Constitution (Wis. Const. art. I, § 25) recognition of the right of the people "to keep and bear arms for security, hunting, recreation, or any other lawful purpose." Ibid.
82. Ibid., 397–98.

83. The Supreme Court's decision in *Mahanoy Area School District, Petitioner v. B.L.*, 141 S.Ct. 2038 (2021) was not discussed because the case was decided on June 23, 2021, over a month after the *N.L.* case was decided. See chapter 2 for a discussion of the US Supreme Court's free speech rulings, including *Mahanoy*.

84. *N.J.*, 536 F. Supp.3d, 400. It is worth noting that the court did not address the second prong of *Tinker*, collision with the rights of others.

85. Ibid., 403 referencing *Hazelwood School District v. Kuhlmeier*, 484 U.S. 260 (1988).

86. *Hazelwood*, 484 U.S., 270.

87. *N.J.*, 536 F. Supp.3d, 405.

88. Ibid.

89. Leonard J. Berkowitz and Anthony Lepage, "Weapons as Aggression-Eliciting Stimuli," *Journal of Personal and Social Psychology* 7 (1967): 202–207.

90. *Jacob*, 37 F.4th, 416.

91. *Hazelwood*, 484 U.S. 260, 270.

92. Ibid., 271.

93. *Jacob*, 37 4th Cir., 425.

94. *Morse v. Fredericks*, 551 U.S. 393, 410 (2007).

95. Richard Fossey and Todd A. DeMitchell, *Student Dress Codes and the First Amendment: Challenges and Policy Issues* (Lanham, MD: Rowman and Littlefield, 2014), 68.

96. *Williams v. Spencer*, 622 F.2d 1200, 1205 (4th Cir. 1980).

97. *Gano v. School District No. 411 of Twin Falls City*, 674 F. Supp. 796 (D. Idaho 1987).

98. Ibid., 797.

99. Ibid., 798.

100. The United States Supreme Court wrote that "a teacher serves as a role mode for [his/her] students, exerting a subtle but important influence over their values and perceptions." (*Ambach v. Norwick*, 441 U.S. 68, 78 (1979).

101. *Jacob*, 37 F. 4th, 423.

102. *Defoe ex rel. Defoe v. Spiva*, 625 F.3d 324, 339 (6th Cir. 2010) (Rogers, J., concurring). The school's dress code read, in pertinent part,

> Clothing and accessories such as backpacks, patches, jewelry, and notebooks must not display (1) racial or ethnic slurs/symbols, (2) gang affiliations, (3) vulgar, subversive, or sexually suggestive language or images; nor, should they promote products which students may not legally buy; such as alcohol, tobacco, and illegal drugs.

Ibid., 326.

6

Clothing Messages about Sex, Abortion, and Sexual Orientation

> In the school setting, competing interests are in tension. Schools should protect all students from physical harm and bullying and from verbal bullying and name calling. Of course, we expect them to teach about democracy, equality, and free speech. In applying these values, should schools protect gay students from the emotional harm of being confronted with anti-homosexual religious messages on t-shirts or in discussions of public policy? Should schools suppress all "intolerant" messages and if so, how should they define them?
>
> This is not a simple problem, either as a matter of theory or law.[1]

As explored in previous chapters, students who come to school displaying messages on their clothing about politics, guns, drugs, and the Confederacy are likely to create some discomfort in the school community. After all, many people hold strong views on such issues as gun ownership, illegal drugs, and antebellum racial attitudes, and students who promote their own political views on such controversial issues while at school are sure to trigger a negative reaction from at least some people. However, these differences on matters of public concern are weighed differently in the special circumstances of the public school.

> "These fundamental values of "habits and manners of civility" essential to a democracy must, of course, include tolerance of divergent political and religious views, even when the views expressed may be unpopular. But these "fundamental values" must take into account consideration of the sensibilities of others, and, in the case of a school, the sensibilities of fellow students. The undoubted freedom to advocate unpopular and

controversial views in schools and classrooms must be balanced against the society's countervailing interest in teaching students the boundaries of socially appropriate behavior. Even the most heated political discourse in a democratic society requires consideration for the personal sensibilities of the other participants and audiences."—*Bethel School District No. 403 v. Fraser*, 478 U.S. 675, 681 (1986)

But sensitive as political issues are when discussed in a school, sexual issues are even more sensitive. Social issues associated with sexual orientation and abortion have long evoked strong reactions. Schools have not been immune from these controversies.

It should not be surprising to find a significant number of court cases involving students who wish to proclaim messages about sex, abortion, and sexual orientation on their clothing. Thus, this chapter is devoted to student clothing messages on sexual topics, organized into three sections: clothing messages that are lewd, vulgar, or contain sexual innuendo; clothing messages on abortion; and clothing messages on sexual orientation.

CLOTHING MESSAGES THAT ARE LEWD, VULGAR, OR CONTAIN SEXUAL INNUENDO

As every high school teacher or parent of a teenager knows, adolescents are afflicted with raging hormones, causing many of them to seem obsessively focused on sex. Thus, it is not surprising to find some federal court cases involve the right of students to proclaim sexual messages on their clothing.

School authorities have clear legal guidance when a student proclaims a sexual message at school that is lewd, vulgar, or indecent. As discussed in chapter 1, the Supreme Court said clearly in the case of *Bethel School District No. 403 v. Fraser* that schools can ban student speech that fits into these categories.[2]

This principle is illustrated in *Pyle v. South Hadley School Committee*, in which Jeffrey Pyle and his brother Jonathan, both students at South Hadley High School in Massachusetts, wore T-shirts during the 1993–1994 school year that displayed messages that school administrators considered vulgar.[3] One T-shirt proclaimed: "See Dick Drink. See Dick Drive. See Dick Die. Don't be a Dick." Another shirt said, "Coed Naked Band: Do It to the Rhythm." In addition, the brothers wore other T-shirts to school with provocative messages and sexual themes.

School authorities banned some of the Pyle brothers' T-shirt messages on the grounds that they violated the school district's dress code, and the brothers sued. They alleged a violation of their right to free speech under the First Amendment and asked a federal court to enjoin school officials from prohibiting them from wearing their sex-themed T-shirts. Their father was a constitutional law professor at a nearby college, which may at least partly explain why this seemingly petty controversy reached a federal court.

A Massachusetts federal trial court acknowledged the seemingly trivial nature of the case, describing it as a "tempest in a teapot," but he took the dispute seriously, conducting a four-day trial on the merits of the Pyle brothers' claims. In the end, the court denied the Pyle brothers' request for an injunction and upheld the school district's decision to ban two of the brothers' T-shirts. In the court's view, the school board, not a federal judge, should determine "when the pungency of sexual foolery becomes unacceptable."[4] The court did, however, invalidate one portion of the school district's speech code that prohibited student speech that was intended to harass individuals.

The Supreme Court's decision in *Bethel School District No. 403 v. Fraser*, upholding a school's authority to ban lewd and vulgar speech in the school environment, was the principal case the federal court relied on when it upheld the South Hadley school committee's ban on the Pyle brothers' T-shirt messages. Today, most school districts have explicit policies banning lewd and vulgar speech at school, secure in the knowledge that the *Fraser* decision supports their position.

Sometimes, it is an easy call for a court to determine that a particular student communication is vulgar and thus capable of being banned by school authorities under the rule laid down by *Fraser*. For example, in *Broussard v. School Board of the City of Norfolk*, a federal judge upheld a school's decision to prohibit Kimberly Broussard, a middle school girl, from wearing a T-shirt to school that proclaimed, "Drugs Suck!"[5] The court concluded that school officials' determination "that the word 'suck' in the context of Kimberly's shirt is lewd, vulgar, or offensive and is not merely a prudish failure to distinguish the vigorous from the vulgar, but rather is a permissible decision by the school to regulate middle school children's language and channel their expression into socially appropriate speech."[6] In the court's view, the word "suck" clearly had a sexual connotation, even though the word was sometimes used merely as an expression of disapproval.

Sometimes, however, it is not easy to determine whether a particular student message is vulgar. For example, in *B.H. v. Easton Area School District*, a 2011 case, officials at a Pennsylvania school district sanctioned two middle school girls who refused to remove bracelets proclaiming the message "I ♥ Boobies" as part of a campaign to promote breast cancer awareness.[7] The girls sued, claiming a violation of their right to free speech.

A federal trial court ruled in the girls' favor. The court concluded that the phrase "boobies" in the context of a communication on the importance of breast cancer awareness had no sexual connotation and was not lewd or vulgar, and thus the bracelets could not be banned on that basis. In an interesting twist, district court judge Mary McLaughlin stated that if the speech on the bracelet had occurred in isolation and was not within the context of a legitimate national breast cancer awareness program, she would have been more open to the bracelets being evaluated under *Fraser*.

The school also argued that the bracelets would likely create a substantial disruption in the school environment, pointing out that the bracelets had led to some inappropriate remarks by middle school boys. But the court rejected this argument. "Such isolated incidents," the court noted, "are well within a school's ability to maintain discipline and order and they did not because a disruption to the School's learning environment."[8]

On the other hand, a federal court in Wisconsin, ruling on similar facts, denied a middle school student's request for an injunction that would permit her to wear "I ♥ Boobies" bracelets at school.[9] "In this court's opinion," the court wrote, "[t]he statement 'I ♥ Boobies! (Keep a Breast)' straddles the line between vulgar and mildly inappropriate."[10] Thus, the court explained, it was reasonable for school officials to conclude that the phrase was vulgar "and inconsistent with their goal of fostering respectful discourse by encouraging students to use 'correct anatomical terminology' for human body parts."[11]

The student speech was the same in both cases. The two federal district courts reached opposite conclusions using the same legal test laid down by the Supreme Court's *Fraser* decision. One judge held that "boobies" was not vulgar or lewd, and the other saw the bracelet as just crossing the line of vulgarity. It is no wonder that educators long for clear direction on the contours of the First Amendment in the school environment. Principals are the legal leaders of their schools, but it is hard to lead when the path is not clearly marked.

The conflict between two courts about the appropriateness of "I ♥ Boobies!" bracelets in a middle school does not change the fact that overall, courts and school officials will usually agree about what types of student expressions are vulgar, lewd, or indecent. Certainly, many judges would agree that "Don't Be a Dick" is an offensive phrase in the school environment and can be banned without violating a student's free speech rights under the First Amendment.

STUDENTS WHO PROCLAIM THEIR OPPOSITION TO ABORTION ON THEIR CLOTHING

Perhaps no social issue is more divisive or inspires more militant advocates than abortion. Given the public response to abortion rights, it is not surprising that debates about abortion have sparked litigation in the education sector—both at the K–12 level and in the universities. For example, in *Pro-Life Cougars v. University of Houston*,[12] a public university in Texas attempted to relegate an antiabortion student group's pro-life photographic exhibit to an out-of-the-way spot on campus rather than a more visible location based on the unilateral conclusion by the dean of students that the pro-life display was "potentially disruptive." A federal court ruled that the university had violated the group's right to free expression under the First Amendment.

For an opposite finding regarding disruption, the Tenth Circuit Court of Appeals addressed the free speech rights of several students who were members of a religious youth group called Relentless.[13] The students planned, without permission, to pass out twenty-five hundred rubber fetus dolls at their high school. The dolls had a card affixed to them with a statement that the dolls represented the actual size and weight of a twelve-week-old fetus. On the other side of the card was a religious message.[14]

The Relentless students offered a fetus to students who were passing the table but allowed students to decline and move along. There was no blockage of the entrance to the school where they set up their distribution table. The assistant principal shut down the distribution after approximately three hundred dolls were distributed. The assistant principal noticed that several students were throwing the dismembered heads of the dolls against the walls of the school.

At the trial, the plaintiff students argued that the "disruptions occurred only because of the behavior of third parties and that no Plaintiffs participated in these activities"[15] and that no substantial disruption had occurred. The court disagreed, applying *Tinker*'s disruption standard. "[T]he District was not obligated to wait until a substantial disruption materialized, so long as its forecast was reasonable," the court ruled.[16]

In at least two court cases, federal judges were called on to decide whether a student in a public high school has a constitutional right to express opposition to abortion on the student's T-shirt. In *K.D. v. Fillmore Central School District*,[17] K.D., a sophomore, repeatedly came to school wearing a provocative pro-life T-shirt. In capital letters, the front of the shirt proclaimed: "ABORTION IS HOMICIDE." The back of the shirt expressed this message:

You will not silence my message.
You will not mock my God.
You will stop killing my generation.
Rock for Life![18]

K.D.'s school had a dress code policy which required students to wear clothing that is "appropriate and [does] not disrupt or interfere with the educational process."[19] At first, principal Kyle Faulkner took a low-key approach to K.D.'s T-shirts, simply asking K.D. to "do him a favor" and refrain from wearing the shirt to school.[20]

However, Faulkner later received complaints from female students about K.D.'s T-shirt. One student said the T-shirt upset her and that she did not "want to be near [K.D.] or anywhere near that shirt."[21] The principal also knew that there were female students in the school who had had abortions or who were contemplating an abortion, and he concluded that each such student "would consider the shirt to be a personal attack on her, but that each girl would not likely come forward to complain."[22]

Finally, on an October school day, Faulkner told K.D. the shirt was not appropriate for school and asked him to cover the shirt's message, turn the shirt inside out, or wear a different shirt. Faulkner gave K.D. the choice of changing his attire or going home for the day. K.D. refused to change his shirt, and he left school.

K.D. sued the school district, alleging a violation of his First Amendment right to free expression. Before a federal judge, K.D. sought a court order directing school officials not to interfere with his right to wear his "ABORTON IS HOMICIDE" T-shirt to school.

School defendants made four arguments in support of their contention that they properly banned K.D.'s T-shirt. First, they claimed that K.D.'s T-shirt message was factually inaccurate because it claims that abortion is homicide. Since abortion is legal, the school authorities reasoned, it is not the unlawful taking of life. Second, the defendants argued that the T-shirt was a direct attack on students who had had an abortion or were contemplating an abortion and that such attacks are inappropriate in the school. Third, they maintained that abortion is a subject which is frequently associated with violence and could be banned on that basis. Finally, Faulkner and the school district contended that abortion is a topic to which elementary students should not be exposed.

In connection with their last argument, the defendants pointed out that K.D. attended a school in which students from pre-kindergarten to twelfth grade were housed in one building. They submitted statements from several parents of elementary school students asserting that they did not want their children exposed to the topic of abortion.

A federal district judge rejected all of these arguments and sided with K.D. In the judge's opinion, K.D. had engaged in passive political speech that had been censored because of its content. The judge said there was insufficient evidence to show that K.D.'s T-shirt had disrupted the school environment, and there was no evidence showing that an elementary school child had actually seen the shirt. Moreover, the judge asserted, it was simply incorrect to say that K.D.'s shirt consisted of a personal attack on students who had had abortions. "That a student may have an opposing view does not make K.D.'s

T-shirt a personal attack on that student for having an opposing viewpoint," the judge reasoned.[23]

Based on these considerations, K.D.'s request for an injunction was granted. The Fillmore Central School District was prohibited from requiring K.D. to remove, turn inside out, or cover the message on his T-shirt, the court ordered, unless it could show that K.D.'s "ABORTION IS HOMICIDE" T-shirt had caused or was likely to cause "a material or substantial disruption of the orderly administration of the school."[24]

Another federal court, this one in California, ruled very differently from the ruling in *K.D. v. Fillmore Central School District.* In *T.A. v. McSwain Elementary School,*[25] a case involving facts like the *Fillmore* case, a trial court denied a student's request for an order permitting her to wear an anti-abortion T-shirt to school.

In this case, a sixth grader wore a T-shirt to school that featured the word "ABORTION" on the front side. Below the word were three squares approximately three inches in height. The first two squares depicted color images of a human fetus in two stages of development. "The third square—containing no image—is filled in with black." Below the three squares, these words appeared: "growing, growing . . . gone."[26]

The back of the shirt proclaimed this message:

American Life League's
Sixth Annual
NATIONAL
PRO-LIFE
T-SHIRT-DAY
APRIL 29, 2008 www.ALL.org[27]

T.A.'s school had a dress and grooming policy that prohibited students from wearing clothing that "present[s] a health or safety hazard or a distraction which would interfere with the educational process."[28] The school also had a "Freedom of Speech/Expression Policy" that prohibited student speech that causes a "substantial disruption of the school's orderly operation."[29]

A teacher spotted T.A. wearing her pro-life T-shirt while eating breakfast at the school. She was taken to the school office, where C. W. Smith, the assistant principal, determined that the shirt violated the school's dress code policy. T.A. was given a temporary T-shirt to wear, and she soon filed a lawsuit.

In responding to T.A.'s motion for an injunction, the school defended its decision to ban T.A.'s shirt on two grounds. First, Smith determined the pictures on T.A.'s T-shirt were "too graphic for the younger students that we have at our school site."[30]

Second, as it happened, T.A. had worn the T-shirt to school during the week that children were taking the STAR test, a state-mandated standardized test. Smith feared the pictures on T.A.'s shirt "would distract students during the time in which they should have been taking the STAR test."[31]

In denying T.A.'s motion for summary judgment on her constitutional claims, the court issued findings favorable to the school district. "Defendants have presented evidence," the court ruled, "that the restriction imposed on [T.A.] was not based on the viewpoint expressed by [T.A.'s] shirt, but rather on the graphic pictures contained on it." In addition, the court ruled, "Defendants have presented evidence that based on their experience and judgment, they believed the shirt would have created a substantial disruption of or a material interference with school activities, especially in the context of the standardized testing being administered at the school on the day in question."[32]

Besides her First Amendment claim, T.A. presented two other constitutional arguments. She claimed the school's dress code was unconstitutionally vague, in violation of substantive due process, and she argued she had been denied equal protection in that the school censored her pro-life message while permitting other views on abortion to be expressed. The court was not persuaded by either argument. In the court's view, the school's policy passed constitutional muster on the vagueness issue. Regarding T.A.'s equal protection argument, the court said the claim that she had been treated differently based on her views would have to be determined at trial.

T.A. v. McSwain Union Elementary School and *K.D. v. Fillmore Central School District* involve similar facts, but the outcomes were different. Indeed, it is interesting to note that K.D.'s T-shirt's rather militant message that "ABORTION IS HOMICIDE" was ruled nondisruptive, while T.A.'s much milder message was viewed as one that could disrupt a school's testing program.[33] It seems likely that the temperaments and dispositions of the ruling judges explain the contrary rulings as much as any distinctions in the facts of the case or judicial interpretations of the law. Unfortunately, little direction is supplied except to the parties as to the boundaries of messages on abortion.

CLOTHING MESSAGES ABOUT SEXUAL ORIENTATION AND SEXUALITY

A second type of sexual-themed student clothing message pertains to student expressions about sexuality and sexual orientation. Usually, students who make pronouncements on the topic of sexual orientation are not doing so to be vulgar or bawdy. Instead, students who proclaim messages on this topic usually do so as a way of communicating their political or religious views.

For example, a sixteen-year-old high school junior filed suit against his high school because school authorities would not let him wear a T-shirt on the student-led annual Day of Silence, which brings attention to the issue of anti-gay bullying and harassment. The T-shirt read, "Jesus is not a homophobe."[34]

It seems clear that students have the right to proclaim their support for gay and lesbian students while at school so long as their expressions s are not disruptive, lewd, or in violation of a valid dress code violation. For example, in *Gillman v. School Board of Holmes County*, high school students in a Florida school district publicly displayed their support for "Jane Doe," a lesbian classmate, after the school principal allegedly harassed Jane because of her sexual orientation.[35] Incorrectly concluding that the principal had suspended Jane, students expressed support for her by writing "GP" or "Gay Pride" on their bodies, wearing T-shirts proclaiming their support for gay rights, shouting "Gay Pride" in the school hallways, and creating signs expressing support for homosexuals.

At some point during this controversy, the principal suspended eleven students for their participation in the so-called Gay Pride movement. The principal interviewed approximately thirty students about the Gay Pride movement, questioning them about their sexual orientation and about their involvement in the planned walkout of a school assembly. He prohibited students from wearing rainbow belts or writing "Gay Pride" or "GP" on their arms and notebooks.[36]

In response to the principal's prohibition of messages expressing support for homosexuals, one student, Heather Gillman, sought clarification from the school board regarding such messages. Specifically, she sought permission from the school board to display various gay-friendly messages, including one proclaiming, "I Support My Gay Friends."

The school board's response to Heather stated that none of the gay-friendly messages she had proposed could be displayed at school. The board justified its decision by claiming that the messages were an indication of membership in an "illegal organization" prohibited by school policy and that the messages were disruptive to the educational process.[37]

Via her mother, Heather sued the school district, claiming that its policies against student expression in support of gay rights violated the First Amendment. The school board responded by arguing that the pro-gay messages could foreseeably cause substantial disruption at the school and therefore could be banned under *Tinker*. Indeed, at trial, the principal testified that students should not be permitted to wear political buttons expressing support for presidential candidates while at school because such expressions might cause "controversy" and unrest."[38]

A Florida federal trial judge rejected the school district's justification for banning pro-gay messages and ruled in Heather's favor. The court noted that the facts of the case were extraordinary: "The Holmes County School Board has imposed an outright ban on speech by students that is not vulgar, lewd, obscene, plainly offensive, or violent, but which is pure, political, and expresses tolerance, acceptance, fairness, and support for not only a marginalized group, but more importantly, for a fellow student at Ponce de Leon [High School]."[39]

This kind of speech, the judge emphasized, is exactly the kind of speech that "is essential in a vibrant, progressive society and is precisely the type of speech that is sacrosanct under the First Amendment."[40] The court emphatically rejected the school district's argument that the pro-gay messages would likely lead to disruption, concluding that the examples of disruption the district put forward were "speculative, theoretical, and de minimis."[41]

Although a student's First Amendment right to express tolerance and support for homosexuals seems well established, a student's constitutional right to express disapproval of homosexuality at school is less clear. One of the most important federal court opinions on this topic is *Harper v. Poway Unified School District*,[42] in which the Ninth Circuit Court of Appeals ruled that there is no such right, but other courts have disagreed with the *Harper* court's analysis.

In *Harper*, school officials at Poway High School permitted the Gay-Straight Alliance, a student group, to sponsor a Day of Silence at the school to promote tolerance toward gays and lesbians.[43] Tye Harper, a high school student, disagreed with the theme of the Day of Silence. On the appointed date for the Day of Silence, he wore a T-shirt expressing his view that homosexual conduct was sinful from a Christian perspective.

The front of Tye's T-shirt proclaimed this message: "I WILL NOT ACCEPT WHAT GOD HAS CONDEMNED." The back of his shirt communicated a similar message: "HOMOSEXUALITY IS HAMEFUL 'Romans 1:27.'"[44]

Apparently, school authorities did not see Tye' T-shirt, and nothing was said to him about it. The following day, however, Tye came to school wearing the same T-shirt, which was emblazoned with an additional message: "BE ASHAMED, OUR SCHOOL EMBRACED WHAT GOD HAS CONDEMNED."[45]

A teacher confronted Tye about the shirt, but he refused to take it off. The teacher gave Tye a dress code violation card and sent him to the front office. At the front office, the principal told Tye that he considered the T-shirt's messages to be inflammatory and that it was the school's "intent to avoid physical conflict on campus." The principal also expressed the view "that it was not healthy for students to be addressed in such a derogatory manner."[46]

Tye refused to remove the T-shirt. Although he twice requested to be suspended, the principal did not suspend him or discipline him. Instead, he required Tye to remain in the front office until the end of the school day.

Tye sued the school district, alleging a violation of his First Amendment right to free speech. His case was dismissed by a federal trial court on the grounds that Tye's T-shirt messages could foreseeably cause a substantial disruption at his school and thus could be banned under *Tinker*. Tye then appealed to the Ninth Circuit Court of Appeals. In a decision issued on April 20, 2006, a three-judge panel of the Ninth Circuit upheld the trial court, with one judge dissenting.

In ruling for the school district, the Ninth Circuit articulated an expansive interpretation of the Supreme Court's *Tinker* decision, an interpretation that surprised many legal commentators all over the United States. In its decision, the court affirmed *Tinker*'s principle that schools can ban student speech that could foreseeably cause a "substantial disruption" in the school environment. This, of course, had been the standard interpretation of *Tinker* by the federal courts for decades and was in no way surprising.

Remarkably, however, the Ninth Circuit focused on a passage in *Tinker* that had generally been overlooked by both courts and scholars. In addition to student speech that causes or is likely to cause a substantial disruption, the Ninth Circuit pointed out, the Supreme Court also said that schools can censor student speech that "intrudes upon . . . the rights of other students" or "collides with the rights of students to be secure and left alone.'"[47]

The Ninth Circuit viewed Tye Harper's antigay T-shirt messages as "'collid[ing] with the rights of other students' in the most fundamental way."[48] The court rejected the argument of Tye's counsel that *Tinker* only intended to protect students from physical confrontations. On the contrary, the court said, "[p]ublic school students who may be injured by verbal assaults on the basis of a core identifying characteristic such as race, religion, or sexual orientation have a right to be free from such attacks while on school campuses."[49] The right to be secure while at school, the Ninth Circuit emphasized, included "not only freedom from physical assaults but from psychological attacks that cause young people to question their self-worth and their rightful place in society."[50]

In the Ninth Circuit's view, student speech that demeaned gay and lesbian students was "detrimental not only to their psychological health and well-being, but also to their educational development."[51] Thus, it is well established, the court said, that attacks on students based on sexual orientation were "harmful not only to the students' health and welfare, but also to their educational performance and their ultimate potential for success in life."[52]

The Ninth Circuit affirmed *Tinker*'s holding that student speech cannot be suppressed simply because some people find it offensive. It pointed out that a student may have a constitutional right to say, "Young Republicans Suck" or "Young Democrats Suck." But—in the Ninth Circuit's view at least—schools do not offend the First Amendment by banning students from engaging in "derogatory and injurious remarks directed at students' minority status such as race, religion, and sexual orientation."[53]

Although the *Harper* decision has been widely criticized for attempting to cut back on *Tinker*'s robust affirmation of students' right to free speech in the school environment, the court's reasoning makes sense to many people.[54] In particular, the following passage of the Ninth Circuit's opinion persuasively argues that demeaning speech directed toward vulnerable students can be harmful:

> Speech that attacks high school students who are members of minority groups that have been historically oppressed, subjected to verbal and physical abuse, and made to feel inferior, serves to injure and intimidate them, as well as to damage their sense of security and interfere with their opportunity to learn. The demeaning of young gay and lesbian students in a school environment is detrimental not only to their psychological health and wellbeing, but also to their educational development.[55]

Based then on these considerations of harm, the Ninth Circuit made clear that school officials have the authority to ban student speech that targets at least three vulnerable groups of students: students targeted because of their race, sexual orientation, or religion. "Those who administer our public educational institutions," the court said emphatically, "need not tolerate verbal assault that may destroy the self-esteem of our most vulnerable teenagers and interfere with their educational development."[56]

Interestingly, although the *Harper* decision inspired a lot of scholarly commentary, its reasoning has not been followed by all federal courts. In fact, in three cases—all involving antigay messages on students' T-shirts—federal courts upheld the right of students to proclaim their opposition to homosexuality based on findings that the critical messages did not disrupt the school environment.

In *Chambers v. Babbitt*, decided several years before the Ninth Circuit's *Harper* decision was handed down, Elliott Chambers, a student at Woodbury High School in Minnesota, wore a sweatshirt to school that proclaimed the message, "Straight Pride."[57] The back of the sweatshirt displayed the image of a man and woman holding hands. Elliott's promotion of heterosexuality and implicit condemnation of homosexuality was informed, at least in part, by his religious beliefs.

Elliott was a member of a Christian student group at the school and used the group as a forum to share biblical passages supporting the claim that homosexuality is sinful.[58] In his testimony, he argued that the school was advocating homosexuality through its tolerance-promoting policies.[59] Thus, it appears that his sweatshirt served as a protest against the school's tolerance for nonheterosexual relationships. At least one student complained to school authorities about the message on Elliott's sweatshirt, and the principal told him not to wear the shirt to school again.

Elliott sued, arguing that the principal's directive violated his constitutional right to express his religious beliefs, and the court granted his request for an injunction prohibiting the school from banning Elliott's sweatshirt message unless it had a reasonable belief that Elliott's message "could lead to substantial disruption of the school environment or material interference with school activities."[60]

In reaching its decision, the court in Elliott Chambers's case relied primarily on its interpretation of *Tinker*'s substantial disruption test. The school district maintained that Elliott's arguably antigay message could disrupt the school environment and cited evidence of eleven fights between students during the school year. The court was not persuaded, however, pointing out that the relationship between the fighting incidents and Elliott's sweatshirt had not been explained.

The court concluded its opinion with an observation about the importance of tolerance toward different points of view. "Our schools, like our communities at large, are invaluably improved by the diversity of their members," the court observed. "All students benefit from the respectful and thoughtful exchange of ideas and sharing of beliefs and practices." In the court's view, "[s]chools, particular, are vital environments that can provide an education of both substance of diversity and the responsible manner with which such diversity is approached and expressed."[61]

The court acknowledged that Elliott's "Straight Pride" sweatshirt message apparently expressed an intolerant attitude toward homosexuals. However, the court pointed out that tolerance includes the tolerating viewpoints such as that expressed by "Straight Pride." Nevertheless, the school had a responsibility "to maintain an environment open to diversity and to educate and support its students as they confront ideas different from their own."[62]

A similar point of view was expressed in the 2005 case *Nixon v. Northern Local School District*.[63] In this case, James Nixon, a middle school student in Licking County, Ohio, wore a T-shirt to school that contained religious messages and disapproval of homosexuality. The front of the shirt proclaimed the word "INTOLERANT," with this added message: "Jesus said . . . I am the way, the truth, and life." The back of the shirt displayed these words: "Homosexuality is a sin! Islam is a lie! Abortion is murder! Some issues are just black and white!"[64]

The school's guidance counselor spotted James wearing his controversial T-shirt and asked him to remove it or wear it turned inside out. James refused, and the counselor escorted him to the principal's office.

At the principal's office, an assistant principal viewed James's shirt and concluded that it was offensive and in violation of school policy. Unless he removed the shirt or wore it turned inside out, the assistant principal told James, he would not be permitted to return to school.

At some point James's father arrived at the school, where he supported his son's right to wear the antigay T-shirt. The father refused to leave the school until he received a satisfactory explanation as to why the shirt was offensive. School authorities called the sheriff's department. A deputy sheriff arrived and took the father's statement, whereupon James and the father left the school.

The school superintendent backed the principal regarding James's T-shirt and affirmed the principal's message that James would be suspended if he returned to school wearing the shirt. The superintendent agreed with the principal that James's shirt violated school policy, which stated that "[a]ny fashion (dress, accessory or hairstyle) that disrupts the education process . . . will not be permitted."[65]

In due course, James and his parents sued the school district, seeking an injunction that would bar school officials from prohibiting James from wearing his controversial T-shirt to school. Before the court, school defendants made two arguments in defense of the decision to ban the shirt on the school campus. First, relying on the *Tinker* decision, school officials argued that the T-shirt had the potential for causing disruption "based on the fact that the school includes students and/or staff members who are Muslims, homosexuals and those who have had abortions."[66] Second, the defendants maintained that James's messages were offensive and could be banned in accordance with the Supreme Court's *Fraser* decision.

A federal court rejected both of the school district's legal arguments and granted James's request for an injunction that would allow him to wear his T-shirt at school. With regard to the school's disruption argument, the court pointed out that there was no evidence that James's shirt had caused a disruption in the school environment or that his shirt was likely to cause a disruption. In the court's view, the mere fact that the school community contained people who were targets of James's messages (Muslims, homosexuals, and women who had had abortions) fell "well short of the *Tinker* standard for reasonably anticipating a disruption of school activities."[67]

Nor, in the court's opinion, could school officials ban James's shirt on the grounds that it was "plainly offensive" under *Fraser*. In the court's view, "plainly offensive," as the Supreme Court and other courts interpreted that phrase, referred to speech that was vulgar, contained sexual innuendoes, or promoted suicide, drugs, alcohol, or murder. Thus, the court concluded, a potentially offensive political speech such as the views expressed on James's T-shirt could not be categorized as "plainly offensive" for purposes of regulation in the school environment.

The *Chambers* and *Nixon* decisions both relied on *Tinker*'s "substantial disruption" standard. It is clear from both of these holdings that the courts required evidence of substantial disruption in the school before they would curtail the students' rights under the First Amendment. In both cases, there was only fear of substantial disruption.[68]

Although the court ruled in James Nixon's favor, it expressed sympathy for school officials who have the responsibility to maintain safe and orderly schools. "In light of the Columbine school shootings and other tragic attacks that have happened on school grounds, the Court wholly understands that school administrators and staff must be extra vigilant in protecting students," the court acknowledged. The court emphasized that its decision in favor of James's right to wear his controversial T-shirt was not "an admonishment of the well-intentioned actions school officials take to ensure a stable educational environment."[69]

In *Zamecnik v. Indian Prairie School District*, decided after the *Harper* decision, the Seventh Circuit Court of Appeals sided with students who were barred from wearing T-shirts to school that proclaimed, "Be Happy, Not Gay," a phrase that expressed mild disapproval of homosexuality.[70] In a previous opinion, the Seventh Circuit had granted the students a preliminary injunction allowing them to wear the shirts, concluding that the shirt's message was "only tepidly negative" and finding no evidence that the shirts disrupted the school environment in any substantial way.[71]

In a later opinion, the Seventh Circuit affirmed a lower court order granting summary judgment to the students. At the appellate level, the school district argued that the lower court had entered summary judgment prematurely, citing evidence that the T-shirts had, in fact, created a substantial disruption and presenting an expert witness's report that supported its position.

The Seventh Circuit found the school's evidence of disruption to be negligible and that some of the disruption consisted of a "heckler's veto," action or speech by people who opposed the T-shirt wearers' point of view. The court gave little credence to the school district's expert report, which contained no reference to the school where the T-shirts were worn. The court noted dryly that the majority of the thirty-eight-page report consisted of the expert's vita and that the substance of the report was only two and a half pages long.

Finally, in a 2010 case, Constance McMillen, a female student in Mississippi, asked school officials for permission to attend prom with her girlfriend and to wear a tuxedo. School officials refused this request.[72] The school district ended up canceling the prom, citing concerns about "the education, safety, and well-being of its students," and hoped that a private group not subject to constitutional constraints would host the prom.[73]

The student sued, arguing that canceling the prom had the effect of banning her "from peacefully conveying her social and political viewpoints that 'it is appropriate for gay and lesbian students to bring same-sex dates to the prom,' and that 'it is appropriate for female students to wear tuxedos despite traditional notions of how females should dress.'"[74]

Applying the four-part test to grant a preliminary injunction requiring the school district to host the prom, the federal district court found that school officials infringed upon the student's First Amendment rights when they did not permit her to bring a same-sex date or to wear a tuxedo. Even though her rights were clearly violated, the court denied her request for a preliminary injunction, asserting that it does meet the public interest standard because of the disruption it would cause. Specifically, it would "confuse and confound the community on the issue" to require the school district to sponsor the prom after the private group had put so much time into planning the dance.[75]

Due to hostility in her local community, Constance transferred to another school district. However, the school district agreed to pay her $35,000, and the court ordered the school district to pay $81,000 in legal fees to Constance's attorneys.[76]

What do the cases tell us regarding whether students have the right to proclaim antigay messages on their clothing while at school? The *Harper* case states flatly that schools can prohibit these messages because they are harmful to vulnerable students. The *Zamecnik* case upheld the right of students to proclaim a mildly gay message—"Be Happy, Not Gay"—on T-shirts but acknowledged that harsh antigay messages could be banned if they fell within the category of "fighting words."

It is interesting to note that in both the *Harper* case and the *Zamecnik* case, the plaintiff students wore antigay messages in response to school-approved activities that supported tolerance toward gays and lesbians. In *Harper*, the Ninth Circuit upheld the Poway school district's ban on students' antigay speech even though the school itself promoted an alternative point of view.

The Seventh Circuit disagreed with the Ninth Circuit on this important point. In the Seventh Circuit's view, "a school that permits advocacy of the rights of homosexual students cannot be allowed to stifle criticism of homosexuality."[77]

The issue of student speech on a controversial topic is compounded when the speech also relates to and in some cases is in direct response to the school's curriculum. Judge Guido Calabresi considered these cases as cutting a path through "the thorniest of constitutional thickets—among the tangled vines of public school curricula and student freedom of speech."[78]

The Seventh Circuit's position is better reasoned than the Ninth Circuit's view. From the perspective of basic fairness, it is questionable whether a school district should take an aggressive position in favor of gay and lesbian rights while stifling student voices that disagree. Judge Alex Kozinski's dissenting opinion in *Harper* captures this concern: It hardly seems fair for a school to introduce a controversial topic into the school environment and prohibit one point of view from being expressed in the marketplace of ideas.[79]

Of course, the restrictions of *Tinker* and *Fraser* should certainly apply with full force in such situations. Certainly, as the Seventh Circuit acknowledged, schools have the authority to censor antigay speech that is hateful, abusive, harassing, or so incendiary that it constitutes fighting words, but a school that promotes tolerance for gays and lesbians should also be able to tolerate nonthreatening student speech that takes an opposite view.

A DRESS CODE WITH NO MESSAGES ALLOWED

The preceding discussion and chapters 3 and 4 discuss dress codes that either target messages or reduce student speech via their choice of clothing. The following case involves a dress code that targets all speech. In some ways it is the perfect transition to the next chapter on school uniforms, which also targets all speech and is thus content neutral.

In August 2009 the Fifth Circuit Court of Appeals issued a decision that may be a game changer with regard to constitutional litigation over students' T-shirt messages. In *Palmer v. Waxahachie Independent School District*,[80] the Fifth Circuit ruled that a Texas school district could bar a high school student from wearing a T-shirt or polo shirt that proclaimed any message other than principal-approved messages pertaining to school spirit, student clubs, or athletic teams.[81] The student, Paul Palmer, had sued to uphold the right to wear two shirts supporting John Edwards for president of the United States and one that displayed the language of the First Amendment.[82]

Without analyzing whether the shirts' messages might be disruptive, which would allow school officials to bar them under *Tinker*'s "substantial disruption" standard, the Fifth Circuit simply ruled that the school district's dress code was a content-neutral regulation and that the district had an important governmental interest in regulating students' clothing while they are at school.[83] The court used the intermediate scrutiny test of *United States v. O'Brien*,[84] a non-education case, for its analysis. This aligns *Waxahachie* with the emerging litigation on school uniforms rather than the T-shirt litigation discussed above.

In concluding that the Waxahachie school district had a substantial governmental interest in its dress code, the Fifth Circuit cited the code's preamble, which stated that the code was adopted "to maintain an orderly and safe learning environment, increase the focus in instruction, promote safety and life-long learning, and encourage professional and responsible dress for all students."[85]

In the Fifth Circuit's view, "improving the educational process" was an important governmental interest,[86] as was "instilling self-confidence, increasing attendance, decreasing disciplinary referrals, and lowering the drop-out rate."[87] And the district had an important governmental interest in encouraging "professional dress" as well.[88] Finally, the court pointed out, "the benefits for the school, such as reducing time spent enforcing the code and promoting school spirit, are also important in promoting better education."[89]

Significantly, the Fifth Circuit did not require the Waxahachie school district to provide quantitative evidence that its dress code furthered the interests that it articulated. "We do not . . . require statistical or scientific evidence to uphold a dress code," the court stated, noting that "improvements in discipline or morale cannot always be quantified."[90] In the Fifth Circuit's view, school authorities were in a better position than the courts to determine the benefits of a dress code.[91]

In short, the Fifth Circuit had no qualms about upholding a school district's dress code that banned all messages on students' shirts unless they pertained to school spirit, athletics, or school clubs. "[S]o long as a dress code does not restrict student dress outside of school and provides them with some means to communicate their speech during school," the court concluded, it passes constitutional muster.[92]

CONCLUSION

The cases reviewed in this chapter illustrate the tensions that exist in public schools about student expression on the controversial topics of sex, abortion, and sexual orientation. As we have seen, two federal courts could not agree regarding whether the phrase "I ♥ Boobies" is vulgar when displayed on a bracelet at school. Two courts could not agree on whether a student has a First Amendment to wear an antiabortion T-shirt to school. And courts are not in agreement about the constitutional right of students to proclaim antigay messages on their clothing in the school environment.

Nevertheless, despite the lack of clarity in the decisions discussed in this chapter, a couple of lessons emerge. First, school authorities should not treat students differently based on their views on a particular issue. Thus, if the school permits students to wear T-shirts endorsing a pro-choice stance on abortion, they should not prohibit other students from wearing T-shirts that proclaim a pro-life viewpoint.

While litigation involving anti-LGBTQ dress code speech appears to have abated, the current moral panic[93] involving instruction and banned books may embolden anti-LGBTQ student speech. Leila Rafei of the American Civil Liberties Union wrote,

> As classroom censorship bills sweep state legislatures, schools are removing books by and about LGBTQ people, BIPOC, and other marginalized groups from curriculums and libraries at an unprecedented rate. This year, more than 111 bills aiming to limit discussions about race and gender in the classroom have been passed or introduced in state legislatures.[94]

An NBC report included interviews of Texas school librarians who spoke of their growing fears of being attacked by parents on social media or threats of criminal charges: "Some said they've quietly removed LGBTQ-affirming books from shelves or declined to purchase new ones to avoid public criticism—raising fears about what free-speech advocates call a wave of 'soft censorship' in Texas and across the country."[95] Within this environment of heightened negative perceptions of LGBTQ persons, students who wear T-shirts with negative statements about the LGBTQ community may provoke a disruptive response that may not have occurred in a less contentious time.[96]

This is reminiscent of the *Tinker* court's admonition: "In our system, students may not be regarded as closed-circuit recipients of only that which the State chooses to communicate. They may not be confined to the expression of those sentiments that are officially approved."[97] This challenge carries with it the seeds of the right of the government through its schools to pursue legitimate ends[98] and the rights of students in public schools to take and communicate a different position. Justice Robert H. Jackson in *West Virginia State Board of Education v. Barnette* in 1943 wrote, "Freedom to differ is not limited to things that do not matter much. That would be a mere shadow of freedom. The test of substance is the right to differ as to things that touch the heart."[99]

"[The] Constitution cannot control such prejudices but neither can it tolerate them. Private biases may be outside the reach of the law, but the law cannot, directly or indirectly give them effect."—*Palmore v. Sidoti*, 466 U.S. 429, 433 (1984).

NOTES

1. Michael Kent Curtis, "Be Careful What You Wish For: Gays, Dueling High School T-Shirts and the Perils of Suppression," *Wake Forest Law Review* 44 (2009): 433. The author writes in the conclusion, "Overtly racist speech is no longer respectable and to an increasing degree overtly homophobic speech is also losing its respectability. Schools are a special and difficult case, but as more and more students join

the crusade for tolerance and acceptance of gays, anti-gay speech becomes less and less acceptable." Ibid., 494.

2. 478 U.S. 675 (1986).
3. 861 F. Supp. 157 (D. Mass. 1994).
4. Ibid., 170.
5. 801 F. Supp. 1526 (E.D. Va. 1992).
6. Ibid., 1537 (internal citations and quotation marks omitted).
7. 827 F. Supp. 2d 392 (E.D. Pa. 2011).
8. Ibid., 409.
9. *K.J. v. Sauk Prairie School District*, 11-cv-622-bbc, 2012 U. S. Dis. LEXIS 187689 (W.D. Wis. 2012).
10. Ibid., *17.
11. Ibid., *22.
12. 259 F. Supp. 2d 575 S. D. Tex. 2003).
13. *Taylor v. Roswell Independent School District*, 714 F.3d 25 (10th Cir. 2013).
14. Ibid., 30.
15. Ibid., 38.
16. Ibid., 39.
17. 2005 U.S. Dist. LEXIS 33871 (W.D. N.Y. 2005).
18. Ibid., *3.
19. Ibid.
20. Ibid., *4.
21. Ibid., *5.
22. Ibid.
23. Ibid., *16.
24. Ibid., *25.
25. *T.A. v. McSwain Union Elementary School*, 2010 U.S. Dist. LEXIS 71973 (E.D. Cal. 2010).
26. Ibid., *4.
27. Ibid.
28. Ibid., *2.
29. Ibid., *3.
30. Ibid., *5.
31. Ibid., *10.
32. Ibid., *11. It is interesting to note that the court found that the school's testing period was important to the issue of disruption. This points to the special nature of the school in that an activity specific to public schools, statewide testing, was dispositive in a free speech determination.
33. A Pennsylvania family sued when their middle school child was told to turn his homemade T-shirt inside out because it proclaimed, "Abortion is not healthcare." The parents sued. The school district agreed to change its dress code policy and paid the Christian legal group Alliance Defense Fund, which represented the student's family, $16,000 in legal fees. A spokesperson for the school board said, "From an economic standpoint, a settlement of this matter is warranted and has been recommended by counsel for the district." Tracy Gordon, "Student, School Settle Abortion

T-Shirt Dispute," Religion News Service (March 19, 2010), https://religionnews.com/2010/03/19/the-family-of-a-pennsylvania-student-who-was-told-by-school-officials-to-tu/.

34. Scott Wegener, "'Jesus Is Not a Homophobe' T-shirt Lands Ohio School District in Federal Court," Newsnet5 (March 4, 2012), http://newsnet5.com/dpp/news/state/jesus-is-not-a-homphobe-t-shirt-ohio-district-in-federal-court.

35. 567 F. Supp. 2d 1359 (N.D. Fla. 2008).

36. Ibid., 1363.

37. Ibid., 1364.

38. Ibid., 1375.

39. Ibid., 1370.

40. Ibid., 1375.

41. Ibid., 1374 (internal citations and quotation marks omitted). The judge took the principal to task, writing, "Davis's conduct, in the capacity of a role model and authority figure is particularly deplorable in light of studies which confirm the vulnerability of gay and lesbian students." Ibid., 1370.

42. 445 F.3d 1166 (9th Cir. 2006).

43. GLSEN (formerly the Gay, Lesbian & Straight Education Network), in collaboration with the United States Student Association, sponsors the National Day of Silence each year. This student-focused event enables students to call attention to anti-LGBT (lesbian, gay, bisexual, and transgender) "name-calling, bullying, and harassment in schools" through their day-long vow of silence. Many students carry cards that read:

> *Please understand my reasons for not speaking today. I am participating in the Day of Silence, a national youth movement bringing attention to the silence faced by lesbian, gay, bisexual and transgender people and their allies in schools. My deliberate silence echoes that silence, which is caused by name calling, bullying and harassment. I believe that ending the silence is the first step toward fighting these injustices. Think about the voices you are not hearing today. What are you going to do to end the silence?*

GLSEN, Day of Silence (2009), http://www.dayofsilence.org/downloads/dos_speaking_card_09. pdf.

In response to the National Day of Silence, the Alliance Defense Fund sponsors a counter-protest called "The Day of Truth." The Day of Truth "seeks to combat anti-gay bias in schools" (The Associated Press, "Group makes noise over Day of Silence" ABC News (April 12, 2005, https://www.nbcnews.com/id/wbna7477978.). During the Day of Truth, some students have chosen to express contrary views about supporting GLBT students. In a few cases, students have worn T-shirts to school condemning homosexuality.

44. *Harper*, 445 F.3d 1171.

45. Ibid.

46. Ibid., 1172.

47. Ibid., 1177, quoting *Tinker v. Des Moines Independent Community School District*, 393 U.S. 503, 508.

48. Ibid., 1178 (internal citation omitted).

49. Ibid.
50. Ibid.
51. Ibid., 1179.
52. Ibid.
53. Ibid., 1183.
54. See Amanda L. Houle, "From T-Shirts to Teaching: May Public Schools Constitutionally Regulate Anti-Homosexual Speech?" *Fordham Law Review* 76, no. 5 (2008): 2477–2510. "This Note further posits that *Harper* properly interpreted *Tinker*, and that schools may regulate anti-homosexual hate speech in the interests of protecting the rights of homosexual students." Ibid., 2503.
55. *Harper*, 445 F.3d 1178–79.
56. Ibid., 1179.
57. 145 F. Supp. 2d 1068 (D. Minn. 2001).
58. Ibid., 1070.
59. The court specifically rejected Elliott's argument that the school was promoting homosexuality. Ibid., 1073. To the contrary, the court stated, "By displaying posters and lists of staff members who are willing to talk about issues of sexuality . . . , the school has made a conscious and commendable effort at creating an environment of tolerance and respect for diversity." Ibid.
60. Ibid., 1074.
61. Ibid., 1073.
62. Ibid.
63. 383 F. Supp. 2d 965 (S.D. Ohio 2005).
64. Ibid., 967.
65. Ibid., 968.
66. Ibid., 973.
67. Ibid.
68. In *Solmitz v. Maine School Administrative District No. 59*, 495 A.2d 812, 815 (Me. 1985), an instructive case on the juxtaposition of a tolerance day and disruption, the Supreme Judicial Court of Maine upheld a lower court ruling denying relief that would have permitted a Tolerance Day at Madison High School. The court upheld the unanimous vote of the school board to cancel the Tolerance Day for the "safety, order, and security" of Madison High School after it received threats to keep children home, of parents intending to monitor the Tolerance Day assembly, picketing the school, and bomb threats and sabotage of the school's furnace. Ibid., 815–16.
69. *Nixon*, 383 F. Supp. 2d 966.
70. 636 F.3d 874 (7th Cir. 2011).
71. *Nuxoll v. Indian Prairie School District*, 523 F.3d 668, 676 (7th Cir. 2008).
72. *McMillen v. Itawamba County School District*, 702 F. Supp. 2d 699 (N.D. 2010).
73. Ibid., 702.
74. Ibid.
75. Ibid., 706.
76. Author, "McMillen v. Itawamba County School District," *American Civil Liberties Union* (n.d.), https://www.aclu.org/cases/fulton-ms-prom-discrimina

tion#:~:text=STATUS%3A%20VICTORY!,a%20judgment%20against%20the%20school.

77. *Zamecnik v. Indian Prairie School District*, 636 F.3d 874, 876 (7th. Cir. 2011).

78. *Peck v. Baldwinsville Central School District*, 426 F.3d 617, 620 (2d Cir. 2005).

79. Kozinski asserted, "As Judge Gilman said in his persuasive dissent in *Boroff v. Van Wert City Board. Education*, 220 F.3d 465 (6th Cir. 2000), 'school officials are not free to decide that only one side of a topic is open for discussion because the other side is too repugnant or demoralizing to listen to." Ibid., 474 (Gilman, J., dissenting) (citing *Tinker*, 393 U.S., 508).' I couldn't have said it better" Ibid., 1194–95 (Kozinski, J., dissenting).

80. 579 F.3d 502 (5th Cir. 2009).

81. Ibid., 505.

82. Ibid., 506.

83. Ibid., 510.

84. 391 U.S. 367 (1968).

85. *Palmer v. Waxahachie Independent School District*, 579 F.3d 510 (5th Cir. 2009).

86. Ibid.

87. Ibid.

88. Ibid., 511.

89. Ibid.

90. Ibid.

91. Ibid.

92. Ibid., 513.

93. See Todd A. DeMitchell, Richard Fossey, and Terri A. DeMitchell, "Moral Panic, Banning Books, and the Constitution: The Right to Direct the Upbringing and the Right to Receive Information in a Time of Inflection," *Education Law Reporter* 397, no. 3 (2002): 905–28.

94. Leila Rafei, "How LGBTQ Voices Are Being Erased in Classrooms," ACLU (June 27, 2022), https://www.aclu.org/news/lgbtq-rights/how-lgbtq-voices-are-being-erased-in-classrooms-censorship. See also, Jeffrey Sachs and Jonathan Friedman, "Educational Gag Orders Target Speech about LGBTQ+ Identities with New Prohibitions and Punishments," PEN America (February 15, 2022), https://pen.org/educational-gag-orders-target-speech-about-lgbtq-identities-with-new-prohibitions-and-punishments/.

95. Mike Hixenbaugh, "Banned: Books on Race and Sexuality Are Disappearing from Texas Schools in Record Numbers," NBC News (February 2, 2022), https://www.nbcnews.com/news/us-news/texas-books-race-sexuality-schools-rcna13886. One school librarian stated, "I'm no saint . . . . I got out because I was afraid to stand up to the attacks. I didn't want to get caught in somebody's snare. Who wants to be called a pornographer? Who wants to be accused of being a pedophile or reported to the police for putting a book in a kid's hand?" Ibid. See also Meghan Roos, "Among Banned Books in U.S. Schools, 41 Percent Have LGBTQ+ Themes: Report,"

Newsweek (September 22, 2022), https://www.newsweek.com/among-banned-books-us-schools-41-percent-have-lgbtq-themes-report-1745557.

96. Todd A. DeMitchell, Richard Fossey, & Terri A. DeMitchell, "A Moral Panic, Banning Books, and the Constitution: The Right to Direct the Upbringing and the Right To Receive Information in a Time of Inflection," *Education Law Reporter* 397 (2022): 905–928.

97. *Tinker v. Des Moines Independent Community School District*, 393 U.S. 503, 509 (1969).

98. See *Rosenberger v. Rectors & Visitors of the University of Virginia*, 515 U.S. 819, 833 (1995) ("when the government appropriates public funds to promote a particular policy of its own it is entitled to say what it wishes.").

99. 319 U.S. 624, 642 (1943).

7

Gendered Dress Codes

"Your Skirt Is Too Short; It Is a Distraction."

> One concern is that many dress codes are explicitly gender-specific, targeting girls but not boys, or at least selectively enforced such that they impact female students disproportionately.[1]

> Boys' dress codes tend toward "Don't promote drinking, drug use, gangs, violence, or racism" while girls' codes imply "Don't be sexy": no shorts, low-cut tops, bare midriffs, thin-strapped tanks, or exposed bra straps.
>
> Most disturbing is the reason given for the girls' rules: Their "provocative" clothing is "distracting" to other students in the learning environment."[2]

This chapter reviews the all-too-prevalent and unfair application of dress codes to female students. Dress code provisions often single out female students to a greater degree than male students. Law professors assert in the *Harvard Civil Rights–Civil Liberties Law Review*,

> The vast majority of school dress codes regulate the appearance of female students much more than male students. There are more rules specifically directed towards young women; more rules that as a practical matter apply only or mostly to women; and more effort exerted enforcing allegedly gender neutral rules against women.[3]

Generally, dress codes are intended to protect the school environment and its students from what is inappropriate, whereas school uniforms are intended to improve the school environment. The Nebraska ACLU asserts that gendered dress code provisions "subject girls to discipline, humiliation and anxiety" as well as inviting biased enforcement.[4]

If this is true, and it is a valid proposition, why do these code provisions target female students to a greater degree than male students? While the answer may be found in the mores of the wider society and traditional expectations for males and females, the issue of student dress is the province of the school's rules and enforcement mechanisms.

Two types of dress codes focusing on female students will be explored. First, what are the types of clothes that females are prohibited from wearing at school, and what do they tell us about the meaning of these targets? In addition to identifying the types of clothing, an exploratory study will be discussed that seeks to identify meaning from the choices of what female students may not wear. The second section will discuss what female students must wear, further identifying the role of females.[5] A school's dress code sends signals and communicates beyond the clothes themselves. What does the prohibition tell us about how the wearer is viewed?

GENDERED DESS CODES: SPAGHETTI STRAPS AND FINGERTIPS

"Girls, particularly those with ample hips and breasts, are almost exclusively singled out, typically told their outfits will 'distract boys.' As if young men cannot control themselves in the presence of a spaghetti strap."—Peggy Orenstein, "Opinion: The Battle Over Dress Codes," *New York Times* (June 13, 2014), https://www.nytimes.com/2014/06/14/opinion/the-battle-over-dress-codes.html

There has been a shift toward asking whether dress codes which on the surface appear to apply equally to both male and female students in effect single female students out for additional scrutiny. University of Chicago professor of law Justin Driver raises the question about the constitutionality of gendered dress codes, writing, "Perhaps predictably, a large number of the school's restrictions can be understood as communicating anxiety about clothing that is thought to display young women's sexuality."[6] Furthermore, he cautions that prohibitions on what students may wear to school present "opportunities for arbitrary discrimination."[7]

For example, a white female teacher discussing the unequal enforcement of a dress code at her high school stated, "When you have a Black girl and a White girl walking down the hall, and the Black girl gets called out. I mean, that's the issue."[8] One area that highlights this inequality, which will be discussed in chapter 8, is grooming provisions of dress codes. Brookings senior fellow Andre M. Perry writes of the 2019 Barbers Hill Independent School

District case in Mont Belvieu, Texas, "To have a backward rule around hair length for boys is bad enough, but the way the policy seems to target Black students is even worse."[9]

It was reported in 2017 that a senior female student at Hickory Ridge High School in Harrisburg, North Carolina, was accused of violating the school dress code because her shirt showed her collarbone and shoulders.[10] In 2018 a seventeen-year-old Florida high school student received a severe sunburn over the weekend. Wearing a bra exacerbated the pain of the sunburn; consequently, she decided not to wear one to school, opting instead to wear an oversized dark shirt. She was dress-coded for not wearing a bra even though there was no specific code section requiring female students to wear a bra.[11]

The issue of whether dress codes unfairly target female students is captured by Peggy Ornstein's *New York Times* op-ed piece above (textbox 7.1). Furthermore, a reporter in Oregon spoke with female students about their experiences with dress codes, reporting,

> The young female students are tired of male teachers warning them they can see their bra straps or having to wear duct tape over ripped jeans. . . . They're frustrated with being told they are distracting the boys if they show their shoulders, and with being taken into the hallway to conduct the "fingertip test" to see if their shorts are long enough. And they're sick of watching their male counterparts break the rules daily, seemingly without consequence.[12]

A new type of challenge to dress codes has surfaced that is not necessarily rooted in free speech: Are dress codes discriminating against female students by singling them out for restrictions based on "gendered" expression?[13] Many of these challenges have been initiated by students. For example, a student petition was circulated at a New England middle school. It stated:

> Dear Mr. XXX,
> I want to bring to your attention the issue among girls regarding the length of shorts required by the dress code. I believe that it should be changed from the bottom of our fingertips to the bottom of our fists or knuckles. In my opinion the dress code for the length of shorts at school needs to be changed.
>
> This past week the weather got up to 85 degrees fahrenheit [*sic*]. On this day there were quite a few girls were wearing leggings or jeans. I talked to them and found that they wore long pants because they did not have any shorts that were dress code. Most shorts either don't fit dress codes or they are so long that they are almost capris. Most girls have to go to many different stores just to find a few pair of shorts that fit the dress code. There is even a price difference between dress code and other shorts. At most stores there is about a five dollar difference. This difference can add up quickly. Just buying five pairs of shorts

can create a 25 dollar difference. This can even represent a financial burden for families.

Not to mention, dress codes targets [*sic*] in unfair ways. It is not fair, boys were never told they couldn't wear their favorite pair of shorts, so why is it fair for girls to be told that they can't wear theirs? By changing it to our fists families can save money, girls don't have to wear jeans in very hot weather, girls won't have to go to several different stores just to get a few pair of shorts, and girls can wear a variety of different shorts without having to worry about being dress coded.

Thank you for your time. I hope you will consider my request of changing the length of shorts to our fists. I appreciate you [*sic*] time and hope you will consider.

Sincerely,
Students of XXX School[14]

Student protests targeted dress code provisions that primarily were aimed at female students, and these types of protests have increased in the last several years.[15] Students also started the movement End Discriminatory Dress Codes in School, which as of November 12, 2022, had garnered 1,317 petitions with 619,275 supporters.[16]

"[The] Constitution cannot control such prejudices but neither can it tolerate them. Private biases may be outside the reach of the law, but the law cannot, directly or indirectly give them effect."—*Palmore v. Sidoti*, 466 U.S. 429, 433 (1984).

Bertram Trail High School in St. Johns County, Florida, similarly became the target of student and parent protests in May 2021. Eighty female students' yearbook pictures were edited with "digitized bars or ill-matching splotches of fabric" to cover bare shoulders or low necklines because the photos were deemed in violation of the student dress code.[17] In the same yearbook, pictures of a group of male students in swimsuits were not retouched.[18] The dress code was changed to gender-neutral language soon after a picture of Riley O'Keefe's yearbook original photo alongside the retouched photo went viral.

A complaint was filed with the US Department of Education Office for Civil Rights (OCR). The complaint included the retouched yearbook pictures of female students. The complaint also included the following:

In addition, the Complainant said staff subject female students to dress code sweeps, in which female students are lined up in the hallways while staff determine whether they are in violation of the dress code. As an example, the

> Complainant described a March 2021 incident at Bartram Trail High School. The Complainant said staff lined up ninth-grade, female students and, if they had on tank tops and a hoodie, told them to remove their hoodie, which then meant they only had on a tank top, which is a dress code violation. The Complainant also said that staff told the female students to hold their hands above their heads to see if their shirt showed their bell[ies].[19]

OCR defined their investigation of the St. Johns County School District on the issue of whether the school district subjected female students to "discrimination on the basis of their sex in connection with enforcing dress code requirements."[20] In other words, the investigation asked whether the district's dress code and the way it was enforced against female students violated Title IX.

ACLU Florida joined the push against the district's dress code policy. The ACLU's July 30, 2021, electronic communication to the board chair and superintendent first commended them for their willingness to adopt a gender-neutral dress code policy. The communication then pivoted to the legal concerns of the policy. Specifically, the ACLU attorneys and president wrote,

> it appears that school officials within the School District have been selectively enforcing the dress code against girls in a manner that reinforces invidious sex stereotypes in violation of the Fourteenth Amendment to the U.S. Constitution, Title IX of the Education Amendments of 1972, Article I § 2 of the Florida Constitution, and the Florida Educational Equity Act.[21]

The Distracted Male: Who Is Responsible?

When she was a Harvard law student in 1982, law professor Mary Whisner pointed out how regulation of female appearance sexual objectifies them. She compared how a federal district court ruled on a dress code case underscored female responsibility for male responses, writing,

> Thus, a federal district court may hold a school's prohibition of dungarees for boys unconstitutional but distinguish that school's "prohibiting scantily clad students because it is obvious that the lack of proper covering, particularly with female students, might tend to distract other students and be disruptive of the educational process and school discipline."[22]

Some forty years later, Sandra Bernadel, a fellow at the National Women's Law Center, stated, "Dress codes are definitely sexist. They put the onus on girls to not be distracting or not call attention to themselves instead of putting the onus on all students to respect everyone's body."[23]

The gendered restrictions are in large part based on the premise that if female students wear *X*, the boys will be distracted from their studies. The argument is that the girls are responsible for the distractibility of boys. In other words, boys cannot help themselves, and the female students therefore must protect boys from themselves by creating a "distraction-free learning zone" for the male students. This argument in a New Jersey dress code protest inspired the hashtag #IAmMoreThanADistraction.[24]

The distracted-male rationale places the interests of males over the interests of females. It "reinforces sexism with the message that girls should cover up or change to meet the needs of the male students."[25] For example, a high school student wrote on a Change.org petition:

> I am going to show my legs, I am going to show my shoulders, I am going to show my stomach. Not only because it is extremely hot outside, but there is nothing wrong with those parts of my body. Nor is there anything wrong with yours. It's not distracting any other students, and if it is we should teach our students not to sexualize and objectify each other. We all have a body and that is okay, we should not have to hide it for the sake of someone else's unjustified discomfort.[26]

The Change.org petition was part of a 2021 protest at Grossmont High School. Some of the students were upset over portions of the dress codes they viewed as misogynistic and sexist. The dress code prohibited about twenty items or styles, most aimed at female students.[27]

In 2022, two eighth grade female students in a West Virginia middle school reported to the school board that their female principal, during an assembly with female students, made inappropriate comments about the dress code. She discussed the ban on wearing pajamas, crop tops, and ripped jeans. But she also stated, according to the students, "that they did not want boys to be distracted by our clothes and they said that if we get touched inappropriately while wearing these clothes to not tell the school because they won't do anything."[28]

The pronoun "they" was not explained. Whether there were more school administrators or teachers who took part in the discussion is not clear. What is clear is the message delivered to the middle school female students: that the boys were going to "touch" girls because of the clothes that they wore and the school would not consider these violations to be worthy of attention. This is an unacceptable response from school authorities tasked with providing a supportive and safe school environment for female and male students.

Body Shaming

One type of discriminating response to female student clothing choices is body-shaming, or as some called it, "slut-shaming."[29] The issue of body-shaming, while prevalent in dress code enforcement, sometimes extends beyond being coded. The case of the altered yearbook photos of Bartram High School students discussed above is one example of this.[30]

The argument around body-shaming is twofold. First, the clothing choices that are available for female students to purchase are limited and not designed to meet school dress codes. Law professor Meredith Johnson Harbach notes that the production and marketing of "sexy" clothing highlights sexuality in child and teen sizes.[31] She cited Catherine Pearlman, a licensed clinical social worker and associate professor of social work, who, tongue-in-cheek, invited the school principal on a blog to go shopping. "To reward you for treating my daughter with such concern, I am cordially inviting you to take my daughter shopping," she wrote. "Now, don't forget that you will have to find something in the stores that also meets with your dress code requirements."[32] Pearlman's five-foot-seven-inch daughter had been cited twice in a row for wearing shorts that were too short according to the fingertip rule.

The second concern is that dress regulations that focus on girls imply that a female student's body is something to be ashamed of, especially if the student is well-developed. Their bodies are the cause of inappropriate thoughts and possible misconduct. Being singled out and being required to wear identifying clothing makes girls self-conscious about their bodies.

Pearlman relayed a story regarding her daughter in which a teacher told her that she could not wear yoga pants "because the boys would get turned on and then be embarrassed." She stated,

> I think there are these subtle messages that sort of carry on that we shouldn't show something. Why shouldn't we show something? Because something's wrong with our body. We need to be teaching the boys what appropriate behavior is instead of teaching the girls that they have to cover up to protect themselves from the boys.[33]

Similarly, a fifteen-year-old who was given in-school detention for wearing shorts to her mid-thigh stated that the school was sending a message that she should cover up and be ashamed. She responded,

> If I show a little bit of my body, I'm considered a bad girl. Just because I'm wearing this doesn't mean that I want people to look at me sexually. I want to be seen as a woman. I don't want to have to feel bad about my body.[34]

Referring to the inequitable application of the dress code, the fifteen-year-old student stated, "If one kid with no boobs can get away with it, so can someone with large boobs."[35]

"Dress codes should be written to support student expression, safety and the overall educational goals of the school. Instead, many dress codes policies are rooted in harmful stereotypes. They imply that girls' bodies are shameful, distracting too other students, need to be covered, must be more regulated than boys' bodies, and that girls can't make their own decisions about their clothing."—"Grading Nebraska's Dress Codes," ACLU of Nebraska (2022), https://www.aclunebraska.org/en/grading-nebraskas-dress-codes

Gendered Dress Codes: A Policy Study*

While gendered dress codes have been challenged in the courts over the years, much of the early litigation centered on boys seeking to wear items that historically have been considered women's attire. For example, in a case involving a second grade male student, a Louisiana court of appeals upheld a school prohibition against boys wearing earrings. The state appellate court held that the gender-based regulation served three "legitimate"[36] objectives: (1) the avoidance of disruption and distraction in the classroom, (2) the fostering of respect for authority and discipline, and (3) the conformation to community standards.[37] Another earring case involving a fifth grade student used the same rationale to uphold the ban of males wearing earrings as "inconsistent with community standards."[38]

However, community standards often change over time. For example, Wisconsin school law scholar Suzanne Eckes and her colleagues note that courts have become increasingly sympathetic to students who desire to wear clothing that conflicts with traditional gender stereotypes: "[R]ecent cases suggest a general trend toward permitting students to wear gender nonconforming attire and accessories."[39] In other words, former taboos are giving way to new norms of acceptance.[40] However, as we note above a stubborn standard that has remained but is being challenged is the number of dress code provisions that target female students.[41]

Discipline based on improper student attire, especially if it involves suspension, must be based on properly adopted dress codes that are clearly communicated to the student body. Consequently, the wording of dress code policies is critical. What types of attire are banned? Does the policy offer general, vague, or overbroad statements that leave the interpretation to school administrators, or does the policy offer such specifics as the width of the strap

* This discussion is based on research on gendered dress code provisions published by Todd A. DeMitchell, Christine Rienstra Kiracofe, Richard Fossey, and Nathan E. Fellman, "Genderized Dress Codes in K–12 Education: A Mixed Methods Analysis of Law and Policy," *Education Law Reporter* 376 (2020): 421–47, 441–46.

of the top and fingertip rules for the length of clothing or the size of a rip in the jeans? I will briefly discuss a recent exploratory study of dress code policies.

For this exploratory study my colleagues and I analyzed dress code policies from New Hampshire, which was selected as a convenience sample. A list of school districts with a high school of at least three hundred students was generated and numbered. A random selection process was used to identify twenty-five school districts. Caution must be exercised in generalizing beyond this sample of school dress code policies. New Hampshire is a relatively racially homogenous population with a small urban population and a significant rural population.

Document analysis is a form of qualitative research that interprets documents. Public records, such as adopted school board policies, are one of the primary types of documents in which this method is used.[42] The analytical procedure involves selecting the policies (convenience random selection of policy manuals), "appraising (making sense of), and synthesizing data contained in the documents . . . organi[zing] [the data] into major themes, categories, and case examples."[43]

First, each dress code policy was reviewed for three categories: gender-neutral statements, sections specific to female students, and sections specific to male students. Statements that did not fit into one of these three categories were discarded as not applicable. The statements for each category were then hand-coded to identify emerging themes. This was an iterative process of winnowing until the final themes were arrived at. Throughout the process, "objectivity (seeking to represent the research material fairly) and sensitivity (responding to even subtle cues to meaning) in the selection and analysis of data from [the] documents" informed the document analysis.[44]

Careful attention was made to what constitutes a gendered policy statement. Males and females often wear clothing that is appropriate for both genders. For purposes of this research, policy sections that do not reference a particular gender or are capable of being applied to either a male or female gender are considered neutral.

Gender-Neutral Policies

While twenty-three of the twenty-five policies have gender-neutral sections, nine of the twenty-five policies do not have any gender-specific provisions. Instead, they rely on statements of purpose and intent. The two outlier policies do not offer any examples of prohibited clothing. One states,

> It is impossible to prescribe dress code regulations that cover every contingency. In the majority of cases, discretion and good taste should be guideline enough. In the event a particular dress style detracts from the educational process/atmosphere, constitutes a threat to the safety or self or others, or is in violation of lawful statutes, the school will take corrective action.

> In the event a particular dress style detracts from the educational process/atmosphere, constitutes a threat to the safety and health of self or others, or is in violation of lawful statutes, the school will take corrective action.[45]

The second policy states,

> All students are expected to be groomed and to dress appropriately with respect to the following criteria: Cleanliness and Safety, Educational Distraction, Offensiveness and Common Courtesy.[46]

These two policies are indicative of the general principles that are found throughout all twenty-five policies. The difficulty with these policies is that they have only general principles, with no examples to assist the school administration in enforcing the policy or students in complying with the policy. Such questions as what constitutes "good taste," "common courtesy," and "distract[ion]" are raised by these potentially vague requirements implicating the due process rights of the students.[47]

Apart from the two school district dress code policies cited above, all of the twenty-three other policies offered examples of prohibitions. The most often cited examples in the category of general, not gender-specific, code sections include the following examples, which are organized into prohibited types of speech, types of student attire, and clothing fit:

DRESS CODE PROHIBITIONS

Types of speech/communicative content

- Statements, depictions, and promotions of alcohol, drugs, tobacco
- Offensive, racist, vulgar language
- Sexual vulgarities/innuendos/explicitness
- Weapons and/or violence
- Promotes gangs and/or gang activity

Types of Student Attire

- Caps, headgear, bandanas, hoodies, and sunglasses
- Nylon and spandex
- Wearing undergarments as outer clothing
- Dangerous clothing like heavy chains, studded belts, and spiked bracelets
- Slippers and wheels attached to footwear

Clothing Fit

- Clothing that is too tight or too loose
- Exposed mid-section, buttocks, clothing covering the body from the armpit to the mid-thigh
- Shorts/tops must cover the top of the pants
- Visible underwear

References to Legal Standards

A number of dress codes in the New Hampshire study as well as dress codes throughout the nation, in addition to specific prohibitions (see the textbox above), include statements of the effects of the attire without specifically stating the content of the attire. These code sections most often reference the *Tinker* test standards. For example, Dress Code Policy #15 identifies the *Tinker* disruption standard as well as content-neutral standards. The policy reads, in pertinent part, "If a student's dress or grooming disrupts the educational process or climate, is unclean, or unsafe, the student will be removed from the class and asked to change."

Furthermore, Dress Code Policy #17 references the second prong of *Tinker*: "While it is the right of the student to express oneself by dressing according to his or her preference, the execution of this right must not interfere with the rights of others." Gender-neutral policies do not single out a student based on their gender, instead focusing on the effect or impact of the attire.

Policy References to Male Students

There are significantly fewer dress code restrictions that target male students to a greater degree than female students. Several can be described as covered by the gender-neutral prohibitions, but the practice seems to be aimed more at male attire. For example, the no-visible-underwear rule applies to female and male students, but the general prohibition also makes a specific reference to sagging pants ("pants worn at the hips"). The other specific prohibitions are muscle shirts and sleeveless undershirts. This statement was part of a gender-neutral section and is an example of targeting a specific gender. The section on inappropriate clothing reads, "Exposed undergarments or clothing meant to be worn as undergarments. This includes men's sleeveless undershirts."[48]

Furthermore, the reference to muscle shirts in the codes is aimed at males. Male-specific dress sections are found in five of the twenty-five dress code policies. As will be explored below, clearly, male students have fewer restrictions associated with their gender than their female peers.

Policy References to Female Students

"In the wake of 'new' styles that girls have been sporting in the late 20th and early 21st centuries, a pervasive panic over dress has ensued in most North American high schools."[49] As seen above, there are some, although very few, specific references to restrictions targeting males, while sixteen of the randomly selected dress codes have sections specific to female students. In these sixteen policies, there are a total of sixty-two specific references to female attire.

Most of the prohibitions do not specifically state that they are targeted at females, but the descriptions of the attire clearly leave the reasonable person to conclude that that the section refers to females. That the categorizing involved a subjective application of the standard "of reasonably associated with females as opposed to males" does not mean that alternative conclusions of exclusion and inclusion of specific sections of the policy are reasonable. With this limitation, we found the following.

The sixty-two female references were sorted into two themes: coverage and sexualization. Coverage refers to covering parts of the body that are usually covered through social convention and in some cases laws on decency. These dress code sections typically refer to covering breasts and buttocks. The second theme of sexualization refers to attire that does cover but has more of an imputed sexuality. For example, straps to a top do not cover breasts or buttocks, but they are prohibited because they are considered "sexy." Similarly, leggings cover but are considered sexy because they accentuate the female body, and backless tops do not reveal breasts but are also considered under certain dress codes to sexualize the student.

An example of the difference between the two themes is found in policies on tank tops. The qualifier applied to tank tops that places them in the coverage theme is "low-cut." The two themes should not be considered separate and distinct, with no bright line distinction. Instead, they are often mutually reinforcing. For example, Dress Code #20 prohibits "[a]pparel that is sexually suggestive, including clothing whereby its brevity or sheerness is sexually explicit. This includes pants, skirts, tops, and other clothing which does not provide appropriate coverage."

Coverage

Coverage refers to the thirty-seven provisions that focus on clothing that is too short and fails to cover specific parts of the female anatomy. Specifically, they refer to breasts, midriffs, and buttocks, as well as skirts, dresses, and shorts that expose the inner thighs. Essentially, these dress code provisions state that a female student must sufficiently cover up body parts that may be considered sexualizing the student and, as some commentators have argued, distracting the male students from their studies.

Examples of coverage sections that pertain to female students include short skirts (eight policies), short shorts (seven policies), exposing breasts/cleavage (seven policies), and transparent clothing (six policies). Length is an important part of many of these dress code sections. The dress code from school district #5 captures coverage and the measurement of coverage for female students. It reads,

> Clothing that is transparent or does not adequately cover the body (spaghetti straps, halter, midriff tops, or low cut tank tops. Shoulder straps will be at least 2″ (or three fingers wide). Short shorts and skirts are inappropriate. Shorts must have an inner seam of 5″ or more. For skirts, stand straight drop hands straight to sides and add an inch of length. When wearing leggings, untucked shirts must cover waist and 1 inch in length. Skin should not be visible any time around the waist.[50]

These types of dress code policies appear to assert that female students must be subjected to measurements, as if moral climate of the school and the responsibility for upholding it and not distracting male students from their proper duty of getting an education can be reduced to inches or the length of fingers.

Sexualization

The second theme of sexualization ($N = 25$) refers to attire that does cover requisite body parts but has more of an imputed sexuality, thus sexualizing the student through her choice of clothing. The majority of these dress code sections focus on what holds up the top the female student is wearing. The terms "spaghetti straps," "tube tops," "halters," "backless," and "strapless" are found in nineteen of the twenty-five provisions.

A master of arts thesis study of fifty-six California high school dress policies and student handbooks found that 109 items out of 288 (38 percent) targeted female students. In addition to sheer/transparent clothing (51.79 percent), the two most cited apparel items were tube/strapless tops (64.9 percent) and spaghetti/string straps (35.71 percent). In addition, restrictions regarding clothing that exposes the student's midriff (82.14 percent) and low-cut necklines (48.21) are prevalent in dress codes.[51]

Finally, it is also important to note that "coverage" and "sexualization" should not be considered as entirely distinct categories. Lack of coverage can be construed as the sexualization of a student. Consequently, there is a dynamic tension between the margins of the categories.

Midriff-revealing tops are one of those crossover apparel items that involve covering, in this case the stomach, presumably because uncovered stomachs are sexually provocative. Nevertheless, as one commentator has noted, "The stomach and belly button are not inherently sexual body parts, as sex is not their primary function."[52]

Pajamas and lingerie were also found in the dress code policies. Both could be considered inappropriate and pajamas could be listed as gender neutral, but lingerie is clearly female attire and is often considered sexy sleepwear.

As seen in the discussion above, there are many prohibitions on student dress that are gender neutral. They are designed to reinforce a "proper" atmosphere for students. However, the dress codes also identify gender-specific clothing, with the majority of gendered sections targeting female students.

As seen in Raby's study, discussed below,[53] female students seek flexibility and equality with their male counterparts in wearing clothing that reflects the weather and allows for comfort, but they are also conscious of and concerned about the self-objectification of female students[54] that can take place through wearing clothing that is inappropriate for school.

However, the problem with this theme is the ascribing of "provocative" to female clothing; in other words, the dress choice of females is presumed to be designed to attract attention from males. Too often women's dress tacitly depicts them "as sexualized objects who have the potential to affect and disrupt men."[55]

THONGS AND TANK TOPS: THE CONUNDRUM OF THE "SLUTTY" LOOK[56]

While there is push for greater latitude for female students' school clothing choices, there are boundaries; while not totally distinct, female students do identify what clothing lays on the other side of the boundary—the slutty look. Professor Felicity Grace Perry, in her focus group research with urban high school students in New Zealand, stated that the "slut" is a prevalent figure in the teen world.[57] Sluts are portrayed as wearing revealing clothes and scantily dressed, with unfavorable assumptions about their sexual practices and intelligence. Perry considers the female students' reactions to the "slut" or "skank" look is highly complex.

The voice of female students, while sprinkled through popular literature, is often scarce as a research artifact. We will next explore their voice by discussing research by Rebecca Raby.[58]

Raby conducted eight focus group sessions during 2004 and 2005 involving secondary school students in Southern Ontario, Canada. While the focus groups gathered to discuss school rules, dress codes received particular attention. Male students were part of the groups; however, Raby focused on how the female participants negotiate dress codes, "both contest[ing] and reproduc[ing] institutional and peer regulation of girls' dress."[59] Her study explored the fine line that girls walk between being "attractive and provocative"[60] in their choice of school attire. While this research is instructive in adding the voice of female secondary students, caution must be exercised in generalizing beyond the four corners of this research.

The plaintiffs in court cases based on free speech often discuss the negative impact that dress codes have on their self-expression. However, the participants in Raby's focus groups argued that "tank tops, spaghetti straps, short skirts and muscle shorts should be acceptable when it is hot rather than mentioning a desire to look good, to be sexy, or to experience pleasure in their dress."[61] Participants focused on the practicality of clothing choices and also stated that the dress code rules on revealing clothing unfairly targeted female students.

For example, participants in Focus Group 1 stated:

Catherine: That's like the spaghetti strap rule is like kind of unfortunate because it's like for boys it's not a problem, and it's just like, "Sorry I am a female like its hot and I would like to wear a spaghetti strap tank top," but it's like "No, no you must not expose skin," which is kind of ridiculous cause—

Janice: You are not even showing anything, just your arm [laughs].

Catherine: Yeah you're really not; it is just your body; it's like "Oh no the human body."

—Rebecca Raby, "Tank Tops Are OK but I Don't Want to See Her Thong: Girls' Engagement With Secondary School Dress Codes," *Youth and Society* 41, no. 3 (2010): 340

A second issue that surfaced in the research was the lack of equity and inconsistency of enforcement of the dress code policy through the application of personal interpretation of what is inappropriate. They identified two groups, which they believe were singled out for more stringent enforcement. First, larger, more developed girls were more likely to be singled out for dress code infractions. The second group, Focus Group 8, noted was that students who wear black were more likely to be coded.

A third theme of Raby's study was the problem of provocative clothing. This section begins with a criticism of the clothing industry and boys' preference for seeming to "prefer to go out with girls who wear sleazy clothes and the fashion industry for shaping girls' dress."[62] Broader cultural patterns impact the decision of what to wear to school.

While wanting the practicality to wear clothes that fit the temperature and the activity, the participants shared a concern and a "hostility" against girls wearing revealing clothing and expressed "a consequent appreciation of dress codes,"[63] at least when targeting revealing clothing. Their criticism was often couched in the language of self-respect. For example, in response to the facilitator's question about provocative dress, "What does that mean, 'something degrading to themselves'?" Crystal from Focus Group 1 responded, "Uh, whorish. [laughing]," and Allison stated, "Basically, 'I have no self-respect, I'm going to flaunt myself in the hope of feeling loved.'"[64]

Despite the criticisms leveled at the dress codes, the participants identified common ground with the dress code goals. They lamented the revealing dress of their peers. The hostility was evident in the language choice of the students: "whorish, slutty, disgusting, disturbing, and wrong."[65] Several focus groups cited the importance of appropriate dress at school, identifying it as a special environment and not the mall or any other social gathering place.

Barbara from Focus Group 4 asked, "Why would you need to attract that kind of attention at school? I mean like who—like who are you there to impress when you're there for, like . . . education."[66] And, possibly in response to the riposte, "Well, if you don't like, don't look," Nicole (Focus Group 3) responded regarding revealing dress, "For me it's disturbing. Like 'great. You're wearing a thong, show it to your boyfriend, show it to someone who cares.'"[67] The participants, like Nicole, talked about the "forced gaze"—the idea that there was nowhere else to look.[68]

Raby concluded that there are gender inequalities in school dress codes. These inequalities are influenced by social factors outside of the school, yet they intrude inside the school environment. Female students are forced to negotiate a path that is ill-defined and fraught with contradictions, yet of consequence. While the obstacle to the practicality of dressing in response to the environment was an aggravation, the participants were not ready to completely abandon dress codes that target revealing clothing, even though the difference between revealing clothing and practical clothing may be difficult to define.

NO PANTS FOR FEMALE STUDENTS? THE AGE OF CHIVALRY IS OVER IN THE FOURTH CIRCUIT

"No, this is not 1821 or 1921. It's 2021. Women serve in combat units of our armed forces. Women walk in space and contribute their talents at the International Space Station. Women serve on our country's Supreme Court, in Congress, and, today, a woman is Vice President of the United

States."—*Peltier v. Charter Day Sch. Inc.*, 8 F.4th 251, 274 (4th Cir. 2021) (Kennan, J., concurring in part and dissenting in part)

One may have thought that an ancient and absurd custom[69]—no pants allowed for female students—would have been banished long ago, but the Fourth Circuit in 2022 in an *en banc* ruling rejected this dress code provision. The *en banc* court first held in what may be decision of first impression that "the plaintiffs have established that CDS acted under color of state law for purposes of Section 1983."[70]

The president and CEO of the National Alliance of Public Charter Schools and the executive director of the North Carolina Association of Public Charter Schools issued the following statement:

> We applaud the U.S. Court of Appeals for the Fourth Circuit's en banc decision today in *Peltier v. Charter Day School*, holding that charter schools are, in fact, state actors for federal equal protection purposes. We believe this is the right outcome, one that's supported by both caselaw and statute.
>
> The importance of this case could not be overstated, as it was the first time a federal appellate court considered whether public charter school students deserve the same constitutional civil rights protections as district public school students. The en banc court clearly and unequivocally affirmed that charter schools are public schools and, accordingly, must be bound by the US Constitution. Moreover, public charter school students have the same constitutional and civil rights as their district public school peers.[71]

It has been approximately fifty years since an Idaho state court said "no" to the no-pants rule; that prohibition has resurfaced. The section will discuss *Peltier v. Charter Day School, Inc.* But first we will first briefly discuss the similar 1973 Idaho dress code case.

The Joint School District No. 60, Bingham County of Idaho adopted a dress code that read, in pertinent part, "Girls are expected to wear dresses or skirts which are not more than two inches above the knee."[72] The board construed the section as banning slacks, pantsuits, and culottes. At the trial level, the school district lost. On appeal the defendant school district asserted that the trial failed to accept the "conclusively established by undisputable facts" that female students wearing culottes, slacks or pantsuits would

- have "a detrimental effect on the morals of the students";
- "result in unsafe conditions and safety hazards at the school";
- "lead[] to insubordination, rebelliousness and lack of respect for authority";

- lead to "an increased amount of physical contact and familiarity between boys and girls";
- result in a "loss of standards of conduct"; and
- have "a detrimental effect on emotional makeup and problems in the school district."[73]

In essence, the school district considered girls in pants threatening.[74]

The Idaho Supreme Court upheld the finding of trial court that there was no evidence to support the school board's contention that culottes, pants, and pantsuits were disruptive to school discipline or instructional effectiveness, nor did they have a detrimental effect on safety or morals. The school district lost and was prohibited from implementing the dress code.

However, in an Arkansas case decided in 1972, one year before *Johnson v. Joint School District No. 60 Bingham County*, while the school district allowed female students to wear pants to school, it had an interesting proviso: If the pants had an open front (a zipper), the student was required to wear a tunic or square-tailed blouse to hide the opening.[75] Side openings did not need to be covered up. One can only puzzle over the motivation for this degree of detail regarding a front zipper on female pants.

The District Court, *Peltier v. Charter Day School, Inc.*: Skirts-Only Dress Code "Perpetuated Harmful Gender Stereotypes"[76]

Charter Day School (CDS), a K–8 school, obtained a charter under state law for North Carolina in 2000. The school is part of four schools operated by Charter Day School, Inc., and managed under a contract by Roger Bacon Academy, Inc. (RBA).

Since its inception the school has "emphasize[d] traditional values," including a "traditional curriculum, traditional manners and traditional respect." For example, CDS teaches a "classical curriculum," utilizing a "direct instruction" method. Overall, as one board member explained, CDS operates "more like schools were 50 years ago compared to now."[77] The charter school trustees, parents, and community sought "to preserve chivalry and respect among young women and men in this school of choice."[78]

"Baker A. Mitchell, Jr., the founder of the school and the owner of the for-profit charter school management responsible for the day-to-day operations of CDS, defined chivalry as 'a code of conduct where women are treated, they're regarded as a fragile vessel that men are supposed to take care of and honor.' Mitchell further explained that, in implementing the skirts requirement, CDS sought to 'treat[] [girls] courteously and more gently than boys.'"—*Peltier v. Charter Day School, Inc.*, 37 F. 4th 104, 113 (4th Cir. 2022).

As part of this educational purpose, CDS implemented a dress code to "instill discipline and keep order so that student learning is not impeded."[79] Among other requirements, all students must wear a unisex polo shirt and closed-toe shoes, "[e]xcessive or radical haircuts and colors" are prohibited, and boys are forbidden from wearing jewelry. Female students are required to wear a "skirt," "jumper," or "skort."

Three sets of parents on behalf of their daughters sued in federal district court alleging a violation of the equal protection and Title IX based on the skirts-only requirement.[80] They asserted that the skirts requirement is a sex-based classification rooted in gender stereotypes that discriminates against them based on their gender. This case sits at the intersection of the growing concern that some dress code sections sexualize and shame female students by holding them to an unreasonable different standard than male students and potential ancient and absurd customs of community standards.

The plaintiffs submitted evidence and testified that the skirt requirement conveyed the message that girls were not equal to boys and that they should be less active than boys, thus empowering boys over girls.[81] The plaintiff students further asserted that the skirt regulation requires girls to wear clothing that is less warm and comfortable than the male students' pants and "more importantly, restricts plaintiffs' physical activity, distracts from their learning, and limits their educational opportunities."[82]

Additionally, they argued that the skirt policy sends a message that the comfort and freedom of the girls to engage in physical activity are less important than that of their male classmates. The plaintiffs asserted,

> The skirts requirement forces [the plaintiffs] to pay constant attention to the positioning of their legs during class, distracting them from learning, and has led them to avoid certain activities altogether, such as climbing or playing sports during recess, all for fear of exposing their undergarments and being reprimanded by teachers or teased by boys.[83]

The board argued that the skirt requirement supported its "traditional values" approach to education that is expressed in its policies and that a change in one policy "risks in advertently changing the broader goal."[84] These policies, the board maintained "work seamlessly together in a coordinated fashion in a disciplined environment that has mutual respect between girls and boys" by allowing students to act more appropriately toward the opposite sex.[85] While the board made much about its test scores and achievements, it did not offer any connection between the skirt requirement and academic achievement.

Judge Malcolm J. Howard concluded that "the skirts requirement causes the girls to suffer a burden the boys do not, simply because they are female."[86] The board failed to demonstrate that there were similar burdens between boys and girls because of the school uniform policy. The judge wrote,

> [The] plaintiffs in this case have shown that the girls are subject to a specific clothing requirement that renders them unable to play as freely during recess, requires them to sit in an uncomfortable manner in the classroom, causes them to be overly focused on how they are sitting, distracts them from learning, and subjects them to cold temperatures on their legs and/or uncomfortable layers of leggings under their knee-length skirts in order to stay warm, especially moving outside between classrooms at the School. Defendants have offered no evidence of any comparable burden on boys.[87]

The plaintiffs' expert, a developmental psychologist, testified that research shows requiring girls to wear skirts reinforcers gender roles in which girls are viewed as passive and lacking personal agency.

The district court held that the defendant charter school was a state actor for purposes of bringing the equal protection claim by the plaintiffs. Therefore, it must respect and protect the constitutional rights of its students. This issue takes on a large role after the *en banc* decision in 2022. Applying an equal protection analysis, the court held that the skirt requirement violated equal protection. But the court found for the charter school, holding that dress codes are categorically exempt from Title IX prohibitions. It held that the withdrawal of a regulation prohibiting discrimination in the application of appearance regulations indicates that there was no legislative history for adding dress codes to Title IX prohibitions.

This is an unusual case in that it was brought under equal protection rather than free speech and is one of the earliest, if not the earliest, cases involving dress regulations and a charter school. In *Peltier*, the concept of "traditional values" as an anchor for dress codes was called into question, as was the use of community norms to decide an equal protection analysis. The days when school authorities could regulate students' clothing based on poorly articulated "traditional values" are waning. As Howard stated, community standards "do not remain fixed in perpetuity."[88]

The Fourth Circuit Court of Appeals Decision: Title IX and Equal Protection

The appeal was argued on March 11, 2021, and decided on August 9, 2021.[89] The appellate court, while acknowledging that the case involved a "host of legal theories," limited its opinion to the complaints arising from the charter school's dress code relative to the Equal Protection Clause and Title IX.

Equal Protection Claim

The court began by holding that the Charter Day School is not a state actor for purposes of promulgating the school's dress code. Therefore, the court noted, "there is no state policy at all that requires, prohibits or regulates uniform policies,"[90] no coercive power of the state can be attributed to the state. Consequently, the charter school is not a state actor. On appeal to the full court of appeals, this central finding is revisited (see below).

Title IX Claim

The defendant charter school asserted that dress codes were not under the purview of Title IX. The circuit first held that the charter school through its private management firm was subject to Title IX regulations and that dress codes are within the authority of Title IX.

Having laid the foundation, the court of appeals turned to its analysis. Echoing the wording of Title IX, the court phrased the question as whether the skirt requirement excluded the plaintiffs from participation, denied them educational benefits, or treated them worse than other similarly situated students. The first two theories were disposed of quickly with a finding that the plaintiffs were excluded from participation and denied benefits, with the court concluding that it was "self-evident" and thus did not require additional analysis. However, the third theory that petitioners were subjected to discrimination on the basis of sex was less self-evident.

To answer the third criterion, the court posited two considerations. First, there must be an objective, individualized harm. Second, the plaintiffs must establish they are objectively worse off than similarly situated peers; they must also show that their sex is a but-for cause of that harm. On remand the plaintiffs carry the burden of demonstrating the presence of these two considerations.

Concurring in Part and Dissenting in Part

Judge Barbara Milano Keenan concurred in part and dissented in part. She agreed with her colleagues with the remand of the Title IX complaint. Keenan noted that she supported the district court's judgment that the skirt requirement harms female students by denying "these girls at this *public* school their constitutional guarantee of Equal Protection under the law."[91]

Keenan set the table for her dissent by emphasizing that Charter Day School was indeed a public school. She disagreed with the majority's finding that the defendant charter school was a private actor and not a state actor, asserting that schools were created by the North Carolina legislature and may only operate under the authority granted to them by the state through their charter. Consequently, CDS is not a government contractor that "builds bridges and dams"; it is "unambiguously" a public entity performing a state function, providing a free public education to its citizens.

Thus, its action of implementing the no-pants restriction was carried out under the color of law, as a state actor. Keenan opined that the petitioners had access to relief under the Equal Protection Clause and indicated she would affirm the lower court's finding that skirt requirement violated the Equal Protection Clause. She asserted that CDS offered only "harmful stereotypes" of how girls should look and behave to justify the sex-based classifications. Keenan concluded, "Therefore, I would hold that if CDS wishes to continue instilling these harmful beliefs in its students, CDS must do so as a private school without the sanction of the state."[92]

Rehearing *En Banc*: No Gender Stereotypes Allowed

> "Courts may not subjugate the constitutional rights of these public-school children to the facade of school choice."—*Peltier v. Charter Day School, Inc.*, 37 F. 4th 104, 123 (4th Cir. 2022).

The Fourth Circuit, sitting *en banc*, found that charter schools are public schools, thus state actors, and the charter school is subject to 42 U.S.C § 1983 lawsuits brought to secure the constitutional rights of its students. The dissent acknowledges this watershed decision while arguing against it, writing, "Prior to today, neither the Supreme Court nor any federal appellate court had concluded that a publicly funded private or charter school is a state actor under § 1983. The majority, however, breaks new ground."[93] This finding that CDS is a public school provides the legal foundation for the plaintiffs' assertion that the no-pants rule violates equal protection and Title IX.

The Fourth Circuit *en banc* court affirmed the district court's summary judgment for the plaintiffs' equal protection claim against CDS. It vacated its summary judgment in favor of the defendants on the Title IX claim and remanded it for further proceedings. We will review each of these findings below.

Charter Day School: A State Actor? Yes, Says the Full Court

Critical to the plaintiffs' equal protection claim under § 1983 was whether the defendants deprived the plaintiffs of a constitutional right and whether it was done under color of state statute, ordinance, regulation, custom, or usage. Merely private action, no matter how wrong or discriminatory, is excluded. The defendant must be a state actor.

CDS responded to the assertion that it was a public school by arguing that the school was merely a private entity fulfilling its contract (charter) with the state. North Carolina had not delegated its responsibility to educate the state's students; rather, the school was just providing a contracted service to the state. The court disagreed.

The majority provided several arguments in support of its conclusion that North Carolina charter schools are public schools. Their analysis included the following under North Carolina General Statute § 115C-218 *et. seq.*:

1. To fulfill the North Carolina Constitution mandate (N. C. art. IX, § 2, cl 1) to "provide by taxation and otherwise for a general system of free public schools . . . wherein equal opportunities shall be provided for all students," the legislature created traditional public schools overseen by a state board of education.
2. Charter schools may only operate under the authority granted to them by their charters with the state.
3. The charter school must design their curriculum to satisfy the state's student performance standards, "a requirement not applicable to non-public schools."[94]
4. The state may revoke a charter for noncompliance with the terms of the charter, poor student performance, or poor fiscal management.
5. Charter schools receive a funding allotment per pupil based on the amount provided for students attending traditional public schools.
6. Employees of charter schools, for purposes of providing certain state-funded employee benefits, are considered public school employees.

And finally, the authorizing charter school legislation clearly stated,

> A charter school that is approved by the State *shall be a public school* within the local school administrative unit in which it is located. All charter schools shall be accountable to the State Board for ensuring compliance with applicable laws and the provisions of their charters. (North Carolina General Statute § 115C-218.15[a])

Consequently, the *en banc* court found that North Carolina charter schools are "clothed with the authority of state law"[95] based on the unambiguous language of North Carolina's state law governing charter schools. Therefore, North Carolina exercised its sovereign authority to exercise a traditionally exclusive governmental function of operating the state's public schools, through its traditional and charter schools, to provide a free education to its citizens. Accordingly, CDS implemented its skirt requirement as part of an educational mission made possible because of state law and its authority granted to the school.

"Under these circumstances, we will not permit North Carolina to delegate its educational responsibility to a charter school operator that is insulated from the constitutional accountability borne by other North Carolina public schools."—*Peltier v. Charter Day School, Inc.*, 37 F. 4th 104, 121 (4th Cir. 2022).

Having determined that CDS is a state actor for purposes of § 1983, the court turned to the equal protection claim and discharged it quickly. Acknowledging that the school's rationale of teaching universal values of respect and kindness as a basis for the skirt requirement is not prohibited by the Equal Protection Clause, the court asserted that perpetuating "archaic" gender stereotypes in pursuit of such values is impermissible. CDS, in the opinion of the majority, "utterly" failed to provide a persuasive justification for the sex-based restriction. Consequently, there is no important government objective supporting the policy; therefore, the policy fails intermediate scrutiny, facially violating the Equal Protection Clause.

The Title IX Claim

The district court held that Title IX does not apply to sex-based dress codes. The plaintiffs' cross-appealed. They argued that the plain language rather than the US Department of Education's rescinding an earlier regulation on dress codes should prevail—no deference should be given to the department's regulatory decision. The defendants disagreed, asserting that the regulatory decision "manifested the agency's reasonable assessment" that dress code regulation is not authorized under the statute. In addition, they argued that the private management firm hired to handle the day-to-day operations, including the adoption of the dress code to meet the school's mission statement, is not a recipient of federal funds and thus not subject to Title IX.

The court disagreed with both of the defendants' arguments. First, the court easily dispatched the argument that RBA is not a recipient of federal funds because the funds flow to CDA. A recipient of federal funds, according to 34 C. F. R. § 106.2(i), is one to whom federal assistance is extended directly or through another recipient which operates an education program or activity. Furthermore, the Supreme Court, the court cited, held that recipients within Title IX are those who receive federal assistance either directly "or through an intermediary."

RBA receives 90 percent of its funding from the four schools operated by Charter Day School, Inc. Nearly all of these funds come from public sources, including the federal government. CDS uses its federal funds as part of the compensation of RBA services at its schools. RBA, the court held, receives federal assistance through an intermediary, CDS, and thus is a recipient and subject to Title IX.

The court next turned to the merits of the Title IX claim. Does Title IX apply to school dress codes that receive federal funds? In 1975, it added a regulation that prohibited discrimination "against any person in the application of any rules of appearance." The U.S. Department of Education revoked this regulation in 1982 in part because the "development and enforcement of appearance codes is an issue of local determination."[96] The majority rejected the argument that the 1982 revocation of the regulation means that Title IX does not apply to dress codes in schools.

Instead, the court argued that the unambiguous language and structure of Title IX encompasses sex-based dress codes. Furthermore, if the Congress had meant to exclude dress codes with gender-based prohibitions, it could have done so. Rather, Congress chose a general prohibition on discrimination followed by specific, narrow exceptions. The fact that Congress did not explicitly prohibit sex based codes does not suggest that such policies are beyond the application of Title IX. The court did not defer to the department rescission of appearance codes to the purview of Title IX.

Consequently, the majority held that the district court erred in granting summary judgment to the defendants and thus vacated and remanded it for an evidentiary proceeding on whether the plaintiffs were treated "worse" than similarly situated male students. In addition, it brought reviews of school dress codes on the basis of alleged discrimination on the basis of sex within the Fourth Circuit under Title IX.

Keenan, writing for the majority, also offered strong language about the ancient and absurd custom of requiring female students to wear skirts as "blatant gender stereotypes about the proper place for girls and women in society."[97] It is a violation of the Equal Protection Clause. The rehearing *en banc* vacated the district court's judgment on Title IX and remanded it for an evidentiary proceeding.

We Concur, We Dissent and The Possible "Parade of Horribles"?

Concurrences

In addition to the majority opinion, there were two concurring opinions and two dissenting opinions. The first concurring opinion primarily responded to the first dissent's position that North Carolina's charter schools are public schools was wrongly decided. The concurrence characterized the concerns voiced in the second dissent as a "parade of horribles" about what will happen as collateral damage with the majority's ruling that charter schools are public, thus entitling its students to constitutional protections like any other public school student.

Judge James Andrew Wynn, who wrote the concurrence joined by Judges Diana Gribbon Motz, Stephanie D. Thacker, Pamela A. Harris, and Keenan, characterized Judge J. Harvie Wilkinson's second dissent as lacking concrete legal or factual arguments. Instead, Wynn stated, Wilkinson "time travels back to the Middle Ages, dons knightly armor, and throws down the challenge gauntlet, presenting two broad policy arguments for why finding state action here is a bad idea."[98]

First, the majority's finding that charter schools are state actors, the dissent argued, will commence a "parade of horribles" leading to the slippery slope to "social homogenization," and mandated uniformity."[99] The supposed damage included curtailing student and parental choice, "extinguish[ing]" the place of historically Black colleges and universities, and the "slow strangulation of litigation" brought on by suing charter schools for unconstitutional conduct.[100]

The second policy argument, the dissent wrote, against finding CDS a public school will lead to charter schools enduring "scurrilous lawsuits" and will "extinguish the vibrancy provided by school choice," and "educational calcification" will "reign supreme."[101] These conclusory statements were offered as outcomes if charter schools are considered public schools with no substantiating evidence to support them. The first concurrence summed the second dissent's argument, writing,

> Stripped of its euphemisms, the second dissent's argument seems to be that subjecting schools like Charter Day to the demands of the Constitution will frustrate parents' imaginary prerogative to send their children to free, state-funded public schools practicing unconstitutional discrimination, thereby "stifling" educational progress. The premise underlying this argument is that state schools must be allowed *to experiment with unconstitutional discrimination* to honor "consumer[ ]" demand and achieve said "educational progress."[102]
>
> In the end, the second dissent's policy arguments must be rejected. The second dissent's borderline insulting insinuations regarding HBCUs do not support its flawed parade-of-horribles argument. And contrary to the second dissent's

insinuations, the specter of parental choice is not a trump card that gives North Carolina public schools license to practice unconstitutional discrimination.[103]

While the first concurrence focused on responding to the first dissent's argument that the CDS did not act under color of state law and thus could not be sued under § 1983 (CDS not being a public school), the second concurring opinion focused on the discriminatory aspect of the dress code requirement. Keenan wrote this opinion with Thacker joining, arguing that the skirt requirement is not "harmless in its effect on CDS' students."[104]

The real question left unanswered in the second concurrence, Keenan asserted, is what "is the full spectrum of success that female students *might have achieved* if they had not been subjected to the pernicious stereotypes underlying the skirts requirement."[105] This concurrence argued that it is irrelevant how well the students performed *despite* carrying the burden of unequal treatment; discrimination cannot be excused because its victims "are resilient enough to persist in the face of such unequal treatment."[106] The CDS imposed "traditional gender roles" on its students holding that its female students are "fragile," communicating a message of inferiority.

The Kennan concurrence concluded:

"But the skirts requirement, harmless as it may seem to the defendants, requires only a pull of the thread to unravel the lifelong social consequences of gender discrimination. In 2022, there is no conceivable basis for allowing such obstacles to girls' progress in our public schools."—*Peltier v. Charter Day School, Inc.*, 37 F. 4th 104, 136–37 (4th Cir. 2022) (Kennan, J., with Thacker, J., concurring)

CDS Is a Public School: The Dissent Says No

Two dissents were filed. The first dissent—CDS is not a public actor; thus its dress code decision is not subject to § 1983—was addressed in the first concurrence. Similarly, the second dissent—the impact of the skirts only provision—resulted in the second concurrence.

The first dissent, authored by Judge A. Marvin Quattlebaum joined by Judges Julius N. Richardson and Allison Jones Rushing, dissented in part from the majority and concurred in part. They concurred with the decision vacating the district court's position on Title IX and remanding the claim for further proceedings. The dissent focused on whether Charter Day School is a state actor.

First, the dissent asserted that the majority breaks new ground by deciding that the Charter Days School is a state actor. It "misconstrues and ignores" guidance from the Supreme Court and sister circuits. Consequently, the "casualty" is not just a dress code; rather, it may well be that all charter schools in North Carolina and in the other states that transform their charter schools as well into state actors, the dissent reasoned.[107] Thus, Quattlebaum asserted that parents would have limited choices. In addition, charter school students would still have legal recourse, just not Constitutional redress, for discriminatory actions by their charter school.

Not surprisingly, the dissent, concurrence, and majority analysis cited the same court cases but reached different conclusions about how the precedents applied to the current controversy. For example, both the majority and the dissent used the much-used 1982 U.S. Supreme Court decision in *Rendell-Baker v. Kohn*[108] to decide whether a private actor's actions are so significant that it is deemed to be that of the state. Specifically, the analysis must demonstrate that the state has outsourced or delegated certain obligations "traditionally the exclusive prerogative of the state."[109]

The dissent found no evidence in its case analysis to support a conclusion that CDS is a public school. The concurrence refuted the dissent's analysis and finding which argued that the state "did not coerce or compel the dress code generally or the skirts requirement specifically."[110] In addition, the dissent argued that providing a free public education is not the exclusive domain of public schools.

However, charter schools, by North Carolina law, cannot discriminate against students in admissions, cannot be affiliated with a religion or religious group, cannot charge tuition, must provide a curriculum that aligns with the state assessments, must administer end-of course tests, and must provide data needed for North Carolina school report cards. This does not even account for the full funding of student attendance consistent with all public schools using the same reporting documents. These requirements of a public school are not required of private schools or of homeschooling. If it walks like a duck and quack likes a duck, it is a public school (see textbox 7.11).

The North Carolina Charter Agreement reads (pursuant to G.S. 115C-218 et seq.) in pertinent part supporting the majority opinion that charter schools are public school:

> 1.2 In accordance with 115C-218.6, the SBE shall review the operations of each charter school at least once prior to the expiration of its charter to **ensure that the school is meeting expected academic, financial, and governance standards**; provided, the SBE may at its discretion review the operations of a charter school at any time the SBE deems it necessary and appropriate.

2.1 Pursuant to Article IX, Section 2, of the North Carolina Constitution and Part 6A of Article 16 of Chapter 115C of the North Carolina General Statute, **a Charter School is a public school and shall be accessible to all North Carolina students eligible to attend public schools under** 115C-218.45(a).

5.1 The Nonprofit shall ensure that the Public Charter School **complies with the Federal and State Constitutions and all applicable federal laws and regulations**, including, but not limited to, such laws and regulations governing employment, environment, disabilities, civil rights, children with special needs, transportation, and student records.

9.2 **The Nonprofit accepts and understands that for purposes of federal and state law, it is obligated to provide free and appropriate education and related services to children with special needs.**

9.4 **The Nonprofit shall be responsible for meeting the needs of English language learners in compliance with State and Federal law.**

12.2 **The Nonprofit is subject to the Public Records Law**, Chapter 132 of the General Statutes. This provision is effective upon the SBE's approval of the Charter Application.

12.3 **The Public Charter School is subject to all the provisions of Article 29 of Chapter 115C, entitled "Protective Provisions and Maintenance of Student Records."**

12.4 **The Nonprofit shall ensure compliance with the Family Educational Right to**

Privacy Act 42U.S.C. §1232g.
16.2 All Public Charter School administrators **must report to the SBE if an employee engages in physical or sexual abuse of a child** as listed in 16 N.C.A.C. 6C.0312.

20.3 The Public Charter School **shall comply with state and federal due process** requirements both in notifying students of conduct for which they may be suspended or expelled and in providing notice and hearing opportunities to students being recommended for exclusion. If the Public Charter School suspends a student with special needs, it shall continue to provide to the student all continuing education services to the extent mandated by federal and state laws and regulations.

23.0 **The Nonprofit agrees to be subject to the Open Meetings law** (Article 33C of

Chapter 143 of the General Statutes). This provision is effective upon the SBE's final approval of the charter application.

—North Carolina Charter Agreement, https://www.dpi.nc.gov/media/10389/open; emphasis added

Both used similar precedents to support their positions, but numbers win, and the majority, including the concurrence, had more numbers. CDS is a public school. The dissent lamented the ramifications of the "expansive" finding North Carolina charter schools to be state actors, stating that the majority's decision would have ramifications beyond North Carolina. The extent of the consequences was not stated, thus sidestepping how a charter school being a state actor harms the states' ability to "improve education by offering innovative educational choices for parents."[111]

Furthermore, Quattlebaum's dissent did not discuss how CDS and other North Carolina charter schools were innovating prior to *Peltier* and how following the *en banc* decision they would no longer be able to innovate. The change is that the charter schools must protect the constitutional rights of its students (e.g., equal protection, due process, search and seizure). The curriculum and instruction as well as the policies of the charter school are not affected by protecting the constitutional rights of students—or, at least, those "innovative practices" should not be predicated upon the removal of protections of a vulnerable student population.

Similarly, the second dissent, authored by Wilkinson and joined by Judges Paul V. Niemeyer and G. Steven Agee, agreed with Quattlebaum's analysis of state action—charter schools are not public schools. This dissent stated that the majority's decision would "drape a pall of orthodoxy over charter schools and shift educational choice and diversity into reverse."[112] The majority "has no clue" and misses the "whole purpose of the development of charter schools"—encouraging innovation and competition within state school systems." Wilkinson, furthermore, asserted,

> [The majority's] opinion is all about conformity. It is essentially dismissive of what charter schools might have to contribute, prejudging them as miscreants that must be brought to heel. *See,* e.g. , Majority Op. at 20 (worrying about the possibility of "blatant, unconstitutional discrimination committed by [charter] schools").[113]

The dissent swiveled from CDS as a public school/state actor to discuss the dress code. This part of the dissent is the focus of Kennan's second concurrence. The second dissent makes several points about "chivalric nature" of the CDS dress code supporting "traditional values," and "cultivating mutual respect among men and women."[114]

- "The [dress] codes are founded upon ideals of 'chivalry'. . . . 'Chivalry' harkens to the age of knighthood, defined as '[t]he brave, honourable, and courteous character attributed to the ideal knight.'"
- "To a great many people, dress codes represent an ideal of chivalry that is not patronizing to women, but appreciative and respectful of them."
- "CDS uses chivalry in an aspirational sense, not to recreate an earlier time in all of its particulars, but to capture the contemporary connotations of a chivalric order as one in which women are due from the very inception of schooling the greatest measure of respect."
- "For CDS, the dress code is an adjunct to an altogether lawful and legitimate view of education that relies upon a 'classical curriculum espousing traditional western civilization values.'"
- "The advent of new possibilities [for women] need not extinguish more traditional gender roles which lend stability to home and family and ultimately to society itself."[115]

Throughout this section of the second dissent, in which the age of chivalry is extolled and the importance of "traditional elements" should not be banished, the relationship between the argument why female students must be required to wear skirts is not made clear. What are these "traditional western civilization values" and how is requiring female students to wear skirts part of them? The requirement that female students wear skirts to school because it supports "traditional western civilization values" implies that for female students to not wear skirts to school is in opposition to the values, which must be stamped out. It is highly doubtful that Western civilization will fall because of female students wearing pants.

How, specifically, is wearing a skirt deserving of respect when wearing pants is not? Where is the "honor" in forcing female students to wear a dress in the second decade of the twenty-first century? The dissent argued for the dress code, stating, "But the new need not banish the old."[116] I agree with the majority and the concurrence that some practices, values, and/or customs should and must be banished as ancient and absurd.

In the last part of the second dissent, Wilkinson writes the epitaph for parental educational choice in the Seventh Circuit because CDS and North Carolina are held to be public schools. Parents will no longer have a choice, charter schools will cease to be innovative and will become just another interchangeable school in the "calcified," "unitary" public school system.

The touchstone parental choice Supreme Court cases of *Meyer v. Nebraska*[117] and *Pierce v. Society of Sisters*[118] were discussed. Together they identified that parents can choose between sending their children to either a public school or a private school (and later homeschooling as the third choice) in order to meet compulsory education laws. These cases and their progeny have not granted to parents the right to control the education that their children receive.[119] Finding that charter schools are state actors does not change the calculus of parental choice in a public school, private school, or homeschooling.

The dissent quoted Chief Justice John Marshall in the seminal 1819 case *Trustees of Dartmouth College v. Woodward* as support for the contention that the majority changed the CDS charter. Wilkinson wrote, "From the fact, then, that a charter of incorporation has been granted, nothing can be inferred, which changes the character of the institution, or transfers to the government any new power over it."[120] The dissent points to no specific section of the charter that was changed by the majority to anchor this charge.

However, according to the court of appeals, the charter schools of North Carolina, including CDS, have operated as public schools since their charters were approved. The enabling legislation has not changed; the law identified charter schools as public schools since their inception. The only change that the dissent has strenuously argued against is that the charter school students' constitutional rights have been recognized; thus, the charter was changed.

What evidence does the dissent provide that supports a proposition that parents will pull or are pulling their children from charter schools because charter schools can no longer abridge their children's constitutional rights? Is the dissent tacitly stating that parents choose charter schools because they are not state actors but will leave after learning that are and have always been public schools? And it was parents who recognized that their children's charter school is a public school brought the lawsuit to secure rights for their children because CDS is a public school.

Wilkinson concluded, "In short, state action doctrine must not be warped to extinguish the vibrancy provided by school choice." Are the floodgates of litigation extinguishing the "vibrancy of school choice," as the dissent fears have been opened, or should this gate be open to children who attend public schools, including charter schools, to protect their rights?

However, the litigation is not over. The defendant, Charter Day School, Inc., filed a writ of certiorari with the US Supreme Court in September of 2022.[121] The question presented to Supreme Court is "[w]hether a private entity that contracts with the State to operate a charter school engages in state action when it formulates a policy without coercion or encouragement by the government."[122] The question is based on the Supreme Court case *Rendell-Baker v. Kohn*, discussed above.[123]

While a number of conservative organizations and a few religious organizations submitted amicus curiae briefs in support of the petitioners, eleven states submitted amicus briefs asking the court to accept the petition. The states argue that the *Peltier* decision threatens government intrusion on the pedagogical independence central to charter schools.[124]

The Supreme Court on January 9, 2023, asked the Biden administration to weigh in on whether the justices should hear the case.[125] Clearly at this stage of the appeal, the court appears posed to hear the case, which would have a wide-ranging effect beyond the specific issue of requiring female students in a publicly funded charter school to wear skirts: "Much more than a mere sartorial regulation is at stake, as demonstrated by the plethora of amicus briefs filed by conservative religious organizations urging the court to take the case."[126]

However, on June 26, 2023 the Supreme Court sidestepped the issue, and denied certiorari. We will have to wait for another day and another Court to resolve the issue of whether charter schools act as state actors (public schools).[127]

As seen in the textbox above, the defendant signed a charter agreement that specifically states its responsibilities not just to the State but also to the students it serves. Students under 5.1 are guaranteed, among other rights, their civil rights. Rights, such as free speech, due process, and equal protection, that cannot be protected are but a shadow of true rights. But essentially the charter school has stated that it does not have to follow that provision and potentially other pedagogical restrictions contained in the charter agreement asserting that it is an interference in their pedagogy.[128]

A dress code case that targets female students appears to be morphing into a broader front by which public charter schools want the freedom to operate as private schools but be secure in their state financial support. There is no parental recourse in private schools for alleged violations of their children's constitutional rights. Will the same be true for public charter schools should the Supreme Court side with CDS?

CONCLUSION

The Fourth Circuit Court's *en banc* affirmation that the skirt requirement for female students is indefensible and is instead an ancient and absurd custom that should be confined to the dustbin of history is correct. The pathway forward for female students is smoothed by these developments but is not yet a completed task and may be made harder depending on the Supreme Court.

Female students must still navigate many unreasonable burdens to equally access a public education.

While ending a skirt requirement may seem trivial at first glance, the message sent by such restrictions has an impact. The elimination of these types of regulations that perpetuate confining and inappropriate stereotypes about how females should look and act is an important task for educators and education. However, this does not mean that the path forward is always clearly marked and free of obstacles.

For example, the previously discussed research on gendered dress codes identified coverage and sexualization as two categories of female specific dress code regulations. While arriving at the conclusion that a skirts-only rule is unsupportable seems reasonable, drawing the boundary between what is an acceptable coverage requirement and what is sexualizing and thus stigmatizing of young girls and young women is much more difficult.

How thick do straps on tops have to be? Should the length of a girl's fingertips be the arbiter of whether their choice of clothing violates the norms of the school? What constitutes cleavage, not as an anatomical description but as a leering focus for male students?

Schools are not just a meeting place for youth for purposes of recreation and social interaction. They are places dedicated to learning, adolescent development, and preparation for informed citizenship. In her doctoral dissertation at the University of Southern California, Jillian Raymond asserts that cultural values are transmitted and perpetuated through organizational policies and practices, of which education is not an exception. Consequently, a school's "dress code sends messages beyond the clothes."[129]

An issue associated with gender that has garnered general attention has focused on transgender and nonbinary students. Dress code polices that target gender raise concerns about whether protections for transgender or nonbinary students are protected. A 2022 US Government Accountability Office report on dress codes found no protections in its review of a nationwide sample of dress codes for these students. Clearly deserving of further discussion among education policymakers as how to best address the concerns of expressions of gender identity in public schools.[130]

We should and must review the content of the messages that we send to our students. How students can and must present themselves in the unique setting of a school is part of the education and preparation for life beyond the schoolhouse gate. The need to provide a suitable, welcoming, and supportive environment necessitates identifying and eliminating ancient and absurd customs; it also requires educators to identify the appropriate and reasonable boundary between the coverage and sexualization of female students and appropriate attire for the school environment.

Table 7.1 Gender-Specific Clothing Prohibitions. Estimated Percentage of Districts That Prohibit Clothing Items Typically Worn by Female and Male Students

Clothing Items	*Percentage*
Female Clothing	
At least one clothing item typically worn by females, e.g., tops with low-cut necklines, shoes with heels of a certain height, nylon and spandex, and clothing that is sheer or transparent/translucent	90.3
Midriff-bearing tops and/or spaghetti straps	75.9
Short skirts or shorts	75.4
Leggings worn as pants	30.7
Male Clothing	
At least one clothing item typically worn by males (no examples were provided)	68.8
Sagging pants	55.6
Muscle shirts	46.2

Source: Jacqueline M. Nowacki, *K–12 Education: Department of Education Should Provide Information on Equity and Safety in School Dress Codes* (Washington, DC: US Government Accountability Office GAO-23-105348 K-12 Education, October 2022), 11, https://www.gao.gov/assets/gao 23 105348.pdf

NOTES

1. Meredith Johnson Harbach, "Sexualization, Sex Discrimination, and Public School Dress Codes," *University of Richmond Law Review* 50 (2016): 1043. The author catalogued several examples of the sexualization of female students, including the following:

> In Evanston, Illinois, school officials banned leggings because they were "too distracting" for boy students. In New Jersey, high school girls were prohibited from wearing strapless dresses to prom because they, too, were "distracting." In Florida, a new student who inadvertently violated her school's skirt rules was made to wear a so-called "shame suit": red sweatpants and an oversized neon yellow shirt that said "Dress Code Violation."

Ibid., 1039–1040; internal citations omitted.

2. Starshine Roshell, "The Ugly Sexism of School Dress Codes," *Week* (July 2, 2016), http://theweek.com/articles/633222/ugly-sexism-school-dress-codes. The author further questions the targeting of female students and male distraction, writing,

> In Montana, a teenager was cited for violating her school's dress code for not wearing a bra under her T-shirt—and told her that her appearance has made a male teacher "uncomfortable." Since her own comfort was the reason she'd gone braless, it must be asked: Whose comfort is a priority? Is requiring bras and different than requiring girls to wear slips or girdles or corsets? And would an A-cup student have been given a pass?

Ibid.

3. Deborah M. Ahrens and Andrew M. Siegel, "Of Dress and Redress: Student Dress Restrictions in Constitutional Law and Culture," *Harvard Civil Rights–Civil Liberties Law Review* 54 (2019): 103–104. The authors further write, "These lopsided

codes not only impose more restraints on the ability of female students to express themselves and to pursue their autonomous choices but also focus a disproportionate amount of female students' attention on policing their own appearance and sexuality." Ibid., 104.

4. "Grading Nebraska's Dress Codes," ACLU of Nebraska (2022), https://www.aclunebraska.org/en/grading-nebraskas-dress-codes.

5. This discussion is based on prior research on the *Peltier* court cases. Richard Fossey and Todd A. DeMitchell, "*Peltier v. Charter Day School*: A Charter School's Regulation Requiring Female Students to Wear Skirts is Ruled Unconstitutional," *Teachers College Record*, ID Number: 22803 (May 22, 2019); Todd A. DeMitchell, Christine Rienstra Kiracofe, Richard Fossey, and Nathan E. Felman, "Skirts, Yes, Pants, No: Gender Specific Dress Codes, and 'Ancient and Absurd Customs'? *Peltier v. Charter Day School, Inc.*," *Education Law Reporter* 471 (2021): 471–82.

6. Justin Driver, *The Schoolhouse Gate: Public Education, the Supreme Court, and the Battle for the American Mind*, (New York: Pantheon Books, 2018), 132 (*see* asterisk).

7. Ibid., 131.

8. Alyssa Pavlakis and Rachel Roegman, "How Dress Codes Criminalize Males and Sexualize Females of Color," *Phi Delta Kappan* (September 24, 2018), https://kappanonline.org/pavlakis-roegman-dress-codes-gender-race-discrimination/.

9. Andre M. Perry, "School Dress Codes and Grooming Codes Are the New 'Whites Only' Signs," Brookings Institution (February 14, 2020), https://www.brookings.edu/blog/brown-center-chalkboard/2020/02/14/school-dress-and-grooming-codes-are-the-new-whites-only-signs/.

10. Galen Sherwin, "5 Things Public Schools Can and Can't Do When It Comes to Dress Codes," ACLU (May 30, 2017), https://www.aclu.org/blog/womens-rights/womens-rights-education/5-things-public-schools-can-and-cant-do-when-it-comes.

11. Jillian R. Friedmann, "A Girl's Right to Bare Arms: An Equal Protection Analysis of Public-School Dress Codes," *Boston Law Review* 60, no. 8 (2019): 2547, n. 4.

12. Natalie Pate, "Salem-Keizer Public Schools to Revamp Dress Code Students Consider 'Archaic' and 'Sexist,'" *Statesman Journal* (Salem, Ore.) (June 18, 2019), https://www.statesmanjournal.com/story/news/education/2019/06/18/salem-keizer-school-district-dress-code-policy-students-protest/1433039001/

13. Kira Barrett, "When School Dress Codes Discriminate," *NEA Today* (July 24, 2018), http://neatoday.org/2018/07/24/when-school-dress-codes-discriminate/. See also Matt Zalaznick, "School Districts Loosen Dress Code after Gender-Bias Complaints," *District Administration* (July 16, 2018), https://www.districtadministration.com/article/school-districts-loosen-dress-codes-after-gender-bias-complaints.

14. Todd A. DeMitchell, Christine Rienstra Kiracofe, Richard Fossey, and Nathan E. Fellman, "Genderized Dress Codes in K–12 Education: A Mixed Methods Analysis of Law & Policy, *Education Law Reporter* 476 (2020): 432.

15. See Linda Ditch, "Feeling Singled Out, Female Students Protest High School's Dress Code," *Kansas Reflector* (September 21, 2021), https://kansasreflector.com/2021/09/21/feeling-singled-out-female-students-protest-high-schools-dress-code/; Emily Bloch, "'We're Not Going to Stop': High School Students across

Jacksonville Demand Dress Code Reform with Protests," *Florida Times-Union* (August 27, 2021), https://www.jacksonville.com/story/news/education/2021/08/27/high-school-students-across-duval-county-protest-dress-code/5614624001/; Nadra Nittle, "Lawsuits, Complaints and Protests Are Upending Sexist School Dress Codes," *The 19th* (January 12, 2022), https://19thnews.org/2022/01/school-dress-code-challenges/; Asia Grace, "Teens Slam School's 'Sexist' Dress Code: 'It Perpetuates Rape Culture," *New York Post* (June 9, 2021), https://nypost.com/2021/06/09/teens-bare-bellies-to-protest-schools-sexist-dress-code/. In protest regarding the dress code prohibition about showing stomachs, students staged a protest by wearing crop tops with the inscriptions written across their stomachs, "Distraction," "It's not my fault," and "Am I distracting?" The protest also included the typed message, "If children's midriffs distract you, you should not be working with children."

16. "Movement—End Discriminatory Dress Codes in School, Change.org (n.d.; accessed November 12, 2022), https://www.change.org/m/end-discriminatory-dress-codes-in-school?source_location=petition_page&source_event=movement_indicator&petition_id=30238411.

17. Suzette Hackney, "Edited Bartram Trail High School yearbook photos are as inherently sexist as they are unsightly," *USA Today* (May 24, 2021), https://www.usatoday.com/story/opinion/2021/05/24/bartram-trail-florida-yearbook-photos-edited/7417017002/. The yearbook company offered reprints of the yearbook with the original pictures of the eighty female students. Joe McLean and Ashley Harding, "Yearbook Company Offers Free Reprints after Bartram Trail High Female Photo Editing Fiasco," News4JAX (June 3, 2021), https://www.news4jax.com/news/local/2021/06/02/yearbook-company-offers-refunds-after-bartram-trail-high-female-photo-editing-fiasco/.

18. Nittle, *supra* note 15.

19. Letter from Michella Vaughn, Office for Civil Rights, Compliance Team Leader to Tim Forson, Superintendent, St. Johns County School District, OCR Complaint No. 04-21-1208 (June 14, 2021), 1–2, https://s3.documentcloud.org/documents/20891249/us-doe-investgiation-of-st-johns-county-dress-code-complaint.pdf.

20. Ibid., 2.

21. Linda S. Morris et al., "ACLU Warns Florida School District Its Dress Code Policies are Discriminatory," ACLU Florida (July 30, 2021), https://www.aclufl.org/sites/default/files/field_documents/st._johns_county_dress_code_aclu_advocacy_letter.pdf.

22. Mary Whisner, "Gender-Specific Clothing Regulation: A Study in Patriarchy," *Harvard Women's Law Journal* 5 (1982): 77, citing *Bannister v. Paradis*, 316 F. Supp. 185,189 (D. N.H. 1970) (emphasis added by Whisner).

23. Isabella Grullon Paz, "'Sexist,' 'Racist,' 'Classist': Georgia 8th Grader Challenges School Dress Code," *New York Times* (September 6, 2021), https://www.nytimes.com/2021/09/04/us/politics/mask-dress-code-protest.html.

24. Brenda Alvarez, "Girls Fight Back against Gender Bias in School Dress Codes," *NEA Today* (January 6, 2016), http://neatoday.org/2016/01/06/school-dress-codes-gender-bias/.

25. Jillian Raymond, *K–12 Dress Codes and Gender Equity: An Examination of Policy and Practice of Dress Code Implementation*, unpublished doctoral dissertation (University of Southern California, 2019), 15.

26. Karen Kucher, Karen Pearlman, and Alex Riggins, "Police Detain, Release Four Grossmont High Students after Dress Code Protest 'Escalated,'" *San Diego Union* (September 13, 2021), https://www.sandiegouniontribune.com/news/public-safety/story/2021-09-13/police-respond-to-grossmont-high-after-student-protest-escalates.

27. Ibid.

28. Madeline List, "Principal Told Girls to Follow Dress Code or Boys May Touch Them, Students in WV Say," *News & Observer* (Raleigh, N.C.) (April 6, 2022), https://www.newsobserver.com/news/nation-world/national/article260171360.html.

29. See Eliza Murphy, "Student Forced to Wear 'Shame Suit' for Dress Code Violation," ABC News (September 4, 2014), https://abcnews.go.com/US/student-forced-wear-shame-suit-dress-code-violation/story?id=25252041 (requiring students to wear red sweat pants and an oversized neon yellow shirt with the statement "Dress Code Violation). See also Laura Bates, "How School Dress Codes Shame Girls and Perpetuate Rape Culture," *Time* (May 22, 2015), http://time.com/3892965/everyday-sexism-school-dress-codes-rape-culture/.

30. Alla Dastagir, "Those Infamous Edited Yearbook Photos and Society's Obsession with Girls' Bodies: 'You Can't Win,'" *USA Today* (May 25, 2021), https://www.usatoday.com/story/life/health-wellness/2021/05/25/sexist-dress-codes-and-altered-yearbook-photos-teach-girls-body-shame/7429562002/.

31. Harbach, *supra* note 1, 1942.

32. Kelly Wallace, "Do School Dress Codes End up Shaming Girls?" CNN, May 30, 2017, https://www.cnn.com/2017/05/30/health/school-dress-codes-body-shaming-girls-parenting/index.html.

33. Ibid.

34. Ibid.

35. Ibid.

36. The US Supreme Court declared that a class based upon gender must survive "intermediate scrutiny." *Reed v. Reed*, 404 U.S. 71 (1971). "To withstand constitutional challenge. . . . classifications by gender must serve important governmental objectives and must be substantially related to achievement of those objectives." *Craig v. Boren*, 429 U.S. 190, 197 (1976).

37. *Jones v. W.T. Henning Elementary School*, 721 S0.2d 530, 532 (La. App. 1998).

38. *Hines v. Caston School Corporation*, 651 N.E.2d 330, 336 (Ind. App. 1995).

39. Suzanne Eckes, Todd A. DeMitchell, and Richard Fossey, "Breaking Social Norms at Prom: Is There a Constitutional Right to Wear Gender Nonconforming Attire at the Prom?" *Principal Leadership* (April 2015): 12.

40. For example, noting some of the dress code restrictions from the study in Todd A. DeMitchell, Richard Fossey, & Casey Cobb, "Dress Codes in the Public Schools: Principal, Policies, and Precepts," *Journal of Law & Education* 29 (2000):

31–49, and comparing them to the New Hampshire random sample of dress code policies found that the following restrictions from 2000 do not appear in the current research: no makeup, no black lipstick, no Butt Naked apparel, no athletic girdles, no cross-dressing, no visible tattoos, no hair rollers, no swimming attire, no beard, and no prescribed hair length for males. Ibid., 44. It is noteworthy that what was forbidden in 2000 was not even mentioned twenty years later in New Hampshire. Twenty years from now, will educators find that now-accepted student dress restrictions were not more than an "ancient and absurd custom"?

41. For example, a 2019 *Wall Street Journal* article noted that "[c]lothing once considered taboo is now permitted as more districts across the U.S. relax student dress code policies, deemed disproportionately targeted at females, and move toward more gender-neutral or suitable dress codes. Tawnell D. Hobbs, "Schools Relax Dress Codes in Bid to End Body Shaming," *Wall Street Journal* (July 13, 2019), https://www.wsj.com/articles/schools-relax-dress-codes-in-bid-to-end-body-shaming-11563010202.

42. "An Introduction to Document Analysis: Triad 3," *Research Methodology in Education* (March 9, 2016), https://lled500. trubox.ca/2016/244.

43. Glenn A. Bowen, "Document Analysis as a Qualitative Research Method," *Qualitative Research Journal* 9 (2009): 28.

44. Ibid., 32.

45. Dress Code Policy #16. The dress code policy is in the files of the author.

46. Dress Code Policy #11. The dress code policy is in the files of the author.

47. For a discussion on vagueness as a principle of due process and the use of the reasonable person standard in a school law student discipline case, see,

> If people of common intelligence must guess at an enactment's meaning and differ as to its application, the law is unconstitutionally vague and is void. Accordingly, an enactment must define the prohibited conduct with sufficient definiteness such that an ordinary individual understands just what conduct is prohibited and must define the prohibited conduct in a manner discouraging arbitrary and discriminatory enforcement.

*Wiemerslage v. Maine Township High Sch. Dist.*207, 824 F.Supp. 136, 139–40 (N.D. Ill. 1993).

48. Dress Code Policy #25. The dress code policy is in the files of the author.

49. Shauna Pomerantz, "Cleavage in a Tank Top: Bodily Prohibition and Discourses of School Dress Codes," *Alberta Journal Educational Research* 53 (2007): 373.

50. Dress Code Policy #5. The dress code policy is in the files of the author.

51. Jaymie Arns, *Undressing the Dress Code: An Analysis of Gender in High School Dress Code Policies*, unpublished master of arts thesis (Sacramento State University (2017).

52. Amber Thomas, "The Sexualized Messages Dress Codes Are Sending to Students," *The Pudding* (February 2019), https://pudding.cool/2019/02/dress-code-sexualization/.

53. Rebecca Raby, "Tank Tops Are OK but I Don't Want to See Her Thong: Girls' Engagement with Secondary School Dress Codes," *Youth and Society* 41, no. 3 (2010): 333.

54. See Lara Winn and Randolph Cornelius, "Self-Objectification and Cognitive Performance: A Systematic Review of the Literature," *Frontiers in Psychology* (January 28, 2020), https://www.ncbi.nlm.nih.gov/pmc/articles/PMC6997128/. The authors write:

- "Objectification theorists posit that exposure to sexually objectifying behavior, images, etc., leads women in particular to adopt an objectifying self-perspective."
- "While self-objectification is often narrowly defined as the adoption of a third-person perspective on the body, the originators of objectification theory define self-objectification as occurring when individuals 'treat themselves as objects to be looked at and evaluated.'" (internal citation omitted)

Ibid.

55. Jessica Wolfendale, "Dangerously Provocative," Dangerous Woman Project (July 4, 2016), http://dangerouswomenproject.org/2016/07/04/dangerously-provocative/.

56. For an insightful analysis of African American female students, see Edward M. Morris, "Ladies or Loudies? Perceptions and Experiences of Black Girls in Classrooms," *Youth and Society* 38, no. 4 (2007): 490–51. In his two-year ethnographic study, he identified the term "hoochie mama" as someone whose clothing is described as "overly provocative" and "inappropriate." In other words, the equivalent of a slutty look.

57. Felicity Grace Perry, "The Slut at School: Sex, Dress and Authenticity," in *Fashion-Wise*, ed. Maria Vaccarella and Jacquelyn Foltyn (Leiden: Brill, 2013): 141–47.

58. Raby, *supra* note 53.

59. Ibid., 334.

60. For a discussion of provocative dress, see Wolfendale, *supra* note 46, 618, writing, "The social privileging of male sexual desire occurs when men's sexual desire is taken as a 'given' that women must try to monitor and negotiate through their behavior and outfits."

61. Raby, *supra*, note 53, 339–40.

62. Ibid, 340. Patricia (Focus Group 1) stated, "But you know what's really wrong though, that all girls' clothes are made to be a slut." Ibid.

63. Ibid., 343.

64. Ibid., 343–44.

65. Ibid., 345.

66. Ibid., 344

67. Ibid.

68. Ibid., 346. Nicole (Focus Group 3) stated about revealing clothing, "This girl that was in my tech class in Grade 9. We all sat on stools, and she'd sit in front of me and she'd pull her thong out of her pants, so you could see it when she sat down. I'm just like [look of surprise]. And then I'd ask her 'could you please not do that,' and she's like 'look somewhere else!' It's like 'where else do you look?' There!" Ibid., 347.

69. See *Morrison v. State Board of Education*, 461 P.2d 375, 383 (Cal. 1969) (citing a list of conduct that was once considered immoral and unprofessional that had come to be considered "ancient and absurd customs.").

70. *Peltier v. Charter Day School, Inc.*, 37 F.4th 104, 123 (4th Cir. 2022).

71. Nina Rees and Rhonda Dillingham, "National Alliance Statement on 4th Circuit Court of Appeals En Banc Ruling on Charter Schools" National Alliance of Public Charter Schools (June 14, 2022), https://www.publiccharters.org/latest-news/2022/06/14/national-alliance-statement-4th-us-circuit-court-appeals-en-banc-review.

72. *Johnson v. Joint School District No. 60 Bingham County*, 95 Idaho 317, 317 (1973).

73. Ibid., 318.

74. Whisner, *supra* note 22, 103.

75. *Wallace v. Ford*, 346 F. Supp. 156, 158 n. 1 (E.D. Ark. 1972).

76. McKenna Oxenden, "Court Sides with Girls Who Sued over School's Skirt Requirement," *New York Times* (June 17, 2022), https://www.nytimes.com/2022/06/17/us/nc-school-dress-code-skirts-lawsuit.html.

77. *Peltier* , 37 F.4th 104, 113 (*en banc*).

78. Ibid. For example, the defendant further explained that "young men were to hold the door open for the young ladies and to carry an umbrella, should it be needed. Ma'am and sir were to be the preferred forms of address. There was felt to be a need to restore, and then preserve, traditional regard for peers." Ibid.

79. Christian Day School, 2019–2020 Parent and Student Handbook, section "Purpose," http://charterdayschool.net/wp-content/uploads/2019/09/CDS-Inc.-Parent-Student-Handbook-2019-20-Updated-0190620.pdf. The section reads,

> *Dress Code*: The School requires all students to wear a uniform to instill discipline and keep order so that student learning is not impeded. The School has designed its dress code to reflect the standards of the community of parents who have chosen to send their children to the School. It has also made sure to do so in a way that actively promotes its educational mission and focus. Use of uniforms also helps promote a sense of pride and of team spirit, as every student is a member of the academic team.

Ibid., 5.

80. *Peltier v. Charter Day School, Inc.*, 384 F. Supp.3d 579, 587 (E.D. N.C. 2019).

81. *Peltier*, 37 F.4th, 114.

82. *Peltier*, 384 F. Supp.3d, 584.

83. Ibid., 587.

84. Ibid., 588.

85. Ibid., 596. This seems to argue that the dress of girls influences the behavior of boys, once again placing the responsibility for boys' behaviors on the actions and decisions of girls. There also did not appear to any data provided to support the asserted causal connection between skirts and the actions of male students toward female students.

86. Ibid., 597.

87. Ibid. Furthermore, the court found that "[w]hile defendants emphasize that the uniform policy is most frequently enforced against boys for failure to wear a belt, there is no evidence that wearing a belt inhibits the boys' ability to fully participate in the programs or activities of the School." Ibid.

88. Ibid., 596.

89. *Peltier*, 8 F. 4th 251.

90. Ibid., 266.

91. Ibid., 275 (Keenan, J., concurring and dissenting) (emphasis in original).

92. Ibid., 281.

93. *Peltier* , 37 F.4th 104, 137 (*en banc*) (Quattlebaum, J., dissenting). Judges Richardson and Rushing join dissenting in part and concurring in part, and Judges Wilkinson, Niemeyer, and Agee join dissenting in part.

94. Ibid., 116.

95. Ibid., 118.

96. Ibid., 128, citing Nondiscrimination on the Basis of Sex in Education Programs and Activities Receiving or Benefiting from Federal Financial Assistance, 47 Fed. Reg. 32,526 (July 28, 1982).

97. Ibid., 130–31 (Wynn, J., with Motz, J., Harris, J., and Keenan, J., concurring).

98. Ibid., 131

99. Ibid.

100. Ibid.

101. Ibid., 133.

102. Ibid. (internal citations omitted) (emphasis in original).

103. Ibid., 135.

104. Ibid. (Keenan, J., with Thacker, J., concurring).

105. Ibid. (emphasis in original). Further writing, "I write separately to emphasize my strong disagreement with this view, which not only is antediluvian but also answers the wrong question."). Ibid.

106. Ibid. (emphasis in original).

107. Ibid., 137 (Quattlebaum, J., dissenting).

108. 457 U.S. 830 (1982).

109. Ibid., 842.

110. *Peltier*, 37 F.4th, 148 (Quattlebaum, J., dissenting in part and concurring in part).

111. Ibid., 150 (Wilkinson, J., dissenting).

112. Ibid. (Wilkinson, J., dissenting).

113. Ibid., 151 (Wilkinson, J., dissenting).

114. Ibid., 152 (Wilkinson, J., dissenting).

115. Ibid., 151–52 (Wilkinson, J., dissenting).

116. Ibid., 152 (Wilkinson, J., dissenting).

117. 262 U.S. 390 (1923).

118. 268 U.S. 510 (1925).

119. See Todd A. DeMitchell and Joseph J. Onosko, "A Parent's Child and the State's Future Citizen: Judicial and Legislative Responses to the Tension over the

Right to Direct and Education," *Southern California Interdisciplinary Law Journal* 22, no. 3 (2013): 591–635. "In short, the federal courts have consistently ruled against extending a parent's right to direct the education of her or his child by molding the school curriculum, no matter how deeply held, religiously or personally held." Ibid., 620 (citations omitted).

120. *Peltier*, 37 F.4th, 155 (Wilkinson, J., dissenting) (citing *Trustees of Dartmouth College. v. Woodward*, 17 U.S. [4 Wheat.] 518, 638 [1819]).

121. Petition for a Writ of Certiorari, *Charter Day School, Inc. v. Bonnie Peltier*, No. 22–238, (September 12, 2022), https://www.aclu.org/petition-writ-certiorari-0.

122. Ibid., i.

123. 457 U.S. 830 (198).

124. Petition for a Writ of Certiorari, *Charter Day School, Inc. v. Bonnie Peltier*, No. 22–238, 19 (September 12, 2022), Brief for the States of Texas, Alabama, Alaska, Arkansas, Kansas, Mississippi, Nebraska, South Carolina, Tennessee, and Virginia as Amici Curiae in Support of Petitioner, https://www.aclu.org/amicus-brief-states-texas-alabama-alaska-arkansas-kansas-mississippi-nebraska-south-carolina-0.

125. Nate Raymond, "Supreme Court Seeks U.S. Government View on Charter School's Skirt Requirement," Reuters (January 9, 2023), https://www.reuters.com/legal/supreme-court-seeks-us-government-view-charter-schools-skirt-requirement-2023-01-09/.

126. Tressa Pankovits, "Charter School Innovation Shouldn't Come at the Expense of Constitutional Protections for Students," *The Hill* (January 8, 2023), https://thehill.com/opinion/education/3802821-charter-school-innovation-shouldnt-come-at-the-expense-of-constitutional-protections-for-students/.

127. Author, "Charter Day School, Inc. v. Peltier," SCOTUSblog (n.d.), https://www.scotusblog.com/case-files/cases/charter-day-school-inc-v-peltier/.

128. The North Carolina Association for Public Charter Schools answers the question "What is a charter school?" Their response is germane to our discussion demonstrating that flexibility in curricular decisions does not mean carte blanche to do as charter school directors choose. The Association writes,

> Authorized by the State Board of Education, charter schools are tuition-free **public** schools of choice that are operated by independent non-profit boards of directors. Because of this level of autonomy, charter schools have more flexibility in their curricula and operations. However, they are still required to meet state testing standards because they are publicly funded.

Rhona Dillingham, "NC Charter School Overview," North Carolina Association for Public Charter Schools (n.d.), https://www.dpi.nc.gov/students-families/alternative-choices/charter-schools; emphasis in original.

129. Raymond, *supra* note 25, 14.

130. Jacqueline M. Nowacki, *K–12 Education: Department of Education Should provide Information on Equity and Safety in School Dress Codes* (Washington, DC: US Government Accountability Office GAO-23–105348 K–12 Education, October 2022), https://www.gao.gov/assets/gao-23-105348.pdf.

8

Braids, Locs, and Hairstyles

Grooming Codes

The First Circuit Court of Appeals speaking to a prohibition on the length of hair in 1970 wrote:

> We see no inherent reason why decency, decorum, or good conduct requires a boy to wear his hair short. Certainly, eccentric hair styling is no longer a reliable signal of perverse behavior. We do not believe that mere unattractiveness in the eyes of some parents, teachers, or students, short of uncleanliness, can justify the proscription.[1]

> Dress codes may have the intention of promoting consistent treatment for all, but they are by no means equitable. From the banning of natural and traditional African and African American hairstyles, as well as extensions, multicolored cuts, and unique hairstyles, to the policing of female bodies, the reality is that dress code violations disproportionately disadvantage minoritized students, including students of color, LGBTQ+ students, and females.[2]

Issues with student dress and appearance at school emerged in the early 1970s. Social and legal issues such as the relaxed dress of young people in the age of Aquarius, the Beatles' haircuts, and the push for constitutional rights of students with *Tinker v. Des Moines Independent Community School District*[3] may have been policy and social streams that converged at this time.

Not all public school dress codes have provisions pertaining to a student's hair. My research with Richard Fossey and Casey Cobb in 2000 found that the mandate for hair to be clean and well-groomed occurred with some frequency while prohibitions against beards and a prescribed hair length for males were rarely occurring provisions.[4] The gendered dress codes research discussed in chapter 7 did not find provisions pertaining to hair restrictions.[5] However, issues regarding hair persist. Length of hair still surfaces as an issue, and recently, prohibitions targeting race and ethnicity have captured the attention of the public, state legislatures, and the courts, where lawsuits have been filed that challenge hair length regulations on constitutional grounds.

Regulations regarding students' hair are different from restrictions on clothing. Clothing that is prohibited at school can be worn when the student is not in school. Likewise, if a student is mandated to wear a school uniform, that uniform can be taken off at home and the student's personal clothing can be put on. A law professor at the University of Pennsylvania wrote in 1969, at the beginning of dress code litigation, describing hair regulations in the following way:

> Long hair is a preexisting condition with which the student enters school and for which the school does not appear responsible. Denying a boy the opportunity to wear long hair in school is a major invasion of his freedom of choice. Flags can be mutilated outside of school, but hair cannot be long outside of school and short in school.[6]

In a nutshell, restrictions on hair, whether it be on length or style (such as braids, cornrows, or locs), intrude in the private, away-from-school life of students in a way that prohibitions involving T-shirts, skirt length, or spaghetti straps do not. While the length of a student's hair emerged as an issue just over fifty years ago, hairstyles associated with Black students have emerged as a matter of public concern. For. example, the federal CROWN Act, which bans discrimination against Black hairstyles in schools and workplaces, was voted down by Republicans twice. Representative Bonnie Watson Coleman (D-NJ) said after the vote,

> Our natural hair is as innate a quality of Black people as the presence of melanin in our skin. Discriminating against our hair is no different is no different than discriminating against the color of our skin. [Black people are] far too often . . . derided or deemed unprofessional simply because their hair does not conform to white beauty standards.[7]

The previous chapters explored student dress prohibitions and mandates. This chapter will discuss student appearance rules, sometimes referred to as "grooming standards," that focus on the length and style of students' hair. Regulations regarding students' hair tend to focus on male students but may also apply to female students. First hair length regulations and then regulations on hairstyles will be explored.

HAIR LENGTH LITIGATION

> "The controversy over the length of male students' hair is becoming an increasing problem for today's high school administrators. School boards have invariably enacted student dress codes that expressly forbid long hair, requiring that it be 'combed and worn so it does not hang below the collar line in the back, over the ears on the side . . . [and] above the eyebrows.'"—"High School Regulations," *Valparaiso University Law Review* 4, no. 2 (1970): 400, citing Williams Bay High School Dress Code, Williams Bay High School, Williams Bay, Wisconsin

On August 2, 2021, the Magnolia Independent School District approved the district's student handbook, which included a student dress and grooming code applicable to all students from kindergarten through twelfth grade. The handbook stated that "hair will . . . [b]e no longer than the bottom of a dress shirt collar, bottom of the ear, and out of the eyes *for male students*," and hair must also "[n]ot be pinned up in any fashion nor be worn in a ponytail or bun *for male students*."[8] Only male students were targeted with this grooming regulation on the length of hair.

Seven students, ages seven to seventeen, brought a complaint against the school district seeking a declaration that the gender-based restrictions (hair and earrings) violate the Equal Protection Clause and Title IX. Six of the students were male, and one student identified as nonbinary and used they/them pronouns. The plaintiffs sought a temporary injunction and permanent injunction against enforcing the restrictions, plus nominal damages and attorneys' fees.

Similarly, the American Civil Liberties Union also filed a Title IX administrative complaint, which includes a Title VI complaint, with the US Department of Education over a gender-based restriction on the length of students' hair. The complaint against the Sharyland Independent School District also referenced a restriction on male students wearing earrings. J.R., a five-year-old kindergartener who is both Latino and Native American, wore his long because of his cultural and religious beliefs. The complaint references the denial of J.R.'s request for a religious exemption from the hair length regulation. As part of the remedy, the complaint sought a gender-neutral dress and grooming policy.[9]

The above lawsuit and Title IX complaint demonstrate that the issue of hair length and grooming standards is still an area of controversy. While it appears that litigation has slowed it has not abated.

In this chapter, student grooming codes are examined where litigation has arisen over student hairstyles or hair length. Lawsuits between school officials and students about student grooming policies began appearing in the 1970s, when long hair was becoming fashionable among young men. School districts often had grooming codes that required male students to cut their hair to an approved length. For example, a school grooming code might specify that a male student's hair must not touch the student's shirt collar or cover his ears.

In lawsuits around the country, male students attested that they had a constitutional right to express themselves through their chosen hairstyle. Louis Fischer, David Schimmel, and Leslie R. Stellman analyzed these cases in the 2003 edition of *Teachers and the Law*.[10] As the authors explained, this litigation was based on several theories. Some students argued that they had a liberty interest in choosing their hairstyle that was protected by the Fourteenth Amendment. Others argued that their choice of hair length was a form of symbolic speech that was sheltered by the First Amendment. Still others argued that hair restrictions applied only to males and thus were a violation of the Equal Protection Clause.

As Fischer and colleagues explained, the federal courts split over the question of whether students had a constitutional right to choose their hairstyle. Some have held that a student's choice of hairstyle enjoys constitutional protection, while others have emphatically ruled that they do not. Below we will explore examples of the early litigation on hair length.

Arnold v. Carpenter (1972)

In *Arnold v. Carpenter*,[11] decided in by the Seventh Circuit Court of Appeals in 1972, a school district appealed a decision by a federal district court enjoining the district from enforcing its student grooming code against Greg Carpenter, a high school student. The code had been adopted after it was developed by a committee of students, teachers, and administrators and approved by a vote of the student body. Nevertheless, the district court ruled that the restrictions on students' hair length violated due process under the Fourteen Amendment.

On appeal, the Seventh Circuit upheld the trial court's ruling. The appellate court pointed out that it had previously held that "the right to wear one's hair at any length or in any desired manner is an ingredient of personal freedom protected by the United States Constitution, and that to limit or curtail that right, the state bore a substantial burden of justification."[12] The court also cited precedent in which it had ruled that long hair did not create a substantial disruption that would allow it to be banned under the *Tinker* standard, which authorizes schools to ban student speech that creates a substantial disruption in the school environment.[13] Nor could a ban on long hair be justified for health and safety reasons.

The school district attempted to distinguish the Seventh Circuit's previous rulings on the grounds that its grooming code had been promulgated through a democratic process. The Seventh Circuit, however, was unpersuaded. "We conclude," the court ruled, "that the democratic process used in adopting the code does not per se justify the denial of Craig Carpenter's right to wear his hair in the mode he chooses."[14] The school district's hair code provision, the court continued, "must have some purpose within the school's competence, such as avoiding substantial disruption of school activities or discipline."[15] In the absence of such justification, the school district's ban on long hair must fail.

Massie v. Henry (1972)

Likewise, *Massie v. Henry*,[16] decided by the Fourth Circuit Court of Appeals in the same year as the *Carpenter* decision, ruled that male students had a constitutional right to wear long hair. In that case, the plaintiffs, students at a North Carolina high school, violated the school district's grooming standards in various ways, including wearing their hair below their collars and over their ears and displaying sideburns that extended below their earlobes.

The Fourth Circuit began by noting that young males had embraced the fashion trend of wearing long hair The court pointed out that the current trend harkened back to earlier times and noted that Ulysses S. Grant and Robert E. Lee wore long hair in a style comparable to the plaintiffs' hair. The court also noted that depictions of Jesus Christ always show him "with hair at least the length of that of the plaintiffs."[17]

The court then went on to survey recent decisions concerning school bans on long hair, acknowledging that some circuits had ruled that a student's preference for wearing long hair did not establish "the existence of any substantial constitutional right."[18]

Nevertheless, the Fourth Circuit ruled, federal court decisions invalidating school prohibitions on long hair were more persuasive. The court recognized that some student plaintiffs had argued that their hair choices constituted symbolic speech that was entitled to the protection of the First Amendment. In the case before it, however, the plaintiffs had merely stated their preference to wear their hair long, without attaching their preference to expression. Therefore, the court ruled, "we prefer, in this case, to treat [the plaintiffs'] right to wear their hair as they wish as an aspect of their right to be secure in their persons guaranteed by the due process clause but having overlapping equal protection clause protection."[19]

King v. Saddleback Junior College District (1971)

On the contrary, in *King v. Saddleback Junior College District*,[20] the Ninth Circuit Court of Appeals upheld hair length regulations for male students at a public high school and a junior college district. In one case, Robert Olff sought an injunction against East Side Union High School District, prohibiting it from enforcing its hair length regulation stating that "[a] boy's hair shall not fall below the eyes in front and shall not cover the ears, and it shall not extend below the collar in back."[21] In a separate lawsuit, Lindahl King, a student at Saddleback Junior College, sued the college, asking for an injunction that prohibited the school from enforcing a hair length policy that was similar to the one that Robert was challenging.

In both cases, federal courts enjoined the enforcement of the hair-length policies. The school district and the junior college district appealed to the Ninth Circuit, which consolidated the two cases.[22] In a 1971 opinion, the Ninth Circuit reversed both the lower courts' injunctive orders.

The Ninth Circuit rejected the students' argument that their hair length choices were protected by the First Amendment. "In the regulations before us, neither of the regulations on its face indicates a conflict with freedom of speech," the court ruled, and there was no evidence suggesting that the school districts passed their hair length policies with the purpose of suppressing speech.[23] Likewise, the appellate court rejected the students' argument that the districts' hair length restriction violated a constitutional right to privacy.

The court also rejected the students' equal protection claim, even though the challenged regulations applied to male students and not females. In the court's view, the fact that boys were treated differently from girls did not "create[e] any substantial constitutional question."[24]

Finally, the court declined to find that the students' due process rights were violated. The two districts were acting under statutory authority to regulate their schools, the court reasoned, and the students had not demonstrated that their hair length rules were unconstitutionally invalid.[25]

The Ninth Circuit concluded its opinion with some policy observations. "This is not a question of preference for or against certain male hair styles or the length to which persons desire to wear their hair," the court emphasized. "This court could not care less."[26] Rather the dispute concerned "the right of school authorities to develop a code of dress and conduct best conducive to the fulfillment of their responsibility to educate, and to do it without unconstitutionally infringing upon the rights of those who must live under it."[27] In the court's view, the two students had not established that any of their substantial constitutional rights had been violated. "A court might disagree with [school authorities'] professional judgment," the court said in closing, "but it should not take over the operation of their schools."[28]

The Ninth Circuit Court of Appeals is generally considered a liberal court,[29] so its decision upholding the right of school authorities to regulate their students' hair length might seem surprising. Nevertheless, *King v. Saddleback Junior College District*, which was decided more than fifty years ago, has never been overruled.

Karr v. Schmidt (1971)

The court's opinion in *Karr v. Schmidt*,[30] decided in 1971, provides another example of a federal circuit court ruling that firmly rejected the notion that a high school student has a constitutional right to choose the length of his hair. In that case, Chesley Karr, a sixteen-year-old student at an El Paso, Texas, high school, attempted to enroll for his junior year but was turned away by school authorities because his long hair violated a school board grooming regulation. Chelsey filed suit in federal court, asserting that the regulation violated his constitutional rights to free speech, equal protection, and substantive due process.

After a four-day trial during which the district court heard testimony from numerous witnesses, the court concluded that the school board's hair length regulation violated Chelsey's rights to due process and equal protection. Indeed, the court concluded that the presence and enforcement of its haircut rule "causes far more disruption of the classroom instruction process than the hair it seeks to prohibit."[31]

On appeal, in an *en banc* opinion, the Fifth Circuit reversed, asserting that Chelsey's asserted right to be free of a school hair length regulation was not cognizable in a federal court. In reaching this decision, the Fifth Circuit's majority considered and rejected each of Chelsey's constitutional arguments. Regarding his free speech claim, the court ruled that the First Amendment's protection did not extend to the wearing of long hair. The court also rejected his argument that the regulation violated his constitutional right to privacy, his right to substantive due process, or his right to equal protection under the Fourteenth Amendment.

In reaching its decision, the appellate noted that federal courts had not ruled consistently regarding the constitutionality of school hair length regulations. "In our view," the court stated, "the validity of hair-length regulations should not turn on the individual view of district court judges."[32]

Therefore, the court concluded, it was necessary to articulate a broad ruling upholding the constitutionality of hair length policies in public schools. "Henceforth," the Fifth Circuit directed, "district courts need not hold an evidentiary hearing in cases of this nature. Where a complaint merely alleges the constitutional invalidity of a high school hair and grooming regulation, the district courts are directed to grant an immediate motion to dismiss for failure to state a claim for which relief can be granted.[33]

This review of *Karr*, *King*, *Carpenter*, and *Massie* demonstrates strong disagreement among the federal circuit courts regarding the constitutionality of school policies that govern the length of a student's hair. Moreover, this disagreement has persisted for more than half a century. Why, then, has the US Supreme Court not accepted one of these cases for review to determine on a nationwide basis whether students have a constitutional right to wear long hair?

Perhaps the answer to that question can be found in Justice Hugo Black's opinion in the *Karr* case, in which he declined to reverse the Fifth Circuit's ruling that lifted the district court's injunction against the El Paso School District pending appeal. "I refuse," Black wrote, "to intervene in these types of decisions best left to the state and its school districts." Black went on to write,

> I confess my inability to understand how anyone would thus classify this hair length case. The only thing about it that borders on the serious to me is the idea that anyone should think the Federal Constitution imposes on the United States courts the burden of supervising the length of hair that public school students should wear.[34]

He concluded by expressing his view that the Supreme Court should not be an arbiter of what length of a student's hair meets constitutional protection: "Perhaps if the courts will leave the States free to perform their own constitutional duties they will at least be able successfully to regulate the length of hair their public school students can wear."[35]

Restrictions on the length of hair, at this point, do not implicate constitutional protections, at least in some federal circuits. However, that does not mean that all restrictions on hair length are beyond judicial scrutiny, even in the Fifth Circuit, where *Karr v. Schmidt* was authored.

Native Americans, Hair Length, Religion, Expressive Conduct

In *Betenbaugh v. Needville Independent School District*,[36] a federal district court in Texas granted an elementary-aged Native American student's motion for a preliminary injunction in a case involving a school policy that prohibited him from wearing his long hair. The district later offered to allow the student to wear his long hair pinned up in a bun or braids so long as the braids were tucked inside his shirt. The student alleged, through his parents, that he was a Lipan Apache and wore his hair in harmony with his Native American religious beliefs. He argued that the school's restriction on long hair (including the accommodations it offered) violated his rights under the Texas Religious Freedom Restoration Act and the US Constitution.

In a 2009 decision, a federal district court permanently enjoined the school district from enforcing its hair length policy against the student.[37] The court found that the braids arguably conveyed a particularized message about his Native American heritage and religion and that others understood the message.[38]

The school district appealed the district court's decision, and the Fifth Circuit Court of Appeals affirmed.[39] The appellate court ruled that the student had a sincere religious belief in wearing his hair visibly long and that a school requirement that he wear his hair in a bun or tucked inside his shirt if braided was a substantial burden on the free exercise of his religious beliefs.[40] The Fifth Circuit also ruled that the school district's interest in teaching hygiene, preventing disruption, and preventing safety hazards was not a compelling interest that justified the burden on the student's religious beliefs.[41] In addition, in the Fifth Circuit's view, the school district's interest in asserting authority and instilling discipline and uniformity were also not compelling interests.

One might ask how the Fifth Circuit's ruling in *Betenbaugh v. Needville Independent School District*, affirming a kindergarten student's right to wear his hair long, squares with *Karr v. Schmidt*, in which the same circuit directed all district courts within its jurisdiction to dismiss all hair length lawsuits without trial, regardless of the theory under which a haircut challenge was brought.

The answer lies in the fact that the Fifth Circuit's ruling in the *Needville* decision was based solely on Texas state law. As the court noted at the beginning of its analysis, "Because we do not decide constitutional claims when a case can be footed on alternative grounds, our analysis begins with state law—specifically, the Texas Religious Freedom Restoration Act."[42]

As the *Needville* ruling illustrates, hair length and style as symbolic speech as an expression of racial ethnic identity as well as religious expression is gaining traction in the courts and legislation.

In *Alabama and Coushatta Tribes of Texas v. Big Sandy Independent School District*,[43] students who were members of the Alabama and Coushatta Native American tribes sued an East Texas school district, charging that the district's hair length policy violated their constitutional rights. They claimed the regulations violated their right to free speech and freedom of religion and their parents' constitutional right to direct the upbringing of their children. They also argued that the regulation violated the Equal Protection Clause.

A federal district court granted the students a preliminary injunction. The court ruled that "the wearing of long hair by Native American students is a protected expressive activity, which does not unduly disrupt the educational process or interfere with the rights of other students. As such, the regulation, as applied to these students, violates the First Amendment free speech clause."[44] The court also ruled that the plaintiffs had stated a violation of their constitutional right to freedom of religion.

In addition, the court was sympathetic to the plaintiffs' argument that the school district's hair length rule violated "the right of the parents and the Tribe to raise and educate their children, to guide their children's religious beliefs, and to instill respect in the young members of the Tribe for their Native American heritage."[45] Based on the evidence presented, the district court agreed that the Native American parents had stated a valid claim that their constitutional right to direct the upbringing of their parents had been violated. (The court rejected the plaintiffs' Equal Protection claim.)

The Big Sandy school district appealed the district court's ruling to the Fifth Circuit Court of Appeals, which remanded the case back to the district court.[46] The appellate court noted that Congress had recently adopted the Religious Freedom Restoration Act (RFRA), which had been signed into law by the president. Thus, the Fifth Circuit suggested, plaintiffs might prevail under that federal statute, which would forestall the need for the court to rule "on a difficult constitutional question when that course of action has become unnecessary."[47] The Fifth Circuit panel directed the lower court to adjudicate the plaintiffs' case in light of the RFRA and allowed the preliminary injunction to stay in place pending reconsideration of the plaintiffs' claims under the RFRA.

Hair Length Regulations in Private Schools

Before leaving the hair length restrictions section for hair style as expression we will briefly explore hair length litigation in private schools. As already discussed, the constitutionality of hair length policies in public schools is unsettled, with some federal circuit courts ruling that a male student's choice to have long hair is entitled to constitutional protection and others holding that school rules restricting a schoolboy's hair choices are not violative of any federal constitutional right. Nevertheless, courts have shown increased sympathy for students who claim their hairstyles and hair length are expressions of ethnic or racial identity.

What about private schools? Have courts restricted private institutions from promulgating hair length restrictions? Private schools are not governmental institutions and are not bound by constitutional restraints; thus, a student at a private school cannot claim that a school rule requiring students to comply with the school's hair length policy violates a constitutional right.

The seminal case on a private school's authority to ban male students from wearing long hair is *Gorman v. St. Raphael Academy*, decided by the Rhode Island Supreme Court in 2004.[48] In that case, Russell Gorman III enrolled as a freshman at St. Raphael Academy in August 2001. His hair extended six to eight inches below his shirt collar, and the school soon demanded that he cut his hair or face expulsion.

His parents filed suit in a Rhode Island court, accusing St. Raphael of breach of contract. The court issued a temporary restraining order against the school, "enjoining St. Raphael from interfering with Russell's normal matriculation and participation at Saint Raphael based on the length of his hair."[49]

In May 2022, as Russell's freshman year was ending, St. Raphael revised its student handbook by adding a hair length rule for boys. The new policy stated as follows:

> All students must keep their hair clean and well groomed. Outlandish hair styles (ex. Any designs, lettering, mohawks, ponytails, etc. engraved/cut into their hair; spiked; hair dye can only be of natural colors, [reds, blues, greens, etc. are not natural colors] are not in keeping with the school's educational mission and will not be tolerated. *A boy's hair may not be longer than the bottom of his shirt collar*. Hair should be neat and not flamboyant for all students. Students who do not conform to these regulations are subject to disciplinary action and possible dismissal if the problem persists.[50]

Russell's parents amended their complaint against the school, again alleging a breach of contract and demanding that Russell be allowed to continue attending St. Raphael under the terms of the student handbook before it was revised with the hair length restriction. After a hearing, the trial court issued an order permanently enjoining the school from enforcing its hair length rule against Russell and awarding attorney fees to Russell and his parents.[51] In the trial court's view, St. Raphael's hair length restriction was arbitrary and capricious, and the school had failed to justify its rule on educational grounds.

On appeal, the Rhode Island Supreme Court reversed. The court began by ruling that St. Raphael's relationship between Russell Gorman and his parents was contractual based on an annually renewable tuition contract and the school's student handbook. The appellate court pointed out that the trial court acknowledged the school's right to change its rules from time to time, although the trial court had ruled that rule changes "should be enacted in good faith and not bespeak the arbitrary or capricious."[52]

In the opinion of the Rhode Island Supreme Court, St. Raphael's hair length policy was not arbitrary or capricious. Nor was it irrational. "More significantly," the appellate court added, "we hold that absent a violation of law or public policy, it is not within the province of the court to inject itself in the rule-making authority of a private school."[53]

Moreover, in the Rhode Island Supreme Court's opinion, the trial court improperly placed the burden of proof on St. Raphael to justify its hair length policy as being rationally related to its educational mission. "Even if the arbitrary or capricious inquiry were the correct standard," the court stated, "the burden of proof rests with the plaintiff to show that a defendant breached the contract."[54]

Rhode Island's highest court concluded its opinion by ruling "that a contractual rule or regulation of a private school is lawful and enforceable as long as it is not against public policy or law." In the case before it, the court noted, "[t]he Gormans did not offer any evidence that a private school rule regulating the length of a student's hair is injurious to the interests of the public, nor that it interferes with the public welfare or safety."[55]

In ruling on the *Gorman* case, the Rhode Island Supreme Court stated that it could find no case law in other jurisdictions that had ruled on the enforceability of hair length regulations at a private school. Nevertheless, its ruling is consistent with decisions in other jurisdictions that have expressed reluctance to interfere in the affairs of private educational institutions.

It is worth noting that most states have laws against sex discrimination and that dress code rules that burden one gender more than others are vulnerable to attack on the grounds of sex discrimination. In a 1998 decision, the Texas Supreme Court ruled that a state statute that prohibited government employees from discriminating on the basis of sex did not apply to a public school's hair length regulation and that different grooming standards for men and women did not violate anti–sex discrimination laws.[56] In the court's view, "[h]air-length restrictions for male students impose no barriers that operate to favor one sex over the other."[57]

The Texas Supreme Court acknowledged that some jurisdictions had ruled differently regarding hair length policies that applied to male students and not females. In *Jacobs v. Benedict*,[58] an Ohio appellate court ruled that a school district could not enforce its hair length policy that applied only to male students, reasoning as follows: "We find, upon a careful review of the record, that the hair regulations are not actually necessary for the government of the schools. Moreover, there is not, actually, evidence that such regulations serve a useful purpose. Further, we note that the regulations do not apply to girl students. Hence, in that context, they are discriminatory as applied to boys."[59]

HAIR STYLE AS EXPRESSION: LITIGATION AND LEGISLATION

When Dyree Williams, a seventeen-year-old senior, transferred from Cincinnati to the East Bernard Independent School District (Texas), his family was unpleasantly surprised to learn that the dress code's prohibition on the length of hair read, "Braided hair or twisted rows/strands will not be allowed" (See EBISD Dress 2021–2022, https://www.scribd.com/document/571889091/East-Bernard-ISD-Dress-Code#).

Dyree's mother's complained about the restriction stating,

- "Once you cut off that hair, you cut off your line to our ancestors, you cut off your lineage, you cut off everything."
- "We don't consider them dreadlocks because we don't dread them, we love them."

The hair policy was reportedly removed from the school's website after the complaint went viral.

—Wendy Medina, "Discriminatory Hair Policy at Texas School Removed After Complaints from Student's Mom Goes Viral," *Black Enterprise* (May 6, 2022), https://www.blackenterprise.com/discriminatory-hair-policy-at-texas-school-removed-after-students-moms-complaints-go-viral/

Above, we explored restrictions on the length of hair. In some situations, the issue of hair length becomes entangled with hairstyle and race. Nowhere is this more evident than the controversy over braids, locs, and other styles associated with Black culture. Journalist Jesse Washington writes, "Hair is Africa's most enduring marker in America, the phenotype most likely to persist through generations of interracial children. Hair is what black folks look at when trying to determine who is one of us."[60] Next, hairstyle restrictions focusing on styles associated with Black culture will be discussed. The chapter will conclude by discussing legislative responses to hair discrimination.

Length, Locs, and Race

Treyvion Gray filed a complaint with the Southern District of Texas Houston Division on April 19, 2022.[61] Treyvion started growing his locs (also referred to as locks or dreadlocks) during his sophomore year in high school. He considers his locs as an expression of his Black identity and culture, stating, "My hair is a part of me, my heritage and my culture."[62] He asserted that his locs did not hinder his academic or extracurricular achievement.

The complaint asserts that effect of the hair length policy disproportionately targets and penalizes Black male students by singling them out for "wearing their hair in its natural state, including locs."[63] This, according to the complaint, has the effect of restricting their mobility in public and private spaces, denying them equal educational opportunities, and negatively impacts the dignity of Black student population within the school district. Consequently, Black students, including Gray, are forced to choose between wearing their hair in "natural formations" and suffer discipline "or conform their hair to Eurocentric hair norms and receive the same educational opportunities as their white counterparts."[64]

Andrew "Drew" Johnson wrestled in the 120-pound weight class for the local high school in the Buena Vista Township in New Jersey. Right before his match, the referee first told Drew that he must shave. Drew went to the locker room, removed the stubble from his sixteen-year-old face, and returned to the mat. The referee next told Drew that he had concerns about his hair. Drew once again withdrew to the locker room and returned wearing a cap. The referee told Drew that the cap did not meet the requirement of being attached to his headgear. The team had not brought an attachable cap because it thought that one was not needed, since Drew had wrestled earlier without wearing a cap.

Finally, the referee cited a rule stating that the wrestler's hair must be in a "natural state"—not that Drew's hair was too long, but that his hair was not in a natural state, deeming that dreadlocks were not natural. The coaches argued Drew's case, but the referee was undeterred in his ruling. "Maloney [the referee] turned his back on them and twirled his finger to start the 90-second injury clock. When it ran out, Drew would forfeit."[65] Drew either had to cut his locs or forfeit the match, which would impact the team. He had the trainer cut his locs in front of the crowd so that could wrestle. When half of the locs had been cut off, the match began. Drew won the match.

The match was over, but the controversy had just begun. The video went viral, and the story was covered on major media outlets. The New Jersey attorney general and the Division on Civil Rights (DCR) investigated the matter. The DCR and the New Jersey Interscholastic Athletic Association agreed to suspend Maloney for the next two wrestling seasons. In addition, the DCR issued a new "Guidance on Race Discrimination Based on Hairstyle." The guidance clarified that "policies banning, limiting or restricting hairstyles closely associated with those of African-American descent—including twists and dreadlocks—may violate New Jersey law."[66]

An earlier controversy at a Boston charter school arose over braids with extensions. Fifteen-year-old twins Deanna and Mya Cook were required to serve multiple detentions, were removed from after-school sports and banned from the prom, and faced suspension for wearing braids with hair extensions. The girl's mother stated that her daughters wore the braided hairstyle as an expression of their Black culture. The girls had worn the braids before without objections.

The school, which serves a diverse school population, asserted that it promotes equity. In a statement, school officials stated,

> Our policies, including those governing student appearance and attire, foster a culture that emphasizes education rather than style, fashion, or materialism. Our policy on hair extensions, which tend to be very expensive, is consistent with, and a part of, the educational environment that we believe is so important to our students' success.[67]

However, the parents argued that the prohibition of hair extensions for braids "disproportionately affects black children."[68]

They also raise the issue of why these restrictions, and specifically ones that have a disproportionate impact on Black students, improve the educational outcomes of students—what impact do nail polish and hair extensions for braids have on math scores?

THE CROWN ACT: CREATING A RESPECTFUL AND OPEN WORLD FOR NATURAL HAIR

WE'RE ENDING HAIR DISCRIMINATION

The CROWN Act was created in 2019 by Dove and the CROWN Coalition, in partnership with then State Senator Holly J. Mitchell of California, to ensure protection against discrimination based on race-based hairstyles by extending statutory protection to hair texture and protective styles such as braids, locs, twists, and knots in the workplace and public schools.

—The Crown Coalition, "The Official Campaign of the CROWN Act Led by the CROWN Coalition," CROWN Coalition (n.d.), https://www.thecrownact.com

Such issues encountered by these students are, unfortunately, not isolated events. And they are not confined to public schools. Too many workplaces also have policies that target their employees' natural hair. For example, a 2019 study of two thousand women, both Black and non-Black, found that 80 percent of the Black women in the study had to change their hair from its natural style to fit in at their workplace.[69] According to the study, Black women's hair is 3.4 times more likely than the hair of nonminority women to be perceived as unprofessional.

"This groundbreaking study," the authors concluded, "confirms workplace bias against hairstyles impacts Black women's ability to celebrate their natural beauty, and how workplace bias and corporate grooming policies unfairly impact Black women."[70] Bias in the workplace based on the natural hair of Black female employees and control of Black male and female students over their natural hair was found to be pervasive in major aspects of Black people's life, school, and work. The confluence of discrimination in critical places for Black people who decided not to follow the grooming standards of non-Black people and embrace their natural hair with the styles of their ancestors and culture led to the rise of antidiscrimination CROWN laws.

CROWN is an acronym for "Creating a Respectful and Open World for Natural Hair." CROWN laws have gained traction across the nation. California passed the first CROWN Act on July 3, 2019. As of February 7, 2023, twenty states had passed CROWN acts, with more than half of the states either filing or prefiling enabling legislation. In addition, more than forty local areas, including Austin, Texas, and Ann Arbor, Michigan, have enacted laws banning discrimination based on natural hairstyles.[71]

AN ACT PROHIBITING DISCRIMINATION BASED ON NATURAL AND PROTECTIVE HAIRSTYLES

(Approved July 26, 2022)

Section 1. Section 7 of chapter 4 of the General Laws [of Massachusetts], as appearing in the 2020 Official Edition, is hereby amended by adding the following 2 clauses:-

Sixty-third. "Protective hairstyle", shall include, but not be limited to, braids, locks, twists, Bantu knots, hair coverings and other formations.

SECTION 2. Chapter 71 of the General Laws is hereby amended by inserting after section 1C the following section:-

Section 1D. A school district, school committee, public school, nonsectarian school, the Massachusetts Interscholastic Athletic Association or any equivalent school organization or an entity or board that provides athletic officials, including, but not limited to, referees and umpires, for school sports or athletic events, shall not adopt or implement a policy or code, including, but not limited to, any policy or code pertaining to a student's participation in sports or athletic events, that impairs or prohibits a hairstyle that is historically associated with race. The department of elementary and secondary education shall provide written guidance for the administration of this section.

—The 192nd General Court of the Commonwealth of Massachusetts (2022), https://malegislature.gov/Laws/SessionLaws/Acts/2022/Chapter117

On March 19, 2021, Representative Bonnie Watson Coleman (D-NJ), supported by 118 cosponsors, introduced H.R. 2116, titled the Creating a Respectful and Open World for Natural Hair Act of 2022.[72] In a speech on the floor of the House of Representatives, Watson Coleman said,

> For too long, Black girls have been discriminated against and criminalized for the hair that grows on our heads and the way we move through and show up in this world. Whether you are a student in a classroom, an employee in the workplace, or the next Supreme Court Justice or the speaker pro [tempore], you deserve to show up as your full self, rocking your crown with your head held high.[73]

The House passed the bill in a 235–189 vote, with fourteen Republicans joining with the Democrats.

Unfortunately, the Senate companion bill, S. 888—CROWN Act of 2021, introduced by Senator Cory Booker (D-NJ), failed to break the Republican filibuster. Following the failure of the Senate bill, Watson Coleman wrote,

> It saddens and angers me that, in the year 2022, something as simple as opposing racial discrimination has become controversial. My colleagues across the aisle were presented with an opportunity to stand united against discrimination. They chose instead to give in to the climate of division and hyper-partisanship.[74]

Is there a rational basis for prohibiting braids, locs, or hair extensions? What positive academic outcomes are associated with such prohibitions? Do they act as an incitement to break disciplinary rules? Without any evidence to the contrary, the prohibition of a student's natural hair does not promote affirmative responses. Therefore, without reasonable justification such prohibitions on natural hair should be removed from dress code policies. And I cannot think of a reasonable justification for enacting or keeping such bans. The CROWN Act is a reasonable and needed antidiscrimination response.

CONCLUSION

As we have seen, students' constitutional rights related to hair grooming decisions have been litigated in the federal courts, with different results. Some federal appellate courts have ruled that a male student's decision to wear his hair long is protected by the First Amendment or the Fourteenth Amendment's Equal Protection Clause, while others have ruled that the school strictures on the length of students' hair are not a matter for judicial intervention.

Passage of the Religious Freedom Restoration Act and various CROWN acts at the state level have opened new avenues of redress for students who wish to challenge school rules that restrict long hair or natural hairstyles. In states that have adopted CROWN acts, it will be very difficult, if not impossible, for school authorities to enforce hair length rules prohibiting ethnic- and racial-inspired hairstyles. Even in states that have not enacted such legislation, educators who wish to regulate their students' hair will be increasingly called upon to justify such regulations based on research and not simply the unsupported attitude that a student's hair grooming disrupts learning or the school environment.

NOTES

1. *Richards v. Thurston*, 424 F.2d 1281, 1286 (1st Cir. 1970).

2. Jennifer L. Martin and Jennifer N. Brooks, "Loc'd and Faded, Yoga Pants, and Spaghetti Straps: Discrimination in Dress Codes and School Pushout," *International Journal of Education Policy and Leadership* 16, no. 19 (2020): 1–2, http://journals.sfu.ca/ijepl/index.php/ijepl/article/view/1047.

3. See, e.g., from chapter 7, the "can of worms" out of which these dress code cases arise was opened by the Supreme Court in *Tinker v. Des Moines Independent Community School District*, 393 U. S. 503 (1969). On the defendants' motion for judgment on the pleadings, which was denied, Griesbach opined on dress code litigation in general. *N.J. by Next Friend Jacob v. Sonnabend*, Case 1: 20-cv-00227-WCG (E.D. Wisc.11/6/20), *5

4. Todd A. DeMitchell, Richard Fossey, and Casey Cobb, "Dress Codes in the Public Schools: Principals, Policies, and Precepts," *Journal of Law and Education* 29, no. 1 (2000): 44.

5. The chapter 8 discussion is based on research published by Todd A. DeMitchell, Christine Rienstra Kiracofe, Richard Fossey, and Nathan E. Fellman, "Genderized Dress Codes in K–12 Education: A Mixed Methods Analysis of Law and Policy," *Education Law Reporter* 376 (2020): 441–46.

6. Stephen R. Goldstein, "The Scope and Sources of School Board Authority to Regulate Student Conduct and Status: A Nonconstitutional Analysis," *University of Pennsylvania Law Review* 117, no. 3 (1969): 400.

7. Zack Linly, "GOP Blocks Anti-Black Hair Discrimination Bill Because 'Divisiveness' Only Counts When White People Are Mad," NEWSONE (March 2, 2022), https://newsone.com/4297849/republicans-block-anti-black-hair-discrimination-crown-act-bill/. The author writes, "So why would all of these *non-divisive* Republicans vote against a simple initiative to stop employers and schools from

banning protective hairstyles like braids and locks or styles like afros which is literally just our hair naturally out of our scalps." Ibid.

8. *A.C., C.P., T.T., T.M., T.B., R.P., and C.W. v. Magnolia Independent School District*, No. 4:21-cv-03466 (S.D. Texas 10/21/21), Complaint, *6, https://www.courthousenews.com/wp-content/uploads/2021/10/seven-male-students-lawsuit-against-magnolia-isd-over-its-hair-policy.pdf; emphasis in original. The handbook further states, "Earrings may be worn only by girls. Earrings worn by boys will be confiscated and may not be returned to the student." Ibid., *7.

9. Complaint letter from Brian Klosterboer, Staff Attorney, ACLU Foundation of Texas (November 10, 2021), https://www.valleycentral.com/wp-content/uploads/sites/39/2021/11/ACLU-Office-of-Civil-Rights-Complaint-against-Sharyland-ISD_Redacted.pdf.

10. Louis Fischer, David Schimmel, and Leslie R. Stellman, *Teachers and the Law*, 6th ed. (Boston: Allyn and Bacon, 2003).

11. 459 F.2d 919 (7th Cir. 1972).

12. Ibid., 941–42 (internal citations and punctuation omitted).

13. 393 U.S. 503 (1969).

14. *Arnold*, 459 F.2d. 943.

15. Ibid.

16. 455 F.2d 779 (4th Cir. 1972).

17. Ibid., 780.

18. Ibid., 781, quoting *King v. Saddleback Junior College District*, 465 F.2d 932, 940 (9th Cir. 1971).

19. Ibid., 783.

20. 445 F.2d 932 (9th Cir. 1971).

21. Ibid., 934–35.

22. Ibid., 933.

23. Ibid., 937.

24. Ibid., 939.

25. Ibid.

26. Ibid., 940.

27. Ibid.

28. Ibid.

29. Dylan Matthews, "How the 9th Circuit Became Conservatives' Least Favorite Court," *Vox* (January 10, 2018), https://www.vox.com/policy-and-politics/2018/1/10/16873718/ninth-circuit-court-appeals-liberal-conservative-trump-tweet. "The [Ninth] circuit's appellate court, which covers California, Washington, Oregon, Arizona, Nevada, Idaho, Hawaii, Alaska, and Montana, has long been stereotyped as a liberal outlier, prone to left-wing rulings that are frequently reversed by the Supreme Court on appeal." Ibid.

30. 460 F.2d 609 (5th Cir. 1972).

31. Ibid., 613.

32. Ibid., 617.

33. Ibid., 617–18. Similarly, the Tenth Circuit ruled that the Constitution does not require federal courts to review school hair length regulations. *Freeman v. Flake*, 448 F.2d 258 (10th Cir. 1971).

34. *Karr v. Schmidt*, 401 U.S. 1201, 1202–1203 (1971) (motion to lift the Fifth Circuit's stay of an injunction pending appeal denied).

35. Ibid., 1203.

36. *Betenbaugh v. Needville Independent School Dist*rict, 701 F. Supp. 2d 863 (S.D. Tex. 2009), *aff'd*, 611 F.3d 248 (5th Cir. 2010).

37. Ibid., 701 F. Supp. 2d 886.

38. Ibid., 882–83.

39. *Betenbaugh*, 611 F.3d 248 (5th Cir. 2010).

40. Ibid., 272.

41. Ibid.,266–68.

42. Ibid., 258.

43. 817 F. Supp. 1319 (E.D. Tex. 1993), *remanded*, 20 F.3d 469 (5th Cir. 1994).

44. Ibid., 1334.

45. Ibid.

46. *Alabama and Coushatta Tribes of Texas v. Big Sandy Independent School District*, 20 F.3d 469 (5th Cir. 2019).

47. Ibid.

48. 853 A.2d 28 (R.I. 2004).

49. Ibid., 31.

50. Ibid.; emphasis added by the court.

51. Ibid., 32.

52. Ibid., 36 (quoting the trial court's opinion).

53. Ibid., 37.

54. Ibid.

55. Ibid., 39.

56. *Bastrop Independent School District v. Toungate,* 958 S.W.2d 365 (Tex. 1997).

57. Ibid., 371.

58. 316 N.E.2d 898 (Ohio Ct. App. 1973).

59. Ibid., 901. See also *Idaho Commission on Human Rights v. Campbell*, 506 P.2d 112 (Idaho 1973) (ruling that Commission had stated a valid claim against a school district that had a policy that restricted male students' hair length, but not female students).

60. Jesse Washington, "The Untold Story of Wrestler Andrew Johnson's Dreadlocks," Andscape (September 18, 2019), https://andscape.com/features/the-untold-story-of-wrestler-andrew-johnsons-dreadlocks/.

61. *Treyvion Gray v. Needville Independent School District*, No. 4:22-cv-02145 (S.D. Tex. April 19, 2022), https://storage.courtlistener.com/recap/gov.uscourts.txsd.1869009/gov.uscourts.txsd.1869009.1.0.pdf.

62. Jadriena Solomon, "Texas Senior Suing School District for Prohibiting Him from Attending Graduation Over His Locs," *Blavity* (May 4, 2022), https://blavity.com/texas-senior-prohibited-from-attending-graduation-over-locs.

63. *Treyvion Gray v. Needville Independent School District*, *2.
64. Ibid., *3.
65. Washington, *supra* note 60. "As a trainer began to hack off fistfuls of locs with a pair of tape scissors, a wave of anguished noise rolled down from the packed bleachers. Shouts of "Noooo!" can be heard on the video." Ibid. The hyperlink in the article can be accessed at https://twitter.com/Complex/status/1076172324301357056.
66. Tom McGurk, "Referee Who Made High School Wrestler Cut Dreadlocks Is Suspended for Two Years," *USA Today* (February 18, 2019), https://www.usatoday.com/story/sports/highschool/2019/09/18/wrestler-dreadlocks-controversy-new-jersey-referee-suspended-two-years/2367239001/.
67. Kay Lazar, "Black Malden Charter Students Punished for Braided Hair Extensions," *Boston Globe* (May 11, 2017), https://www.bostonglobe.com/metro/2017/05/11/black-students-malden-school-who-wear-braids-face-punishment-parents-say/stWDlBSCJhw1zocUWR1QMP/story.html.
68. Ibid.
69. "The CROWN Research Study," Dove (2019), https://static1.squarespace.com/static/5edc69fd622c36173f56651f/t/5edeaa2fe5ddef345e087361/1591650865168/Dove_research_brochure2020_FINAL3. pdf.
70. Ibid.
71. Matt Gonzales, "CROWN Act: Does Your State Prohibit Hair Discrimination?" SHRM (February 7, 2023), https://www.shrm.org/resourcesandtools/hr-topics/behavioral-competencies/global-and-cultural-effectiveness/pages/crown-act-does-your-state-prohibit-hair-discrimination.aspx.
72. H. R. 2116—Creating a Respectful and Open World for Natural Hair Act of 2022, Congress. Gov, https://www.congress.gov/bill/117th-congress/house-bill/2116/text.
73. Veronica Stracqualirsi and Rachel Janfaza, "What Is the CROWN Act and What Do Advocates Say It Will Do?" CNN Politics (April 30, 2022), https://www.cnn.com/2022/04/30/politics/crown-act-hair-discrimination/index.html.
74. "Senate Republicans Block Passage of CROWN Act," Bonnie Watson Coleman (December 14, 2022, press release), https://watsoncoleman.house.gov/newsroom/press-releases/senate-republicans-block-passage-of-crown-act.

9

School Uniforms

The Mandated Appearance

> School uniforms may not be the most effective way to improve student behavior and engagement.[1]

Laws, policies, rules, regulations, and procedures are pervasive and ubiquitous in public education. Policies frame responsibilities and rights, articulate procedures and process, and state what is important to be pursued by the organization. They allocate scarce resources. A policy[2] often solves a problem, clarifies a situation, and directs behavior that seeks consistency. Policy drives our educational system.

Neither government nor public schools can address all of the issues that parents, citizens, and educators want solved. Consequently, the agenda-setting process narrows the conceivable public issues to the set that becomes the focus of attention of government officials. So how does an issue get on the public's agenda for attention and resolution? The public agenda is small and crowded. The number of issue partisans clamoring for a place to be heard is large.

John W. Kingdon's classic work on policy streams and policy windows provide a scheme for understanding how issues get on the public agenda and become public problems. He starts his work with the question, "How does the public know that an ideas time has come?[3]

Kingdon identified three streams that are constantly flowing and occasionally converge to open a policy window. First, there is problem stream: gaining recognition for your problem is important. This often occurs in which critical or prominent events or data/research help to focus attention on a problem.

Second, there is a stream of proposals seeking problems to attach to so that they can be implemented. The last stream is politics: the ongoing search to gather scarce resources through competition and coalition building. This stream consists of political factors and actors who gain power and judge the political climate and mood as well as voices of advocacy and voices of opposition. When these streams merge, a window of opportunity opens. When windows open, solutions can be grafted onto problems and a new policy is developed. These windows do not stay open long, and advocates rush to take advantage of the opening.

"Public school districts across the country have increasingly turned to the adoption of mandatory dress policies, sometimes referred to as 'school uniforms policies.' In an effort to focus student attention and reduce conflict."—*Jacobs v. Clark County School District,* 526 F.3d 419, 422 (9th Cir. 2008).

THE POLICY ARGUMENTS OVER MANDATORY SCHOOL UNIFORMS*

The federal government is an actor in the stream of education politics. The United States Department of Education asserted that a safe and disciplined environment is a requirement for a good school. It further states that "many parents, teachers, and school officials have come to see school uniforms as one positive and creative way to reduce discipline problems and increase school safety" and that "the adoption of school uniform policies can promote school safety, improve discipline, and enhance the learning environment."[4]

Furthermore, former president Bill Clinton and former secretary of education Richard Riley supported the role of school uniforms in reducing violence and establishing an environment for students and adults that is conducive to learning.[5] School uniforms have been advanced as a positive strategy to reform schools—behavior, academics, and school climate. One middle school principal referred to school uniforms as the remedy to student "draggin, sagging, and laggin."[6]

---

* This chapter draws on the earlier work Todd A. DeMitchell and Richard Fossey, *The Challenges of Mandating School Uniforms in the Public Schools* (Lanham, MD: Rowman and Littlefield, 2015).

ASSERTED POTENTIAL BENEFITS OF SCHOOL UNIFORMS

The US Department of Education offers the following potential benefits for implementing a school uniform policy:

- Decreasing violence and theft—even life-threatening situations among students over designer clothing or expensive sneakers
- Helping prevent gang members from wearing gang colors and insignia at school
- Instilling students with discipline
- Helping parents and students resist peer pressure
- Helping students concentrate on their schoolwork
- Helping school officials recognize intruders who come to the school

—US Department of Education, (n.d.), *Manual on School Uniforms*, https://files.eric.ed.gov/fulltext/ED387947.pdf

The benefits of school uniforms asserted by their proponents include improvements in the problems safety and discipline aas well as establishing an enhanced learning environment.[7] One commentator wrote on these claims, "Student behavioral change, school cultural change, and higher achievement, all for little to no cost, [school uniforms] must be the holy grail of school remedies."[8]

However, despite the rhetoric of the efficacy of wearing mandated school uniforms, it is questionable as to whether they are perceived as a major solution for educational problems. While growing in numbers from 1999 to 2000, school uniform policies are far from universally adopted. Table 9.1 displays data from the National Center for Education Statistics (NCES) on the adoption of school uniforms and dress codes. (Note that NCES uses the term "strict dress codes," which I have used for this discussion of the data.)

The data show that the school uniforms increased in use from 1999–2000 to 2015–2016. School uniform adoption increased 9.7 percent, to a high 21.5 percent in 2015–2016. Dress code usage increased 11.1 percent, to a high of 58.5 percent in 2013–2014. Both declined from their high-water mark. There was a 2.7 percent decline for school uniforms, but an increase of 23 percent from 1999–2000. Dress codes declined 14.8 percent, a point which is lower than its 1999–2000 starting point. However, comparing the lowest figures for dress codes compared to the highest for school uniforms shows that schools preferred dress codes by a two-to-one margin (21.5 percent and 43.7 percent, respectively).

Table 9.1 National Center for Education Statistics: Safety and Security Measures

Strict Dress Codes & Mandatory School Uniforms		
Year	Mandatory School Uniform—% of Schools	Strict Dress Code—% of Schools
1999–2000	11.8	47.4
2003–2004	13.8	55.1
2005–2006	13.8	55.3
2007–2008	17.5	54.8
2009–2010	18.9	56.9
2013–2014	20.4	58.5
2015–2016	21.5	53.1
2017–2018	19.8	48.8
2019–2020	18.8	43.7

Source: National Center for Education Statistics, "Table 233.50 Percentage of Public Schools with Various Safety and Security Measures: Selected years, 1999–2000 through 2019–20," *Digest of Education Statistics* (October 2021), https://nces.ed.gov/programs/digest/d21/tables/dt21_233.50.asp

While the percentage of schools adopting school uniform policies is larger in 2020 than in 2000, even while it has declined from its high point, the distribution of those policies across school districts appears to be uneven. For example, the US Government Accountability Office in an October 2022 report on dress codes found that schools with certain characteristics had a higher percentage of school uniform policies. Schools with higher percentages of Black and Hispanic students had school uniform policies. Urban schools (40 percent) had more policies than suburban schools (18 percent) and rural schools (7 percent). In addition, the GAO estimated that 23 percent of elementary schools, 18 percent middle schools, and 10 percent of high schools required their students to wear a school uniform. And 64 percent of charter schools required uniforms.[9] Mandatory school uniform policies are not widely distributed throughout the nation's public schools.

Not All Schools Embrace School Uniform Policies

A 2015 University of New Hampshire policy brief reviewed responses from New Hampshire superintendents regarding whether they either had adopted a school uniform or were contemplating adopting such a policy in the near future. While the response rate is cautionary (32 percent +), it found that no responding superintendent had instituted a school uniform policy and none had definite plans to implement one. One superintendent said he or she may consider it in the next two years and another responded that the idea comes up every year, but there have been no serious talks about developing such a policy, and one superintendent wrote that there were "too many other issues to deal with."[10]

Furthermore, Kate Zernike in a 2002 *New York Times* article noted that schools in California, Utah, Florida, and Kansas had "abandoned" school uniform policies.[11] Similarly, New York City mayor Michael Bloomberg scrapped his plan to require uniforms in the city's schools when his report on school uniforms concluded that school uniform policies had not "reaped benefits in other cities."[12]

School uniforms have made it onto school board agendas with different results. In one case, the Somerset County Board of Education in Maryland was set to require the students at its two elementary schools to wear khaki pants and dress shirts starting in the fall of 2009. The school board hoped the change of clothes would improve the education system.

School board chair Jack Willing stated that the new policy would lead to fewer distractions in the classroom and less stress for parents, faculty, and students. "Parents stress out about buying expensive clothes, students stress out about what they are going to wear that day in trying to keep up with their peers," said Willing. "The faculty have to worry about being fashion police and determining whether something is appropriate or not."[13] Implementing a school uniform was, according to the school board chair, the perfect reform strategy.

However, the Long County Board of Education in Georgia rejected a recommendation from its superintendent to implement a school uniform policy.[14] Oddly enough, the faculty and school administrators were in favor of implementing a school uniform policy, but the parents were not. Similarly, but with an opposite conclusion, the Bradford County School Board in Florida voted to continue its school uniform policy at the middle school despite a parent survey that was nearly two to one against the policy.[15]

Similar problems, same proposal, but different politics resulted in different outcomes. This may be the lesson of policy streams: the same or similar problem (student learning, discipline, and school culture) and same proposal (mandatory student uniforms), but different politics mean that one proposal cannot be easily transposed from one community into the politics of another community.

"[T]he [Waxahachie Independent School District] noted that it had considered adopting school uniforms but decided not to do so, because it still wanted students to have some freedom to choose their clothing."—*Palmer v. Waxahachie Independent School District*, 579 F.3d 502, 505 note 2 (5th Cir. 2009)

For example, the Education Commission of the States concluded that "[a] ccording to this *Policy Report #15–02*, research on the effects of dress code and school uniform policies are inconclusive and mixed. Some researchers find positive effects, others claim no effects or only perceived effects."[16]

Educational polices, especially ones that engender controversy from students, parents, and community members, should be based on research. Many of the assertions about the efficacy of school uniforms and bringing about systemic and cultural change in schools may not be grounded in research and instead provide a narrative of false hope and vain promises of change.

Selected student comments about wearing a mandated school uniform:

"If someone wants to do well in school, they will without the help of dull and useless pieces of cloth."—Laura Wicki, responding to an online petition to stop Pinkerton Academy (Derry, New Hampshire) from adopting a school uniform policy. "Pinkerton Academy 'Unified Dress Code' (Uniforms): Stop the Uniform Proposal," Change.org (2013), https://www.change.org/petitions/pinkerton-academy-unified-dress-code-uniforms-stop-the-uniform-proposal

"[B]ecause nobody likes uniforms. [I] would look like an 85 year old woman."—Ocean Valdez, responding to an online petition against the proposed Pinkerton Academy school uniform policy. Ibid.

Westside High School (Houston Texas) student Raven Dugas commented on her high school newspaper's article on a proposed school uniform policy. She wrote (February 5, 2016), "Also, uniforms wouldn't increase academic success, if a student doesn't want to learn, a polo shirt with a Westside logo is not going to change that." And, "Let us solve our OWN problems, let us grow independently because in college we won't be wearing uniforms. Prepare for the future, leave uniforms in the past, that's for middle and elementary schools." (emphasis in original)— Karolina Benitez, Diana Carreon, & Kitzia Diago, "The Uniform Debate, (January 25, 2016), https://howlernews.com/1631/news/the-uniform-debate/.

SCHOOL UNIFORMS: THE LEGAL CONTROVERSY

The issue of what to wear to school has traveled from the clothes closet to the courtrooms across the United States, including New Hampshire. The twist in the morning ritual is not what clothes can be selected; rather, the issue—both political and legal—is that the decision has been taken from students by the public school policies about what must be worn.

However, while mandating uniform dress for students may have solved the morning question of what to wear, it has not resolved the issue of student expressive rights. Does a required school uniform abridge the free speech rights of public school students? Is it good public policy for a school district to adopt such a requirement? These two legal and policy issues continue to vex students, parents, and educators and to fill court calendars.

The legal arguments against public school policies which mandate a school uniform are the similar as those asserted for challenges to school dress code policies. Students who assert that a mandatory school uniform policy abridges their First Amendment right to wear clothing of their choice must argue that choosing one's clothing has some expressive content, possibly some symbolic expression.

Expressive conduct, as used in this commentary, is an activity such as wearing an article of clothing intended as a message. Expressive conduct usually does not involve the typical verbal or written communication most often associated with speech.[17] Expressive conduct is often symbolic, nonverbal speech.

As discussed in chapter 2, the test used by the courts to analyze expressive conduct were developed by non-education cases. For example, there two related elements are explored: Is there "[a]n intent to convey a particularized message . . . and in the surrounding circumstances the likelihood [must be] great that the message would be understood by those who view it."[18]

For example, in a 2022 case, a school administrator of the Mystic Valley Regional Charter School (Massachusetts) wrote up an eighth grade student for a uniform violation. The student wore a hijab to school. The school recognized that religious attire is "an expression of their sincerely held beliefs" but asks students to provide a letter "expressing this desire from a member of their clergy." The administration admitted that they mishandled the situation.[19]

While the US Supreme Court has recognized that speech at school may be symbolic, it does not automatically mean that all choices of what to wear is symbolic, expressive expression. For example, as discussed in chapter 3, Shermia Isaccs's argument that her decision to wear a headwrap in defiance of a school policy against wearing headgear violated her symbolic speech about celebrating her African American and Jamaican heritage failed in federal court.[20]

Similarly, a federal district court in North Carolina upheld a principal's prohibition against wearing blue jeans to a graduation ceremony, finding no violation of the student's constitutional rights.[21] Blue jeans, in this case, did not involve discernible expression worthy of constitutional protection.

A second free speech argument asserts that compelling students to wear a school uniform is tantamount to compelled speech reminiscent of the compelled flag salute of *West Virginia State Board of Education v. Barnette*.[22] For example, the plaintiff students in *Jacobs v. Clark County School District* argued that wearing a mandatory uniform forced them to convey a message of uniformity with which they disagreed.[23]

School uniform policies define what is proper attire; all other attire is improper. More certainty is achieved with a school uniform policy, and educator discretion in deciding what is appropriate is reduced as a consequence of the certainty. The amount of litigation on school uniforms compared to dress codes is quite small, but it is growing. As more schools adopt uniforms, it is expected that the pace of litigation will likely grow rather than contract, absent a definitive statement from the US Supreme Court.

Before discussing the cases that specifically addressed the issue of whether a school uniform policy violates students' constitutional rights, we will take a quick look at two cases related to school uniforms. These two cases are free speech cases aimed at school uniforms.

Nonspeech Challenges Related to School Uniforms

Interestingly, two cases involving school uniforms were heard in federal court, but the issue was not whether mandatory uniforms abridged free speech; the issue was whether students had the free speech right to protest against the school uniform policy. *Lowry v. Watson Chapel School District*[24] addressed the issue of the constitutionality of the discipline of students who wore black armbands protesting the school uniform policy.[25] The protest bands were worn on the wrist, forearm, or bicep and did not cover up any portion of the uniform. The school administrators instituted discipline, believing that the students were trying to defeat the school uniform policy. The students sued.

Using *Tinker*, the district court and the court of appeals found that the school had violated the students' free speech rights with their nondisruptive symbolic protest. The school district was permanently enjoined from "disciplining any student who wears a band substantially similar to the ones plaintiffs wore around the wrist."[26] The school uniform policy was not disturbed by the ruling, but the school district had to pay $37,500 in attorneys' fees to the student plaintiffs.[27] (See below for the district court analysis of the Watson Chapel School District school uniform policy.)

The second case was about buttons. Two fifth grade students at two different elementary schools in the Bayonne School District in New Jersey wore a button to protest the school uniform policy. The buttons had the phrase "No School Uniforms" and a red circle with a slash through it over a background picture appearing to portray a picture of Hitler Youth dressed in the same uniform and facing the same direction.[28] The school district sent letters home to the students' parents stating that the pictures were offensive and did not constitute speech. The parents brought suit.

The court held that the buttons were not school sponsored, thus *Kuhlmeier* did not apply. *Morse* did not apply because the button did not reference illegal drug activity. The court turned to *Fraser*.

Analyzing *Fraser*, the court developed a narrow definition of lewd, vulgar, indecent, or plainly offensive. These terms relate to the content of Matthew Fraser's nominating speech, which was replete with sexual innuendo. Suspect speech under a *Fraser* analysis fits between obscene at one end and offensive at the other end. Most often *Fraser* has been applied to speech that has implicit or explicit sexual content. Consequently, plainly offensive language without a sexual connotation does not fit within a *Fraser* analysis. The buttons, the court reasoned did not reach the level articulate in *Fraser* of sexual innuendo or profanity. The message was protected speech even though the court acknowledged that the Hitler Youth picture may be found by some to be offensive and in poor taste.[29]

Nevertheless, the button did not meet the *Fraser* standard of lewd or vulgar, and the application of *Tinker* supported the free speech rights of the students. There was no disruption and there was no reasonable forecast of a disruption; however, if a disruption occurred the school, officials may respond, the court concluded. As with *Lowry*, the school uniform code was left in place. The student plaintiffs were allowed to wear their protest buttons, but, in an odd ruling, they were not allowed to distribute the buttons at school.[30]

Up until 2014, all courts, including those that heard protest speech aimed at school uniform policies, have upheld the constitutionality of the school uniform policies. The one exception, *Frudden v. Pilling*,[31] will be discussed last. The state courts will be discussed first followed by the federal courts, concluding with the school uniform case on compelled speech.

SELECTED SCHOOL UNIFORM CASES: STATE COURTS

Arizona: *Phoenix Elementary School District No. 1 v. Green*, (1997)

On September 6, 1995, the Phoenix Preparatory Academy, a public inner-city middle school, instituted a mandatory uniform policy. On the day of implementation, two students wore clothing which did not comply with the policy. One student wore a T-shirt with a United States flag and logos stating, "I support my country" and "America." The other student wore a T-shirt with a picture of Jesus Christ and the Bible with the words "The School of Higher Learning." The parents of the students informed the school authorities that day that their children would never comply with the mandatory uniform policy and insisted that they were entitled to opt out of the policy. The school district responded by transferring the students out of the academy school to another school, which did not have a mandatory uniform policy. The following day, the parents and the students marched onto the academy's campus, entered the classrooms without permission, and distributed literature to other students disparaging the dress code. Both sides soon sued, seeking declaratory and injunctive relief.[32]

Consolidating the cases as *Phoenix Elementary School District No. 1 v. Green*, the trial court started with the forum analysis of *Cornelius v. NAACP Legal Defense and Educational Fund*, a non-education case decided by the US Supreme Court.[33] *Cornelius* distinguishes between public and nonpublic forums. A traditional public forum is a place or means of communication "which by long tradition or by government fiat [has] been devoted to assembly and debate." Street corners and public parks are typically perceived as public forums. Government's restriction of speech in a public forum must further a compelling state interest. Under *Cornelius*, government can restrict access to the forum "as long as the restrictions are reasonable and [are] not an effort to suppress expression merely because public officials oppose the speaker's view."[34]

The trial court's application of *Cornelius* found that the dress code regulated the medium of the message—choice of clothing—not the content of the message. It also found that the academy was not a public forum, and thus government could reserve the forum for its intended function: the education of students. Furthermore, the policy requiring a uniform was reasonable and an appropriate matter of concern for the school board. Finally, the trial court, balancing the interests of the entire student body, found those interests outweighing the plaintiffs' freedom of expression rights.

The court of appeals disagreed with the appellants as to whether the more stringent standard of *Tinker* was applicable and agreed with the trial court that the *Cornelius* analysis was appropriate. The court of appeals further agreed with the trial court that under the *Cornelius* standard, the mandatory uniform policy's content-neutral restrictions do not contravene the First Amendment. The appellate court affirmed that a school is generally not considered a public forum. To ascertain the reasonableness of the regulation, the court turned to *Hazelwood*, observing that school officials have great latitude to regulate activities in a manner reasonably related to legitimate pedagogical concerns.[35] The court accepted that the mandatory uniform regulation bears a reasonable relation to the pedagogical purpose of the school:

1. Promotes a more effective climate for learning
2. Creates opportunities for self-expression
3. Increases campus safety and security
4. Fosters school unity and pride
5. Eliminates "label competition"
6. Ensures modest dress
7. Simplifies dressing
8. Minimizes costs to parents[36]

Last of all, the court of appeals turned to the *Cornelius* analysis, which involves consideration of whether there are alternative avenues of expression. The appellate court noted that the dress code provided students with such alternative methods of expression as jewelry, buttons, non-uniform days, and petitions. The court concluded the school district's content-neutral mandatory uniform policy constitutionally regulated the students' First Amendment speech in the nonpublic forum of their school. It regulated a method, not a message, and was reasonable in view of the pedagogical mission of the school. It treated all content of speech neutrally, neither supporting nor opposing competing ideas.

This school uniform case is one of first impression. The focus of the case was less on the speech of the student than on the restrictive power of the school. The court did not explore the contours of whether the selection of clothing meets the threshold of speech. It may be inferred from the use of *Cornelius* that student clothing has some protected communicative properties, but the extent and margins of that speech were not charted. It may be that the constitutional issues typically raised with dress codes are sidestepped by mandatory uniform policies because a uniform policy is content neutral.

Furthermore, the court of appeals used the legitimate pedagogical test to determine reasonableness under *Cornelius*. The court also noted that the students had alternative methods of expression including wearing buttons. The U.S. Supreme Court in *Rosenberger v. Rector & Visitors of University of Virginia*[37] made clear that *Hazelwood*'s legitimate pedagogical concern governs only when a student's school-sponsored speech could reasonably be viewed as speech of the school itself. If the mandatory school uniform becomes identified with a particular school, would anything worn on the uniform be associated with the school?

In other words, would the button's message carry the imprimatur of the school, thus possibly embroiling the school in speech it may choose not to support? The alternative is that the school could disassociate itself from the speech, as per *Hazelwood*, by compelling the student to remove the button.

Would this act, then, reduce the alternative methods of expression available to students causing the school to run afoul of *Cornelius*?

The *Green* decision is conspicuous for its lack of a mandatory opt-out provision. Some have argued that an opt-out provision is necessary for a mandatory uniform policy to stand on constitutionally firm ground. One legal commentator argued that this lack of a need for an opt-out provision would help to overcome a major hurdle of instituting a uniform policy in high schools.[38] According to *Green*, whether the student's clothing is speech is immaterial because the forum is content neutral: all speech is treated the same, and government does not favor one idea over another.

Connecticut: *Byars v. City of Waterbury* (2001)

Byars v. City of Waterbury,[39] a school uniform case in Connecticut raises a constitutional question separate from the free speech argument, which has thus far dominated litigation on school uniforms. The Waterbury Public Schools approved a pilot program in 1997 to try out a school attire policy that limited students to wearing clothing of prescribed styles and colors—basically a uniform. The following year, the board of education adopted the pilot study school attire policy.

The policy in 1998–1999 school year provided an opt-out provision, allowing parents to exempt their children from the requirements concerning style and color but not the list of prohibited items, which included wearing blue jeans. In 1999–2000, the opt-out provision was eliminated, making the uniform policy mandatory. The policy differentiated the elementary and middle schools from the high school. The high school policy was less restrictive. Violations of the policy resulted in suspensions, with ten suspensions resulting in an expulsion recommendation.

After forty-nine suspensions for violations of the school attire policy, Teshana Byers was expelled on July 20, 1999. She was assigned to an alternative school operated by the school district. She was allowed to wear blue jeans—the basis for the suspensions—at the alternative school but was home-schooled by her parents instead during the 1999–2000 school year. Teshana, through her parents, sued the school district in April of 1999.[40] The original complaint was amended in May 2000 after the school board eliminated the opt-out provision. Teshana claimed, among other complaints, that the mandatory uniform policy deprived her of her liberty, protected through the Fourteenth Amendment, to wear blue jeans. However, she did not allege that the uniform policy violated her right to free speech. Instead, she based "her claim on the fourteenth amendment's prohibition against actions which, in substance, rather than procedure, constitute a denial of due process of law."[41] The judicial analysis under a substantive due process claim is different than the traditional free speech analysis of *Tinker*, *Fraser*, *Hazelwood*, and *Morse*.

The court first decided which level of scrutiny is most appropriate. "When the right infringed is 'fundamental,'" the court wrote, "the governmental regulations must be 'narrowly tailored to serve a compelling state interest.'"[42] Fundamental rights are central to our concept of "ordered liberty." Speech, voting, and childbearing are examples of fundamental rights requiring the strict scrutiny of the government's intended regulation. Governmental actions reviewed under this strict scrutiny analysis must be necessary to achieve a compelling state interest. Actions that do not involve fundamental rights are reviewed by a lesser standard. Under this lower standard, government actions are valid if they are rationally related to a valid governmental objective.

Clearly, it is easier for governmental policies to survive the standard of rationally related to a valid governmental objective. Strict scrutiny analysis makes it more difficult for government to prevail because the action must be "necessary"—a higher standard than rational—and the government objective being served by the policy must be compelling as opposed to simply legitimate. Government has a heavy burden when the courts employ strict scrutiny. "The court in the present case found that there is no fundamental right to wear blue jeans to school, and that only the rational relationship test applies to the challenged regulation."[43]

Rational basis was used to ascertain if the mandatory uniform policy was valid under substantive due process. The analysis started with the government goal. The court found that the goals of the uniform policy were to "reduce disruption, taunting, theft and loss of attention to course work."[44] Through testimony from the school's educators, the judge found that prohibition of blue jeans was rationally related to the stated goals.[45]

It is interesting and germane to our discussion that the court in *Byars* held that *Tinker* "approved the authority of school officials to regulate dress"[46] so long as the right to engage in specific fundamental rights such as political speech was not subject to unjustified regulations. In other words, the court asserted that the mere selection of what to wear to school does not necessarily implicate free speech. This position supports not only mandatory uniforms but also, to a possibly lesser degree, dress codes.

SELECTED SCHOOL UNIFORM CASES: FEDERAL COURTS

Louisiana: *Canady v. Bossier Parish School District* (2001)

In 1997, the Louisiana State Legislature amended its law to allow parish school boards the discretion to implement mandatory uniforms, provided the school board gives the students' parents written notice explaining the uniform requirements. In the 1998–1999 school year, the Bossier Parish School Board required sixteen of its schools to adopt mandatory uniforms as a pilot study to determine the effect of uniforms on the learning environment.

After receiving favorable results, the school board implemented a mandatory school uniform policy for all of its schools beginning in the 1999–2000 school year. The mandatory uniform was similar to the one in Arizona and consisted of a choice of two colors of polo or oxford shirts and navy or khaki pants.

Several parents filed suit in federal court seeking an injunction against the enforcement of the uniform policy. The parents claimed that the uniform policy violated their children's First Amendment rights to free speech, failed to account for religious preferences, and denied their children's liberty interest to wear clothing of their choice.

The parents and the school board filed for summary judgment. The school board offered statistics showing a reduction in disciplinary actions and a rise in test scores after the implementation of the uniform policy. The court entered summary judgment for the school district, and the parents' appeal followed.

The parents in *Canady v. Bossier Parish School District*[47] put forward a two-pronged appeal. First, they argued that the trial court erred by concluding that enforcement of the school uniform policy did not violate their children's constitutional rights. Second, they asserted that the trial court abused its discretion by denying them additional time to conduct discovery.

The appellate court started from the proposition that before reviewing the specifics of the uniform policy it must first be determined whether a person's choice of attire qualifies as speech protected by the First Amendment. The court used *Texas v. Johnson* a non-education Supreme Court case.[48] According to the test, first, the actor must intend to convey a particularized message, and second, there must be a great likelihood that the message would be understood by those who observe the conduct.

The court of appeals noted that the lower court relied on *Karr v. Schmidt*[49] and concluded that choice of clothing is a matter of taste or style and is not afforded First Amendment protection.[50] While *Karr* focused on hair length and communicative content, the district court equated hair length and clothing as essentially the same for purposes of constitutional protection.

The appellate court disagreed. It found that a "person's choice of clothing may be predicated solely on considerations of style and comfort, an individual's choice of attire also may be endowed with sufficient levels of intentional expression to elicit First Amendment shelter."[51] Conduct coupled with communicative intent raises First Amendment concerns, the court opined: "However, the First Amendment does not safeguard a limitless variety of behavior."[52]

Despite the statement above, the court took an expansive view, asserting that a person's choice of clothing is infused with intentional expression on many levels. Words printed on clothing qualify as pure speech and are protected under the First Amendment, the court asserted. Clothing may symbolize ethnic heritage or religious beliefs. Citing *Tinker*'s armband as authority, the court argued that color patterns or styles may be speech if worn with intent to express a particular message: "The choice to wear clothing as a symbol of an opinion or cause is undoubtedly protected under the First Amendment if the message is likely to be understood by those intended to view it."[53]

The court further asserted that students often choose attire with intent to signify the social group to which they belong and to communicate their attitude toward society in general and the school environment in particular. The audience for the message need not be adults, which may hold the message as of little value. However, "it has a considerable affect, whether positive or negative, on a young person's social development."[54] The court concluded that expression of one's identity and group affiliation through choice of clothing may meet the threshold for protected speech. Accordingly, the court of appeals disagreed with the district court's "blanket assertion that, like the length of a male student's hair, clothing does not contain sufficient communicative intent."[55]

The court offered several cautions regarding their analysis, lest it appear that it imbues all clothing choices with expressive protection. First, in a footnote, the court stated that "[w]e do not conclude that every choice of clothing expresses a particularized message."[56] Second, even if the forms of expressive conduct are protected speech, that protection is not absolute, "especially in the public school setting." The public school was carved out as a niche occupying a special place in First Amendment protection. The court noted that educators have an essential role in regulating school affairs and establishing appropriate standards of conduct and this must be balanced with the civil liberties of students. Citing the Supreme Court in *Hazelwood*, the Fifth Circuit wrote, "School boards, not federal courts, have the authority to decide what constitutes appropriate behavior and dress in public schools."[57]

In *Canady*, the court found that the facts of the case do not readily conform to either of the three categories addressed by the Supreme Court—*Tinker*, *Fraser*, and *Hazelwood*; *Morse* had not yet been decided but would likely not be used in this instance. The Bossier Parish School Board's mandatory uniform policy is viewpoint neutral on its face and as applied. In *Tinker*, the school regulation targeted the viewpoint of the antiwar movement. Unlike *Fraser*, students were not punished for lewd, obscene, or patently offensive words or pictures. Finally, a student's choice to wear certain apparel to school is neither a school-sponsored activity nor is it related to the school curriculum (*Hazelwood*).

Rejecting the three major student free speech Supreme Court cases at the time, the Fifth Circuit was left with the need to fashion an appropriate test. The court argued that because (1) choice of clothing is personal expression that happens to occur on the school premises and (2) the school board's uniform policy is unrelated to any viewpoint, a level of scrutiny should apply that is higher than the standard in *Hazelwood* but less stringent than the burden in *Tinker*. The court adopted the *O'Brien* intermediate scrutiny test.

Under the *O'Brien* analysis, the mandatory uniform policy passes constitutional scrutiny if it furthers an important or substantial government interest, if the interest is unrelated to the suppression of student expression, and if the incidental restrictions on First Amendment activities are no more than is necessary to facilitate that interest.

First, improving the educational process is undoubtedly an important governmental interest furthered by the uniform policy. The court cited school board statistics showing that one year after implementing the school uniform policy in several schools, "discipline problems drastically decreased and overall test scores improved."[58]

Second, the court asserted that purpose behind the school uniform policy—reduction of discipline problems and increase test scores—is unrelated to the suppression of student speech. While restricted from wearing clothing of their choice at school, the court noted, students are free to wear what they want after school. Third, students are also free to express their views through other means throughout the school day. The Fifth Circuit Court of Appeals did not state what those speech mediums might be. In a two-paragraph application of the *O'Brien* test, the court affirmed the district court's order granting summary judgment in favor of the Bossier Parish School Board.

In a similar case, *Long v. Board of Education of Jefferson County*,[59] involving a restrictive dress code instead of a uniform policy, a federal district court utilizing the *O'Brien* test found the dress regulation to be on constitutionally firm ground. In an apparent departure from *Tinker*, the court stated that it is "unnecessary to require the School to show that the Dress Code was necessary to stop an actual disruption."[60] As with *Canady*, the *Long* court distinguished the application of *Tinker*, *Fraser*, and *Hazelwood* and opted for the "less stringent" standard of *O'Brien*. The court concluded that the dress code was reasonable and therefore did not violate the plaintiffs' First Amendment rights.

Texas: *Littlefield v. Forney Independent School District* (2001)

The Forney Independent School District, acting under the Texas Education Code, passed a mandatory school uniform policy in 1999. Prior to the implementation of the code, the school district had a dress code that prohibited certain types of clothing deemed unsafe, immodest, or otherwise inimical to the educational process. There was no reported finding that the dress code policy was ineffective.

Nevertheless, the uniform policy was adopted to promote school spirit and school values, promote the decorum of a school as a place of order and work, and promote respect for authority. It was also asserted that the uniform policy was designed to decrease socioeconomic tensions, to increase attendance, and to reduce dropout rates. The relationship between these outcomes and wearing uniforms was not stated. Failure to comply with the uniform policy resulted in disciplinary action up to expulsion.

Suit was brought in 2000 against the policy, claiming a violation of students' free speech rights. The plaintiffs in *Littlefield v. Forney Independent School District* argued that the uniform policy acts as a form of coerced speech conveying a state-approved message and that it acts as a prior restraint preventing the students from expressing any message at all through their attire.[61]

The defendant school district asserted that the choice of clothing is not expressive conduct protected by the First Amendment. The school district also contended that "the wearing of school uniforms does not convey a sufficiently particularized message to be considered coerced speech."[62]

Under *Canady*, discussed above, a person's choice of clothing is infused with intentional expression and may amount to protected speech.[63] Also following *Canady*, the court of appeals applied the *O'Brien* test. The court first easily found that that the school district had the power to implement a uniform policy pursuant to state law; "[s]econd, improving the educational process is undoubtedly an important and substantial interest of Forney and the school board;"[64] and third, the plaintiffs did not establish that the school district's goal was to suppress expression. Consequently, the court of appeals found that the mandatory uniform policy "survives First Amendment scrutiny under the *O'Brien* test."[65] Thus, the school uniform policy was found to be constitutional.

Arkansas: *Lowry v. Watson Chapel School District* (2001)

We return to the *Lowry* discussion started above. Watson Chapel School District adopted a mandatory school uniform policy in the spring 2006 "to equal educational opportunity though economic access to appropriate and orderly, uniform apparel standards for students."[66] A number of students and parents opposed the policy.

On October 6, 2006, several students wore black armbands, reminiscent of *Tinker*, to protest the policy. The students did not wear the black armbands over any part of their school uniform in accordance with the policy, which allowed students to wear jewelry, including wristbands, as long as they were not worn over any part of the school uniform. The students were disciplined, and a suit in federal court followed four days later.

The court granted the students' motion for preliminary injunction. On February 22, 2007, the plaintiffs amended their complaint, adding allegations that the school uniform policy violated the freedom of expression in that it is a prior restraint on speech, that the enforcement of the policy violated the students' due process rights, and that the student literature policy violated their freedom of expression.[67]

The federal district court began its analysis acknowledging that neither the Supreme Court nor the Eighth Circuit had decided a school uniform or dress code case on First Amendment grounds. Lacking precedent, the court turned to the Sixth Circuit in *Blau v. Fort Thomas Public School District*[68] and the Fifth Circuit in *Littlefield v. Forney Independent School District*.[69]

First, the court found that the school uniform policy is unrelated to the suppression of expression. While students must wear the school uniform while students are at school, they are "absolutely free of the school uniform policy" after school, on the weekend, during holidays, and during vacations.[70] They can wear what they want during those times, expressing themselves in any way that they want. The second prong asks whether the policy furthers an important governmental interest. The policy is intended to further important governmental interests such as bridging socioeconomic gaps between families in the school district, focusing attention on learning rather than fashion, and improving school security.

The third prong, which requires that the policy not burden speech any more than necessary, is met by the policy. The district court opined that the policy is not pretext to suppress opinion and the uniform "requirement does not bar the 'important' personal inter-communication among students' necessary to an effective educational process."[71] In other, the school uniform policy does not foreclose all the means of communication available to students while they are in school. Having met the standards of *O'Brien*, the court concluded, "the school uniform policy adopted by the Watson Chapel School District contravenes no provision of the United States Constitution."[72]

Nevada: *Jacobs v. Clark County School District* (2008)

Jacobs v. Clark County School District, a Ninth Circuit Court of Appeals case,[73] involved high school students. The student plaintiff brought suit for violations of First Amendment expressive rights; the court used the *O'Brien* analysis, upholding the school district's school uniform policy.

The Clark County School District adopted Regulation #5131, creating a dress code for all of its students. The regulation also allowed individual schools to adopt a more stringent school uniform code. The school uniform policies were to be established "for the purpose[s] of increasing student achievement, promoting safety, and enhancing a positive school environment."[74]

The Liberty High School uniform regulation required all students to wear solid khaki-colored bottoms and solid-colored polo, T-, or button-down shirts (blue, red, or white) with or without Liberty logos. Kimberly Jacobs, an eleventh grader at Liberty High School, violated the uniform policy five times, resulting in twenty-five days of suspension. Educational services were provided during the suspensions.[75]

Kimberly brought suit against the school district seeking declaratory relief that the school uniform policy violated her free speech rights among other allegations, expunge the disciplinary records, and award her appropriate damages. Jacobs won her preliminary injunction but moved to another school district. Concerned about the viability of the lawsuit, a number of students and their parents joined the suit, seeking declaratory and injunctive relief and appropriate damages. However, on summary judgment, the defendant school district prevailed.

On appeal, the plaintiffs alleged that the implementation of the school uniform policy prevented them from engaging in pure speech[76] and expressive conduct,[77] and that it compels them "to 'speak' in a particular manner."[78] The court began with a review of whether the stricter standard of *Tinker* applies to a school uniform case, which has content-neutral regulations on expressive conduct rather than pure speech. The court of appeals found that the stricter standard of *Tinker*'s substantial interference test applies to pure speech but not to expressive conduct. The court selected the intermediate scrutiny of *O'Brien*. Nothing in the school uniform regulation, the court opined, was directed at suppressing "the expression of particular ideas[79] "or [] manipulat[ing] the public debate through coercion rather than persuasion."[80]

Instead, the regulation was directed at (1) promoting safety by "reducing the ability to hide weapons, drugs, or alcohol; (2) allowing students and staff to focus more attention on increasing student achievement; (3) eliminating dress differences that emphasize different income levels; and (4) simplifying daily school preparation and maintenance for families."[81] The appellate court found that the school uniform policy was content neutral "despite [the] allowances for clothing containing school logos."[82]

The intermediate scrutiny of *O'Brien* involves a three-step analysis.[83] As applied to the Clark County School District mandatory school uniform policy, the court found that it furthers important governmental interests of "increasing student achievement, promoting safety, and enhancing a positive school environment."[84] The second prong of *O'Brien*'s intermediate scrutiny analysis asks whether the school district's interests are unrelated to the suppression of free expression. The court asserted that on their face, the "District's goals have nothing to do with quelling speech or limiting expression."[85] The district's policy, the court argued, is not a pretext "for an underlying desire to limit free speech."[86]

The third prong requires that the school uniform policy does not restrict more speech than necessary. A school uniform restricts the clothing choices of students, which limits students' ability to express themselves by way of their choice of clothes to wear at school. However, students retain the ability to express themselves through the school day via other means such as verbal conversations, publishing articles in the school newspaper, and joining student clubs. Furthermore, students can wear what they want when school is not in session.

The Clark County School District mandatory uniform policy withstood intermediate scrutiny; therefore, students' free speech rights were not abridged.

The plaintiff's last allegation was the school uniform policy compelled students to express support for the school district's message of conformity. The plaintiff's argument is that wearing a uniform conveys symbolic messages of conformity and community affiliation.[87] The court disagreed, finding it unlikely that a person viewing a student's uniform would understand it to be a message of conformity.

The Ninth Circuit Court of Appeals upheld the district court's grant of summary judgment in favor of the school district.[88] School uniforms prevailed again.

Indiana: *Derry v. Marion Community Schools* (2008)

One of the arguments advanced by school uniform advocates is that school uniforms will save parents money in that they do not have to buy a lot of expensive clothes, feeding into the designer wars that are often waged in schools. This tenet was tested in an Indiana case. Soon after a school uniform policy was adopted for McCulloch Middle School, parents brought suit seeking a preliminary injunction against its implementation on the grounds that the cost of the uniforms would place an undue burden on their family, thus violating due process and equal protection.[89] They did not pursue a free speech argument.

The school uniform policy specifies that color and types of clothes that can be worn and the clothes that students are restricted from wearing.[90] Exceptions are made for physical conditions or religious affiliations. The school administration conducted research on school uniforms and found that uniforms, among other findings, helped to prevent gang-related clothing issues and increased the focus on learning, and that "uniforms helped to level the playing field between students who can and cannot afford brand name clothing."[91]

The parents of the two middle school students preferred to buy new clothes for their children and planned to purchase five sets of uniforms for each child so they could have a different uniform for each day of the week. Their equal protection argument asserted that the uniform policy was not relationally related to improve education and to address disciplinary problems. Because some students had opt-out provisions, they argued that it did not makes sense to have the two groups intermingle at school functions and extracurricular events. They asserted their fundamental right to make decisions regarding the "care, custody, and control of their children."[92] (This is an argument unsuccessfully asserted by cases discussed previously, *Blau v. Fort Thomas Public School District* and *Littlefield v. Forney Independent School District*).

The court used the rational basis analysis and not strict scrutiny analysis reserved for suspect classifications and fundamental interests. The federal district court held parents "do not have a fundamental right to direct the dress code and school uniform policy."[93] McCulloch Middle School, the court found, was a low-performing that had not shown adequate yearly progress in the previous five years and that in the prior year it had three thousand disciplinary referrals. The court argued that the school was acting rationally to address the problems, and trying a school uniform "experiment" was tailored to the problems. The nexus between the policy and goals need not be perfect.

Finding a rational basis for the school uniform policy, the court held that parents were not required to purchase a minimum number of uniforms, nor did the policy require the uniforms be purchased from particular stores. In addition, parents could access the free uniform program. Therefore, parents retained considerable control over the costs of the school uniforms. The equal protection claim failed, and because it failed, the due process claim failed as well. The school uniform withstood constitutional scrutiny.

Nevada: *Frudden v. Pilling* (2012 and 2014)

Roy Gomm Elementary School (RGES) in Reno, Nevada, passed a school uniform policy in May 2011, with two-thirds of the families voting to approve the mandatory school uniform policy.[94] Students were required to wear red or navy polo-style shirts and tan or khaki bottoms during school hours. Students were not allowed to alter the uniform. The exemption to the mandatory school policy was wearing a uniform from a nationally recognized youth organization such as the Boy Scouts or the Girl Scouts. The uniform shirts had the Roy Gomm logo of a gopher with the words "Roy Gomm Elementary School," with the school motto—"Tomorrow's Leaders"—above it. The school uniform was objected to, and the motto "Tomorrow's Leaders" became the focus of the ensuing lawsuit.

In early fall, soon after the policy was implemented, the Frudden children (a fifth grade boy and a third grade girl) did not wear the required uniform; no action was taken by the school. Approximately two weeks later, they wore uniforms from the youth soccer organization. The students were asked to change because there was neither a meeting of the organization nor a practice that day. The same thing happened following day, with the same result. On the following day, September 14, 2011, the fifth grade boy wore his uniform shirt inside out so that the logo was not visible. When he was asked to turn it right side out, he complied. The Fruddens sued.[95]

Aside from the four student free speech cases, two other Supreme Court cases help to frame the discussion in *Frudden v. Pilling* of the school uniform's "Tomorrow's Leaders" motto as compelled student speech. The controversy was framed by two concepts. First, the right to speak connotes a complementary right to refrain from speaking.[96] Second, in a teachers' union case, the Supreme Court wrote that "at the heart of the First Amendment is the notion that an individual should be free to believe as he will, and that in a free society one's beliefs should be shaped by his mind and his conscience rather than coerced by the State."[97] In other words, concomitant with the right to speak is the right not to be compelled to speak.

The Ninth Circuit Court of Appeals (2014)

The federal district court granted the defendant school district' motion to dismiss the case, thus finding that the school uniform policy did not violate the plaintiffs' constitutional rights. Among other findings,[98] the court found the motto[99] with the picture of a gopher, while slightly complex, was innocuous and that there was no meaningful risk that the students would be conveying a message of conformity.

The plaintiffs alleged the school uniform compelled students to wear an expressive statement that is not viewpoint neutral "and that the very fact of wearing a uniform compels the expression of support for group affiliation."[100] The district court disagreed and granted the defendant school district's motion to dismiss. The Fruddens appealed.

There were two issues before the Ninth Circuit. First, is the required logo "Tomorrow's Leaders" unconstitutionally compelled speech on leadership?[101] Second, does the policy contain a content-based exemption for nationally based student organizations, such as the Boy Scouts and the Girl Scouts?

Compelled Speech Analysis

Frudden came on the heels of another Ninth Circuit case involving a mandatory school uniform: *Jacobs v. Clark County School District* (see above).[102] In that case, the appellate court upheld the school's school uniform policy. Some of the schools displayed the school logo but none of the school uniforms had written communications. Therefore, the defendant schools did not force students to communicate any message, "much less one expressing conformity or community affiliation."[103] The policy merely required students to wear solid-colored tops and bottoms.[104] Consequently, the *Frudden* court distinguished the *Jacobs* court holding. However, the *Jacobs* court noted that the school uniform did not convey a symbolic message.[105]

This analysis starts with the Supreme Court case *West Virginia Board of Education v. Barnette*,[106] the classic flag salute case in which a state law requiring students to stand and recite the Pledge of Allegiance was found to be unconstitutional. The Supreme Court held that the compelled flag salute violates the Bill of Rights, which protects individuals' right to speak their own mind and not be compelled by the government "to utter what is not in [their] mind."[107]

The court asserted that the mandatory pledge required an "affirmation of a belief and an attitude of mind."[108] The pledge was characterized as an "observance of ritual,"[109] analogizing the flag salute to a "coerced uniformity of sentiment"[110] and a "compulsory unification of opinion."[111] Essentially, the court that the individual right of conscience and intellect is inviolable by government. Government cannot compel individuals to espouse that which the individual does not hold.

Thirty-four years after the *West Virginia* case, the Supreme Court heard another case of compelled speech, *Wooley v. Maynard*,[112] in which New Hampshire's license plate inscription, "Live Free or Die," was the subject of the free speech case. Were the plaintiffs compelled by government to express a position by carrying the license plate with a motto they felt was "repugnant to their religious and political beliefs"?[113] The plaintiffs became the instrument, through the license plate motto, to convey government's normative statement, a statement with which the plaintiffs disagreed. This is the essential reasoning of *West Virginia*.[114]

Similarly, the Fruddens argued that the mandated written motto conveys two viewpoints: first, that "leadership should be celebrated (or at least valued above being a follower), and second, Roy Gomm Elementary School is likely to produce '[t]omorrow's leaders.'"[115] The court of appeals agreed that the motto on the mandatory school uniform conveyed a message to which the Fruddens disagreed but were compelled to passively advocate.

The court held that the motto was not meaningfully distinguishable from the New Hampshire license plate.[116] The school uniform with its mandated motto violated the free speech of the plaintiffs through compelled speech.

"Practically speaking, RGES [Roy Gomm Elementary School] compels its students 'to be an instrument' for displaying the RGES motto. Had the RGES uniforms consisted of plain colored tops and bottoms, as in *Jacobs,* RGES would have steered clear of any First Amendment concerns. However, by mandating the written motto on the uniform shirts, the RGES policy compels speech under *Wooley.*"—*Frudden v. Pilling*, 742 F.3d 1199, 1205 (9th Cir. 2014).

Content-Neutral Policy?

The plaintiffs next argued that the school uniform policy exemption for nationally recognized youth organizations is not content neutral. When government favors the content of one speech over another with a different content, it comes before the courts with an exacting test it must meet. The classic example of content-neutral restrictions are time, place, and manner restrictions. The burden is placed on the government/school district to meet the burden of its restriction on speech based on the content of the speech.

The court asserted that the exemption favors the speech of some organizations (nationally recognized student organizations) but not others (locally or regionally recognized youth organizations).[117] "Therefore," the RGES school uniform policy's "exemption indicates a content-specific distinction between favoring certain clothing-related speech."[118]

Reversed and Remanded

The Ninth Circuit Court of Appeals held for the plaintiff Fruddens' finding that the motto on the school uniform constituted compelled speech. The court also asserted that the exemptions were not content neutral. Furthermore, the policy must reviewed using the highest level of review – strict scrutiny analysis.

This analysis asks whether the goal of the policy serves a compelling state interest and whether the means (a school uniform policy) are narrowly tailored to serve the interest. Therefore, the court reversed the decision of the district court and remanded it back to the lower court to allow the school district the opportunity to justify placing the written motto on the uniforms and the exemption in the policy.[119]

On remand, the district court used strict scrutiny analysis rather than intermediate scrutiny to analyze the motto and exception, as directed by the appellate court. The lower court awarded summary judgment to the school district. The district court held that the motto was narrowly tailored to a compelling state interest and thus survived strict scrutiny. It also found that the individual defendants were entitled to qualified immunity because there was not a clearly established right against compelling students to wear a motto. It did not reach the issue of whether the exemption also survived strict scrutiny because the Fruddens did not suffer any damages. Jon Frudden appealed.[120]

Back to the Court of Appeals (2017)

The 2017 appellate panel disagreed with the earlier panel, asserting that intermediate rather than strict scrutiny should be applied to the policy. However, their call for an *en banc* failed. Thus, the 2017 appellate court was bound to use strict scrutiny following the 2014 ruling.

Applying strict scrutiny analysis to the motto "Tomorrow's Leaders," the court found that the two government interests of "promoting student achievement and preventing bullying or distractions arising out of differences in student's socioeconomic backgrounds" is important but did not find authority that they are compelling.[121] The appellate panel, however, was willing to find that these interests "can hardly be more compelling than fostering children's educational achievement and providing a safe and supportive educational environment."[122] However, the court "reluctantly" concluded that the display of the motto on the mandated school uniforms does not serve those interests.

The appellate court affirmed the decision that the school uniform motto failed the strict scrutiny analysis test. The school uniform with the school's motto is unconstitutional, therefore, compelling speech which the plaintiff students disagreed. The court also affirmed the district court's finding that the individual defendants were entitled to qualified immunity. It affirmed the district court's finding that the individual defendants were entitled to qualified immunity.[123] However the appellate court remanded to the lower court to determine damages to the institutional defendants (the school district and the Parent-Faculty Association).

Because *Frudden* is both new and novel in its asserted cause of action, its impact is hard to forecast with any precision. One outcome, at least at this point, that appears to be clear is that a school should refrain, at least in the Ninth Circuit, from having a motto on its uniforms. Second, given that the exemptions were not considered content neutral, thus raising the level of review, it may be more prudent for a school to not allow any exemptions, thus not allowing for any speech. Another outcome may be the reluctance by school authorities to assert the school's position, aspirations, and message through broad-based means for fear of lawsuits. The school district spent more than $100,000 in legal fees, not counting the amount of educator time required, to address whether "Tomorrow's Leaders" is compelled speech.[124]

This case is interesting and instructive on several levels.

Compelled Speech

- The compelled speech section of the *Frudden* court's holding raises issues. If mottos and their use in schools are constructed liberally, the application of compelled speech may proliferate beyond school uniforms. While the students in *West Virginia v. Barnette* suffered expulsion for their decision to violate the policy on the flag salute, the Fruddens suffered no such adverse action, and discipline was not central to their case. While the Fruddens suffered no state-sanctioned adverse action, as opposed to *Barnette* (expulsion)[125] and *Wooley* (imprisonment),[126] the court considered a lack of adverse state action to be irrelevant. Therefore, no additional harm other than compelled speech is necessary under *Frudden* to assert a cause of action.
- *Frudden* introduced, at the federal appellate level, compelled speech, which has not surfaced in any meaningful way since *West Virginia v. Barnette*. Once a cause of action has entered the court system, the tendency is for it to proliferate beyond the original fact pattern. For instance, if a school has students who violate the dress code and are told to wear a T-shirt in place of or over the questionable attire or face suspension and that T-shirt states something more than the name of the school, is it compelled speech?
- Do all aspirational statements/mottos, such as "Everyone Successful Everyday," "Where Kids are #1," and "*Scientia*, *Concordia*, *Sapientia*: Knowledge, Harmony and Wisdom," or even such descriptions as "Home of the Warriors" or "Home of the Crusaders" constitute speech? And under *Frudden*, if they are speech, it may constitute compulsion to carry the statement on school materials or to recite the non-"ideological speech"? Does a required school identification card with the school's motto constitute compelled speech?
- A statement about the students being the leaders of tomorrow is innocuous. Yet it is considered compelled speech. The unresolved issue that both *Frudden* and *Jacobs* dodged was whether the logo (the gopher in *Fridden*) constitutes speech and thus can be compelled speech. If the logo is compelled speech, the constitutional protection may reach beyond school uniforms

to any other identification with the school that students may encounter in which they wear, carry, or identify their school.

- It is problematic whether the slogan "Tomorrow's Leaders" will survive strict scrutiny analysis. Does it serve a compelling state interest, and is it narrowly drawn? Will any motto or slogan reach this exacting and high standard? Will any hortatory statement about the goals of the school reach this standard?

Content-Neutral Exemptions

The requirement for greater specificity for exemptions may involve an attempt to narrow exemptions through a tighter definition or to expand them to include everything. The proper response may be to not allow any restrictions, much like *Palmer v. Waxahachie Independent School District*,[127] which banned all messages on student clothing. This content-neutral finding may not be specific to just exemptions for school uniforms. Is an exemption for religious beliefs content neutral or does it favor religious beliefs over other kinds of beliefs (or no beliefs)?

Wearing a school uniform with the motto "Tomorrow's Leaders" is not the same as being compelled to stand and recite a pledge that is not held by the individual, nor is it of the same degree of infringement as being compelled to affix a license plate to your vehicle forcing the owner "to be an instrument for fostering public adherence to an ideological point of view he finds unacceptable."[128] Schools are special places where deference is often afforded to school authorities to establish acceptable and reasonable expectations for student behavior. Becoming tomorrow's leaders is an aspiration, possibly a teaching opportunity to remind students of the potential they carry within them. It is not a pledge of allegiance in support of nationalism, nor is it a license plate affixed to one's property proclaiming a particular normative position favored by government.

Frudden restricts the ability of school authorities to make reasoned and rational decisions regarding student behavior. Another hurdle has been placed in front of educators, who must have at their fingertips the constitutional knowledge and application of legal concepts that do not abridge a student's constitutional rights; for example, what constitutes lewd and vulgar language, what constitutes a matter of public concern, when is the student speaking as a student and not as a citizen who just happens to be at school, what constitutes a prior restraint, and what off-campus internet/electronic communication requires on-campus discipline. And now educators may have to possibly parse what constitutes compelled speech.

The court's holding on compelled speech is particularly problematic and may result in mischief. *Frudden* provides little guidance for school administrators who must almost daily chart a path through the thicket of First Amendment rights and still manage the culture of the school, provide a safe environment, and meet curricular demands. Today's leaders are ill served by the ruling on "Tomorrow's Leaders."

CONCLUDING REMARKS

The comparison between dress code litigation and school uniform litigation is stark. Dress codes have a spotty record of constitutional survival, whereas school uniforms have a near-perfect record. Litigation involving dress codes tends to look more like potpourri than an articulated and unified body of litigation. The more restrictive policy of mandated dress fared better than the more flexible attire policy of dress codes.

In addition to the near-perfect win/loss record for school uniforms, of note is the judicial standards that have been used by these cases. With dress codes, we have seen *Tinker* used predominantly to ascertain if student speech can be sanctioned for causing or reasonably forecasting a disruption as the major standard used by the courts. *Fraser* and *Hazelwood* have also been used, and to a much lesser degree so has *Morse*. However, we are seeing the use of the non-education standards being used more often.

The lesson for dress codes from a review of school uniform cases may be found in *Palmer v. Waxahachie Independent School District*, in which all student speech is stopped through content-neutral policies and which survived constitutional muster.[129] Less student speech may be the outcome.

School uniform cases have not followed the traditional four student free speech cases. Instead, the courts have used the non-education Supreme Court cases of *O'Brien*, *Spence*, and *Johnson*. *O'Brien* is used to judge whether the uniform policy passes intermediate scrutiny for content-neutral policies. Every time it has been used, the school uniform policy passed the test. *Spence* and *Johnson* are used to ascertain what expressive conduct rises to the level of speech and thus follows under the penumbra of the First Amendment protection.

With *Frudden*, we see the intersection of two Supreme Court cases: one arising in public education (*West Virginia Board of Education v. Barnette*) and the other involving adult free speech (*Wooley v. Maynard*). It is foreseeable that *O'Brien*, *Spence*, and *Johnson* will continue to influence student free speech issues associated with student attire. The impact of *Frudden* could be relatively short-lived if schools make the motto voluntary. However, compelled speech may surface in other venues.

To Require a School Uniform or Not?

This book is not advocating for student uniforms in the public schools. Coupled with other school reform strategies, school uniforms may play a role in reshaping a school's culture and creating a school environment that is perceived as more orderly and more focused on academics. But school uniforms alone offer a vain hope and false promise of change and will likely produce disappointing results unless they are introduced as part of a wider and encompassing effort to achieve change.

Should a school district decide to explore the fit of a mandatory school uniform with the culture of its school(s), the following considerations should help to guide school authorities before and while adopting a student uniform policy.

Political Considerations

A. Keep in mind that a constitutionally firm policy is not the same as an educationally sound policy or a politically viable and enforceable policy.[130]
B. Be cognizant of the challenges of change, especially changes that have high visibility and impact beliefs and practices. Expect resistance; almost any change is threatening to some school constituents, and schools should expect at least some parents to consider school uniforms to be a threat to family's right to make their own decisions about what their children wear to school.
C. Involve parents early and throughout the process. Do not leave the public out of this public education discussion and decision.
D. Make sure that you have worked with the faculty, staff, and administrators to answer their questions, to listen carefully to them, and to look for advocates within the schools. What exactly are the problems that school uniforms are intended to address and why do you think, beyond mere speculation and hope, that school uniforms will appropriately and adequately address those concerns?
E. Keep your school board advised at every stage of the school uniform adoption process. School board members will face the same type of public scrutiny and heat that the school administration will face. Are board members supportive of the proposed policy? If not, address their concerns before going too far down the implementation road. What do they need to know? Make sure school board members can publicly articulate an educational justification for mandating school uniforms.

Organizational Considerations

A. Gather research studies that look at both the pros and cons of school uniform policies. Develop readable position statements for and against adopting a school uniform policy based on research and public input. Make those findings easily available prior to community meetings.
B. Know the case law on school uniforms and have it handy for responding to questions.
C. Ensure that there are multiple venues that allow for community input.
D. Make sure that your meetings are well organized and well run. Choose your moderator carefully. It is best to have someone without a stake or position in the outcome.
E. Parents are conscious of the cost of school uniforms. They must provide two sets of clothes, those for school (the uniform) and those for out-of-school activities. What allowances can be made for parents who have reasonable fiscal constraints and concerns about purchasing a uniform? What are some of the local costs of the uniform?
F. Be wary of specifying suppliers for uniforms. Requiring that school uniforms be purchased from a specific retailer reduces options for parents with limited economic means.

Legal Considerations

A. What exemptions/opt-out provisions will you allow? As reviewed in *Frudden v. Pilling* above, you should include a carefully crafted exemption for religious reasons. A school uniform policy may substantially burden the free exercise of a student's religion. Allowing yarmulkes for Jewish male students and headscarves for female students who are practicing Muslims are a good start in crafting religious exemptions.
B. In light of the discussion of non-education cases in chapter 3, what alternative means of expression will you allow for student speech if students are required to wear uniforms? Will you allow pins, buttons, sashes, or caps? Are there topics that will not be allowed at school (think dress code restrictions)? Will you allow sagging uniforms similar to *Bivens*? Will you allow students to wear pins that proclaim their opposition to abortion, homosexuality, or the school uniform policy itself?
C. Given the decision in *Frudden*, will your school uniform include the school's motto or name? The Fruddens objected to being required to wear the school's motto because it allegedly celebrated leadership over followership and because they disagreed with the motto's claim that the school is likely to produce tomorrow's leaders.[131]

Including the school's mascot as part of the school uniform, at this point, seems to be safe. However, out of an abundance of caution, schools may want to consider making their mascot and logo optional, allowing students to purchase patches to affix to their uniform if they choose.

As stated above, this analysis is neither an advocacy piece for uniforms nor a lobby against them. However, as outlined, the road to adopting a school uniform policy is fraught with peril, and school administrators who attempt to implement such a policy would be wise to prepare for opposition.

Courts often accept the school district's assertion that mandatory school uniforms support the school district's stated student academic and social outcomes, thus a compelling interest is served by the uniforms. However, this has often occurred without an analysis of data to support the connection. As research accumulates on the impact of school uniforms, research will be introduced that either establishes the nexus or questions whether a change of clothes is, as school uniform researchers David L Brunsma and Kerry A. Rockquemore analogize, "cleaning and brightly painting a deteriorating building in that on the one hand, it grabs our immediate attention; on the other hand, it is only a coat of paint."[132]

School uniforms to date have consistently passed constitutional muster, with the exception of the *Frudden* coerced speech case. As schools and school districts focus on this record of successfully responding to student lawsuits, many may equate legal success with school uniform success. This may be premature, as two education law commentators have stated: "School uniforms may well be a symbolic reform rather than a substantive reform. The jury is literally still out."[133] We do not know yet know what effect, if any, school uniforms have on student achievement and behavior.

NOTES

1. Jeff Grabmeier, "School uniforms don't improve child behavior, study finds," Ohio State News (December 20, 2021), https://news.osu.edu/school-uniforms-dont-improve-child-behavior-study-finds/.

2. A policy is a set of values issued with authority and expressed in written form or words. It is authoritative when there is sufficient power to induce a shift in behavior toward achieving specified values. Catherine Marshall, Douglas Mitchell, and Frederick Wirt, *Culture and Education Policy in the American States* (New York: Falmer Press, 1989). Policies consiss "of a web of decisions and actions that allocate values." David Easton, *The Political System* (New York: Alfred A. Knopf, 1953), 130.

3. John W. Kingdon, *Agendas, Alternatives, and Public Policies*, 2nd ed. (New York: Longman, 1995).

4. US Department of Education, *Manual on School Uniforms* (n.d.), 1, https://files.eric.ed.gov/fulltext/ED387947.pdf.

5. William Jefferson Clinton, "Remarks by President on School Uniform Program. Jackie Robinson Academy, Long Beach, California (February 24, 1996), cited in Alison Mitchell, "Clinton Will Advise Schools on Uniforms, The New York Times (February 25, 1996), https://www.nytimes.com/1996/02/25/us/clinton-will-advise-schools-on-uniforms.html.

6. Reported in Todd A. DeMitchell, "Commentary: School Uniforms: There Is No Free Lunch," *Teachers College Record* (December 14, 2006), ID 12891.

7. Troy Y. Nelson, "If Clothes Make the Person, Do Uniforms Make the Student? Constitutional Free Speech Rights and Student Uniforms," *Education Law Reporter* 118 (1997): 1 (school uniforms can support a safe school if part of an overall safety program).

8. DeMitchell, *supra* note 6.

9. Jacqueline M. Nowacki, *K–12 Education: Department of Education Should Provide Information on Equity and Safety in School Dress Codes* (Washington, DC: US Government Accountability Office GAO-23–105348 K–12 Education, October 2022), 23, https://www.gao.gov/assets/gao-23–105348. pdf.

10. Todd A. DeMitchell, "School Uniforms in New Hampshire Public Schools: Hype or Hope," *Policy Brief #15–02* (University of New Hampshire, Department of Education, November 2015), 1–13. "New Hampshire schools, as noted by Ted Comstock, Esq. Executive Director of the New Hampshire School Board Association, have not joined the national uptick in adopting school uniform policies, instead most have opted for "school dress codes that are quite general in scope." Ibid., 3.

11. Kate Zernicke, "Plaid's Out Again, as Schools Give up Requiring Uniforms," *New York Times* (September 13, 2002), http://www.nytimes.com/2002/09/13/us/plaid-s-out-again-as-schools-give-up-requiring-uniforms.html.

12. Jennifer Steinhauer, "Bloomberg, with Promises to Keep, Says He Kept Many," *New York Times* (February 11, 2003), http://www.nytimes.com/2003/02/11/nyregion/bloomberg-with-promises-to-keep-says-he-kept-many.html.

13. Brie Jackson, "Two Somerset County Schools to Start Wearing Uniforms," WBOC (May 29, 2009), http://www.wboc.com/Global/story.asp?S=10439682&nav=MXEF.

14. Mike Riddle, "Log BoE Nixes Student Uniforms," *Coastal Courier* (Hinesvilla, Ga.) (May 29, 2009), https://coastalcourier.com/news/long-boe-nixes-student-uniforms/.

15. Mark J. Crawford, "Board Ignores Survey to Support Uniforms," *Bradford County Telegraph* (Starke, Fla.) (May 28, 2009), http://www.zwire.com/site/news.cfm?newsid=20321977&BRD=2150&PAG=461&dept_id=377017&rfi=6.

16. Education Commission of the States, *School Safety: Uniforms and Dress Codes*, http://www.ecs.org/html/IssueSection.asp?issueid=101&subissueid=331&ssID=0&s=Selected+Research+% 26+Readings, cited by Howard Johnson, "Research Brief: Student Dress Codes and Uniforms," *Education Partnerships* (November 2, 2009), https://files.eric.ed.gov/fulltext/ED537953.pdf.

17. See *R. A. V. v. St. Paul*, 505 U.S. 377 (1992).

18. *Spence v. Washington*, 418 U.S. 405, 410–11 (1974).

19. "Massachusetts Student Receives Uniform Violation for Hijab," AP News (August 19, 2022), https://apnews.com/article/religion-massachusetts-charter-schools-trending-news-6e63c101a1b294116a02d0f2b53e8c86. Five years earlier, the charter school came under intense scrutiny for disciplining two fifteen-year-old Black female students for violating a policy banning hair braid extensions while white students had not been punished for violations of hairstyle regulations. Ibid. In July 2022, a law prompted by this incident was passed banning discrimination based on natural hairstyles.

20. *Issacs v. Board of Education of Howard County, Maryland*, 40 F. Supp.2d 335 (D. Md. 1999). See also *Brandt v. Board of Education of City of Chicago*, 480 F.3d 460, 465 (7th Cir. 2007), *cert. denied*, 128 S.Ct. 441 (2007) (middle school students designed a T-shirt for school; "clothes are certainly a way in which people express themselves, clothing as such is not-not normally at any rate-constitutionally protected speech.").

21. *Fowler v. Williamson*, 448 F. Supp. 497 (W.D. N.C. 1978).

22. 319 U.S. 624 (1943).

23. 526 F.3d 419, 428 (9th Cir. 2008).

24. 508 F. Supp. 2d 713 (E. D. Ark. 2007), *aff'd* 540 F.3d 752 (8th Cir. 2008), *cert. denied*, 129 S.Ct. 1526 (2009).

25. The school policy also stated that "[n]o towel, scarf, bandana, do-rag, shirt, string, chain, jewelry, special button, insignia, label, marking, different-colored stitching, fringe, brad, stud, picture, logo, ribbon, embroidery, initials, monogram, special buckle, or any other form of adornment may be worn on or over any part of the uniform, except the school name, school logo, or school insignia." *Lowry v. Watson Chapel School District*, 540 F.3d 752, 756 note 6 (8th Cir. 2008).

26. Ibid., 762.

27. Ibid., 766.

28. *DePinto v. Bayonne Board of Education*, 514 F.Supp.2d 633, 636 (D. N.J. 2007).

29. Hitler was, said the court, "one of history's greatest miscreants." Ibid., 644.

30. Ibid., 650.

31. *Frudden v. Pilling*, 742 F.3d 1199 (9th Cir. 2014).

32. *Phoenix Elementary School District No. 1 v. Green*, 943 P.2d 836 (1997).

33. 473 U.S. 788 (1985).

34. Ibid., 798.

35. *Phoenix Elementary School District No. 1 v. Green*, 943 P.2d at 839, quoting *Hazelwood School District v. Kuhlmeier*, 484 U.S. 260, 273 (1988).

36. Ibid.

37. 515 U.S. 819 (1995).

38. Jennifer Starr, "School Violence and Its Effect on the Constitutionality of Public School Uniform Policies," *Journal of Law and Education* 29 (2000): 118.

39. 47 Conn. Supp. 342 (2001, Conn. Super.).

40. Ibid.

41. Ibid., 361.

42. Ibid., 362.
43. Ibid., 364.
44. Ibid., 363.
45. The court did not require that there be a demonstration that the goals be met through a demonstration of statistically significant improvement, Ibid., 365.
46. Ibid.
47. 240 F.3d 437 (5th Cir. 2001).
48. 491 U.S. 397 (1989).
49. 460 F.2d 609 (5th Cir. 1972).
50. *Canady v. Bossier Parish School District*, 240 F.3d 439–40. See also *Richards v. Thurston*, 424 F.2d 1281, 1285 (1st Cir. 1970) (stated that "a school rule that which forbids skirts shorter than a certain length while on school grounds would require less justification than one requiring hair to be cut, which affects the student twenty-four hours a day, seven days a week, nine months a year"). For a similar argument, see *Issacs v. Board of Education of Howard County, Maryland*, 40 F.Supp.2d 335, 339 (D. Md. 1999) (distinguished hairstyle regulations from dress code regulations. "Headgear, like other clothing and unlike hair, is easily removed and replaced. Shermia is free to wear her headwrap outside of school and, apparently, is even free to wear the headwrap to and from school. The school rules simply require that she leave the headwrap in her locker during the school day").
51. *Canady*, 240 F.3d 440.
52. Ibid.
53. Ibid., 441.
54. Ibid.
55. Ibid.
56. Ibid., 441, fn. 3. "Our analysis simply acknowledges that certain choices of clothing may have sufficient communicative content to qualify as First Amendment activity" Ibid. However, the court expressly declined to define the contours of the "extent or type of clothing necessary to communicate a discrete message in order to afford First Amendment protection." Ibid.
57. Ibid.
58. Ibid., 443.
59. 121 F.Supp.2d 621 (W.D. Ky. 2000).
60. Ibid., 627.
61. *Littlefield v. Forney Independent School District*, 268 F.3d 275, 283–84 (5th Cir. 2001). ("Regarding the 'coerced speech' argument, the students argue that mandatory uniforms convey a particularized message that the school district wishes to express, namely that students have respect for the authority of teachers and administrators, have Forney school and civic pride, and support school policies" [fn. 8]).
62. Ibid., 284.
63. Ibid., 285.
64. Ibid., 286.
65. Ibid., 287.

66. *Lowry v. Watson Chapel School District*, 508 F. Supp 2d 713, 715 (E.D. Ark. 2007).

67. Ibid., 716.

68. 401 F.3d 381 (6th Cir. 2005).

69. 268 F. 3d 275 (5th Cir. 2001).

70. *Lowry v. Watson Chapel Sch. Dist.*, 508 F. Supp. 2d, 719.

71. Ibid., 720 citing *Canady v. Bossier Parish Sch. Dist.*, 240 F.3d 437, 443 (5th Cir. 2001).

72. Ibid.

73. *Jacobs v. Clark County School District*, 526 F.3d 419, 423 (9th Cir. 2008).

74. Ibid., 422.

75. Ibid. Interestingly, Kimberly Jacobs's grades improved during her suspensions.

76. Ibid., 427 ("prohibit[s] students from displaying any printed messages on their clothing, save for, in some cases the school logo").

77. Ibid., 428 (school uniform policy restricts students' ability to "express [their] individuality through forced uniformity").

78. Ibid. (plaintiffs "being forced to convey a message of uniformity . . . by wearing the same clothing as . . . classmates").

79. Ibid., 432.

80. Ibid., 433.

81. Ibid., 432.

82. Ibid., 433 ("the District considered the logo to be an identifying mark, not a communicative device").

83. *United States v. O'Brien*, 391 U.S., 376–77.

84. *Jacobs v. Clark County. School District*, 526 F.3d, 435. ("Indeed, it is hard to think of a government interest more important than the interest in fostering conducive learning environments for our nation's children"). Ibid., 435–36.

85. Ibid., 436.

86. Ibid.

87. Ibid., 438.

88. Ibid., 441. Judge Sidney R. Thomas dissented, arguing that the case should have been analyzed under *Tinker*. Ibid., 443.

89. *Derry v. Marion Community Schools*, 790 F.2d 839, 842 (N.D. Ind. 2008).

90. The policy restricts hoodies, denim clothing, clothing with altered openings, bandanas, buttons, and attire signifying gangs. Ibid., 845.

91. Ibid., 846. The research was cited in the court case.

92. Ibid., 850.

93. Ibid.

94. *Frudden v. Pilling*, 742 F.3d 1199, 1201 (9th Cir. 2014).

95. The Fruddens originally brought suit on July 1, 2011, prior to their children's actions. On October 18, 2011, they amended their complaint alleging sixteen complaints. Ibid.

96. *Riley v. National Federation of the Blind, Inc.*, 487 U.S. 781, 797 (1988).

97. *Abood v. Detroit Board of Education*, 431 U.S. 209, 234–35 (1977).

98. The Fruddens alleged violations of First Amendment expressive rights, First Amendment associational rights, procedural and substantive due process, equal protection, and viewpoint discrimination. The plaintiff lost on all counts. *Frudden*, 742 F.3d 1273–78.

99. The district court stated that the motto was "one team, one community" *Frudden v. Pilling*, 842 F. Supp. 2d 1265, 1274 (D. Nev. 1012). The Ninth Circuit Court of Appeals stated that the logo was "Tomorrow's Leaders." *Frudden*, 742 F.3d, 1201. No explanation for the difference in logos was offered by the appellate court. An internet search showed the use of the "Tomorrow's Leaders" logo.

100. *Frudden*, 842 F. Supp. 2d 1274.

101. *Frudden*, 742 F.3d 1202.

102. 526 F.3d 419 (9th Cir. 2008).

103. Ibid., 438.

104. Ibid., 438.

105. Ibid. (quoted by *Frudden*, 742 F.3d 1204).

106. 319 U.S. 624 (1943). The plaintiff students who refused to stand and salute the flag had been expelled and their parents had been prosecuted for "causing delinquency." Ibid., 629–30.

107. Ibid., 634.

108. Ibid., 633.

109. Ibid., 634.

110. Ibid., 640.

111. Ibid., 641.

112. 430 U.S. 705 (1977).

113. Ibid., 707–708.

114. The Supreme Court in *Wooley* reasoned that "[c]ompelling the affirmative act of a flag salute involved a more serious infringement upon personal liberties than the passive act of carrying the state motto on a license plate, but the difference is essentially one of degree." Ibid., 715 (quoted by *Frudden*, 742 F.3d 1203).

115. *Frudden*, 742 F.3d 1204.

116. "[B]y mandating the written motto on the uniform shirts, the RGES policy compels speech under *Wooley*." Ibid., 1205.

117. Ibid., 1206. Furthermore, the court raised the issue of what criteria are used to determine national recognition.

118. Ibid., 1207.

119. Ibid., 1207–1208.

120. *Frudden v. Pilling*, 877 F.3d 821, 824 (9th Cir. 2017).

121. Ibid., 829.

122. Ibid.

123. The court responded to the plaintiff and *amicus* argument that the prohibition against the logo was well established in *Barnette* and *Wooley*. The court found that the cases were analogous to *Frudden*. Although both involved written words, the logo was an "anodyne" phrase, while Barnette involved the compelled oral recitation of a pledge to fidelity to national unity. The court also distinguished *Wooley*'s "Live Free or Die" vehicle license from the logo. It noted that the motto

has little substantive content and was only displayed on a school uniform as opposed to the license plate that was publicly displayed wherever the vehicle was driven. Ibid., 432.

124. Siobhan McAndrew, "Proposed Washoe Policy Addresses School Uniforms," *Reno Gazette-Journal* (May 12, 2014), http://www.rgj.com/story/news/education/2014/05/12/proposed-washoe-policy-addresses-school-uniforms/8985163/.

125. *West Virginia*, 319 U.S., 630.

126. *Wooley*, 430 U.S. 708.

127. *Palmer v. Waxahachie Independent School District*, 579 F.3d 502 (5th Cir. 2009).

128. *Wooley*, 430 U.S. 715.

129. 579 F.3d 502 (5th Cir. 2009). See my discussion, with my colleagues Richard Fossey and Suzanne Eckes, about how Waxahachie may be used in dress codes to achieve a similar result to school uniforms. Richard Fossey, Todd A. DeMitchell, and Suzanne Eckes, "The End of the T-Shirt Wars in the Public Schools? *Palmer v. Waxahachie Independent School District*," *Teachers College Record* (September 28, 2009), ID 15775.

130. For a discussion on challenges that may have politic al consequences, see Todd A. DeMitchell and Richard Fossey, *The Challenges of Mandating School Uniforms in Public Schools: Free Speech, Research, and Policy*, (Lanham, MD: Rowman and Littlefield (2015): 124–27.

131. Debra Cassens Weiss, "School Uniforms with 'Tomorrow's Leaders' Motto Amount to Compelled Speech, 9th Circuit Says," *ABA Journal* (February 18, 2014), http://www.abajournal.com/news/article/school_uniforms_with_tomorrows_leaders_motto_amount_to_compelled_speech_9th/.

132. David L. Brunsma and Kerry A. Rockquemore, "Effects of Student Uniforms on Attendance, Behavior Problems, Substance Use, and Academic Achievement," *Journal of Educational Research* 92, no. 1 (1998): 60.

133. Todd A. DeMitchell and Mark A. Paige, "School Uniforms in the Public Schools: Symbol or Substance?" *A Law and Policy Analysis, Education Law Reporter* 250 (2010): 879.

10

Policy Implications of Student Dress and Grooming Codes

Balancing Rights and Responsibilities

> Gone are the days when government could constitutionally regulate appearance without rhyme or reason.[1]

Schools are special places recognized by the courts.[2] The rights of students and educators[3] are greater outside the schoolhouse gate than inside. Students' free speech rights "are not co-extensive with adults,"[4] and speech that may be allowed in other settings may not be allowed in the schools. As expressed by Judge Jon O. Newman and quoted by the Supreme Court, "the First Amendment gives high school students the classroom right to wear Tinker's armband, but not Cohen's jacket."[5] And educators' right to free speech in school is contingent upon their speech being on a matter of public concern.[6]

While individuals walking the sidewalks, strolling the public parks, playing on their lawns, or sitting on their front porches may have great latitude in what they chose to wear, students do not have that same essentially unfettered right. A school is a special place reserved for learning and the inculcation of civic values, and it is a place of business. What may be tolerated in public spaces may not need to be tolerated in the classroom. Lewd messages and advertisements for alcohol or legalized marijuana may be acceptable on the public boardwalks of our beaches, but our public school hallways are another matter.

Students have rights and schools have responsibilities. Finding the balance by properly placing the fulcrum is a challenge. It is not unreasonable for school officials to ensure that the school environment is free from disruptions that undermine learning. This, among other tasks, entails monitoring clothing choices, given the special circumstances of the school.

Examples of appropriate and legally defensible regulations include rules that prohibit messages that promote drugs, alcohol, or violence; clothing that clearly identifies gang affiliations or gang territory; and clothing that proclaims other messages that are likely to create a disturbance or are immodest or inappropriate in a school or workplace.

"In the public school setting, the First Amendment protects the nondisruptive expression of ideas. It does not erect a shield that handicaps the proper functioning of the public schools."—Sypniewski v. Warren Hills Regional Board of Education, 307 F.3d 243, 259 (3d Cir. 2002), *cert. denied*, 538 U.S. 1033 (2002)

Indeed, as we have discussed, developing, implementing, and enforcing a reasonable, fair, and equitably applied dress code policy is a daunting challenge. How to find the proper balance is the question. Some school districts have approached student dress and appearance with the "precision" of inches and fingertips, some have removed reference to gender, and some have remained silent. The intervention—the inspection of a student's dress and appearance—impacts students; it is not just the response of turning clothes inside out, covering messages with duct tape, wearing a required T-shirt identifying the student as a violator, detention, and suspension that are felt by students. For many its impact is felt at a deeper level.

Without regard to what the policy says or whether there is a policy, the challenge is how the educators in the school perceive and define what is in-bounds and what is out-of-bounds for dress and appearance. Cultural expectations of role, including gender, both in the school and in the community shape, perceptions, which in turn influence actions. Consequently, developing a new or revising an existing dress code policy is not just an administrative decision; it is a political act, and an endorsement of particular values as to what is and is not appropriate student dress and grooming in the school environment. It prohibits and allows types of expression and choice. Dress and grooming codes that prohibit or mandate what is allowed often sit on the edge of competing visions of the individual's place within the special characteristics of the public schools. This political act of enacting and enforcing how a student presents themself at school seeks to balance the rights of minors and the responsibilities of government. These conflicts may seem in miniature to some, but they play an important part in defining the culture of the school.[7] Organizational culture and the assumptive worlds of individuals interact with and resist change. Norms are stubborn things, but stubbornness should not be rewarded with acquiescence. Despite the challenges, they must be confronted.

Dress codes, as stated above, must be reasonable, fair, and equally applied. Students must not be targeted because of their gender, body type, race, or ethnicity. Embracing these two propositions is the starting point—they must not be just espoused theories; they must be theories in practice.[8] One approach to reforming dress that has received a lot of attention is the 2016 Oregon NOW Model Student Dress Code (2016). It is worth exploring.

THE OREGON NOW MODEL SCHOOL DRESS CODE

Throughout the various chapters of this book, we have explored a number of issues associated with dress codes, including gendered dress code provisions. A national dress code was developed by the National Organization for Women (NOW) for the Portland School District, which updated school dress code policies to "support equitable educational access without reinforcing gender stereotypes."[9] The Oregon NOW Model Student Dress Code (hereafter the Model) is a response to dress codes which are arguably overreaching and detrimental to some K–12 students. The Model spread from Portland, Oregon, across the nation and was probably propelled by student and parent protests that were publicized by both mainstream and social media.[10]

The dress code starts with a statement of the values that inform the Model. The values are:

- All students should be able to dress comfortably for school without fear of unnecessary discipline or body shaming.
- All students and staff should understand that they are responsible for managing their own personal "distraction" without regulating individual students' clothing/self-expression.
- Teachers can focus on teaching without the additional and often uncomfortable burden of dress code enforcement.
- Students should not face unnecessary barriers to school attendance.
- Reasons for conflict and inconsistent discipline should be minimized whenever possible.[11]

Essentially, the Model seeks to leave the clothing choices up to students; "parents can decide with their children what is appropriate to wear to a public school."[12] The Model is organized into five sections: Goals of a Student Dress Code; Recommended Dress Code Policy; Training for School Administrators, Teachers and Students; Dress Code Enforcement at Schools; and Teaching about Consent and Sexual Harassment: A Step beyond Dress Code.

The Recommended Dress Code Policy starts with a basic principle: Certain body parts must be covered for *all* students. Genitals, buttocks, and nipples must be covered with opaque material, but cleavage should not require coverage.[13] The policy is organized into what students *must* wear (a top, a bottom, and shoes); what students *may* wear (e.g., midriff-baring shirts, pajamas, leggings, yoga pants, and tank tops, including spaghetti straps, halter tops, and tube (strapless) tops; and what students *cannot* wear (e.g., clothing that displays violent language or images, clothing that promotes drugs or alcohol, hate speech, and language or images that creates a hostile or intimidating environment based on a protected class).[14]

The enforcement section addresses student concerns about the unequal application of a dress code policy—"A school dress code is only as effective and fair as its enforcement."[15] This section prohibits shaming (including kneeling or bending over to check attire), being removed from the classroom for a dress code violation, requiring students to wear extra clothing, or calling parents to come to school with alternative clothing. The policy explicitly states that no students will be disproportionately affected by dress code enforcement because of gender, race, body size, or body maturity. This guidance on dress code enforcement makes sense and is fair. The section on what cannot be worn also makes sense.

However, there are a couple of elements in the policy that I find problematic. First, I am not sure about a position that cleavage cannot be regulated. Also, the code indicates that pajamas are appropriate clothing for a student to wear to school. I disagree. A school is a workplace, not an environment where sleepwear is appropriate.

The coverage section is consistent with existing dress codes and general community expectations. However, the issue of cleavage may not be consistently enforced, with more fully developed female students receiving more scrutiny. There are dress codes that prohibit showing cleavage, and there are ones that are silent on the issue. The prohibition against displaying cleavage is often a discretionary call regarding what constitutes cleavage; a top that shows some separation between breasts may be allowed by some educators, while some may hold that anything that shows a natural separation between breasts is prohibited.

This issue of coverage runs the gamut from the Bartram Trial High School controversy, in which the high school yearbook pictures of female students were retouched to cover cleavage,[16] to Rebecca Raby's research in which female students discussed the "slutty" look associated with some clothing choices.[17] A line of research on sexual encounters may provide some support for Raby's research. This line of research seeks to understand why women sometimes view women and girls pictured in revealing clothing in a negative light.[18] What amount of coverage is reasonable and appropriate for school may be a difficult consistent discipline call for administrators and a tangled and difficult endeavor for writing a dress code policy.

A rigid interpretation of dress code sections can result in not only embarrassment to a female student who is dress coded; it can cause shame and emotional issues about body image among adolescent female students. However, the sexualization of students that may occur with a focus on such issues as the width of straps and inches is often in tension with truly sexually, provocative dress at school: both the sexualization of female students and truly provocative clothing meant to accentuate sexual features are inappropriate. The sexualization tends to arise from the policies and practices of dress code enforcement while the intent to wear clothing that emphasizes attire that is inappropriate for the special environment of a school. This section of dress codes must be approached with sensitivity for the student and an awareness of the negative impact of overtly sexual dress by both female and male students as well as protecting the proper environment for education. It calls for a thoughtful and careful balance of the rights of students to secure their constitutional rights, which are applied in the "special characteristics of the school environment"[19], as well as being mindful of their nascent development, and the responsibility to all students to provide a proper environment for learning. Dress codes must be approached with sensitivity for the student and an awareness of the negative impact of overtly sexual attire. This section of dress codes must be approached with sensitivity for the student and an awareness of the negative impact of overtly sexual dress by both female and male students.

The "may" section in the Model captures the in-school issues along with their enforcement concerns. The types of contested applications of dress codes are centered in the "cannot" wear section. The Model does not resolve the controversy over what speech found on student attire is protected and what speech is out-of-bounds.

While not a silver bullet, the Model is a step in the right direction. It provides a usable template for constructing a student dress code that balances the right of students to choose what they will wear to school against the responsibility of school authorities to maintain an orderly school environment that is conducive to learning. What is needed is the skill to maintain balance. This involves communication between staff members to reach an agreement as to not only the purpose of the restrictions but also what they cover, articulated with as much specificity as possible.

CONCLUDING THOUGHTS ON FINDING THE BALANCE

The constitutionality as well as the wisdom of implementing dress codes and school uniform policies has been adjudicated and debated over a period of several decades. Most of this litigation juxtaposes the constitutional right of students to express themselves in the clothes and accessories that they wear to school with the school's interest in providing a climate that supports instruction and that is appropriate for children and adolescents who are not adults and who do not possess the full panoply of rights guaranteed to adults. The challenge is one of finding the right balance between students' rights and school authorities' responsibilities when drafting a student dress code.

A legal commentator asserted that the "'Achilles Heel' of dress codes is the difficulty of defining what is proper attire in the classroom without violating the basic constitutional rights of students."[20] Thus, while students possess free speech rights, when those rights are exercised within the special environment of the public school, they must be balanced. The following section explores my findings for seeking the proper balance between rights and responsibilities.

School Uniforms

Thus far, students have been far more successful in challenging dress codes than mandatory school uniform policies, with the exception of *Frudden*. The paradox is that students have some success contesting the lesser restrictions of a dress code and almost no success in contesting the more restrictive mandatory school uniform policies, either through a free speech analysis or a substantive due process analysis.

A constitutionally valid policy is not the same as an educationally sound policy. Transforming schools involves heavy lifting by educators. Do school uniform policies contribute to the task? Is a change of clothes the magic bullet? I think not. There is scant research to support adopting a mandatory school uniform that will meet the lofty goals stated in chapter 9. Without more substantive changes to improve student learning and the culture of the school, uniforms offer a vain hope and a false promise of meaningful reform. Chapter 9 offers political, organizational, and legal considerations to help frame the discussion, planning, and implementation.[21]

A Perspective on Dress Codes

Should students be able to wear anything they want to school? The consistent answer is no. While individuals outside of school have great latitude in what they chose to wear, students do not have that same unfettered right.

As has been emphasized throughout this volume, the school is a special place reserved for learning. It is also a place of business—the business of education. Crop tops, exposed underwear, and pajamas may be tolerated at a shopping mall but need not be tolerated in the classroom. Bathing suits are accepted on the beach, but in school they are appropriate only in a swimming class or a school's swim team, and even then, the style is controlled. Invitations and advertisements for sexual or illegal activity may have to be accepted at the mall, but not in our public school hallways.

Dress codes in schools are a legitimate exercise of the educational responsibility of the state. There are probably few individuals who would argue that elementary schools, middle schools, and high schools should allow students to wear anything that they want or as little as they want while on a school campus. In an earlier study, a principal from a rural area, when asked about the need for dress codes, responded, "Some would come Nude without it."[22]

Schools do not only teach manners and habits of civility; they also prepare students for their entry into an adult world of work, where employers may enforce strict dress and grooming standards. Preparation for the workplace is one of the recurring reasons stated for adopting dress codes.

Reasonable school dress codes define boundaries that students will likely encounter in the work world. It is reasonable to give students some latitude about their clothing choices, but license is another matter. The classroom is a work environment for students and educators. To expect that students' and educators' attire reflect the importance of that work environment is not unreasonable.

The constitutionality as well as the wisdom of implementing dress codes and school uniform policies has been adjudicated and debated for several decades. Most of this litigation juxtaposes the constitutional right of students to express themselves in the clothes and accessories that they wear to school with the school's interest in providing a climate that supports instruction and is appropriate for children and adolescents who are not adults and who do not possess the full panoply of rights guaranteed to adults.

Dress regulations that target lewd, vulgar, sexual language (*Fraser*) on attire, scanty clothing, bedroom and beach wear, promotions for drugs, alcohol (*Morse*) and tobacco, and dangerous objects like chains and dog collars are reasonable and consistent with a school's in loco parentis responsibility. Attire that creates or is likely to create a material and substantial disruption (*Tinker*), such as the attire that displays the Confederate flag, has also been successfully banned.

Issues that are less clear include speech on a student's attire, especially messages that touch on topics of public concern. Bans associated with abortion, sexual identity, and weapons have had mixed results when tested in the courts. These legal disputes often revolve around *Tinker*'s material and substantial disruption standard and its admonitions "in our system, undifferentiated fear or apprehension of disturbance is not enough to overcome the right to freedom of expression"[23] and "students may not be regarded as closed-circuit recipients of only that which the State chooses to communicate. They may not be confined to the expression of those sentiments that are officially approved."[24]

However, educators must be careful not to interject their personal biases when evaluating students' speech or enforcing a dress code regulation. As the US Supreme Court stated in the important flag salute case during World War II,

> If there is any fixed star in our constitutional constellation, it is that no official, high or petty, can prescribe what shall be orthodox in politics, nationalism, religion, or other matters of opinion, or force citizens to confess by word or act their faith therein. If there are any circumstances which permit an exception, they do not now occur to us.[25]

Educators have a responsibility to create, support, and maintain the environment of the school, educating students in a civil society within the schoolhouse gate. This mission can intersect with the *Morse v. Fredericks* standard.[26] Confederate flags, drugs, alcohol, and the depiction of weapons may run counter to the mission of the school, as was found in *Morse* regarding a student's message that celebrated the use of drugs.[27] There may be other messages that students want to display on their clothing that run counter to the school's instructional mission. Indeed, the Supreme Court in *Hazelwood School District v. Kuhlmeier* admonished that a "school need not tolerate student speech that is inconsistent with its basic educational mission."[28]

Consistent with the mission of the school and antidiscrimination laws, school administrators must consider the impact that dress codes have on all of their students, including transgender and/or gender-nonconforming students. Consideration must be given as to whether a dress code regulation or decision singles out these students based on their protected characteristics.[29]

A parent complained that a teacher at Tocoi Creek High School in St. Johns County, Florida, wore a T-shirt to school that read,

PROTECT TRANS KIDS

The school's principal spoke to the teacher about his T-shirt and the teacher changed shirts. No disciplinary action was taken. The school district's rules stated,

> Employees while on duty at school or on school property are not allowed to wear buttons or apparel, that display a written message

> of any kind, except for names, logos and slogans related to a District school, the District, or school or District related organizations, events or activities. Employees shall not wear apparel with a political logo (elephant, donkey, etc.). However, employees shall have the right to participate in political activities in their individual capacity when they are not scheduled for duty and are not on District property or at a school-sponsored event or activity.
>
> —Sheldon Gardner, "St. Johns County Teacher Wears 'Protect Trans Kids' Shirt, Is Asked to Remove It," *St. Augustine Record* (April 1, 2022), https://www.staugustine.com/story/news/local/2022/04/01/st-johns-county-teacher-asked-change-after-wearing-trans-t-shirt/7246845001/

Revising a Dress Code

To revise a dress code, a critical review of the dress code is the starting point. First, involve the faculty, parents, and students in the process early and often. The dress code is a reflection of the school community's culture. Next, ascertain what the staff are willing to enforce consistently and fairly. A rule that is not consistently and fairly applied soon ceases to be a rule and becomes a mere suggestion or a choice made at the whim of a school official. Is the rule reasonable and does it protect learning and students by providing some protection for female students from self-objectification,[30] or does it reflect "ancient and absurd customs"?

For example, the principal of a high school in Las Vegas found when she and her faculty discussed the controversy over wearing leggings that no one knew why the school had the rule: "She didn't see how leggings would keep a student from learning. So, with the agreement of her school board, she got rid of the rule."[31]

Furthermore, what provisions sexualize students and what prohibitions unnecessarily result in embarrassment? Does a two-inch strap really impact the school as opposed to a three-inch strap? Search out gender-neutral policies that do not target female students. A policy for all students that clothing must cover the body from mid-thigh to the armpits and not be made of transparent material and that underwear must be covered by such lower garments as pants, skirts, and/or dresses are examples of gender-neutral rules.

What provisions implicitly single out students based on their race or ethnicity? Is a ban on locs and braids important to the education of students? They are well-recognized and accepted hairstyles seen throughout society and protected in many states and locales through CROWN acts. (See chapter

8 for a discussion of the CROWN Act.) If the style is genuinely distracting, *Tinker* can be used rather than a blanket prohibition. Grooming prohibitions must not target race and ethnic hairstyles, which runs counter to the school's antidiscrimination mission.

Controversies over grooming restrictions such as hair length and braids or locs typically share a common denominator. The disciplinary issue which leads to the legal controversy is not one of whether the student violated the regulation but whether the regulation itself is valid.[32]

The dress code must be flexible enough to allow for students' movement, comfort, and modesty; they also should be considerate of the weather. And finally, staff need opportunities to train together on the application of the dress and appearance provisions. They are the ultimate enforcers of student dress and grooming rules and need a shared view for consistent and fair implementation of dress codes.

Developing a reasonable dress code that protects the special environment of the school, provides meaningful insight into the norms and mores that the students will face upon graduation, and is supportive of students during their developing years is the first major challenge. The second is the consistent enforcement of the policy. No group should be singled out for heightened scrutiny or given an easy pass. No student or group of students should enjoy privileged status in the classroom, in the hallway, or on the playing field. It is imperative that students believe that faculty and staff care for them for who they are and that rules governing student attire are fair and are enforced fairly.

An NBC reporter interviewed nine high school female students following the February 2023 release of the Centers for Disease Control's *2021 Youth Risk Behavior Survey*. The CDC report found that teenage girls were suffering through sexual violence and traumatic experiences leading to persistent sadness and a sense of hopelessness seriously affecting their mental health. While the CDC report did not specifically address school dress codes, the NBC correspondent wrote of her interviews:

> Several mentioned that they think their bodies are policed at school in a way male students' bodies aren't, with girls subjected to dress codes and told their bodies are a distraction to classmates — particularly boys.
>
> "Your body is changing in and of itself at this time, and to add the stressors of society and men putting you into boxes … it isn't talked about as much as it should be," said Omalina Wolfe, 18.

These interview anecdotes are not meant to assert cause or correlation with dress codes and the mental health of teenage girls. However, they do give one pause that it would be brought up as a concern in interviews over feelings of sadness and hopelessness.

—Kalhan Rosenblatt, "What's Really behind the Wave of Sadness among Teenage Girls? We Asked 9 of Them," NBC News (February 23, 2023), https://www.nbcnews.com/health/mental-health/cdc-report-teen-sadness-girls-respond-rcna71073

An example of the concern about fair enforcement of dress code regulations is highlighted in a complaint filed on January 5, 2023, in the US District Court, Southern District of Georgia. In that case, three students brought a civil rights action against the Effingham County School District. Their complaint alleges discriminatory and unconstitutional actions by school administrators. In addition to the complaint of deliberate indifference to acts of racial animosity toward Black students is an allegation of "viewpoint discrimination in its dress code and the inconsistent administration of disciplinary policies to the detriment of Black students."[33]

The school district's dress code prohibits students from "wearing and displaying expressive items on the uniform that may contribute to disruption by substantially interfering with discipline or rights of others."[34] The complaint alleges in the statement of facts that administrators interpreted the policy as excluding "Black Lives Matter" but allowing Confederate flag attire as well as paraphernalia supporting former president Donald Trump. The plaintiffs were told that "Black Lives Matter . . . constituted a disruption" but "the Confederate flag represents 'heritage not hate' and is point of pride rather than disruption."[35] As explained in chapter 4, I disagree with school administrators' interpretation of Confederate symbols.[36] This case bears close watching as it moves through the judicial system.

Standards of behavior are expected and necessary for the special circumstances of the classroom and school to assure the delivery of efficient and effective learning experiences and providing a safe environment for students. Clear, reasonable standards, fairly enforced, for what is appropriate student dress can be part of those expectations. What is the educational purpose behind a dress code provision? Are the means of enforcing the policy fair, efficient, and effective? Good policy not only seeks to find the right balance of rights and responsibilities but also actually achieves the purpose behind the policy.

NOTES

1. Jennifer L. Greenblat, "Using the Equal Protection Clause Post-VMI to Keep Gender Stereotypes out of the Public School Equation," *UC Davis Journal of Juvenile Law and Policy* 13 (2009): 282. Greenblat's commentary reviews a public school's dress code policy for potential equal protection violations. For example, she found the following two rules that likely run afoul of the Equal Protection Clause. She asserts that "Rule 3, Highlights/lowlights must be Blond in color for girls" does not serve "any legitimate goal" and that "Rule 4, Highlights/lowlights are not allowed for boys" restricts "boys from adopting 'girly' hairstyles is almost certainly the impetus behind Rule 4 and is likewise unconstitutional." Ibid., 293, 295.

2. See *Tinker v. Des Moines Independent Community School District*, 393 U.S. 503, 506 (1969) ("First Amendment rights, applied in light of the special characteristics of the school environment, are available to teachers and students").

3. Educators' constitutional protections are not as robust inside the schoolhouse gate as outside the gate. For example, the US Supreme Court case *Garcetti v. Ceballos*, 547 U.S. 410 (2006) restricted the First Amendment rights of public employees, including educators, when they are speaking in their official capacities in the workplace.

4. *Bethel School District No. 403 v. Fraser*, 478 U.S. 675, 682 (1986).

5. Ibid., 683. In *Thomas v. Board of Education, Granville Central School District*, 607 F.2d 1043, 1057 (2nd Cir. 1979), Judge Newman referred to Paul Robert Cohen's jacket which had "Fuck the Draft" lettered on the back of his jacket which he wore into a US Postal Office, citing *Cohen v. California*, 403 U.S. 15, 21 (1971).

6. A matter of public concern is part of the *Pickering* test, which balances the employee's interests in free speech with the employer's interest in the efficiency of the services provided to the public. The US Supreme Court in *Pickering* articulated the interest of the employee narrowly "as a citizen, in commenting upon matters of public concern." *Pickering v. Board of Education*, 391 U.S. 563, 568 (1968). The third case in the *Pickering* balancing test is *Connick v. Myers*, 461 U.S. 138, 146 (1983). In *Connick*, the court tightened the definition of a matter of public concern, writing, "When employee expression cannot be fairly considered as relating to any matter of political, social, or other concern to the community, government officials should enjoy wide latitude in managing their offices, without intrusive oversight by the judiciary in the name of the First Amendment."

7. See Edgar H. Schein, *Organizational Culture and Leadership*, 4th ed. (San Francisco: Jossey-Bass, 2010).

8. See the seminal work of Chris Argyris and Donald Schon, *Theory in Practice: Increasing Professional Effectiveness* (San Francisco: Jossey-Bass, 1974).

9. "Oregon NOW Model Student Dress Code, 2016," National Organization for Women, (February 2016), https: //noworegon.org/wp-content/uploads/sites/12/2018/01/or_now_model_student_dress_code_feb_2016__1_. pdf.

10. See Sabrina Rojas Weiss, "These School Districts Are Actually Changing Their Dress Codes in Response to Student Complaints," Yahoo! Life (August

8, 2018), https://www.yahoo.com/lifestyle/school-districts-actually-changing-dress-codes-response-student-complaints-225203474. html; Nadra Nittle, "Students Are Waging War on Sexist and Racist Dress Codes—And They're Winning," *Vox* (September 13, 2018), https://www.vox.com/the-goods/2018/9/13/17847542/students-waging-war-sexist-racist-school-dress-codes.

11. Oregon NOW, *supra* note 9, 1.

12. Samantha Matsumoto, "Oregon's 'Model Dress Code' Aims to Make School Policies More Fair," OPB (Portland, Oregon) (September 21, 2018), https://www.opb.org/radio/programs/thinkoutloud/segment/oregon-model-dress-code-portland-public-schools/ ("And more and more schools are listening to these protests, adopting guidelines that reflect a new understanding of what constitutes "appropriate" student dress").

13. Oregon NOW, *supra* note 9, 2; emphasis in original.

14. Ibid., 3.

15. Ibid., 4.

16. See chapter 7, nn. 17 and 18.

17. See ibid., nn. 53 and 54.

18. Beth Ellwood, "Women Who Dress Provocatively Are Judged Negatively by Other Women Due to Perceptions of Promiscuity," *PsyPost* (May 25, 2022), https://www.psypost.org/2022/05/women-who-dress-provocatively-are-judged-negatively-by-other-women-due-to-perceptions-of-promiscuity-63188.

19. Hazelwood School District v. Kuhlmeier, 484 U.S.260, 266 (1988)].

20. Rob Killen, "'The Achilles Heel' of Dress Codes: The Definition of Proper Attire in Public Schools," *Tulsa Law Journal* 36 (2000): 459. Killen asserts that dress codes "suffer from a number of inherent weaknesses, such as being too vague, being overbroad, not completely addressing the problems that they were created to solve, and repeated litigation of similar issues throughout various jurisdictions." Ibid. He argues for the use of school uniform policies "instead of relying on inherently weak dress codes." Ibid., 486.

21. For those administrators and school board members considering adopting a school uniform policy, I recommend that they also consider the seven challenges of enforcement; waivers; alternative speech; the differences between elementary, middle, and high schools; uniform-free days; political heat; and adult uniforms, discussed in Todd A. DeMitchell and Richard Fossey, *The Challenges of Mandating School Uniforms in the Public Schools: Free Speech, Research, and Policy* (Lanham, MD: Rowman and Littlefield, 2015), 124–28.

22. Todd A. DeMitchell, Richard Fossey, and Casey Cobb, "Dress Codes in the Public Schools: Principals, Policies, and Precepts," *Journal of Law and Education* 29, no. 1 (2000): 45. My coauthors and I included an open-ended question: "In your own words, succinctly state why a dress code policy is needed or not needed at your school." We concluded in our analysis of the 107 responding principals' comments the following:

> There was a high degree of support for dress codes among school principals. Eighty-five percent of the principals believed that a dress coded was needed at their school, while fifteen percent did not. Elementary school principals had the highest percentage of responses

of not needed, while middle/junior high school and high school principals overwhelmingly supported dress codes.

Ibid.

23. *Tinker*, 393 U.S. 503, 509.

24. Ibid., 508.

25. *West Virginia State Board of Education v. Barnette*, 319 U.S. 624, 642 (1943). Furthermore, see *Burnside v. Byars*, 363 F.2d 744 (5th Cir. 1966), a case involving wearing "freedom buttons" in a public school. The Fifth Circuit recognized the right to make reasonable regulations but said that "school officials cannot ignore expressions of feelings with which they do not wish to contend." Ibid., 749.

26. *Morse v. Fredericks*, 551 U.S. 393 (2007).

27. As Chief Justice John Roberts summarized in *Morse*, "The question thus becomes whether a principal may, consistent with the First Amendment, restrict student speech at a school event, when that speech is reasonably viewed as promoting illegal drug use. We hold that she may." Ibid., 403.

28. 484 U.S. 260, 266 (1988)

29. See, for example, Suzanne Eckes, Todd DeMitchell, and Richard Fossey. "Breaking Social Norms at Prom: Is There a Constitutional Right to Wear Gender Nonconforming Attire to the Prom?" *Principal Leadership* (April 2015): 10–13; Deanna J. Glickman, "Fashioning Children: Gender Restrictive Dress Codes as an Entry Point for the Trans* School to Prison Pipeline," *Journal of Gender, Social Policy and the Law* 24, no. 2 (2016): 264–84. Glickman writes,

> Dress codes are a method of reinforcing gender norms and rely heavily on a binary system which leaves no space for those whose gender identities and expressions do not conform to the two dominant categories. . . . Gendered dress codes are a specific point of entry for the school to prison pipeline because clothing choice is an integral part of gender identity and expression.

Ibid., 276.

30. For a brief discussion of self-objectification see chapter 8, n. 53.**[AQ83]** The authors do not expressly address school dress codes; their analysis pertains to the gender gap in cognitive performance it may help to inform the discussion on dress codes. They write,

> At the same time, appearance monitoring may impede women's performance through the monopolization of cognitive resources. Moreover, appearance monitoring is likely to activate self-objectification, which may further impede performance and fundamentally undermine women's aspirations.

Lara Winn and Randolph Cornelius, "Self-Objectification and Cognitive Performance: A Systematic Review of the Literature," *Frontiers in Psychology* (January 28, 2020), https://www.ncbi.nlm.nih.gov/pmc/articles/PMC6997128/.

31. Lee Hale, "Dress Coe Drama: What's a Principal to do?" NPR (September 16, 2015), https://www.npr.org/sections/ed/2015/09/16/438852964/dress-code-drama

-whats-a-principal-to-do. The principal of a middle school in Camas, Washington approached leggings from a different perspective:

> Her students were upset they couldn't wear ripped jeans. So she invited some students to her office and they reached a compromise: If the students wore leggings underneath, they could wear jeans with as many rips as they wanted. The solution may seem obvious or simplistic, she says, but the students were excited that their voices had been heard.

32. See *Conyers v. Glenn*, 243 So. 2d 204, 208–9 (Fla. Dist. Ct. App. 1971) (writing, "Conyers[, the student plaintiff,] admits the violation but denies the validity of the regulation. Under such circumstances an action for injunction is appropriate. This situation is to be contrasted with that in which the student seeks an administrative hearing on the question whether there has been a violation). This is an early case using *Tinker* on a student hair length regulation in which the appellate court reversed the lower court and reinstated a temporary of temporary injunction and remanding the case on the issue of disruption. The majority wrote, "While the school authorities may have ample cause to suspend a pupil who uses long hair—or well developed muscles, for that matter—in a disruptive way, there is nothing in the record at this stage to justify this regulation." Ibid., 208.

33. *J.K. v. Effingham County School District*, Case No. 4:23-cv-00005-WTM-CLR (S. D. Georgia 01/05.23), *2, https://www.wsav.com/wp-content/uploads/sites/75/2023/01/Effingham-court.pdf.

34. Ibid., *8.

35. Ibid., *9.

36. See Todd A. DeMitchell and Richard Fossey, "Scrubbing the Confederacy from the Public Schools: Now Is the Time," *Education Law Reporter* 378 (2020): 15–16, writing, "In the conflict between symbols of heritage and symbols of oppression, many civic leaders and courts since the mid 1970s are siding with the findings that Confederate flags, statues, and symbols are perceived as symbols of oppression."

Appendix A

Example Dress Code

Gulf District Schools
Port St. Joe, Fl 32456
https: //gulfcoschools.com/students/dress-code/

DRESS CODE

The dress code is designed to insure [*sic*] the health and safety of students and to avoid distractions to the educational process, while preserving the basic rights of individuals. Unsafe or inappropriate is defined as anything which could undermine the morale or endanger the physical well being of a student. It is our belief that good taste and judgment are keys to proper attire and appearance. The dress code puts focus on academics, not fashion and allows students to express themselves through personality and individual achievement. Dressing appropriately creates a sense of school pride and belonging as well as reducing discipline issues and distractions. Student are asked to dress in a manner that demonstrates they have respect for themselves and for others.

- Shorts / skorts may be worn to school if they are no shorter than five (5) inches above the top of the kneecap. No biking shorts, spandex, or tight fitting shorts.
- Jeans with holes are not permitted.
- Skirts or dresses may be worn to school if they are no shorter than three (3) inches above the top of the knee cap [*sic*] (slits or openings in skirts or dresses cannot extend beyond three (3) inches above the top of the

kneecaps). IF TIGHTS, JEGGINGS OR LEGGINGS ARE WORN, THEY MUST BE WORN UNDER SHORTS, SKORTS, SKIRTS OR DRESSES THAT MEET DRESS CODE LENGTHS. LEGGINGS WORN UNDER BLOUSES ARE ONLY ACCEPTABLE IF BLOUSES MEET DRESS CODE LENGTH OF SKIRTS/DRESSES. [emphasis in original]

- K–2 students should wear shorts beneath skirts and dresses.
- Shirts, blouses and/or dresses must be worn at all times and must be long enough in length to cover the stomach and back completely.
- Necklines may not expose cleavage.
- Girls may wear sleeveless tops having a minimum two (2) inch wide shoulder strap.
- Boys are not allowed to wear tank tops.
- Pajamas must not be worn except on designated days.
- Blouses made of sheer fabric may be worn only as an over blouse to tops that meet previously stated guidelines.
- Pants must be worn at the waistline. Low riding, sagging pants are not allowed. If belts are worn they must be buckled.
- Hoods, hats, caps, head stockings, hair rollers, sunglasses, bandanas, combs, wide headbands, and other types of headwear shall not be worn except in designated areas and on designated days.
- Shoes must be worn at all times. Bedroom slippers or shower shoes are not to be worn. All students must wear soft soled athletic shoes in PE classes. Hard soled shoes are not permitted in gymnasiums.
- Clothing or accessories bearing profane, suggestive, offensive, obscene or gang related language, symbols, slogans or advertising alcoholic beverages, tobacco products or unlawfully controlled substances are not permitted.
- Appropriate undergarments must be worn at all times and must not be seen.
- Beach attire is not to be worn at school.
- Wallet chains, dog collars, or other inappropriate chains or accessories will not be allowed on campus.
- Trench coats and other distracting oversized clothing will not be allowed on campus.

Exceptions to the dress code shall be permitted when:

- A student's parent requests a reasonable accommodation to address the student's disability.
- The wearing of clothing in compliance with the dress code violates a student's sincerely held religious beliefs. Such students and the student's

parents shall submit a signed affidavit setting forth the religious issues and the requested exemption to the policy.

The school administration is the final authority regarding the appropriateness of dress and grooming. The student code of conduct will be applied to violations of the dress code.

Appendix B

Example of a Gender-Neutral Specific Dress Code

Murietta Valley Unified School District
Murricta, CA 92562
Administrative Regulation
https: //www.murrieta.k12. ca.us/cms/lib/CA0100
0508/Centricity/Domain/5/5132AR.pdf

DRESS AND GROOMING AR5132(A)

In cooperation with teachers, students and parents/guardians, the principal or designee may establish school rules governing student dress and grooming which are consistent with law, Board policy, and administrative regulations. These school dress codes shall be regularly reviewed.
(cf. 0420—School Plans/Site Councils)

Minimum Safe Attire

Student attire and grooming must permit the student to participate in learning without posing a risk to the health or safety of any student or school district personnel.

1. Students must wear clothing including both a shirt with pants or skirt, or the equivalent (for example dresses, leggings, or shorts) and shoes.
2. When the body is standing straight, clothing must cover the chest, back, torso, stomach, and lower extremities from armpit to mid-thigh (at no time may any part of a student's buttocks be exposed). Tops must have a strap.

3. Clothing must cover all undergarments. No underwear or undergarments may be visible at any time. Clothing may not be seen through.
4. Clothing must be suitable for all scheduled classroom activities including physical education, science labs, shop classes, field trips and other activities where unique hazards or specialized attire or safety gear is required. Bare feet are not permitted at any time.

Dress Code Enforcement

No list of dress and appearance guidelines for students can be written that will anticipate all potential dress and grooming extremes. In the case of questionable dress or grooming that is not specifically covered in the list above, the administration will make the final decision. Appropriate action will be taken at that time, and when necessary, contact will be made seeking parental cooperation and assistance.

School-directed changes to a student's attire or grooming should be the least restrictive and disruptive to the student's school day. Any school dress code enforcement actions should minimize the potential loss of educational time. Administration and enforcement of the dress code shall be gender neutral and consistent.

The administration retains the sole discretion to make the final determination whether clothing, jewelry, accessories and/or appearance meet acceptable standards. All school certificated and classified personnel shall be responsible for reporting violations of this dress code. When a dress code violation occurs, the student will be required to change into proper attire. Continued violations of the dress code will be considered defiance and will be referred to administration for disciplinary action.

No grade of a student participating in a physical education class shall be adversely affected if the student does not wear standardized physical education apparel because of circumstances beyond the student's control. (Education Code 49066)

Students shall be allowed to wear sun-protective clothing, including but not limited to hats, for outdoor use during the school day. (Education Code 35183.5)

Gang-Related Apparel

At individual schools that have a dress code prohibiting gang-related apparel at school or school activities, the principal, staff and parents/guardians participating in the development of the school safety plan shall define "gang-related apparel" and shall limit this definition to apparel that reasonably could be determined to threaten the health and safety of the school environment if it were worn or displayed on a school campus. (Education Code 32282)

Because gang-related symbols are constantly changing, definitions of gang-related apparel shall be reviewed at least once each semester and updated whenever related information is received. As necessary, the school shall collaborate with law enforcement agencies to update definitions of gang-related apparel.

Uniforms

In schools where a schoolwide uniform is required, the principal, staff and parents/guardians of the individual school shall jointly select the specific uniform to be worn.
(Education Code 35183)

At least six months before a school uniform policy is implemented, the principal or designee shall notify parents/guardians of this policy. (Education Code 35183)

Parents/guardians shall also be informed of their right to have their children exempted.

The Superintendent or designee shall establish criteria for determining student eligibility for financial assistance when purchasing uniforms.

The Superintendent or designee shall establish a method for recycling or exchanging uniforms as students grow out of them.

Students who participate in nationally recognized youth organizations shall be allowed to wear organization uniforms on days when the organization has a scheduled meeting. (Education Code 35183)

Regulation approved: revised: revised:

Regulation	**MURRIETA VALLEY USD**	
Approved	March 10, 1994	Murrieta, California
Revised	February 13, 1997	
Revised	October 10, 2019	

Appendix C

Table of Court Cases

FEDERAL CASES

Cases	*Chapters*
U.S. Supreme Court	
Abood v. Detroit Board of Education	9
Beauharnais v. Illinois	2
Bethel School District No. 403 v. Fraser	1, 2, 6, 9, 10
Board of Education v. Earls	2
Board of Education v. Pico	2
Board of Education v. Rowley	2
Brandenburg v. Ohio	2
Broaderick v. Oklahoma	3
Chaplinsky v. New Hampshire	2
Cohen v. California	10
Connally v. General Construction Company	3
Cornelius v. NAACP	1, 2, 9
Craig v. Boren	7
Board of Education v. Pico	2
Gilbert v. State of Minnesota	2
Ginsberg v. New York	2
Goss v. Lopez	2
Grayned v. Rockford,	2
Hazelwood School District v. Kuhlmeier	2, 5, 9, 10
Ingraham v. Wright	2
In re Gault	2
Karr v. Schmidt	8
Linmark Associates, Inc. v. Township of Willingboro	2
Lovell v. City of Griffin	2
Mahony Area School District v. B.L.	2, 5

(*continued*)

Cases	Chapters
Meyer v. Nebraska	3, 7
McIntyre v. Ohio Elections Commission	2
Miller v. California	2
Mills v. Alabama	2
Morse v. Frederick	2, 5, 10
New Jersey v. T.L.O	2
New York v. Ferber	2
New York Times Company v. Sullivan	2
Palko v. Connecticut	2
Perry Education Association v. Perry Local Educators' Association	2
Pierce v. Society of Sisters	3, 7
Poulos v. New Hampshire	2
R.A.V. v. St. Paul	2, 9
Reed v. Reed	7
Rochin v. California	5
Riley v. National Federation of the Blind, Inc.,	9
Rosenberger v. Rectors & Visitors of the University of Virginia	6, 9
San Antonio Independent School District v. Rodriguez	2
Shelton v. Tucker	2
Simon & Shuster, Inc. v. Members of the New York State Crime Victims Bd. 2	
Smith v. Goguen	3
Snyder v. Phelps	2
Spence v. Washington	2,3, 9
Terminello v. Chicago	2
Texas v. Johnson	2
Tinker v. Des Moines Independent Community School District	1, 2, 3, 4, 5, 6, 7. 9, 10
United States v. O'Brien	2, 3, 6, 9
Vernonia School District 47J v. Acton	2
Virginia v. Black	2
Ward v. Rock Against Racism	2
West Virginia State Board of Education. v. Barnette	2, 4, 6, 9, 10
Whitney v. California	2
Wooley v. Maynard	9
Federal Court of Appeals (Circuit)	
First Circuit	
Brown v. Hot, Sexy and Safer Productions, Inc.	3
Richards v. Thurston	8, 9
Second Circuit	
Guiles v. Marineau	2, 5
Peck v. Baldwinsville Central School District	6
Thomas v. Board of Education, Granville Central School District	2, 10

(*continued*)

Cases	Chapters
Third Circuit	
Sypniewski v. Warren Hills Reg. Board. of Education	2
Fourth Circuit	
Crosby v. Holsinger	4
Hardwick v. Heyward	4
Massie v. Henry	8
Newsome v. Albemarle County School Board,	2, 5
Peltier v. Charter Day School Inc	7
Williams v. Spencer	5
Fifth Circuit	
Alabama and Coushatta Tribes of Texas v. Big Sandy Indep. Sch. Dist.	8
A.M. v. Board of Trustees of Burleson Independent School District	4
Betenbaugh v. Needville Independent School District	8
Canady v. Bossier Parish School Board	2, 9
Karr v. Schmidt	8
Littlefield v. Forney Independent School District	3, 9
Morgan v. Swanson	2
Palmer v. Waxahachie Independent School District	2, 6, 9
Sixth Circuit	
Barr v. Lafon	4
Blau v. Fort Thomas Public School District	2, 3, 9
Boroff v. Van Wert City Board of Education	2, 3, 5, 6
Defoe Ex Rel. Defoe v. Spiva	4
Melton v. Young	4
Seventh Circuit	
Arnold v. Carpenter	8
Banks v. Muncie Community Schools	4
Brandt v. Board of Education of City of Chicago	5, 9
Jacob v. Sonnabend	5
Miller v. School District	1
Nuxoll v. Indian Prairie School District	6
Zamecnik v. Indian Prairie School District	6
Eight Circuit	
B.W.A. v. Farmington R-7 School District	4
Stephenson v. Davenport Community School District	3
Ninth Circuit	
Frederick v. Morse	2
Frudden v. Pilling	9
Harper v. Poway Unified School District	2, 6
Jacobs v. Clark County School District	2, 9

(continued)

Cases	Chapters
King v. Saddleback Junior College District	8
LaVine v. Blaine School District	2
Tenth Circuit	
Sypniewski v. Warren Hills Regional Board of Education	5
Taylor v. Roswell Independent School District	6
Eleventh Circuit	
Scott v. School Board of Alachua County	4
Federal District by State	
Alaska	
Frederick v. Morse	2
Arkansas	
Lowry v. Watson Chapel School District	9
Wallace v. Ford	7
California	
Dariano v. Morgan Hill Unified School District	5
Jeglin v. San Jacinto Unified School District	3
T.A. v. McSwain Elementary School	6
Florida	
Denno v. School Board of Volusia County	2
Gillman v. School Board of Holmes County	6
Moms for Liberty v. Brevard Public Schools	2
Georgia	
J.K. v. Effingham County School District	10
Idaho	
Gano v. School District No. 411 of Twin Falls City	5
Illinois	
Olesen v. Board of Education of School District No. 228	1
Indiana	
Bell v. Anderson Community Schools	3
Derry v. Marion Community Schools	9
Griggs v. Ft. Wayne School Board	5

(continued)

Cases	Chapters
Kansas	
West v. Derby Unified School District #260	4
Kentucky	
Long v Board of Education of Jefferson County	2, 9
Louisiana	
Smith v. St. Tammany Parish School Board	4
Maryland	
Isaacs v. Board of Education of Howard County	3, 9
Sons of Confederate Veterans, Inc. v. Glendening	4
Massachusetts	
Pyle v. South Hadley School Committee	1, 2, 6
Michigan	
Barber v. Dearborn Public Schools	5
Minnesota	
Chambers v. Babbitt	6
New Hampshire	
Banister v. Paradis	3
Governor Wentworth Regional School District v. Hendrickson	2, 5
New Jersey	
DePinto v. Bayonne Board of Education	9
New Mexico	
Bivens v. Albuquerque Public Schools	1, 2, 3
New York	
Grzywna v. Schenectady Central School District	3
K.D. v. Fillmore Central School District	6

(continued)

Cases	*Chapters*
North Carolina	
Fowler v. Williamson	9
North Dakota	
McMillen v. Itawamba County School District	6
Ohio	
Harper v. Edgewood Board of Education	1
Hines v. Caston School Corporation	1
Pennsylvania	
B.H. v. Easton Area School District	6
Miller v. Penn Manor School District	5
South Dakota	
Dreaming Bear v. Fleming	1
Texas	
A.C., C.P., T.T., T.M., T.B., R.P., and C.W. v. Magnolia Indep. Sch. Dist.	8
Chalifoux v. New Caney Independent School District	3
Madrid v. Anthony	5
Pro-Life Cougars v. University of Houston	6
Treyvion Gray v. Needville Independent School District	8
Virgina	
Broussard v. School Board of the City of Norfolk	6
Wisconsin	
K.J. v. Sauk Prairie School District	6
N.J. By Next Friend Jacob v. Sonnabend	5
Schonecker v. Koopman	5
STATE COURTS	
Cases by State	Chapters
Arizona	
Phoenix Elementary School District No. 1 v. Green	9

(*continued*)

Cases	Chapters
Arkansas	
Pugsley v. Sellmeyer	1
California	
Morrison v. State Board of Education	7
Connecticut	
Byars v. City of Waterbury	9
Florida	
Conyers v. Glenn	10
Idaho	
Idaho Commission on Human Rights v. Campbell	8
Johnson v. Joint School District No. 60 Bingham County	7
Indiana	
Hines v. Caston School Corporation	7
Iowa	
Valentine Independent School District	1
Louisiana	
Jones v. W.T. Henning Elementary School	7
Maine	
Solmitz v. Maine School Administrative District No. 59	6
Mississippi	
Jones v. Day	1
Rhode Island	
Gorman v. St. Raphael Academy	8
Texas	
Bastrop Independent School District v. Toungate	8
Wisconsin	
State ex rel. Dresser v. District Board of Sch. Dist. No. 1	2

Index

About the Author

Todd A. DeMitchell (BA, MAT, University of La Verne; MA, University of California, Davis; EdD, University of Southern California; Post-Doctorate, Harvard Graduate School of Education) is professor emeritus of education law and labor at the University of New Hampshire. He previously held the John & H. Irene Peters Endowed Professor of Education and the Lamberton Endowed Professor of Justice Studies positions. In addition, he was named Distinguished Professor at the University of New Hampshire. He also received the Excellence in Teaching Award from the College of Liberal Arts and the University Graduate Mentor Award. He has authored/coauthored more than two hundred books, law review articles, commentaries, and education articles. Prior to joining the faculty at the University of New Hampshire, he spent eighteen years in the public schools holding such positions as teacher, principal, director of personnel and labor relations, and superintendent.

www.ingramcontent.com/pod-product-compliance
Ingram Content Group UK Ltd.
Pitfield, Milton Keynes, MK11 3LW, UK
UKHW012043150926
475560UK00001B/156